305.8009 Jacobson, Matthew
JAC   Frye, 1958-

          Whiteness of a
          different color.

$29.95

DATE			

Whiteness of a Different Color ⋐

WHITENESS OF A DIFFERENT COLOR

European Immigrants and the Alchemy of Race

Matthew Frye Jacobson

Harvard University Press
Cambridge, Massachusetts
London, England   1998

Library of Congress Cataloging-in-Publication Data

Jacobson, Matthew Frye, 1958–
    Whiteness of a different color : European immigrants and the
alchemy of race / Matthew Frye Jacobson.
        p.   cm.
    Includes bibliographical references and index.
    ISBN 0-674-06371-6 (alk. paper)
    1. European Americans—Race identity.
    2. Whites—United States—Race identity.
    3. Immigrants—United States—History.
    4. Racism—United States—History.
    5. United States—Race relations.
    I. Title.
    E184.E95J33   1998
    305.8'00973—dc21
    98-15754

To Fran, Nick, and Tess

Contents

Illustrations

following page 199

Note on Usage

It has become customary among academics to set words like "race," "races," "Anglo-Saxons," or "whiteness" in undermining quotation marks. The practice certainly suits the spirit of this book, whose central theme is the social fabrication of "race" and "races." But I have forgone the quotation marks except in those instances where the words in question are in fact a quotation—as, for instance, when I want it to be clear that a certain author actually did refer to "Nordics," "Hebrews," "Teutons," and "Anglo-Saxons." Otherwise I have left out the quotation marks altogether, even where I do refer to archaic categories like Nordic, Hebrew, Teuton, and Anglo-Saxon.

This began as a stylistic decision: scarcely a sentence went by in which one phrase or another did not seem to require quotation marks, and this, I felt, became distracting. More important than style, however, is the inconspicuous racial logic of the practice itself. I notice that few of the writers who put "race" in quotation marks also put "Caucasian" in quotation marks, and I wonder about the unexamined racial certainty that this denotes. For my own part, as I went through the manuscript to streamline the punctuation, I found that I had always set "Caucasian," "Anglo-Saxon," "Hebrew" and many other appellations in quotes, and almost always "race," "racial," or "races," but only sometimes "white" or "black." I wonder about the unexamined racial certainty that this denotes, too. All these designations belong on the same epistemological footing, and so they appear before you now without any stylistic marker to separate archaic fabrications from current ones. If you are inclined to supply your own as you go, I only invite you, too, to note the patterns in your own choices. A principled consistency on this score is rendered very difficult by the culture within which we operate.

Hardly two [scientists] agree as to the number and composition of the races. Thus one scholar makes an elaborate classification of twenty-nine races; another tells us there are six; Huxley gives us four; Kroeber, three; Goldenweiser, five; and Boas inclines to two, while his colleague, Linton, says there are twelve or fifteen. Even my dullest students sometimes note this apparent contradiction.

—Brewton Berry, "A Southerner Learns about Race,"
Common Ground (1942)

Caucasian Variety. I have taken the name of this variety from Mount Caucasus, both because its neighborhood, and especially the southern slope, produces the most beautiful race of men, I mean the Georgian; and because all the physiological reasons converge to this, that in that region, if anywhere, it seems we ought with greatest probability to place the autochthones of mankind . . . That stock displays . . . the most beautiful form of the skull, from which, as from a mean and primeval type, the others diverge . . . Besides, it is white in color, which we may fairly assume to be the primitive color of mankind, since . . . it is very easy to degenerate into brown, but very much more difficult for dark to become white.

—Johann Fredrich Blumenbach, *On the Natural Varieties of Mankind* (1775)

Of all the odd myths that have arisen in the scientific world, the "Caucasian mystery" invented quite innocently by Blumenbach is the oddest. A Georgian woman's skull was the handsomest in his collection. Hence it became his model exemplar of human skulls, from which all others might be regarded as deviations; and out of this, by some strange intellectual hocus-pocus, grew up the notion that the Caucasian man is the prototypic "Adamic" man.

—Thomas Henry Huxley, "Methods and Results of Ethnology" (1868)

Introduction: The Fabrication of Race

We tend to think of race as being indisputable, *real*. It frames our notions of kinship and descent and influences our movements in the social world; we see it plainly on one another's faces. It seems a product not of the social imagination but of biology. Like some mid-century liberals who saw race as a "myth" or a "superstition," however, scholars in several disciplines have recently shaken faith in this biological certainty. The conventions by which "race mixing" is understood, they point out, is one site where the unreality of race comes into view. Why is it that in the United

States a white woman can have black children but a black woman cannot have white children? Doesn't this bespeak a degree of arbitrariness in this business of affixing racial labels?[1]

The history of racial classification over time is a second such site: entire races have disappeared from view, from public discussion, and from modern memory, though their flesh-and-blood members still walk the earth. What has become of the nineteenth century's Celts and Slavs, for instance? Its Hebrews, Iberics, Mediterraneans, Teutons, and Anglo-Saxons? This book tells the story of how these races—these public fictions—rose and fell in American social consciousness, and how the twentieth century's Caucasians emerged to take their place.

In Philip Roth's *Counterlife* (1988) a Gentile woman chances to comment that she seldom repays the attention of Jewish men "because there are enough politics in sex without racial politics coming into it." "We're not a race," objects her Jewish listener. The ensuing exchange cuts to the very heart of "difference" and the epistemology of race.

> "It *is* a racial matter," she insisted.
>
> "No, we're the same race. You're thinking of Eskimos."
>
> "We are *not* the same race. Not according to anthropologists, or whoever measures these things. There's Caucasian, Semitic—there are about five different groups. Don't look at me like that."
>
> "I can't help it. Some nasty superstitions always tend to crop up when people talk about a Jewish 'race.' "
>
> ". . . All I can tell you is that you *are* a different race. We're supposed to be closer to Indians than to Jews, actually;—I'm talking about Caucasians."
>
> "But I am Caucasian, kiddo. In the U.S. census I am, for good or bad, counted as Caucasian."
>
> "*Are* you? *Am* I wrong?"[2]

This passage beautifully conveys the seemingly natural but finally unstable logic of race. The debate over Jews' racial identity begins merely as a matter of conflicting classification: at the outset stable, meaningful categories are assumed, and the question is simply where a particular group belongs—which pigeonhole do Jews fit into, Caucasian or Semite? But the question itself points to a more profound epistemological crisis: if he is certain that he is a Caucasian, and she is certain that he is not, then what does it mean to call a person a Caucasian in the first place? And where does all this certainty come from?

Once the two characters recognize the slippage in what they had each thought an uncompromising natural fact, both scramble to appeal to some higher authority in order to uphold their initial views. She invokes science ("according to anthropologists . . ."); he invokes the state ("in the U.S. census . . ."). They thus identify what, historically, have been two key actors in the creation and enforcement of these public fictions called races. (Not incidentally, the narratives and images of popular culture, like Roth's best-seller itself, represent another.) Caucasians are not born, these combatants now seem to understand; they are somehow made. It's just a question of who does the making.

If both characters are dubious as to the origin of these distinctions, they do seem to grasp the inherent stakes. Although each seems to be talking about race as a neutral feature of the natural landscape—tree, rock, pond, Caucasian, Eskimo—the conversation nonetheless becomes highly charged, as an element of value is inescapable in these allegedly neutral observations. That the woman is perhaps too insistent is indicated in her heated, italicized speech—it *is* a racial matter, we are *not* the same race. The man's condescending "kiddo" is retaliatory. Likewise, neither character's conception of the Caucasian race is itself entirely innocent: his understanding of "Caucasian" integrity is constituted by excluded "Eskimos," just as hers is constituted by excluded "Indians" and "Semites." Although they suppose that they are talking about scientific facts, they also intuit the supremacist baggage attached to the term. In this respect it is not merely incidental that the issue came up in the context of interracial sexuality in the first place. The policing of sexual boundaries—the defense against hybridity—is precisely what keeps a racial group a racial group. As Glenda Gilmore has written of the Jim Crow South, from the perspective of white supremacism interracial liaisons "resulted in mixed race progeny who slipped back and forth across the color line and defied social control."[3] Thus sexuality is one site at which all the economic advantages, political privileges, and social benefits inhering in a cultural invention like *Caucasian* converge and reside.

Roth himself is most interested here in the idea of Jewishness—the poor bastard, as one of his own characters puts it, "has Jew on the brain"—and certainly the notion of racial Jewishness, like anti-Semitism, has an independent history of its own. But the vicissitude of Jewish whiteness is intimately related to the racial odysseys of myriad other groups—the Irish, Armenians, Italians, Poles, Syrians, Greeks, Ruthenian's, Sicilians, Finns, and a host of others—who came ashore in the United States as "free white persons" under the terms of reigning naturalization law, yet whose racial credentials were not equivalent to those of the Anglo-Saxon "old stock" who laid proprietary claim to the nation's founding documents and hence to its stewardship. All of these groups became Caucasians only over time; and all of them, like Roth's fictional Caucasian/Semite, faced certain challenges to their racial pedigrees along the way.

As races are invented categories—designations coined for the sake of grouping and separating peoples along lines of presumed difference—Caucasians are made and not born. White privilege in various forms has been a constant in American political culture since colonial times, but whiteness itself has been subject to all kinds of contests and has gone through a series of historical vicissitudes. In the case of *Rollins v. Alabama* (1922), for instance, an Alabama Circuit Court of Appeals reversed the conviction of one Jim Rollins, a black man convicted of the crime of miscegenation, on the grounds that the state had produced "no competent evidence to show that the woman in question, Edith Labue, was a white woman." Labue was a Sicilian immigrant, a fact that, this court held, "can in no sense be taken as conclusive that she was therefore a white woman, or that she was not a negro or a descendant of a negro." Although it is important to underscore that this court did not find that a Sicilian was necessarily nonwhite, its finding that a Sicilian was inconclusively white does speak volumes about whiteness in 1920s Alabama. If the court left room for the possibility that Edith Labue *may* have been white, the ruling also made clear that she was not the sort of white woman whose purity was to be "protected" by that bulwark of white supremacism, the miscegenation statute.[4]

This ruling is not an oddity of the Alabama courts, but part of a much broader pattern of racial thinking throughout the United States between the mid-nineteenth century and the mid-twentieth. The racially inflected caricatures of the Irish at mid-century are well known, as when *Harper's* depicted the "Celt" and the "Negro" weighing in identically on the scales of civic merit, but in the 1890s even the Irish novelist John Brennan could write that the Irishness of the emigrants' children showed in their "physiognomy, or the color of their countenances."[5] When in 1891 a *Detroit News* reporter asked a Negro whitewasher whether or not he worked with any white men, the laborer answered (in a dialect provided by the journalist), "No, dere's no wite men. Dere's some Polacks, but dey ain't wite men, you know. Ha! ha! ha!"[6] In his 1908 study *Race or Mongrel?* Alfred Schultz lamented in unambiguously biological language:

The opinion is advanced that the public schools change the children
of all races into Americans. Put a Scandinavian, a German, and a
Magyar boy in at one end, and they will come out Americans at the
other end. Which is like saying, let a pointer, a setter, and a pug enter
one end of a tunnel and they will come out three greyhounds at the
other end.[7]

In her 1910 study of Homestead, Pennsylvania, the sociologist Margaret Byington broke the community down along the "racial" lines of
"Slav, English-speaking European, native white, and colored."[8] H. L.
Mencken later casually alluded to the volume of literature crossing his
desk by "Negro and other non-Nordic writers," by which, evidently, he
meant people like John Fante and Louis Adamic. In *The Sheik* (1921),
Rudolph Valentino traded on his physiognomical ability to be both the
exotic, racial Other and the acceptable, chivalric European—first, as a
"savage" Arab, kidnapping Agnes Ayers, and later (safely revealed to be
of English and Spanish descent), rescuing her from an even darker African
foe. When *Porgy and Bess* appeared (1935) critics broadly attributed
George Gershwin's talent for "American-Negroid music" to the "common
Oriental ancestry in both Negro and Jew."[9]

The contest over whiteness—its definition, its internal hierarchies, its
proper boundaries, and its rightful claimants—has been critical to American culture throughout the nation's history, and it has been a fairly untidy
affair. Conflicting or overlapping racial designations such as *white, Caucasian,* and *Celt* may operate in popular perception and discussion simultaneously, despite their contradictions—the Irish simians of the
Thomas Nast cartoon, for example, were "white" according to naturalization law; they proclaimed themselves "Caucasians" in various political
organizations using that term; and they were degraded "Celts" in the
patrician lexicon of proud Anglo-Saxons. Indeed, this is the nature of
ideological contest. Such usages have had regional valences as well: it is
one of the compelling circumstances of American cultural history that an
Irish immigrant in 1877 could be a despised Celt in Boston—a threat to
the republic—and yet a solid member of The Order of Caucasians for the
Extermination of the Chinaman in San Francisco, gallantly defending U.S.
shores from an invasion of "Mongolians."

There has been a tendency on the part of late-twentieth-century scholars, when confronted by the many jarring expressions of an earlier era's
race consciousness, simply to dismiss the discrepancy as a shift in the

meaning of the word "race." But a closer examination of the vicissitudes of "difference" is in order. Racism, as Alexander Saxton writes, is "fundamentally a theory of history."[10] It is a theory of who is who, of who belongs and who does not, of who deserves what and who is capable of what. By looking at racial categories and their fluidity over time, we glimpse the competing theories of history which inform the society and define its internal struggles. Despite the slippages in American racial thinking, some broad patterns are discernible across time. This book proposes to map the significance of the racial designations that have framed the history of European immigration—white and Caucasian on the one hand, and narrower distinctions such as Anglo-Saxon, Celt, Hebrew, Slav, Alpine, Mediterranean, or Nordic on the other—in order to make sense of pervasive racial articulations that scholars have too conveniently passed over simply as *mis*uses of the word "race." The patterns in literary, legal, political, and graphic evidence suggest that it was not just an archaic meaning of the word "race" but rather an archaic perception of "difference" by which Emma Lazarus wrote of the "Oriental blood" of the Jew and John Brennan described the distinct physiognomy and skin color of the Celt.

American scholarship on immigration has generally conflated race and color, and so has transported a late-twentieth-century understanding of "difference" into a period whose inhabitants recognized biologically based "races" rather than culturally based "ethnicities." But in the interest of an accurate historical rendering of race in the structure of U.S. culture and in the experience of those immigrant groups now called "Caucasians," we must listen more carefully to the historical sources than to the conventions of our own era; we must admit of a system of "difference" by which one might be both white *and* racially distinct from other whites.

Two sorts of anachronism have resulted from the general failure to recover the historical processes of racial mutability. First, historians have most often cast the history of nineteenth-century immigration in the logic of twentieth-century "ethnic" groups—"race" did not really *mean* "race" back then, in other words. This blithe disbelief not only distorts the historical record but also carries with it some troubling baggage. Tacitly assuming that "race" did not mean "race"—that Hebrews, Celts, Mediterraneans, Iberics, or Teutons were *really* Caucasians—is worse than merely underestimating the ideological power of racialism: it is surrendering to that power. To miss the fluidity of race itself in this process of becoming Caucasian is to reify a monolithic whiteness, and, further, to

cordon that whiteness off from other racial groupings along lines that are
silently presumed to be more genuine. Failure properly to theorize the
transmutation of white races into Caucasians has left open the way for a
second kind of anachronism: seizing upon their forebears' status as racial
Others, writers like Michael Novak and Michael Lerner now disavow
any participation in twentieth-century white privilege on the spurious basis of their parents' and grandparents' racial oppression. Novak wrote the
Bible of the "ethnic revival" decades ago; but the move toward reclaimed
otherness has become more common in recent years, in part in response
to group-based social policies like affirmative action. As one African-
American leader of a seminar on racism put it when, one by one, his class
explained away their whiteness ("I'm not white; I'm Italian"), "Where are
all the white people who were here just a minute ago?"[11]

The sociologists Michael Omi and Howard Winant assert that the contending forces of class formation and racial formation in American political culture produced "the institutionalization of a racial order that
drew a color line *around* rather than *within* Europe."[12] True enough, and
a useful corrective to those who would disavow their whiteness even while
they live lives predicated upon its privileges. But between the 1840s and
the 1920s it was not altogether clear just where that line ultimately *would*
be drawn. Just as it is crucial to recognize the legal whiteness undergirding
the status of the white races in the United States, so is it crucial to reckon
seriously with the racial othering that overlaid that whiteness. One way
of doing that is to examine the relationship among competing ideas such
as *white, Caucasian, Nordic, Anglo-Saxon, Celt, Slav, Alpine, Hebrew,*
Mediterranean, Iberic, Latin, and so on.

The vicissitudes of race represent glacial, nonlinear cultural movements. Nonetheless, the history of whiteness in the United States is divisible into three great epochs. The nation's first naturalization law in 1790
(limiting naturalized citizenship to "free white persons") demonstrates the
republican convergence of race and "fitness for self-government"; the
law's wording denotes an unconflicted view of the presumed character
and unambiguous boundaries of whiteness. Fifty years later, however, beginning with the massive influx of highly undesirable but nonetheless
"white" persons from Ireland, whiteness was subject to new interpretations. The period of mass European immigration, from the 1840s to the
restrictive legislation of 1924, witnessed a fracturing of whiteness into a
hierarchy of plural and scientifically determined white races. Vigorous
debate ensued over which of these was truly "fit for self-government" in

the good old Anglo-Saxon sense. Finally, in the 1920s and after, partly because the crisis of over-inclusive whiteness had been solved by restrictive legislation and partly in response to a new racial alchemy generated by African-American migrations to the North and West, whiteness was reconsolidated: the late nineteenth century's probationary white groups were now remade and granted the scientific stamp of authenticity as the unitary Caucasian race—an earlier era's Celts, Slavs, Hebrews, Iberics, and Saracens, among others, had become the Caucasians so familiar to our own visual economy and racial lexicon.

The 1965 immigration act, passed by the first Congress in U.S. history in which Roman Catholics constituted a plurality, consecrated the massive and theretofore problematic immigration of the pre-1924 period by giving preference to those immigrants' relatives. Indeed, a few years earlier the election of John F. Kennedy, a Celt whose "Papist" allegiances were questioned, but whose racial character never was, marked the ascendance and utter hegemony of this third paradigm. The crossing over of the scientific appellation "Caucasian" into the vernacular with increasing regularity in the mid-twentieth century marks a profound readjustment in popular thinking as to the relationship among the immigrant white races. *Becoming* Caucasian, then, has been crucial to the politico-cultural saga of European migration and settlement, and the process by which this came about touches the histories of every other racially coded group on the American scene.

Two premises guide my approach to these questions. First, race is absolutely central to the history of European immigration and settlement. It was the racial appellation "white persons" in the nation's naturalization law that allowed the migrations from Europe in the first place; the problem this immigration posed to the polity was increasingly cast in terms of racial difference and assimilability; the most significant revision of immigration policy, the Johnson-Reed Act of 1924, was founded upon a racial logic borrowed from biology and eugenics; and, consequently, the civic story of assimilation (the process by which the Irish, Russian Jews, Poles, and Greeks became Americans) is inseparable from the cultural story of racial alchemy (the process by which Celts, Hebrews, Slavs, and Mediterraneans became Caucasians). The European immigrants' experience was decisively shaped by their entering an arena where European-ness—that is to say, whiteness—was among the most important possessions one could lay claim to. It was their *whiteness*, not any kind of New World magnanimity, that opened the Golden Door. And yet, for those who arrived between 1840 and 1924, New World experience was also decisively stamped by their entering an arena where race was the prevailing idiom for discussing citizenship and the relative merits of a given people.[13]

The second premise guiding this work is that race resides not in nature but in politics and culture. One of the tasks before the historian is to discover which racial categories are useful to whom at a given moment, and why. Nor is this simply a case of immigrants' insisting upon their whiteness while nativists tarred them as "Hebrews" or "Slavs." Immigrants were often as quick to recognize their racial distance from the Anglo-Saxon as vice versa. Immigrant nationalisms were particularly prolific in generating and sustaining distinct racial identities—the Irish Race Conventions of the 1910s, for example, represent another instance where "race" really meant "race."[14] Racial categories themselves—their vicissitudes and the contests over them—reflect the competing notions of history, peoplehood, and collective destiny by which power has been organized and contested on the American scene.

This is not to argue that race is freighted the same way from period to period or from case to case. No one who has looked into this country's maze of segregation statutes, miscegenation codes, housing covenants, slavery laws, or civil rights debates could ever suppose that being a "Celt," say, was tantamount to being some kind of European "Negro." My point here is not to equate one racial experience with another, but rather to demonstrate the inadequacy of modern notions of "ethnicity" in rendering the history of whiteness in American social and political life. Ultimately, I would argue, this treatment of the racial history of European immigration counters any facile comparisons of the African-American experience with the white immigrant experience: it is not just that various white immigrant groups' economic successes came at the expense of nonwhites, but that they owe their now stabilized and broadly recognized whiteness *itself* in part to these nonwhite groups.

And so this history of whiteness and its fluidity is very much a history of power and its disposition. But there is a second dimension: race is not just a conception; it is also a perception. The problem is not merely how races are comprehended, but how they are seen. In her 1943 obituary of Franz Boas, Ruth Benedict recounted how Boas the physicist, having gone to the Arctic to study the properties of water, became Boas the anthropologist upon discovering that his observations did not at all match those of the Eskimos he encountered. Remarked Benedict, "He returned with an abiding conviction that if we are ever to understand human behavior we must know as much about the eye that sees as about the object seen. And he had understood once and for all that the eye that sees is not a mere physical organ but a means of perception conditioned by the tradition in which its possessor has been reared."[15]

If this passage sums up Boas's understanding of the power of culture, it also nicely sums up the properties of race itself. In racial matters above all else, the eye that sees is "a means of perception conditioned by the tradition in which its possessor has been reared." The American eye sees a certain person as black, for instance, whom Haitian or Brazilian eyes might see as white. Similarly, an earlier generation of Americans *saw* Celtic, Hebrew, Anglo-Saxon, or Mediterranean physiognomies where today we see only subtly varying shades of a mostly undifferentiated whiteness. (If pressed, we might come to a consensus on the physiognomical properties of Irishness, Slavicness, or Jewishness, but at a glance these certainly do not strike most Americans with anything like the perceptible force that they did a century ago, or that live racial distinctions do today.) Although much of this study is given over to the history of various conceptions of racial "difference," the second half of the equation consists of the ways in which those conceptions of difference successfully masquerade as nature. The awesome power of race as an ideology resides precisely in its ability to pass as a feature of the natural landscape. Perhaps the most far-reaching ambition of this book, then, is to help loosen the grip of race by laying bare the moribund, and now quite peculiar, circuitry of an earlier era's racial conceptions and perceptions.

I initially identified a number of well-delineated arenas for this investigation of race and its workings: science, law, politics, popular culture, and the literary work of immigrants and natives, Caucasians and non-Caucasians. But these arenas did not remain well delineated at all. This was the source of much excitement and consternation as my research progressed. Franz Boas wandered out of his niche in "science" and into the arena of "law," testifying in court as to the Caucasian origins of a group of Armenian immigrants petitioning for citizenship. Local conflicts such as the lynching of eleven Italians in New Orleans surfaced well beyond the pale of "political conflict," now recast as "literature" in Mark Twain's *Pudd'nhead Wilson*. Political debates over slavery, naturalization law, and immigration drew on the sciences of anthropology and eugenics, but these bodies of knowledge had arisen in answer to questions about peoplehood generated by the politics of exploration, expansion, colonialism, slavery, and republicanism in the first place. Scientists and politicians freely cited the first-hand accounts of white travelers in order to assert this or that truth about Africa or Asia, and yet those accounts—like the travelers' experiences—had already been structured by technologies, modes of seeing, a set of social relations, and an epistemology entwined in the project of Euro-American exploration and imperial expansion.

How, then, to render something at once so thick and so vaporous as *ideology* in a thin black line of linear prose? The eight chapters that define the structure of this book represent an experimental answer. My narrative takes three separate tacks on the problem, each illuminating one particular dimension of race and its workings in American culture: race as an organizer of power whose vicissitudes track power relationships through time; race as a mode of perception contingent upon the circumstances of the moment; and race as the product of specific struggles for power at specific cultural sites.

More than once in the process of this research I have been reminded of Oscar Handlin's famous remark, "Once I thought to write a history of the immigrants in America. Then I discovered that the immigrants *were* American history."[16] Race and races are American history, it now seems to me; that is, to write about race in American culture is to exclude virtually nothing. A word, then, on some of the choices I have made along the way. As race is a public fiction, I have confined myself to public images and expressions with the power both to articulate and to influence racial conceptions. Since race is a kind of social currency, it seemed most useful to begin with an analysis of its public exchange. My conclusions derive from patterns observed in the racial logic of novels, films, and print journalism; from legal codes, colonial charters, and state constitutions; from congressional debates over citizenship, immigration, expansionism, and civil rights; from the court records of various naturalization and miscegenation cases; from published tracts in ethnology and anthropology; from immigrant journalism; from political speeches and nativist lectures; from cartoons and engravings; from travel literature; from newspaper coverage of sensational events like the Leo Frank case and the draft riots, and from coverage of more mundane affairs, like the daily police blotter. This study is of necessity structured something like a pointillist painting: the separate points, in this case, consist of close readings and historical analyses of an idiosyncratic assemblage of texts, events, images, and utterances. Some choices will be predictable, others less so; but taken together, I hope, they add up to a suggestive tableau of coherent ideological and cultural patterns across a rather large sweep of time—the *Grande Jatte*, as it were, of American race thinking.

My intent here is to join scholars like David Roediger and Karen Brodkin Sacks in moving race to the foreground of historiography on European immigration and assimilation. The saga of European immigration has long been held up as proof of the openness of American society, the benign and absorptive powers of American capitalism, and the robust health of American democracy. "Ethnic inclusion," "ethnic mobility," and "ethnic assimilation" on the European model set the standard upon which "America," as an ideal, is presumed to *work;* they provide the normative experience against which others are measured. But this pretty story suddenly fades once one recognizes how crucial Europeans' racial status as "free white persons" was to their gaining entrance in the first place; how profoundly dependent their racial inclusion was upon the racial *ex*clusion of others; how racially accented the native resistance was even to *their* inclusion for something over half a century; and how completely intertwined were the prospects of becoming American and becoming Caucasian. Racism now appears not anomalous to the working of American democracy, but fundamental to it.

I focus on the historical contingency of Europeans' racial identities not so that so-called white ethnics can conveniently disassociate themselves from the historic legacies of white privilege. On the contrary, recognizing how that privilege is constituted depends upon our first understanding how whiteness itself has been built and maintained. Recasting the saga of Europeans' immigration and assimilation in the United States as a *racial* odyssey is a first step in that direction.

THE POLITICAL HISTORY
OF WHITENESS

Scholars in several disciplines have discovered that racial whiteness can be quite changeable. The nineteenth-century antagonism between the English and the Irish, for instance, was at the time a racial conflict between Anglo-Saxons and Celts, though few today would invoke the language of race in recounting the "Troubles." Having emigrated to North America, moreover, many maligned Celts took on a new racial identity, now participating in a politics of white supremacy in groups like The Order of Caucasians, often right alongside the Anglo-Saxons with whom, in other settings, their racial equality was so vigorously denied.

These observations raise a number of questions in their turn. If whiteness is indeed changeable, under what circumstances does it change? What have been the historical patterns that characterize whiteness and its vicissitudes? What does the racial history of European immigration look like across the chronological sweep of U.S. history?

The three chapters of part one sketch the history of whiteness through three periods in the American setting. The contending forces that have fashioned and refashioned whiteness in the United States across time, I argue, are capitalism (with its insatiable appetite for cheap labor) and republicanism (with its imperative of responsible citizenship). Citizenship was a racially inscribed concept at the outset of the new nation: by an act of Congress, only "free white" immigrants could be naturalized. Yet as immigration soared in the second half of the nineteenth century, incoming "white" peasants and laborers from unanticipated regions of Europe aroused doubts about this equation of "whiteness" with "fitness for self-government." Over the latter half of the nineteenth century a second regime of racial understanding emerged in response, cataloguing the newcomers as racial types, pronouncing upon their innate, biological distance from the nation's "original stock," and speculating as to their fitness for citizenship. This regime culminated in the racially based and highly restrictive immigration legislation of 1924, which in its turn laid the way for yet a third racial regime.

The period from the 1920s to the 1960s saw a dramatic decline in the perceived differences among these white Others. Immigration restriction, along with internal black migrations, altered the nation's racial alchemy and redrew the dominant racial configuration along the strict, binary line of white and black, creating Caucasians where before had been so many Celts, Hebrews, Teutons, Mediterraneans, and Slavs.

To track racial whiteness across time is to depict American political culture in its major adjustments, as shifting demographics have chafed against the more rigid imperatives of this fragile experiment in self-governance. To trace the process by which Celts or Slavs became Caucasians is to recognize race as an ideological, political deployment rather than as a neutral, biologically determined element of nature.

1

"Free White Persons" in the Republic, 1790–1840

In *Modern Chivalry* (1792), Hugh Henry Brackenridge's extended meditation on republican government, the Irish servant Teague O'Regan undergoes a dramatic transformation. When he is introduced in the novel's
opening paragraph, the servant is but a cipher—"an Irishman," according
to Brackenridge's contemptuous narrator, "whose name was Teague
Oregan [later O'Regan]. I shall say nothing of the character of this man,
because the very name imports what he was." By the closing lines, some
eight hundred pages later, O'Regan has become the novel's central character, he has pursued with some success the plums made available by the
new nation's democratic politics, and the narrator is reflecting on the
possibility that, in some future volume, "my bog-trotter" might even venture to England as the U.S. ambassador.[1]

This transformation reflects not only the Irishman's mobility of station
but also a certain alchemy of race. The "aborigines of Ireland," Brackenridge avers, "are far from being destitute of talents, and yet there is a
certain liability to blunders, both in their words and actions, that is singular." Here as elsewhere the narrative testifies to certain immutable

truths about "the national character of the aboriginal Irish." Indeed, there is a certain ideological alignment in the classification of the "aboriginal Irish" (as distinct, presumably, from their Anglo-Irish rulers) on the one hand, and the *North American* aborigines on the other: an Indian treaty-maker approaches O'Regan's employer, for example, with the scheme of "borrowing" the Irishman to play the part of an Indian chief for the staging of a treaty. Teague O'Regan, according to this script, will be "king of the kickapoos" for a treaty highly beneficial to white settlers. He is well suited to the part of Indian chief because he happens to speak the "necessary gibberish."[2]

And yet it is by his favorable contrast to these same Indians, ultimately, that the bog-trotter O'Regan becomes an acceptable member of the white polity. His political fortunes first begin to turn after he delivers a rousing speech on the question of how to deal with "de vile savages":

> I have heard of dese Indians; plase your honours; dey come out of de woods, and stale shape, like de rabbers in Ireland, and burn houses, and take scoolps; trate wid dese! I would trate wid dem, wid a good shelelah, or tomahawk to break deir heads. Give dem goods! by Shaint Patrick, I would give dem a good bullet hole in deir faces; or shoot dem trough de backside for deir pains. If I was in Cangress, and God love your shouls, I wish you would put me dere, I would make a law to coot dem aff, every one o' dem . . . Trate wid dem! Trate wid de wolves or de bears, dat roon troo de woods: I would trate wid a good knock in dere troat, and be doon wid dem.

These sentiments, so forcefully spoken, go a long way in making a proper republican of the Irish aboriginal. Indeed, "those particularly who were for using force against the savages, thought the Irish gentleman had spoken very well."[3]

Later, while serving in a war party, O'Regan accidentally sacks a detachment of Indians after he happens upon them in his own ill-fated attempt to get away: he appears fearlessly to be advancing even in his haste to beat a retreat; his shouts of alarmed surprise are taken for shouts of confidence. He becomes the accidental victor: "When the party of the whites came up to the brow of the hill, and saw the bog-trotter in possession of the ground and the booty, they took it for granted, that singly, and alone, he had discomfitted the Indians."[4] On the strength of such heroism, he is named a commissioner for executing future treaties: rather than representing the Indians by playing "chief," he will now represent the white settlers. His transformation is complete. Thus, in spite of himself, does O'Regan become a hero in this crucible of Indian warfare, and thus does he traverse the social distance separating "bog-trotters" from "the party of whites" that is the New World polity.

Modern Chivalry thus anticipates one of the throughlines of American political culture for decades to come: republicanism would favor or exclude certain peoples on the basis of their "fitness for self-government," as the phrase went, and some questionable peoples would win inclusion based upon an alchemic reaction attending Euro-American contact with peoples of color. "Can a bog-trotter just from Ireland like you be supposed to be cognizant of the genius of the people sufficiently to form a constitution for them?" one character asks, as O'Regan's appetite for political participation piques. Brackenridge's final answer is, no, perhaps the "genius" of the people will ever elude the bog-trotter, and yet, nonetheless, O'Regan can number himself among "the people" by his essays in Indian-hating. (Years later James Hall rendered this dynamic with admirable economy: "I believe that in killing the savage I performed my duty as a man and served my country as a citizen.")[5]

"Whiteness" has recently received important scholarly attention, and yet the reigning paradigms among historians—coming primarily from the direction of working-class or labor history—have not yet exhausted its full complexity. Most notable in this regard are Theodore Allen's *Invention of the White Race* and David Roediger's *Wages of Whiteness.*[6] Allen's is a brilliantly conceived study of the "relativity of race" documenting how the Irish who had been downtrodden "Celts" on one side of the Atlantic became privileged "whites" on the other. But however nuanced Allen's depiction of an ever changeable racial Irishness, his argument remains at bottom a rather rigid economic argument about "racial oppression and social control." Race here operates primarily to create an "intermediate buffer social control stratum" that bolsters the capitalist order by winning the allegiance of the potentially disaffected: "Propertyless classes are recruited into the intermediate stratum, through anomalous 'racial' privileges not involving escape from propertylessness." Hence the moment the oppressed Celts set foot on American soil, "however lowly their social status might otherwise be they were endowed with all the immunities, rights, and privileges of 'American whites,' " and thus became "enrolled in the system of racial oppression of all African-Americans."

Politics in the United States thus reiterates the "perfectly devilish inge-
nuity," in James Connolly's phrase, by which the allegiance of economically oppressed laborers was won through racial privilege.[7]

Roediger's *Wages of Whiteness* similarly opens up important terrain in
the problematics of whiteness, and it does so with tremendous subtlety
when it comes to the intersections of political economy, class formation,
and psychology. Yet because Roediger also comes at this problem from
the angle of labor history, his work, too, remains wedded to economic
models in its handling of the question. In Roediger's account the attri-
bution of whiteness does not depend on a natural—nor even a static—
condition, but rather represents "a way in which white workers responded
to a fear of dependency on wage labor and to the necessities of capitalist
work discipline." The key to his argument is W. E. B. Du Bois's formulation that, despite a low monetary wage, white workers were compen-
sated by a "public and psychological wage" involving "public deference"
and their preferential "personal treatment" by key social and political
institutions.[8]

Both works convey in important and ingenious ways the instability and
relativity of race, but, in focusing upon class and economics as the primary movers of race, they fall short in three respects. First, neither captures the full complexity of whiteness in its vicissitudes: what are the
significant points of divergence and alignment among categories such as—
taking the Irish as an example—*white, Caucasian,* and *Celt?* How do the
three ideas operate at a given moment? How do they differ? What does
each accomplish in the social order, and for whom? What is at stake in
these competing versions of racial reality?

Second, though both Allen and Roediger nicely melt down the seeming
fixities of race to reveal its fluidity at certain moments, neither sets whiteness against a broad historical backdrop. This is especially debilitating
for Roediger's argument as it relates to the escalating salience of whiteness
for Irish workers at mid-century: the phrase "free white persons" had been
on the books since 1790, and was indeed responsible for their possibility
of naturalized citizenship in the first place. Did whiteness assume a new
place in American systems of "difference" in the 1850s, 1860s, and 1870s,
or was it simply cast in bolder relief by new political, social, economic,
and demographic circumstances? Were Americans *seeing* whiteness dif-
ferently in the 1870s than they had in the 1790s? Than they would in the
1920s? Because the certainties represented by race are bound in a wildly

complex skein of political, economic, cultural, ideological, psychological, and perceptual strands, their movements are glacial rather than catastrophic, uneven rather than linear or steady. Thus the historical twists and turns taken by a racial idea like *white, Celt,* or *Caucasian* are best charted across more time rather than less—scores and even hundreds of years rather than mere decades.

Finally, and most important, neither Roediger nor Allen adequately depicts the struggle over defining whiteness and apportioning its privileges outside the economic arenas of class concern and social control. Economic models may indeed explain the racial valences of "self-respect" in nineteenth-century America and the nexus between working-class, largely Irish, aggrieved entitlement on the one hand, and the eager embrace of a self-affirming whiteness on the other. Allen's "social control" model, likewise, may reveal quite a lot about the "spontaneous allegiance" of Irish workers, and their claim to prior rights over the "Negro," summed up in the insistence—as New York's *Weekly Caucasian* had it in the 1860s—that "this Government was made on the WHITE BASIS . . . for the Benefit of WHITE MEN." Economics alone, however, cannot explain why this government was made on the "white basis" to begin with; nor can economics alone explain why native elites again and again tried to deny peoples like Celts (and Jews and Armenians and Italians and Slavs) a full share in whiteness itself—that is, why native elites tried to deny them the "public and psychological wage" that was allegedly holding these potentially rebellious masses in check. Economics alone cannot explain why, as patrician New Yorkers looked out their windows at Irish rioters in 1863, they saw, not so many "white men," but "thousands of barbarians in our midst every whit as ferocious in their instincts as the Minnesota savages"—the multiplied, essentialized "Celt," whose "impulsiveness . . . prompts him to be foremost in every outburst."[9] Nor, most important, can economics alone explain why the Irish themselves, like the novelist John Brennan, often commented upon their racial distinctiveness from other whites on the American scene.

One need look further, at the complex crosscurrents at the confluence of capitalism, republicanism, and the diasporic sensibilities of various racially defined groups themselves. In his satiric novel *The Man Who Knew Coolidge* (1928), Sinclair Lewis pointed out one of the critical integers in the equation of race and economics. Amid a harangue about the political debates surrounding birth control, Lewis's "Nordic Citizen" remarks,

One faction claims that the superior classes like ourselves, in fact the great British stock, had ought to produce as many kids as possible, to keep in control of this great nation and maintain the ideals for which we and our ancestors have always stood, while these lower masses hadn't ought to spawn their less intellectual masses. But then again, there's them that hold and maintain that now we've cut down immigration, we need a supply of cheap labor, and where get it better than by encouraging these Wops and Hunks and Spigs and so on to raise as many brats as they can?[10]

The Nordic's crass statement of the conflict between the ideal "control of this great nation" on the one hand and the ever-pressing need for "cheap labor" on the other fairly sums up a tension between the imperatives of democracy and the imperatives of capitalism that is integral to American political culture. Historically this tension has heavily inflected American race thinking. Categories of race have fluctuated, not only in response to the imperatives of a segmented labor market, or to the "spontaneous allegiance" of white workers based on their own perceived whiteness, but also to perceptions of "fitness for self-government." The very "inferiority" that suits a given group to a particular niche in the economy, for instance, may raise serious questions about its participation in a self-governing democracy; the very "psychological wage" of whiteness that might win workers' allegiance to capitalism confers a degree of political entitlement altogether threatening to the republic. In short, the idea of a wage economy established "on the white basis" may be useful, whereas a *government* "on the white basis" may be quite dangerous. Hence a major element of the contest over whiteness: the Celt may be white, but he is nonetheless a savage. (A second element, of course, is the white immigrants' own view of their relative consanguinity with native whites. Many came ashore bearing historical baggage of racial thought and racial perception themselves; Celtic or Hebrew identity was not merely pressed upon them from without by native republicans convinced of Anglo-Saxon virtue, but was a *self*-ascription as well—a politically useful idiom in the service, say, of Irish nationalism or Zionism.)

This is not to minimize the significance of economics and class in racial formation. Race and class are intertwined in ways that even Roediger and Allen have yet to explore fully. First, republican notions of "independence" had both racial and economic valences; the white men's movement for "Free Labor, Free Soil, and Free Men" was but the flipside of certain racial notions such as a belief in the Indian's innate "dependency." Second, racial stereotypes like inborn "laziness," as applied to Mexicans or Indians, were economic assessments that had economic consequences (in the form, typically, of dispossession). Third, race has been central to American conceptions of property (who can own property and who can *be* property, for example), and property in its turn is central to republican notions of self-possession and the "stake in society" necessary for democratic participation. Fourth, political standing, doled out on racial terms (such as the naturalization code limiting citizenship to "free white persons"), translates immediately into economic realities such as property rights or labor-market segmentation. And fifth, in cases in American political culture ranging from the Mexican population of Old California to the immigrant Jews of New York's Lower East Side, class markers have often been read as inborn racial characteristics: members of the working class in these groups have been viewed in more sharply racial terms than have their upper-class compatriots.[11]

It is not my interest, then, to minimize the significance of class and economics; rather, since class has received most of the attention afforded questions of whiteness in the scholarship thus far, I will go into other areas more fully—especially the areas of national subjectivity and national belonging—as they both inflect and are inflected by racial conceptions of peoplehood, self-possession, fitness for self-government, and collective destiny.

Reviewing the Dillingham Commission Report on Immigration, which significantly constricted whiteness as it bore on eligibility for naturalized citizenship, the eugenicist Harry Laughlin of the Carnegie Foundation remarked, "We in this country have been so imbued with the idea of democracy, or the equality of all men, that we have left out of consideration the matter of blood or natural inborn hereditary mental and moral differences. No man who breeds pedigreed plants and animals can afford to neglect this thing."[12] On the contrary, the "idea of democracy" had never neglected "this thing" about the matter of blood or natural inborn differences, and contested notions of "inborn difference" are themselves as traceable to the imperatives of democracy as they are to the imperatives of capitalism. Chinese Exclusion and the precarious political status of free blacks in the North are two of the more obvious evidences of this. The topography of American politics from the Revolution through the twentieth century has been a contest over the "inborn differences" among various groups—not least, among the "free white persons" who entered the polity under the terms of the naturalization law of 1790. The eighteenth century's free white persons became the nineteenth century's Celts, Slavs, Hebrews, Iberics, Latins, and Anglo-Saxons, who in turn became the twentieth century's Caucasians, as popular recognition of consanguinity or racial difference fluctuated in response to national, regional, and local circumstances.

Whiteness and Citizenship

In 1790 Congress enacted "that all free white persons who, have, or shall migrate into the United States, and shall give satisfactory proof, before a magistrate, by oath, that they intend to reside therein, and shall take an oath of allegiance, and shall have resided in the United States for one whole year, shall be entitled to the rights of citizenship."[13] So natural was the relationship of whiteness to citizenship that, in the debate which followed, the racial dimension of the act remained unquestioned. Members of the first Congress argued over the one-year requirements (should it have been two or three?); they wondered whether Jews and Catholics should be eligible; they entertained a proposal for a period of political "probation" for newcomers and pondered limitations on the right to hold political office; they argued over foreigners' rights of land-holding and inheritance; they worried about the potential threat posed by "monarchists," former "nobles," and criminals from other lands. They debated the naturalization process and wondered whether they had made citizenship "much too easy" to attain—should claimants be required, for example, to provide witnesses to their good character? In general the nation's first legislators saw the law as too inclusive rather than too exclusive, and nowhere did they pause to question the limitation of naturalized citizenship to "white persons."[14]

Modern commentators ranging from Gunnar Myrdal to Judith Shklar have offered some version of the argument that a democracy built upon systematic disenfranchisements is politically hypocritical. The political history of inequality represents a "dilemma," an uncomfortable betrayal of the "American Creed," according to Myrdal; American society has been "actively and purposefully false to its own vaunted principles," argues Shklar. But "hypocrisy"—even Pierre van der Berghe's condemnatory *Herrenvolk democracy*—is too simple a frame to do justice to the historical conjunction of racialism and American democracy.[15] Exclusions based upon race and gender did not represent mere lacunae in an otherwise liberal philosophy of political standing; nor were the nation's exclusions simply contradictions of the democratic creed. Rather, in the eighteenth and nineteenth centuries these inclusions and exclusions formed an inseparable, interdependent figure and ground in the same ideological tapestry of republicanism.

That whiteness would be so entwined with ideas of citizenship as to be invisible during the congressional debate was overdetermined. The practical and ideological meaning of color in the early republic is worth examining. Most important was the practical issue of what was required of a citizen. Political identity was rendered racial identity at least implicitly in the earliest documents establishing a European political order in the New World, the colonial charters, inasmuch as the limits of the polity, the duties of its members, and its mission as a community were articulated in the context of encounter. References to the New World's "barbarous" or "savage" inhabitants were standard in the charters' articulations of political necessity. The Third Charter of Virginia (1611–1612), for instance, dedicated the colony to "the propagation of the Christian Religion, and Reclaiming of People barbarous, to Civility and Humanity." The Declaration of Proposals of the Lord Proprietor of Carolina (1663) similarly declared "a pious and good intention for the propagation of the Christian faith amongst the barbarous and ignorant Indians," while the Charter of Rhode Island and Providence Plantations (also 1663) committed the members of that colony to "pursuing, with peacable and loyall mindes [the] sober, serious, and religious intentions . . . [of] the gaineing over and conversione of the poore ignorant Indian natives."[16]

Whereas in these documents the presence of "savages" or "barbarous nations" defines the boundaries of a polity of *un*savage, *un*barbarous Englishmen, in the Charter of New England (1620) the very absence of such peoples defined the new political community in this "wilderness," although to much the same effect. We have been given "certainly to knowe," ran the text, that

> there hath by God's Visitation raigned a wonderfull Plague, together with many horrible Slaugthers and Murthers, committed amongst the Savages and brutish people there, heertofore inhabiting, in a manner to the utter Destruction, Devastacion, and Depopulacion of the whole Territorye . . . whereby We in our Judgment are persuaded and satisfied that the appointed Time is come in which Almighty God in his great Goodness and Bountie towards Us and our People, hath

thought fitt and determined, that these large and goodly Territoryes, deserted as it were by their natural Inhabitants, should be possessed and enjoyed by such of our Subjects and our People as heertofore have and hereafter shall by His Mercie and Favour, and by His Powerfull Arme, be directed and conducted thither.[17]

Where "savage" peoples were not evoked in the charters as a field of opportunity for the work of propagating Christianity, they were evoked as probable foes on an imagined field of battle. The Charter of Maryland (1632) granted power to the baron of Baltimore to raise an army "because, in so remote a region, placed among so many barbarous Nations, the Incursions as well of the Barbarians themselves, as of other Enemies, Pirates and Ravagers, probably will be feared." This army was "to wage War, and to pursue even beyond the Limits of their Province, the Enemies and Ravagers aforesaid, infesting those parts by Land and by Sea, and (if God shall grant it) to vanquish and captivate them, and the Captives to put to Death, or, according to their Discretion, to save [them]." The power to muster an army was likewise included in the Grant of the Province of Maine (1639), "because in a Country soe farr distant and seated amongst soe many barbarous nations the Intrusions or Invasions aswell of the barbarous people as of Pirates and other enemies maye be justly feared." The Preamble to the Georgia Charter (1732), perhaps more vividly than any other, demonstrates the meaning of "polity" and the responsibilities of citizenship in the New World:

Our provinces in North America, have been frequently ravaged by Indian enemies; more especially that of South Carolina, which in the late war, by the neighboring savages, was laid waste with fire and sword, and great numbers of English inhabitants, miserably massacred; and our loving subjects who now inhabit them, by reason of the smallness of their numbers, will in case of a new war, be exposed to the late calamities; inasmuch as their whole southern frontier continueth unsettled, and lieth open to said savages.[18]

This colonial line of thinking culminated in July 1776, in the Declaration of Independence: among the "injuries and usurpations" attributed to the king, he has "endeavored to bring on the inhabitants of our frontiers the merciless Indian savages, whose known rule of warfare is an undistinguished destruction of all ages, sexes, and conditions."

These colonial documents do not use the word "white," but between the charters of the early seventeenth century and the naturalization law of the late eighteenth, the word "white" did attain wide usage in New World political discourse, and it was written into an immense body of statutory law. In the colonies the designation "white" appeared in laws governing who could marry whom; who could participate in the militia; who could vote or hold office; and in laws governing contracts, indenture, and enslavement. Although there were some exceptions, most laws of this kind delineated the populace along lines of color, and the word "white" was commonly used in conferring rights, never in abridging them (with the single exception of proscribing whom "whites" could marry).[19] The designation "white" appeared in the Articles of Confederation as well, though not in the Constitution.[20] As scholars like Leon Higginbotham, Jr., have suggested, in practice the idea of citizenship had become thoroughly entwined with the idea of "whiteness" (and maleness) because what a citizen really was, at bottom, was someone who could help put down a slave rebellion or participate in Indian wars. This meaning of citizenship emerged, for instance, in congressional debate over the relationship of Americans' land-holdings to their former nations of residence: "A person owing no allegiance to a sovereign, ought not to hold lands under its protection, because he cannot be called upon and obliged to give that support which invasion or insurrection may render necessary."[21] In other words, the potential for "invasion or insurrection" and its attendant "necessities" came to define citizenship for the New World polity.[22]

Nor is it surprising that when Congress first penned "An Act more effectually to provide for the National Defence by establishing an Uniform Militia throughout the United States" (1792), the new militia's participants were defined as "each and every free able-bodied white male citizen of the respective states." It was unlikely that a Negro or an Indian should be required to "provide himself with a good musket or firelock, a sufficient bayonet and belt, two spare flints, and a knapsack, a pouch with a box therein to contain not less than twenty-four cartridges."[23] The very notion of "providing for the common defence" was inherently racial in the context of slaveholding on the one hand and frontier settlement on the other. Thus when the legislators of 1790 limited naturalization to "free white persons," they were employing language that had become familiar—for instance, in Georgia's limitation of the franchise to "all male white inhabitants" (1777), or in South Carolina's requirement that every voter and officeholder be a "free white male."[24]

In addition to the racially inflected question of "common defense," as scholars like Benjamin Ringer and Ronald Takaki have shown, whiteness was tacitly but irretrievably written into republican ideology as well.[25] The American Revolution radically altered the lines of authority from the Crown to "the people," these scholars argue, but it left entirely untouched various Enlightenment assumptions about who "the people" properly ought to be. The experiment in democratic government seemed to call for a polity that was disciplined, virtuous, self-sacrificing, productive, far-seeing, and wise—traits that were all racially inscribed in eighteenth-century Euro-American thought. With its abolition of monarchic power and its disruption of strict, top-down lines of political authority, the new democratic order would require of its participants a remarkable degree of *self-possession*—a condition already denied literally to Africans in slavery and figuratively to all "nonwhite" or "heathen" peoples in prevailing conceptions of human capacity. In his study of the Roman precedents for American republican ideology, M. N. S. Sellers enumerates the elements of classical republicanism this way:

> (1) pursuit of justice and the common good, through (2) the rule of law, under (3) a mixed and balanced government, comprising (4) a sovereign people (5) a deliberative senate, and (6) an elected magistracy. Americans in every faction endorsed this basic conception of republican government and the patrician vision of (7) ordered liberty and (8) public virtue it sought to protect.

This was to be an empire "of law and reason, not arbitrary will or passion"; and indeed in this configuration *passion* itself is among the chief villains or potential tyrants. And unbridled passion, if difficult enough to keep under control among Europeans, was the veritable hallmark of "the savage."[26] As John R. Commons summed it up in 1907, "It is not enough that equal opportunity to participate in making and enforcing the laws should be vouchsafed to all—it is equally important that all should be capable of such participation."[27] Thus does the republican ideal of "the consent of the governed" become inextricably linked to its unfortunate shadow, the gendered, almost always racial question of "fitness for self-government."[28]

Gordon Wood, perhaps the foremost student of the Revolutionary generation's republicanism, illumines the extent to which inclusions and exclusions based on whiteness did not contradict, but rather *constituted*, republican principles, though he himself is little concerned with race. Wood's gloss of popular republicanism contains several features that dovetail with broader Euro-American racial assumptions of the period. Among them are, first, an inclination to see "Anglo-Saxon" England as the seat of political genius in the world, thus removing the English to a special political plane; second, a conception of humanity as suspended precariously between vice and virtue, between reason and passion—a struggle whose outcome was scarcely in question for "savages" and "barbarous nations," however perfectible these may have been in theory; and third, a conception of the "public good" that depended upon the polity's constituting "a homogenous body whose interests when candidly considered are one," and upon individual members' capacity for reflection, restraint, and self-sacrifice. In the political thinking of the period, according to Wood, " a republic was such a delicate polity precisely because it demanded an extraordinary moral character in the people."[29] With its emphasis upon community and self-sacrifice, Wood elsewhere elaborates, with its reasoned suppression of "private desires" for the sake of "the public interest," republican government placed "an enormous burden" on individual members and "demanded far more of . . . citizens than monarchies did of their subjects."[30] (This at a time when the definition of the word "Negro" in a Philadelphia encyclopedia could include "idleness, treachery, revenge, debauchery, nastiness and intemperance.")[31]

It should be emphasized here that this was merely the dominant, not the monolithic, view of the relationship between republican government and race in the period. The Revolution laid the groundwork for abolitionism, as Wood notes, in that "the republican attack on dependency [of all kinds] compelled Americans to see the deviant character of slavery and to confront the institution as they never had to before."[32] The attorney general of Maryland, for one, insisted in 1788 that slavery was "inconsistent with the *genius* of *republicanism* and has a tendency to *destroy* those *principles* on which it is *supported* as it *lessens* the *sense* of the *equal rights* of *mankind,* and habituates us to *tyranny* and *oppression.*"[33] Generations later an abolitionist like Theodore Parker could assert, "If slavery continues, democracy goes down; every form of republicanism, or of constitutional monarchy, will perish; and absolute military despotism take their place at last."[34]

But however potent republican logic could prove for egalitarian argumentation, the anti-egalitarian dimension of republicanism was ratified again and again in the political conduct of the new nation. The formulae that maintained this dual civic terrain of the "fit" and the "unfit" for self-government included the white-supremacist naturalization law of 1790;

later, the anomalous construction of American Indians neither as "nations" nor as "citizens," but as "domestic dependent nations"; later still, the enforced alienation of Asian immigrants as "immigrants ineligible for citizenship"; and even in the wake of Emancipation, the Black Codes passed at the local level in various places to keep African-Americans in a political region somewhere well short of true freedom.

Most telling in this respect is not the conquest of American Indians and the policy of removal, nor even the seeming contradiction of slaveholding in a democratic republic, but rather the political status of *free* blacks in the antebellum period.[35] Within this republican framework of racially recognized "fitness for self-government," *free* blacks, not enslaved blacks, represented the greater political anomaly; indeed, according to one legal scholar, *free black* was a "schizophrenic description" in the American setting.[36] During the late-eighteenth-century debates over slavery and abolition, bondage itself represented only one half of the equation; the political fate of freed slaves was another, in some ways thornier issue. Even setting aside the questions of abstract moral principle, states' rights, and slaveholders' rights in property that framed discussions of abolition, the question remained, what was to become of the ex-chattel? And in most discussants' minds Emancipation decidedly would not imply blacks' equality as citizens. Thus it was that even the most radical blueprints for the abolition of slavery involved, in one way or another, the *disappearance* of the freed slaves—either a colonization scheme would remove them to some distant land, or, by the magic of eighteenth-century ethnological principles, "in the process of time the very color would be extinct and there would be none but whites."[37]

"It will probably be asked, Why not retain and incorporate the blacks into the state?" wrote Thomas Jefferson in his *Notes on the State of Virginia*. "Deep rooted prejudices entertained by the whites; ten thousand recollections, by the blacks, of the injuries they have sustained; new provocations; the real distinctions which nature has made; and many other circumstances, will divide us into parties, and produce convolutions which will probably never end but in the extermination of the one or the other race." The republican emphasis upon a homogeneous polity did figure in Jefferson's thinking. But he went on to detail "the real distinctions which nature has made" between the two races. He rhapsodized over the greater beauty of whiteness; he noted with unelaborated portent "the preference of the Oranootan for the black woman over those of his own species"; and he asserted that "in reason [blacks] are much inferior" and "in imagination they are dull, tasteless, and anomalous."[38]

Jefferson's comments in *Notes on the State of Virginia*—"proving that negroes were by nature an inferior race of beings," as one legislator had it—were quoted in support of a pro-slavery position during the first Congress's consideration of an abolitionist memorial presented by the Quakers. As William Smith (S.C.) characterized Jefferson's thinking, according to the transcript, "that respectable author, who was desirous of countenancing emancipation, was on a consideration of the subject induced candidly to avow that the difficulties appeared insurmountable." Blacks would of necessity "continue as a distinct people," a prospect intolerable in a self-governing republic.[39]

Indeed, African-American political standing in the "free" states of the North underscores the extent to which citizenship and whiteness were conjoined. Whether or not *slavery* was just became a point of much contention, summoning good republicanist arguments on both sides. But human bondage aside, white republicans came to a much easier consensus on the question of whether free blacks should or could participate in the republic as full citizens—whether, that is, they were "fit for self-government." Alexis de Tocqueville noted in 1831 that "the prejudice of race appears to be stronger in the states that have abolished slavery than in those where it still exists; and nowhere is it so intolerant as in those states where servitude has never been known." As Leon Litwack has documented, well after abolition in the Northern states whites continued jealously to guard the distinction between legal protections on the one hand—the right to life, liberty, and property—and full political equality on the other. At a Constitutional Convention in Pennsylvania in 1837, for instance, during a rousing speech on the benefits of extending the right of suffrage—"that right, sacred and dear to every American citizen"—one delegate could unproblematically add the limiting clause: "I use the word citizen as not embracing the coloured population."[40] Or again, an 1842 Senate committee in the "free" state of Michigan could comfortably assert that "our government is formed by, for the benefit of, and to be controlled by the descendants of European nations." Negro suffrage would thus be "inexpedient and impolitic."[41] Like the usage of the word "white" in the 1790 naturalization law, moreover, restrictions on the rights of free blacks in the North were characteristically adopted without much debate, as a matter of common assumption. By the time Justice Roger Taney handed down the *Dred Scott* decision in 1857, in which he asserted that blacks possessed no rights "which the white man was bound to respect"—a decree often singled out for its shockingly glib violation of democratic ideals—a long history of social and political practice, North and South, was on his side.[42]

Although merely implicit in much of the writing of the Revolutionary period, this critical link between race and republicanism would become increasingly explicit as the nineteenth century wore on, and especially as the slavery question gained prominence in public discussion. As J. H. Van Evrie, a vociferous pro-slavery propagandist, argued, the presence of the "inferior" Negro and American Indian in North America actually *led to* America's grand experiment in democracy: their presence "led directly to the establishment of a new system and a new civilization based on foundations of everlasting truth—the legal and political equality of the race, or of all those whom the Almighty Creator has Himself made equal."[43] Stephen Douglas made the same point at several junctures in his debates with Abraham Lincoln, asserting not only that "this government of ours is founded on the white basis," but also that "a negro, an Indian, or any other man of inferior race" should be permitted only those "rights, privileges and immunities which he is capable of exercising consistent with the safety of society." The framers, he argued, had "no reference either to the negro, the savage Indians, the Fejee, the Malay, or any other inferior and degraded race, when they spoke of the equality of men."[44]

Deeply embedded racial assumptions of republican ideology, then, in combination with the practical "necessities" of a slaveholding, settler democracy on a "savage" continent, led to an unquestioned acceptance of whiteness as a prerequisite for naturalized citizenship. In the wake of the 1790 naturalization law, the word and idea "white" appeared in a variety of state laws governing voting, officeholding, and apportionment. Laws governing the marriage or sexual relations of "whites" with "blacks" or "Indians," too, were extended in some of the newly formed states, and created anew in certain others.[45] Legal and statutory references to "whites" after 1790 ranged from boiler-plate references to "white inhabitants" or "free white male inhabitants," as in the state constitutions of Alabama and Arkansas (1819, 1836), to the rather extraordinary language of the Illinois constitution (1848), which not only provided that the militia "shall consist of all free male able-bodied persons (negroes, mulattoes, and Indians excepted)," but also mandated that the General

Assembly shall "pass such laws as will effectually prohibit free persons of color from immigrating to and settling in this State."[46]

In the first half of the nineteenth century, politically restrictive uses of the word "white" likewise appeared in the constitutions of Missouri (1812), Mississippi (1817), Connecticut (1818), California (1849, 1879), and Minnesota Territory (1849). Conversely, eighteen state constitutions specifically classed blacks as "dependents," thus assigning them the same political status as white women and children of all colors.[47] Although popular prejudices certainly did exist against *certain* groups of "white persons"—Jews and Catholics in many areas, for instance—still the alchemy of slaveholding and the frontier was powerful enough that in general Europeans, like Brackenridge's "bog-trotter" Teague O'Regan, became simply "white persons" in matters of race and the rights and responsibilities of citizenship.

Whiteness and Science

The racist practices that normalized the connection between whiteness and citizenship by 1790 had been carried out, as it were, without the assistance of modern racism. From the early 1600s to the early 1800s Euro-American policies of conquest, Indian removal, slave-trading, and disenfranchisement relied on a logic of "civilization" versus "barbarism" or "savagery," or of "Christianity" versus "heathendom." Peoples might be displaced because of their benighted beliefs or their barbarous customs—their nomadic indifference to the benefits of enclosing and "improving" land, for instance; or their legitimate enslavement might be understood as owing to the mark they bore of God's curse on Ham.[48] Religion itself carried physical markers, as far as seventeenth-century Euro-Americans were concerned, as when James Otis, a dissenter on the slavery question, wondered in 1764 whether " 'tis right to enslave a man because he is black? Will short curled hair like wool *instead of Christian hair* . . . help the argument? Can any logical inference in favor of slavery be drawn from a flat nose?"[49] God's judgments and biological facts were operating terribly closely here, but this was not racial, exactly. Although Blumenbach had lighted upon his most lovely Georgian skull and so had spoken the group "Caucasians" into existence in the late eighteenth century, it was not until the nineteenth that the language of racism proper— the language of "genus," "species," "types," "poly-" and "monogenesis," "craniometrics," "phenotypes," and "genotypes"—would frame discussion of human groups, their capacities, and their proper relationship to one another.

If the political meaning of whiteness seems barely to have changed with the advent of scientific inquiry into human types, the epistemological basis of whiteness and its "others" did change drastically. The historian Audrey Smedley has nicely delineated the rise of scientific racialism in five elements that distinguished it from earlier understandings of human diversity, regardless of how similar the consequences for social and political relationships between, say, slaves and masters were. It entailed (1) the classification of human groups as "discrete and biotic entities" measured by physical and behavioral variations; (2) an inegalitarian ethos that required hierarchical ordering of human types; (3) the belief that outer physical characteristics were but markers of inner intellectual, moral, or temperamental qualities; (4) the notion that these qualities were heritable; and (5) the belief that "the imputed differences, believed fixed and unalterable, could never be bridged or transcended," so distinctly had these populations been created.[50]

Although the scientific outlook represents a new way of viewing "difference," the development of such an outlook on human types was not a complete break from the conquests and enslavements of the past. On the contrary, the new sciences that arose to theorize the relationship among the world's peoples—ethnology, anthropology, craniometry, anthropometry, and phrenology among them—owed a great deal to precisely those social questions generated by Euro-American expansionism and the intensifying slavery debate. In his instructions to the explorer Meriwether Lewis, for instance, Thomas Jefferson had asserted that "the commerce which may be carried on with the people inhabiting the line you will pursue, renders a knolege of those people important." He went on rather frankly to instruct that, "considering the interest which every nation has in extending & strengthening the authority of reason and justice among the people around them, it will be useful to acquire what knolege you can of the state of morality, religion, & information among them; as it may better enable those who may endeavor to civilize and instruct them." Decades later, in his paean to westward expansion, "A Passage to India," Walt Whitman would appropriately number the ethnologist among the "noble inventors," "scientists," "chemists," and "geologists" who were at the helm of the new, expansive epoch.[51]

The development of various scientific schemes for the understanding and classification of humanity, wrote Franz Boas, one of the most creative and prolific participants in the project of modern anthropology, owed much to "the passions that were aroused by the practical and ethical aspects of the slavery question."[52] The imperialism question weighed in heavily, too. The rising nineteenth-century regime of ethnological knowledge, produced by Euro-American expansionism and slave-trading from its beginnings, in its turn created new epistemologies of human difference and thus buttressed a political order based upon physicality and its "recognition." As David Spurr has observed, once " 'knowledge' of racial difference is made a condition for political power . . . such knowledge loses its status as an independent, a priori basis for practice, and becomes instead a mere aspect of practice, a construct produced by the same practice it would claim logically to precede."[53] Thus the racial sciences were in fact *racializing* sciences, ever responding to the political imperatives of the slavery question, questions of territorial expansion, and, later, the vexing immigration question, and at the same time creating in their wake new kinds of "certainty" that "explained" slavery, expansion, and the trouble with immigrants.

Within the context of European and American exploration, trade, expansionism, enslavement, and conquest, then, a rising genre of scientific explication emerged to enumerate, describe, and ultimately to rank the world's peoples. In the long view, science provided an alternative vocabulary to the polarities of "heathendom" and "Christianity" of religious discourse—a vocabulary keyed to physicality and "nature" rather than to belief, yet marking peoples nonetheless as possessing an inherent degree of righteousness, now refigured as innate *capacity*. Scientific debate between the late eighteenth century and the late nineteenth shifted from natural sciences that merely classified types, toward biological models that apprehended, explained, and thus ranked these types; it also shifted away from static conceptions of various types, toward more dynamic, evolutionary models of diversification through constant change. The scientific controversies and arguments couched within these general intellectual shifts included a bitter debate between adherents of "monogenesis" (who believed in a single origin for all human types) and adherents of "polygenesis" (who argued that human types themselves were so divergent as to indicate separate origins); between hereditarians and environmentalists; and between Darwinians and Lamarckians. These controversies have been ably documented elsewhere.[54]

Most important for the present purposes is the extent to which these scientific models altered the epistemology of race, lent a new authority to popular notions of "difference," and thus altered the understanding of whiteness. The relationship between the politics of expansionism and slavery on the one hand, and scientific "knowledge" on the other, is nowhere as clear as in the writings of Josiah Nott. Among the chief propagandists for polygenesis in the United States, Nott frankly rooted his scientific observations in the context of the social relations that had produced them. In a letter to J. D. B. DeBow, printed as a preface to his *Two Lectures on the Relationship between the Biblical and Physical History of Man* (1849), Nott articulated the close connection between his scientific understanding of diverse peoples and the daily rhythms of antebellum Mobile, Alabama: "Born in a slave state, and having passed our childhood and manhood in daily intercourse with the white and black races, it is but natural that you and I should have become deeply impressed not only by the physical but also by the moral and intellectual differences which exist between them: nor is it less natural that a doubt as to their common origin should suggest itself to our minds." Nott's polygenetic view thus both justifies and derives from the fact that the slave-holding South was his laboratory writ large. "The Almighty in his wisdom," he continued to DeBow, "has peopled our vast planet from many distant centers, instead of one, and with races or species originally and radically distinct."[55]

Nor are Nott's scientific assessments of white supremacism limited to the "proofs" and "justifications" of black slavery. He also assigned science itself a key role in the imperialist enterprise—here, again, relying upon the "data" of domination for his justification of further domination: "The numberless attempts by the Caucasian race, during several thousand years, to bring the Mongol, Malay, Indian, and Negro, under the same religion, laws, manners, customs, etc., have failed, and must continue to fail, unless the science of Ethnography can strike out some new and more practical plan of operation."[56] Or again, demonstrating the tortuous circularity of empire, slave-trading, travel, scientific knowledge, and political necessity, Nott in *Types of Mankind* (1855) described the peoples of the eastern coast of Africa,

> each [tribe] presenting physical characters more or less hideous; and, almost without exception, not merely in a barbarous, but superlatively savage state. All attempts toward humanizing them have failed. Hopes of eventual improvement in the condition of these brutish

families are entertained by none but missionaries of sanguine temperament and little instruction. Even the slaver rejects them.[57]

Given the circumstances in which such research was undertaken—the power relations which supported it, the social and political necessities which defined it—it is no surprise that scholars who vigorously disagreed with one another on many theoretical and conceptual issues were virtually unanimous in the white supremacism of their scientific findings. Thus scholars on both sides of the Atlantic like Samuel Morton, Arthur Comte de Gobineau, and James Cowles Prichard, who took quite different positions on the question of single or diverse human origins, nonetheless made strikingly similar pronouncements regarding that "uppermost" division of humanity, the "white" or "Caucasian" race. The polygenist Morton declared in his *Crania Americana* (1839) that the "Caucasian" race was "distinguished for the facility with which it attains the highest intellectual endowments." Gobineau, for his part, would take the position of the agnostic on origins, even if he was convinced of "the inequality of human races" (as the title of his best-known work put the matter). Although "there are both scientific and religious reasons for *not* believing in a plurality of origins of our species," he wrote, "the various branches of the human family are distinguished by permanent and irradicable differences, both mentally and physically. They are unequal in intellectual capacity, in personal beauty, and in physical strength." His assessments of the world's peoples, moreover, were forged in a political ambience: he found that "white" peoples, for instance, "are gifted with relative energy, or rather with an energetic intelligence . . . greater physical power . . . extraordinary instinct for order . . . remarkable, even extreme, love of liberty, and are openly hostile to the formalism under which the Chinese are glad to vegitate, as well as to the strict despotism which is the only way of governing the Negro."[58]

Prichard, for his part, was a strict monogenist, finding in the biological facts of interracial fertility undeniable proof that "all tribes of men are of one family." But his argument, too, was frankly bounded by the politics of the day. Although he noted that abolitionism was an object of scorn among most polygenists, for whom "the ultimate lot of the ruder tribes is a state of perpetual servitude," Prichard himself merely marshaled his *mono*genesis—his view of the similarity of human types—toward imperialism of a more benevolent stripe:

We contemplate among all the diversified tribes who are endowed with reason and speech, the same internal feelings, appetites, aversions . . . We find everywhere the same susceptibility . . . of admitting the cultivation of these universal endowments, of opening the eyes of the mind to the more clear and luminous views which Christianity unfolds, of becoming moulded to the institutions of religion and of civilization.[59]

The question, then, is simply whether white stewardship is to be benign or not—the *tenor* of European supremacy, not the fact of it, is the ultimate stake in the poly- versus monogenesis debate, so far as Prichard is concerned.

Political questions of slavery, expansion, and conquest continued to be highly visible in scientific writings about race as static conceptions of human difference gave way to a more dynamic view based on principles of evolution. Euro-American expansionism was clearly a significant part of Charles Darwin's laboratory as he theorized "the competition of tribe with tribe, race with race." "When civilized nations come into contact with barbarians the struggle is short," he averred, for instance, "except where a deadly climate gives its aid to the native race . . . We can see that the cultivation of the land will be fatal in many ways to the savages, for they cannot, or will not, change their habits." Nor was a stubborn clinging to old "habits" the chief crime of such "savages." Darwin gave voice to a supreme imperialist vision, when, in the closing lines of *The Descent of Man* (1871), he asserted, "I would as soon be descended from that heroic little monkey, who braved his dreaded enemy in order to save the life of his keeper; or from that old baboon, who, descending from the mountains, carried away in triumph his young comrade from a crowd of astonished dogs—as from a savage who delights to torture his enemies, offers up bloody sacrifices, practices infanticide without remorse, treats his wives like slaves, knows no decency, and is haunted by the grossest superstitions."[60]

Because scientific inquiry was so rooted in the politics and practices of white supremacism, these writings tended to ratify the profound separation of whiteness from nonwhiteness that characterized pre-scientific (and hence merely protoracist) colonial policies and statutes. Among those who now seized upon scientific views to buttress political arguments were publicists like Van Evrie. His singular contribution to the scientific discourse of race involved not substance but simply volume. In tracts like his *Negroes and Negro Slavery* and in the pages of his pro-slavery *Weekly*

Caucasian, Van Evrie tirelessly popularized the scientific basis of white supremacism, though always peppering his science with a good dose of Biblical authority as well. Whereas Blumenbach had merely praised the physical beauty of "Caucasians" and held them out as an ideal type, Van Evrie now scanned the physiognomical surfaces for signs of a deeper, more abiding racial superiority. Thoroughly blending the aesthetic with the moral (and the patriarchal), Van Evrie waxed rhapsodic on the inner virtues betokened by the subtle beauties of the "Caucasian" face. "What is there at the same time so charming and so indicative of inner purity and innocence," he asked,

> as the blush of maiden modesty? For an instant the face is scarlet, then . . . paler than ever in its delicate transparency; and these physical changes, beautiful as they may be to the eye, are rendered a thousand times more so by our consciousness that they reflect moral emotions infinitely more beautiful. Can anyone suppose such a thing possible to a black face? that these sudden and startling alterations of color, which reflect the moral perceptions and elevated nature of white woman, are possible to the negress?

Van Evrie later added that, although whiteness itself was "essential" in reflecting noble passions, "without the deeply cut and distinctly marked features of the Caucasian, color would be comparatively useless in reflecting the grander emotions of the soul."[61]

The crux for Van Evrie was that "the Almighty has obviously designed all His creatures—animal as well as human—for wise, beneficent, and useful purposes." Blacks were slaves not only by religious right and by longstanding American tradition, but by *nature*—slavery represented their "normal condition" and the "natural relation" between the races. As for the "Caucasian," meanwhile, "the flowing beard . . . projecting forehead, oval features, erect posture and lordly presence, stamp him the master man wherever found."[62]

Thus, of course, the distinction between whiteness and nonwhiteness never fully lost its salience in American political culture. Mexican annexation, black Emancipation, Reconstruction, Jim Crow practices, Indian Wars, Asian immigration and Exclusion, Hawaiian and Puerto Rican annexation, and Philippine conquest—all would keep whiteness very much alive in both the visual and the political economies. But upon the arrival of the massive waves of Irish immigrants in the 1840s, whiteness itself would become newly problematic and, in some quarters, would begin to lose its monolithic character—notwithstanding the rights and privileges that continued to inhere in whiteness, and the assertions of various John Van Evries that "in modern times there are no white barbarians. In all modern history, wherever found, white men are much the same."[63]

The Famine Migration announced a new era in the meaning of whiteness in the United States, an era greeted by many as a full-blown political crisis. In response, some would begin to question the monolithic quality of whiteness, and, again, science would provide the language and the models for understanding this natural fragmentation *within* the "white race." As Samuel Morton had written of the "Celts" in 1839, "In some locales their physical traits, their moral character and their peculiar customs, have undergone little change since the time of Caesar. It is probable that the most unsophisticated Celts are those of the Southwest of Ireland, whose wild look and manner, mud cabins and funereal howlings, recall the memory of a barbarous age."[64]

By the 1860s the Irish would seem to some to be so many "thousands of barbarians in our midst, every whit as ferocious in their instincts as the Minnesota savages."[65] (It is worth recalling, in this connection, that the "wild Irish" and the violent colonization of Ireland had provided the template for English understanding of North American savages and the course of North American colonization in the first place. "The wild *Irish* and the *Indian* doe not much differ," one English observer who was familiar with both had written in 1646, "and therefore [they] should be handled alike.")[66] The white-over-dark dynamic of racial theorizing would retain its purchase in Euro-American thought, to be sure, but the fracturing of whiteness (the splitting off of "unsophisticated Celts," for instance), would become an ever more salient feature of racial discourse as the massive immigrations of the nineteenth century progressed. The untroubled republican equation of whiteness with fitness for self-government, which had informed colonial thinking and had reigned in the new nation since 1790, then, became increasingly untenable as "free white persons" of undreamt-of diversity and number dragged ashore in the 1840s and after.

It is for the Republican institutions of America that we hope and fear most.

—"Immigration into the United States," *DeBow's Review,* 1848

There may be those who can contemplate the addition to our population of vast numbers of persons having no inherited instincts of self-government and respect for law; knowing no restraint upon their own passions but the club of the policeman or the bayonet of the soldier; forming communities, by the tens of thousands, in which only foreign tongues are spoken, and into which can steal no influence from our free institutions and from popular discussion. But I confess to being far less optimistic.

—"Restriction of Immigration," *Atlantic Monthly,* 1896

 2

Anglo-Saxons and Others, 1840–1924

With two centuries of hindsight, the first thing one is likely to notice about the 1790 naturalization law is its fierce exclusivity. Indeed, this is no small matter. The limitation of naturalized citizenship to "free white persons" profoundly shaped Asian-American history, for instance. It was this law, still in effect in the 1870s and 1880s, that denied Chinese immigrants the political might with which to challenge the rising tides of exclusionism or to protect themselves against the violent white mobs of a Rock Springs or a Tacoma. It was this law, still in effect in 1942, that left Japanese immigrants so vulnerable to the wartime hysteria that would become a federal policy of internment. John Okada brilliantly rendered the enduring salience of the inclusions and exclusions of 1790 in his novel *No-No Boy* (1957), when Ichiro Yamada ruminates upon the fateful apostrophe separating the Irish O'Hara from the Japanese Ohara in American political culture.[1] Clearly, the exclusivity of the 1790 law was of profound consequence.

What is too easily missed from our vantage point, however, is the stag-

gering *in*clusivity of the 1790 naturalization law. It was this law's unquestioned use of the word "white" that allowed for the massive European
migrations of the nineteenth century, beginning with the Famine Migration from Ireland, and ultimately including the '48ers from Germany, the
Scandinavian pioneers, and then successive waves of East European Jews,
Italians, Greeks, Poles, Ruthenians, Slovenians, Magyars, Ukrainians,
Lithuanians—none of whom the framers had ever envisioned swelling the
polity of the new nation when they crafted its rules for naturalization.
This law, its unexamined inclusivity, and its unforeseen consequences set
the stage for a nineteenth-century political crisis of remarkable urgency
and scope.

Even as early as the eighteenth century there were some who saw whiteness not as monolithic but as variegated. In what was to become a standard political refrain in the nineteenth century and beyond, for instance,
Benjamin Franklin wanted to know in 1751 why Pennsylvania, "founded
by English, [should] become a colony of aliens, who will shortly be so
numerous as to Germanize us, instead of our Anglifying them, and will
never adopt our language or customs any more than they can acquire our
complexion?" "The number of purely white people in the world is pro-
portionably very small," he lamented in this essay on human population.

> All Africa is black or tawny; Asia chiefly tawny; America (exclusive
> of the newcomers [that is, the English]) wholly so. And in Europe,
> the Spaniards, Italians, French, Russians, and Swedes are generally
> of what we call a swarthy complexion; as are the Germans also, the
> Saxons only excepted, who, with the English, make the principal
> body of white people on the face of the earth. I could wish their
> numbers were increased.[2]

But such concerns never found their way into the debate over the first
naturalization law, probably because legislators at the time were so con-
sumed by the legal problems posed by slavery, whiteness, and blackness.
Consequently, whiteness in the early decades of the republic remained a
legislative and conceptual monolith that left the gates open to all European comers.

The perceived over-inclusivity of the first naturalization law and the
dawning political problem of whiteness itself in the mid-nineteenth century are nicely encapsulated in Richard Henry Dana, Jr.'s, sea-voyaging
memoir *Two Years before the Mast*. A patrician New Englander who had
dropped his studies at Harvard to go to sea in the early 1830s, Dana

published a travelogue of his journey around the cape to California in 1840. A shift in the languages of peoplehood in this text indicates the profound cultural reorientation that had taken place between the book's initial publication and the time of Dana's added postscript for the 1859 edition. Throughout the original manuscript, Dana refers to Europeans and Euro-Americans as "whites" and "white men"—most often in contradistinction to the "drawling, lazy half-breeds" of San Pedro, to the Pacific's "primitive" Kanakas only recently "advanced [from] barbarism," or to the "darkies" among the ship's crew itself. In the postscript of 1859, however, the phrases "English race" and "Anglo-Saxon race" appear in the text for the very first time. Significantly, these alternative racial appellations crop up within a paragraph of this remark: "The Cathedral of St. Mary . . . where the Irish attend, was . . . more like one of our stifling Irish Catholic churches in Boston or New York, with intelligence in so small a proportion to the number of faces."[3] This racial refinement from "white" to "Anglo-Saxon" is neither accidental nor idiosyncratic; rather, it reflects a political revision of whiteness in Dana's New England during the two decades bracketing the Famine in Ireland and the tremendous Celtic exodus to North America.

Whereas the salient feature of whiteness before the 1840s had been its powerful political and cultural contrast to nonwhiteness, now its internal divisions, too, took on a new and pressing significance. The main currents in this period (c.1840s–1920s) included, first, a spectacular rate of industrialization in the United States, whose voracious appetite for cheap labor—combined with political and economic dislocations across industrializing Europe—brought unprecedented numbers of migrants to New World shores; second, a growing nativist perception of these laborers themselves as a political threat to the smooth functioning of the republic; and third, consequently, a fracturing of monolithic whiteness by the popular marriage of scientific doctrines of race with political concerns over the newcomers' "fitness for self-government."

This increasing fragmentation and hierarchical ordering of distinct white *races* (now in the plural) was theorized in the rarified discourses of science, but it was also reflected in literature, visual arts, caricature, political oratory, penny journalism, and myriad other venues of popular culture. It was this notion of variegated whiteness that surfaced in 1863, for instance, when the New York *Tribune* characterized the rioting Irish in New York as a "savage mob," a "pack of savages," "savage foes," "demons," and "incarnate devils." It was this notion of variegated whiteness that undergirded Henry Cabot Lodge's claim, in 1891, that Slovak immigrants "are not a good acquisition for us to make, since they appear to have so many items in common with the Chinese." It was this notion of variegated whiteness that prompted one Colorado congressman, during an exchange on the merits of an immigration-restriction bill in the 1920s, to offer this cautionary fable:

> Suppose we should move out of the United States all the hundred and six million people who are here now and put in their places a hundred and six million people who are to-day vegetating in darkest Africa. How long do you suppose that America would retain any similarity to its condition of the present time?
>
> The picture appears plain enough when we paint it in such broad lines of black and white. But is it not essentially the same picture if we use shades—if instead of bringing in people who are entirely different we bring in people who are somewhat different?[4]

As these comments indicate, the older, supremacist meaning of whiteness was not completely overthrown by the new paradigm of plural white races. The key here is in his implicit ranking of human difference by degree—peoples who are "entirely" different and those who are "somewhat" different. But even if painted in "shades" rather than in stark, black-and-white polarities, the importation of "different" peoples posed a terrible threat to the well-being of the republic.

Thus race is not tangential to the history of European immigration to the United States but absolutely central. "Fitness for self-government," a racial attribute whose outer property was whiteness, became encoded in a naturalization law that allowed Europeans' unrestricted immigration and their unhindered (male) civic participation. It is solely because of their race, in other words, that they were permitted entrance. But the massive influx borne of this "liberal" immigration policy, in its turn, generated a new perception of some Europeans' unfitness for self-government, now rendered racially in a series of subcategorical white groupings—Celt, Slav, Hebrew, Iberic, Mediterranean, and so on—white Others of a supreme Anglo-Saxondom. This does not simply represent a shift in American thinking "toward racism," as John Higham, still the premier historian of American nativism, would have it.[5] Rather, the political history of whiteness and its vicissitudes between the 1840s and the 1920s represents a shift from one brand of bedrock racism to another—from the unquestioned hegemony of a unified race of "white persons" to a contest over political "fitness" among a now fragmented, hierarchically arranged series of distinct "white races." Race has been among the central organizers of the political life of the republic all along, and the racial reclassification of various European immigrants as their numbers swelled is among the most salient reminders of how powerful its sway has been.

Rethinking Whiteness

The demographics of the republic began to change dramatically in the mid-nineteenth century. In the early decades of the republic, immigration had been calculated by the mere thousands per year—an influx of 8,385 from all sending countries combined in the year 1820, for instance. But these yearly figures climbed to the tens of thousands per year by the mid-1820s, and to the hundreds of thousands per year by the 1840s. In 1847, among the worst years of the Famine in Ireland, total immigration to the United States leaped to 234,968, of whom nearly half (105,536) were from Ireland. From 1846 through 1855 a total of 3,031,339 immigrants came ashore in the United States, including 1,288,307 from Ireland and another 976,711 from Germany, the two new leading sources of immigration. By 1860 (that is, by the time "Anglo-Saxon" had displaced "white" in Dana's racial lexicon) the foreign-born population of the United States was more than 4 million, of whom 1,611,304 had been born in Ireland, and 1,276,075 in Germany. Over the next several decades the economic and political dislocations across Europe continued to send increasing numbers of migrants to American shores, with each region furnishing its own statistical curve of migration slopes and peaks: Irish migration peaked at 221,253 in 1851; German migration peaked at 250,630 in 1882; Italian migration peaked at 285,731 in 1907; and Russian (largely Jewish) migration peaked at 258,943 also in 1907. By 1920 the "white" foreign-born population was more than 13.5 million, most of whom would not have qualified for Benjamin Franklin's appellation "Saxon" (nor, indeed, "lovely white," if even the Swedes are "swarthy").[6]

It is against this backdrop that the history of political whiteness took shape and that the fluidity of certain groups' racial identities became apparent. The crosscurrents here are terribly complex. The Mexican War, slavery and Emancipation, Reconstruction, Indian wars, anti-Chinese agitation, Pacific expansion, and popular accounts of Pacific, Asian, and African exploration all kept vividly alive the crucial distinction in American political culture dividing white from nonwhite populations, as did hiring practices, most labor agitation, and miscegenation statutes. And yet the multitudes of European immigrants who arrived in waves beginning in the 1840s, it was said, posed a new threat to democratic institutions. This emerging political crisis lent a new, multifaceted character to whiteness itself.

Thus, on the one hand, in *The Inequality of Human Races* (1855) Arthur Comte de Gobineau could look across the Atlantic at the United States and predict the decline of the Anglo-Saxons, who now found themselves suddenly overwhelmed by "the most degenerate races of olden day Europe. They are the human flotsam of all ages: Irish, cross-bred German and French, and Italians of even more doubtful stock." Although penned in Europe, this sentiment would become increasingly common in North American discussion whenever immigration was the question of the moment. But when questions pertaining to slavery or expansion took center stage, on the other hand, racial differences among white populations receded. As Van Evrie put it, "Irishmen, Germans, Frenchmen, etc., come here, settle down, become citizens, and their offspring born and raised on American soil differ in no appreciable or perceptible manner from other Americans . . . [But the Negro is] as absolutely and specifically unlike the American as when the race first touched the soil and first breathed the air of the New World." Or again, setting the Europeans' environmentalist potential for change against the Africans' hereditary stasis, Van Evrie declared, "The coarse skin, big hands and feet, the broad teeth, pug nose etc. of the Irish and German laborer pass away in a generation or two."[7]

There was hardly consensus on the prospect of immigrant "difference," marked by physicality ("coarse skin," "pug nose"), merely "passing away" with time. As had been the case with public debates over slavery and the displacement and extermination of American Indians, the gathering debate over immigration and the crisis it represented drew upon "knowledge" of peoples derived from the sciences. Indeed, as Ruth Benedict has remarked, the proportion of racialist literature in American intellectual history that deals with purportedly white peoples is staggering (perhaps, as she proposes, because "our treatment of the Negro conforms so closely to the predilections of these authors that they doubtless had little to suggest"). From Samuel Morton's 1839 comment on the "unsophisticated Celts" of southwest Ireland, who "recall the memory of a barbarous age," to the ascendent eugenics movement of the early twentieth century, the relative merits of the white races of Europe and America represented one of the abiding concerns of American ethnological sciences, anthropology, sociology, literature, politics, and historiography. As Gobineau noted on the tenor of white supremacism at mid-century, "The most ardent democrats are the first to claim superiority for the *Anglo-Saxons* of North America over all the nations of the same continent." And indeed, even a staunch abolitionist like Theodore Parker could intone, "No tribe of men has done such service for freedom as the Anglo-Saxons, in Britain and America." (Elsewhere Parker would present an elaborate interpretation of world history, based upon a racial scheme of "five great powers of the civilized Christian world": Russia, "a great Slavic people"; France, "a great Celtic people, variously crossed with Basque, Roman, and Teutonic tribes"; Germany, "a great Teutonic people"; England, "a great Saxon-Teutonic people"; and the United States, "a great English-Saxon-Teutonic people.")[8]

Josiah Nott was among the first in this country to invest the discourse of white races with full polygenetic implications. Objecting to the construction of a more or less unified "Caucasian" race presented in Samuel Morton's *Crania Americana* (the category "Caucasian" was known in scientific discourse at this time, but was still rare in popular discourse), Nott commented that "the Teuton, the Jew, the Hindoo, the Egyptian, &c., have all been included under the term Caucasian; and yet they have, as far as we know, been through all time as distinct in physical and moral characters from each other, as they have from the Negro races of Africa and Oceanica." The differences among the races were so pronounced, in Nott's view, that "nothing short of a *miracle* could have evolved all the multifarious Caucasian forms out of one primitive stock . . . There must have been many centers of creation, even for Caucasian races, instead of one center for *all* types of humanity."[9]

Engaged as they were in both scientific inquiry and social observation, writers like Nott and the more avowedly polemical Van Evrie faced a complex task when it came to comprehending the divisions and rankings within the superior "white" race. For these authors slavery, not immigration, was the pressing question of the day and the real point of scientific inquiry into human types. Whether or not "all the multifarious Caucasian forms" could have developed from a single "primitive stock," white supremacism did entail its own imperatives—especially at a time when slavery as an institution was under attack. Like Van Evrie, Nott considered slavery to be fully "consistent with the laws of God." Thus standing firmly upon a bedrock of religiously and scientifically explained white supremacism generated within the context of slaveholding Mobile, Alabama, he could only greet racial findings generated in the nativist Northeast or in the British Empire with some caution. For example, a contemporary English observer had described certain native Irish as "pot-bellied, bow-legged, and abortively featured; and [they] are especially remarkable for open, projecting mouths, with prominent teeth and exposed gums, their advancing cheekbones and depressed noses bearing barbarism on the very front. In other words, within a short period they seem to have acquired a prognathous type of skull, like the savages of Australia." Nott responded by pointing out that "a healthy, well-developed race of men, like our domestic animals, (horses, cattle, and sheep) may be much more quickly and certainly altered for the worse than for the better." These poor Irish merely represented a "diseased stock," he argued, and their "abortive features" could be brought back "to their original type" in better circumstances: "It is wonderful how rapidly the lower class of Irish ... do improve in America when they are well fed and comfortably lodged."[10]

By the 1860s Van Evrie was even more pronounced in his efforts to redeem the European immigrant, viewing the Irish as key constituents in a Northern, pro-slavery coalition. "Something like five hundred millions of money" had been funneled to the antislavery cause in Britain, he lamented, "money taken from Irish laborers within the last seventy years and expended for the assumed benefit of the negro." The Irish, by this account, were so many "unfortunate white people" who should have been saved.[11] Thus, as would be the case in the pan–white-supremacist agitation against Chinese immigrants in California in the 1870s, recouping or shoring up "Celtic" whiteness was among the chief tasks of political coalition-building among pro-slavery Northerners.

But as the discussions of Semites, Teutons, Slavs, or Anglo-Saxons on the part of Morton, Nott, and Gobineau suggest, notwithstanding the pressing slavery question these white races were subject to the new epistemological system of difference—a new visual economy keyed not only to cues of skin color, but to facial angle, head size and shape, physiognomy, hair and eye color, and physique. As the first to immigrate in huge numbers at once well within the literal language but well outside the deliberate intent of the "free white persons" clause of 1790, Irish and German arrivals of the 1840s and after drew special attention in discussions of race and its implications for assimilability and citizenship. In popular perception German immigrants generally remained the less racially distinct—or dangerous—of the two. By longstanding tradition in the high discourse of race, the Anglo-Saxon and Teutonic traditions were closely aligned; indeed, by many accounts Anglo-Saxons traced their very genius to the forests of Germany—Anglo-Saxondom represented one branch of a freedom-loving, noble race of Germanic peoples.[12]

Further, in contrast with the Irish, a large proportion of German immigrants settled not in the polyglot, industrializing Northeast, but in the West. Thus even if in theory the various "New Germanys" of the West were to "keep the German settlers racially and culturally distinct," they were nonetheless subject to the racial alchemy of a "frontier" society that saw the world divided between whiteness and others. As one scholar remarked in 1909, the historian "will find the German element on the frontier line at every single stage of its progress westward, securing and defending it." German immigrants themselves also were less likely than their Irish counterparts to find the notion of a unified German race either terribly appealing or politically useful. According to one historian, the religious diversity of the German immigration in particular "made it very difficult for German Catholics . . . to see themselves as part of a larger 'German' entity" defined by race. Hence the Germans did not participate very actively in their own racial formation as non–Anglo-Saxons.[13]

Even so, ascriptions of Germanic racial identity were not uncommon. Richard Henry Dana could describe the '48er Carl Schurz as a "red-bearded Teuton"; the *Ohio Republican,* a Know-Nothing paper, could lament that Germans were driving "white people" out of the labor market; and Henry Cabot Lodge could glibly conclude that Germans "produced fewer men of ability than any other race in the United States." Nor was racial self-ascription unknown among German immigrants: even in addressing assimilationism, speakers often turned to a language of "racial amalgamation." After the failure of one "New Germany" in the West, a writer for the *Illustrierte Welt* (1859) identified racial amalgamation as the solution to the German problem: "Wouldn't it be wiser to seek the cultural-historical task of the German emigration in a melting of Germanic idealism with the realism of the Anglo-Saxon?" According to one Anglo-American observer in the 1880s, German newspapers and German clubs fairly rattled with the question, "Will the Teutonic race lose its identity in the New World?" Even by World War I, however, it had not: one speaker at a Swiss festival in Philadelphia called for "the final, decisive victory of the Teutonic race," while Germans in Chicago greeted war with Russia as a "war of the Teutonic race against the Slavic" and classed Slavs as the "natural serf races of Europe." Another writer, more inclined toward the allies, averred, "German blood has flowed freely in past times for the American union. It will flow as freely again if the Union again calls on its sons of the German race to be its sword and its buckler in its hour of danger."[14]

But by far the more powerful language of racial differentiation applied to the Irish. As Dale Knobel has amply demonstrated, beginning in the 1840s American comment on the "Irish character" became not only more pejorative but also more rigidly cast in a racial typology. During the mid-1840s, Knobel notes, American discussion of Irish immigration and urban social conditions rested upon the unquestioned fact of "something contemporaries had begun to call 'Irishism'—an alleged condition of depravity and degradation habitual to immigrants and maybe even their children." Negative assessments of Irishism or Celtism as a fixed set of inherited traits thus became linked at mid-century to a fixed set of observable physical characteristics, such as skin and hair color, facial type, and physique. The Irishman was "low-browed," "brutish," and even "simian" in popular discourse; a *Harper's Weekly* piece in 1851 described the "Celtic physiognomy" as "distinctly marked" by, among other things, "the small and somewhat upturned nose [and] the black tint of the skin." This comprehension of racial Irishness would surface in a wide range of contexts, including popular jokes, political speeches, newspaper cartoons, constabulary reports, and social policy guidelines. The Massachusetts State Board of Charities, for example, identified the immigrants' "inherited organic imperfection, vitiated constitution, or *poor stock*" as the chief cause of their pauperism and public dependency. Ultimately such racial conceptions would lead to a broad popular consensus that the Irish were "constitutionally incapable of intelligent participation in the governance of the nation."[15]

Racialism thus provided a powerful frame for interpreting and explaining Irish immigrant behaviors of all sorts, and for rearticulating at every turn the unbridgeable chasm separating natives (Anglo-Saxons) from immigrants (Celts). Whereas Irish nationalists themselves invoked their own yearning for liberty and fondly drew parallels between their cause and the glories of the American Revolution, native commentators often saw only chaos and irresponsibility in Irish political conduct. In the wake of an abortive Fenian raid on Canada in 1866, the *Atlantic Monthly* concluded, "All the qualities which go to make a republican, in the true sense of the term, are wanting in the Irish nature." To the "Celtic mind," the journal explained, "when anything comes in the guise of a law, there is an accompanying seizure of moral paralysis." The Irish rebel lives "in a world of unrealities almost inconceivable to a cool Saxon brain." Or again, in response to violence involving the radical Molly Maguires in 1877, the New York *Tribune* identified the Irish as "a race with more wholesome and probably unreasonable terror of law than any other." "Is there no other way [besides violence] to civilize them?" this editorialist wanted to know.[16]

Toward the century's end, Irish immigrants' innate "unfitness for self-government" would be familiar enough in the lexicon of America's public sphere to serve as the stuff of casual satiric allusion in works of fiction. Of the immigrant vote, one character in Marion Crawford's *An American Politician* (1884) remarks, "It is the bull in the china shop—the Irish bull amongst the American china—dangerous, you know." An *Atlantic Monthly* piece in 1896 similarly noted that "the unscrupulousness of the Irish in politics arises from the Celtic ardor and partisanship with which he pursues his objects . . . A Celt . . . lacks the solidity, the balance, the judgement, the moral staying power of the Anglo-Saxon." By their very peculiarities of "Celtic blood," in this estimation, the Irish posed a threat to the republic; but even more so in their eagerness to assimilate: the Celt "imbibes with avidity the theory of equality, and with true Celtic ardor pushes it to excess . . . there are many Irish-Americans, young men growing up in our cities, who are too vain or too lazy to work, self-indulgent, impudent, and dissipated."[17]

But because the animosity between Celts and Anglo-Saxons drew upon a long, racially accented European history of Saxon conquest, this racial divide was evoked and respected on the Celtic side as well. Many of the Irish in America, in other words, fundamentally agreed with American commentators like the editorialists of *Harper's* and *Atlantic Monthly* that a discernible racial chasm separated the Celt from the Anglo-Saxon; and though these Irish observers rejected the argument of Celtic inferiority in all its shades, they rejected the idea of Celtic racial difference not at all. For them no less than for their Anglo-Saxon contemporaries, physical differences marked an inner, natural "difference" separating the two races undeniably. This is a dimension of the overall racial picture of immigrant life that has gone largely unnoted.[18]

As Hugh Quigley wrote with considerable race pride, "The modern Irish are the most genuine, unmixed, and unchanged Celtic people that exist on the globe. Even the most prejudiced writers against the Irish . . . acknowledge that Ireland, today, is the land where the world-renowned race is to be found in its purity and its ancient characteristics." John Brennan's passage on the "physiognomy" of Irish-American children underscores the extent to which the category *Celt* reflected not simply how "difference" was conceived, but how it was actually seen. As in the case of other racial categories, the social meanings and distinctions surrounding the Celt were so ideologically thick as to translate into an immediate perception of discernible physicality. The biological dimension of Celtic identity was expressed most clearly by the Irish editor James Jeffrey Roche, who answered the anxieties of "race suicide" articulated by Anglo-supremacists like Teddy Roosevelt and Edward A. Ross with a rather mirthful argument we might properly call "race *homicide*." "Let the Anglo-Saxon call the roll of his relations," Roche wrote with some satisfaction, "and confess, with shame, that a grand race like that of the Puritan and pilgrim is vanishing . . . The fittest will always survive when they care to do so." Roche thus characterized the genetic contest between Saxon host and Celtic immigrant in the very same terms as the staunchest of American Anglo-Saxonists.[19]

Among self-ascribed Celts it was the discourse of nationalism above all that carried and enforced the racial meanings of Irish identity. Irish nationalism, of course, has a complex history of its own, but for the present purpose the specific ins and outs of Irish nationalism as a political program are less important than the more diffuse currents of myth and sensibility that were embedded in Irish immigrant culture. Elizabeth Gurley Flynn recalled the ubiquity of street-level nationalism in her autobiography, *The Rebel Girl:* "The awareness of being Irish came to us as small children through plaintive song and heroic story . . . As children we drew in a burning hatred of British rule with our mother's milk." This highly nationalist "awareness of being Irish" was carried not only in song and story but in the strains of Irish Catholicism and its hagiography; in the outlook of the Irish-American press; in holidays, festivals, and celebrations like St. Patrick's Day; in the martial tones of associational life (groups like the Clan na Gael and the Ancient Order of Hibernians were steeped in an ethos of national regeneration); and in popular entertainments such as vernacular theater and even parish dramas.[20] This "awareness of being Irish," in addition to being heavily nationalistic, was frequently accented by the racialism of a distinctly "Saxon" brand of historic oppression and a uniquely "Celtic" (or sometimes "Gaelic") brand of impoverishment and resilience. It was a worldview in which the Irish and the English on both sides of the Atlantic were racially distinct and thus shared a mutual animosity rooted in nature.

Confronting the proposition that his "mad" hatred for the British stemmed from his experience in British prisons, for example, the physical force nationalist Jeremiah O'Donovan Rossa remarked, "That kind of talk is all trash of talk. What I am now, I *was,* before I ever saw the inside of an English prison. *I am so from nature.*" Elsewhere, in describing his parents' reflexive hatred for the English, he suggested, "That kind of instinct is in the whole of the Irish race today." This language of racial unity was among the staples of Irish nationalist polemic, and nationalist leaders continually sounded the chords of racial obligation and a race-bound group destiny in their efforts to keep the overseas Irish oriented toward the homeland and toward the promise of its eventual liberation. As Robert Ellis Thompson wrote in the 1890s, "The greater Ireland [that is, the diaspora] which English misgovernment and deportation has created, sends its confirmation back to the old Ireland of its love and its hate. From every quarter of the inhabited world the Irish race watch and wait for the hour of deliverance." This sense of collective memory, injury, and desire was expressed in a variety of locutions, from the compact trope of "the sea-divided Gael," to the poet's refusal of an "Anglo-Saxon" America because "you are not of the self-same race / Nor blood of the self-same clan," to the Irish Race conventions of the 1910s.[21]

These Irish nationalist and American republicanist dimensions of Celtic racial identity fed off one another, even if they arose independently. On the one hand, the Anglo-Saxonist strains of American political culture replicated and thus reinvigorated the Irish sense of Celtic injury that had been cultivated across the Atlantic. As Rossa put it, "I cannot feel that America is my country . . . the English power, and the English influence and the English hate, and the English boycott against the Irishman is today as active in America as it is in Ireland."[22] On the other hand, the heated speech and the brash actions of Irish nationalists seemed to confirm Anglo-Saxon doubts about Celtic reason; and so nationalist manifestations fed back into the loop of dominant racial discourses on republican virtue.

In the matter of racial character, then, naturalization law allowed Irish immigrants entrance as "white persons," and the labor competition under capitalism may frequently have encouraged an aggressive embrace of that whiteness. And yet both U.S. and Irish nationalisms generated a racial crosscurrent that placed a high premium indeed upon the differences between distinct white races, the Anglo-Saxon and the Celt. This racially inscribed experience of the Irish on New World shores marked a more general shift in the ideological and visual lexicons of whiteness that affected a number of other groups of "free white persons" between the mid-nineteenth and the mid-twentieth centuries.

The White Other

Because racial classifications so successfully masquerade as features of the natural landscape, they are seldom commented upon overtly. But there have been certain moments when commentary on racial boundaries does present itself for examination. Three moments of violence and civic unrest surrounding three different white races between the 1860s and the 1910s provide glimpses of the assumptions attending this period's regime of variegated whiteness: the largely Irish uprising known as the New York City draft riots (1863), the lynching of eleven Italian prisoners in New Orleans by a white mob (1891), and the lynching of the Jewish "outsider" Leo Frank by an avenging mob in Atlanta (1915) each afford an unusually clear view of the contests over power and meaning that attended the question of racial difference in the case of European immigrant groups.

In recreating the New York City draft riots for *Harper's Magazine* (1867), Eleanor Leonard recalled, "A great roaring suddenly burst upon our ears—a howling as of thousands of wild Indians let loose at once . . . the cry arose from every quarter, 'The mob!' The mob! The Irish have risen to resist the draft!' " Her reference to "wild Indians" was neither accidental nor entirely metaphorical. Indeed, the "savage" nature of the Irish became a point of much discussion. Those days of violence in the wake of the 1863 Conscription Act raised many questions about class and the burdens of war; about Republican leadership; about unity in the North; and about Northern whites' willingness to make sacrifices perceived to be for the benefit of Southern blacks. According to one contemporary account, for example, a particularly visible leader of the mob denounced "this damned abolition draft," whereas others "threatened to kill every Black Republican-nigger-worshipping s—— of a b——, and burn their houses." Among the most dramatic acts of violence during the rioting, too, was the burning of a Colored Orphans' Asylum.[23]

But as the *Times* announced on the fourth day of violence, "it is a fact, patent to anyone who has seen anything of the mob, that it is composed almost exclusively of Irishmen and boys," and hence chief among the questions that lingered in civic discussion as the violence waned was, Just who *are* these Irish? Were they, as they had proclaimed by their actions, so many aggrieved "whites"? Or, on the contrary, were they, as some native New Yorkers openly wondered, a "savage" people, as Leonard had implied, like "wild Indians let loose" in the city streets? Thomas Nast had put the matter most compactly: a cartoon of the rioters later in the summer bore the caption, "A Gorilla on the Loose."[24] The riots thus became the occasion for a contest over the racial meaning of Irishness itself—an assertion of pan–white supremacism on the one hand, versus vigorous denials of Celtic equality with the Anglo-Saxon on the other.

Although the class antagonisms that were played out during July 1863 are significant, as Iver Bernstein has shown, the riots themselves nonetheless enacted a deeply embedded race politics, a violent racial melodrama. As Bernstein points out, racial antagonisms ran high during the spring because of the decision of local shipping companies to break a longshoremen's strike by employing black labor.[25] The local pro-slavery paper, the *Weekly Caucasian,* announced at the head of every issue that it stood "firmly for WHITE SUPREMACY, a defense of the rights and welfare of the Producing and Working Classes, now imperiled by the doctrine of Negro Equality."[26]

And indeed the rioters' actions over the course of the week were in part a violent enactment of this brand of whiteness itself. Rioters targeted their perceived enemies among prominent Republican politicians, to be sure, but they vented much of their fury in such a way that the rioting itself seems a racial ritual of civic differentiation. "It would have been far from safe for a negro to have made his appearance in [the Eleventh Ward]," reported the *Herald,* "for the laboring classes there appear to be of the opinion that the negroes are the sole cause of all their trouble, and many even say that were it not for the negroes there would be no war and no necessity for a draft." Common enough were reports that "the rage of the mob was exclusively directed against colored people," or, again, that a certain black woman had been "badly beaten about the head by Irishwomen."[27]

But the rioters' assaults were not directed solely at blacks; nor was their insistence upon whiteness drawn only by a contrast with blackness. According to the *Herald,* one rioter had "endeavored to lead an attack on a house . . . where negroes visited white women. Ambitious to regulate the races and prevent amalgamation, his hostility was not confined to Africans." He had also destroyed the furniture of a white man who "had married a squaw." Here antiblack feeling verged on a more general expression of white supremacism aimed at any person or community defined as "nonwhite"—whose equality, in the logic of the *Weekly Caucasian,* imperiled the producing and working classes. Hence "having caused a general exodus of negroes," as one reporter observed, "[rioters] turned their attention to the Chinese who delight to reside in that precinct. The celestials had been found guilty of uniting with white wives, and their headquarters were sacked. The John Chinamen escaped, but in some instances their inconstant consorts have not followed them." The crowd descended on the Chinese neighborhood of the Fourth Ward after one speaker urged that the Chinese represented "a modification of the negro."[28] When the violence subsided, casualties were found to include one Ann Derrickson, "a white woman, the wife of a colored man," and Peter Heuston, a Mohawk Indian "with dark complexion and straight black hair." According to one witness, Heuston had been murdered because "a gang of ruffians . . . evidently thought him to be of the African race because of his dark complexion." But not necessarily: as the antidraft protest became an unleashing of white-supremacist violence, merely being "dark" was sin enough.[29]

If the actions of the rioters seem to have embodied a working-class entitlement based both on race (white entitlement) and on class (their privileged status as producers in a producers' republic), many non-Irish onlookers and commentators, in their turn, registered their own republican claims by questioning the rioters' full status as "white persons." In response to a New York *Herald* piece that referred to the rioters as "the people," a *Times* editorialist objected that those who could rightly lay claim to that title "regard with unqualified abhorrence the doings of the tribe of savages that have sought to bear rule in their midst." The *Times* went on to decry the "barbarism" of the riots and to characterize the rioters themselves as "brute," "brutish," and "animal."[30]

This quickly became the reigning paradigm within which the rioters' actions were interpreted and described in genteel quarters. A second *Times* article two days later asserted, "Few imagined that there was such a race of miscreants extant . . . In spite of our Christian institutions we have thousands of barbarians in our midst, every whit as ferocious in their instincts as the Minnesota savages, and never wanting anything but the opportunity to copy every Indian deed of horror." A Brooklyn minister averred that "the cruelties of the aboriginal savages can hardly rival those of the brutal mob that has disgraced [New York]." The *Tribune* reported that "a white gentleman (the son of a missionary), born in the East Indies . . . said, when he saw the rioters yesterday, 'I am proud of the heathen.' " The *Tribune* routinely characterized the Irish as a "savage mob," a "pack of savages," "savage foes," "demons," and "incarnate devils." In his rousing account *The Bloody Week*, an anonymous "Eye Witness," too, chimed in that the mob consisted of "barbarians and inhuman ruffians." (The language here is strikingly similar not only to colonial rhetoric regarding Indians, but to contemporary accounts of the Indians in the West. That same month, July 1863, for instance, the *Oroville Union* [California] would refer to Indians as "devils of the forests.")[31]

Even *Harper's Weekly,* which early on had tried to dispel the notion that the riot derived from "the perversity of the Irish race," and which had argued that "there was nothing peculiar . . . to the Irish race in this riot," later suggested that "the impulsiveness of the Celt . . . prompts him to be foremost in every outburst, whether for a good or an evil purpose." By summer's end writers at *Harper's* were noting the "riotous propensities" of the Irish and comparing them unfavorably to African-Americans: "Where, either in our colonial or our national history, have the Irish, as a race, won so clear a title to the gratitude of the people of the United States as the negroes have won within the past three months?"[32]

Given that the uprising took place during a time of war—and a war for the liberation of slaves, no less—it was perhaps inevitable that discussion would turn to the imperatives of citizenship and the Celt's "fitness for self-government." As one commentator put it in a book review of *The Wrong of Slavery* for the *Atlantic Monthly* in 1864, "The emancipated Negro is at least as industrious and thrifty as the Celt, takes more pride in self-support, is far more eager for education, and has fewer vices. It is impossible to name any standard of requisites for the full rights of citizenship which will give the vote to the Celt and exclude the Negro."[33] The comment is double-edged: like the cartoon years later (1876) that would place the Celt and the Negro on the scales of civic virtue and find them weighing in identically, here an argument on the Negro's behalf seems to make as strong a case for actually *stripping* the rights and privileges that have already been conferred upon the Celt as a "free white person." The war, which was going to entail some revisions in the notions of American citizenship, was a most fitting occasion for some reflection upon the civic virtues of the Celtic immigrants and their contribution to the republic.

This image of Celtic savagery was revived and pressed into service as a cautionary metaphor years later, in the wake of the Haymarket affair, when an anonymous "Volunteer Special" outlined the perils to "Americanism" posed by unchecked immigration. In his suggestively titled *Volcano under the City* (1887), "Volunteer" resurrected the Irish mob of 1863 as "whooping, yelling, blaspheming, howling, demonic, such as no man imagined the city to contain . . . none of them seem to be Americans." And conditions had only worsened since 1863. Among the most pressing problems faced by the republic were the ever-expanding "race-colonies" of unmetabolized, un-Americanized Europeans now in every major city.[34]

Whereas in New York in 1863 an Irish mob action seemed to ratify a common conception of Celtic "savagery," in New Orleans in 1891 a perception of immigrant Italians as "savage" led to an anti-Italian mob action. The racial discourse within which the events were comprehended and narrated, however, was similar. Is an Italian a white man? a journalist asked a West Coast construction boss in the 1890s. "No sir," he answered, "an Italian is a Dago." Similarly, a *Harper's Magazine* piece offered a guided tour of "Italian Life in New York," in which the exoticized accounts of the human landscape echoed then-current travel accounts from Africa or the Levant: "It is no uncommon thing to see at noon some swarthy Italian . . . resting and dining from his tin kettle, while his brown-skinned wife is by his side." (The exotic body's swarthy surfaces, of course, contain "the quick intuition of Italian blood.")[35]

In New Orleans in 1891 such perceptions of Italians' racial distinctness became deadly. In the wake of a spectacular murder trial whose verdict was widely believed to have been "fixed" by local Mafiosi, a popular understanding of Italians' *innate* criminality not only allowed, but indeed prompted, the brutal lynching of eleven immigrants accused of conspiring to murder the police chief of New Orleans. So blithely was the guilt of the immigrants presumed, that, utterly without irony, even a Northern journal like the New York *Times* could refer to the lynch mob as consisting of the city's "best element." So fused in popular perception were the issues of Mafia conduct and Italian racial character that, in editorials about the affair, the *Times* would cast Italian immigrants' behavior as racially determined and question their fitness for citizenship. "These sneaking and cowardly Sicilians," pronounced one editorial, "who have transplanted to this country the lawless passions, the cutthroat practices, and the oathbound societies of their native country, are to us a pest without mitigation. Our own rattlesnakes are as good citizens as they."[36]

The social location of Italian immigrants in Louisiana in this period points up just how complex the vicissitudes of race can be. It was not the case that the various probationary white races of the nineteenth century were invariably "whitened" by the presence of nonwhite Others in the cultural and political crucible of a given locale. Although it is true that whiteness *could* emerge by its contrast to nonwhiteness (as seems to have been the case with Celts in California during the anti-Chinese campaign of the 1870s, for instance), immigrants who were white enough to enter the country as "free white persons" could also lose that status by their association with nonwhite groups. This was precisely the case with Italians in New Orleans.

In certain regions of the Jim Crow South Italians occupied a racial middle ground within the otherwise unforgiving, binary caste system of white-over-black. Politically Italians were indeed white enough for naturalization and for the ballot, but socially they represented a problem population at best. Their distance from a more abiding brand of social whiteness (what Benjamin Franklin might have meant by "lovely white") was marked by the common epithet "dago"—a word whose decidedly racial meaning was widely recognized at the time and was underscored by the more obviously racial "white nigger."[37]

It was not just that Italians did not look white to certain social arbiters, but that they did not *act* white. In New Orleans Italian immigrants were stigmatized in the post–Civil War period because they accepted economic niches (farm labor and small tenancy, for instance) marked as "black" by local custom, and because they lived and worked comfortably among blacks. According to one social historian, by their economic pursuits alone, which often set them side by side with black laborers, "Italian immigrants assumed the status of Negroes . . . [and] Southern thinking made no effort to distinguish between them." Italian immigrants ran further afoul of white supremacists in the region when they "fraternized with local blacks and even intermarried," and when—like blacks—they supported Republican and Populist candidates instead of the party of white supremacy. From being "like Negroes" to being "as bad as Negroes" was but a trifling step in dominant Southern thinking; and hence in states like Louisiana, Mississippi, and West Virginia, Italians were known to have been lynched for alleged crimes, or even for violating local racial codes by "fraternizing" with blacks. (It is worth noting that the execution of the eleven Italian prisoners in New Orleans was carried out by the White League, a Reconstruction-era terror organization much like the better-known Ku Klux Klan.)[38]

After the sensational trial of the eleven immigrants for the murder of

Police Chief Hennessy, and after the even more sensational vigilante raid on the jailhouse and the retaliatory murder of the prisoners themselves, one of the first questions to arise in the press and elsewhere was the relationship of these events to the Italian character. Did Italian racial character have anything to do with the original crime? Did the mob murder the prisoners because they were Italian? When Italians across the country (and, indeed, across the Atlantic) denounced the lynching as a brutal act of persecution and racial violence, the New York *Times* responded that, no, these Italians had *not* been persecuted "as Italians." In an editorial striking for its success in combining a tone of cool, irreproachable rationality with an argument that *lauded* the lynch mob, the *Times* went on to warn that, if Italians failed to fall in behind other "decent" American citizens and to applaud the mob's success in doing away with the "criminals" (even while deploring the lawlessness of the lynchings), then Americans would draw the conclusion that all Italians were lawless ruffians with Mafia ties. Then, indeed, all Italians would be persecuted "as Italians," "and this would not be a prejudice, but a sentiment founded upon facts and sustained by reason." The men who were murdered were guilty, the *Times* flatly asserted; "there is no doubt whatever." "This is a fact that the Italians in Italy are not supposed to know, but that the Italians in this country have no excuse for not knowing."[39]

Others were even more blunt in their condemnations of the Italian immigrants and more forthcoming in their commendation of the New Orleans mob. As one merchant characteristically put it, "The Italian colony in New Orleans . . . is a menace to American citizenship and good government. Why, I had rather have a thousand Chinamen than one Italian. They are treacherous, revengeful, and seek their revenge in most foul and cowardly manners. They have no regard for the truth . . . The lynching, terrible as it was, is a blessing for New Orleans." One local judge, R. H. Marr, Jr., pointed to the racial clannishness of the Italian colony to explain the community's fierce outpouring of anti-Italian sentiment in the wake of the Hennessy murder. Convictions in crimes involving Italians had been notoriously scarce, he charged, because, when questioned, "any number of Dagoes . . . swear to the most positive and circumstantial alibi" on behalf of the accused. "Until the killing of Hennessy," moreover, "these people had so far as the public knew, confined their operation to their own race." Even journals as far from the crime scene as the Portland *Oregonian* were inclined to depict the behavior of the New Orleans Italians in racial terms—"an explosion of cheap Latin fury and braggadocio."[40]

Another dimension of this apprehension concerning lawless or degenerate "dagoes" was a certain racial pride in the masterly bearing of the "Anglo-Saxon" lynch mob. At a moment when the "patriotism of race" uniting Great Britain and the United States was just beginning to find its adherents in both countries, the lynching could be assimilated to self-flattering, chivalric narratives of virile Anglo-Saxon manhood. A letter to the editor of the *Pall Mall Gazette* (England), reprinted in the New York *Times,* commended "the men on the Mississippi who are not spoiled by the spirit of submission to the letter of the law, which has done so much to emasculate the human race." The *Gazette* criticized the letter, but nonetheless did conclude that "one branch of the Anglo-Saxon race does not differ from another in this matter. The citizens of New Orleans, finding that the jury did not do its duty, said: 'We must by one means or another put crime down.' " (In another telling twist on the alchemy of race, it is worth noting the significance here in "Anglo-Saxon" New Orleans' being represented by the *Irish* Police Chief Hennessy in this racial drama. As one social historian argues, Irish immigrants represented 13 percent of the local population by 1890, and, unlike Italians, they had thoroughly assimilated to the "white" population—thus becoming, one might say, honorary Anglo-Saxons.)[41]

Significantly, Italian comment, too, reflected a racial interpretation of the entire affair. Secretary of State James Blaine received telegrams from Italian organizations all over the country protesting the "outrage" at New Orleans and demanding that "all Italian citizens of the United States be properly protected against violence and race prejudice." Grasping at once the racial significance of American ("Anglo-Saxon") rhetoric, Italian protestors themselves mobilized a racially accented language of "barbarism" and "civilization" in addressing the wrongs perpetrated in New Orleans. Not only must Italian protest be "noble, dignified, and measured," counseled the Italian journal *Cristofero Colombo;* further, "it must impress upon Americans the mark of savage people; it must be the lesson of a civilized nation to one that is not so." Likewise, *L'eco d'Italia* urged that since the United States had shown "unexampled barbarism" toward the immigrants, therefore "let us answer by setting before them our example of true civilization." It is not clear whether such spokespersons shared the Anglo-Saxons' deep-rooted concern for "civilization" and "savagery," or simply recognized the rhetorical purchase of this language in American political culture. In either case, however, it is clear that they recognized the significance of the ideology of diverse peoplehood that framed the lynching itself and provided the terms for national discussion in its after-math.[42]

As the event lingered in public memory, racial understanding of Italian character inevitably tended toward the period's broader discussion of immigration and its consequences for the republic. Most forceful in this connection was "Lynch Law and Unrestricted Immigration," Henry Cabot Lodge's essay for the *North American Review*. Lodge was as quick to defend the anti-Italian hysterics from the charge of racism as he was to defend ordinary, law-abiding Italian immigrants from blanket racial charges of lawlessness or proneness to violence. "The killing of the eleven prisoners had in it no race feeling whatever," he assured. "There has been no hostility to the Italians in America, as such." Various "dangerous societies" among immigrants—like the Mafia, the Molly Maguires, anarchists, and "Secret Polish Avengers"—derived not from "race peculiarities," Lodge explained, but from "the quality of certain classes of immigrants from all races." He did go on, however, to blame the Italian victims for the mob violence in New Orleans: the lynching had been a reasonable response of good citizens to the immigrants' offensive secret organizations and their lamentable power. Such mob scenes were destined to be repeated—and here is the real relationship between "lynch law and unrestricted immigration"—*if the tide of immigration were not stemmed*.[43]

Lodge's protestations notwithstanding, the gist of his *North American Review* article was indeed to vent a certain "hostility to the Italians of America, as such." Although he insisted that "race" was not at issue, Lodge took the occasion to quote at length from a State Department report on immigration which insisted, among other things, that "the immigration of those races which had thus far built up the United States, and which are related to each other by blood or language or both, was declining, while the immigration of races totally alien to them was increasing." Lodge, for his part, insisted to the end that it was Mafia behavior and not Italian character that lay at the heart of the New Orleans affair. He nonetheless asserted that "not only was our immigration changing in point of race, but . . . it was deteriorating."[44]

Such views on immigration made it into even the lightest, most popular and lurid renditions of the New Orleans tragedy. The first treatment of the lynching in fiction appeared only weeks after the event, in the April 1891 number of the New York Detective Library, *The New Orleans Mafia: or, Chief of Police Hennessy Avenged*. Though geared toward a thrill-seeking audience and not necessarily a politically engaged one, this account retained all the key elements common to the New York *Times* editorials and the piece by Henry Cabot Lodge: the depiction of the Italian colony as not properly white; the question of good citizenship; and, hence, the ultimate righteousness of the lynch mob.

The racial dimension of the story is announced in the opening pages, when the boy hero, Tom Duff, first comes upon the villains: "The upper half of their countenances were covered by black half-masks, out of the eyeholes of which gleamed the snakiest of black eyes." Notwithstanding their obscured visages, "it was evident to the boy that both were Italians for the color of their skin and the contour of their features amply proclaimed their nationality. 'Dagoes!' he muttered." Lest the reader mistake the implication, the narrative likewise compares the Italians to another nonwhite group ("Like the Negro," we are told, "the favorite weapon of the Sicilian is the razor"), and offers some observations on their essential racial character ("the Sicilians have always been the most bloody-minded and revengeful of the Mediterranean races . . . These traits are probably owing to their Saracen origin, murder and intrigue being natural with them").[45]

These racial traits alone are enough to commend the rising nativist argument that Italians are not such stuff as republicans are made of, and to exonerate the lynch mob for its lamentable but finally necessary brand of rough justice in New Orleans. *The New Orleans Mafia* does both. Early passages establishing the scene and setting the stage for the story's central drama include a fictional letter to local officials, in which the "Chief of the U.S. Secret Service" opines, "Italian immigration should receive the same check as the Chinese has . . . Legislation should suppress what is becoming a menace to the country." And at the story's end, Tom Duff, who had emerged as one of the key figures in the "avenging" lynch mob, appears enviably unconflicted in his role in the violence: given the characters involved and the deeds they had committed, "he did not feel guilty of having done any more than his duty."[46] Nativist misgivings at the Italian presence and remorseless support for the chivalric lynch mob, then, are the two primary sentiments bracketing this adventure tale; racialism is the ideological undercarriage that lends shape to both.

Finally, the episode was reworked yet again, in less direct fashion, in Mark Twain's set piece "Those Extraordinary Twins," later a subplot for *Pudd'nhead Wilson* (1894). Surely the New Orleans affair was somewhere in the back of Twain's mind when, after one of the novel's white

characters has an altercation with "that derned Italian savage" and another (who happens to be—like Hennessy—a city official) has been murdered, the twins land in jail to await their lynching. Luigi is indicted for
the murder and Angelo is held as accessory (echoing the New Orleans
case); the two are "in constant danger of being lynched" until Pudd'nhead
Wilson himself is able to discover the real murderer. Most telling, however, is that the tale would surface here, in *Pudd'nhead Wilson,* Twain's
tortured exploration of race itself as a "fiction of law and custom." The
Italians perfectly embody the problematic status of the "racial Italian" in
a bifurcated political culture: one was "dark-skinned . . . up to all kinds
of mischief and disobedience when he was a boy, I'll be bound"; and the
other was "blonde," with "such kind blue eyes, and curly copper hair and
fresh complexion."[47]

Italians long continued to occupy that middle ground in the racial order.
As late as 1925, a study of immigrants and the justice system could conclude that Italians "are by nature emotional and demonstrative," and
"should not be allowed to drift into racial communities [ghettos], forming
habits of thought . . . that are limited and warped." The more famous
expression belongs to William Faulkner: in *Light in August* (1932), in
response to his "confession" that he is a Negro, a woman casually says
to Joe Christmas, "I thought maybe you were just another wop or something."[48] (The court in *Rollins v. Alabama* basically concurred with this
candid confusion, ruling in essence that the Sicilian Edith Labue might
have been just another Negro or something.)

Decades after the New Orleans affair, as Georgia was abuzz with news
of the Jew Leo Frank's alleged misdeeds in Atlanta, Tom Watson's *Jeffersonian* called for a "vigilance committee," reminding readers of the clarity
and decisiveness with which New Orleans had dealt with the Italian "mur-
derers" in 1891. Watson finally did get his wish. It may well be, as Seth
Forman has recently argued, that Jews in the former slaveholding states
of the South were the first Jews in North America to see themselves as
"white." But, as the Leo Frank case demonstrated, even in the context of
strict, white-over-black social bifurcation, complete with its own imperatives, rituals, etiquette, and patterns of deference and domination, Jews
could be racially defined in a way that irrevocably set them apart from
other "white persons" on the local scene. The evidence and nature of the
testimony in the case, public sentiment, questions of the relative veracity
of the accounts of the Jewish defendant and a key black witness, and
questions of Frank's character, his alleged "perversion," and his status as

a social "outsider," all combined to form one overarching question of race and the identity of the Jew. As one black journalist asked at the time, in puzzling out the complex public sentiments, "Is the Jew a White Man?"[49]

Leo Frank's ordeal began in April 1913, when the body of a fourteen-year-old white girl, Mary Phagan, was discovered in the basement of a pencil factory in Atlanta, Georgia. Frank, a young graduate of Cornell University, was part-owner and manager of the factory. A note the girl had allegedly scrawled—presumably as she died—seemed to point to a night watchman named Newt Lee as the assailant. But after a long and sensational trial, Frank himself was eventually convicted, largely on the testimony of a Negro janitor named Jim Conley. In August 1915, after the lame duck governor of Georgia commuted Frank's sentence, a mob descended upon the prison where Frank was being held, took him to the outskirts of Marietta, and hanged him. As the Fulton County coroner told a reporter soon after, the lynching reminded him of "the old Ku Klux Klan days"—and he had been a member.[50]

During an interview in the aftermath of Frank's murder, incoming Governor Nathaniel Harris gave the lynching a chivalric twist: "There is something that unbalances men here in the South where women are concerned," he explained. "Let a strong man use his strength to force a helpless woman to yield to him, and there is something that arouses the tiger in Southern men . . . It is something that goes with this," he said, tapping his "white cheek," according to the interviewer. "It goes with the white man's skin and I have even seen it in some cases among niggers." Southern chivalry, not anti-Semitism, explained the lynching of Leo Frank, argued Harris, in rebuttal of the common Northern interpretation. But the Frank case itself had generated a new level of anti-Semitism in Georgia, Harris had to concede: there was now an uncomfortable feeling among Georgian Gentiles that Jews had "banded themselves together as a race or a religion to save a criminal," and had thus "ranged themselves in opposition to men of other races and religions."[51]

Harris's syntax reveals the indeterminacy of the Jewish position in Georgia's local knowledge of race. That Jews had banded together "as a race or a religion" itself raises the question of who, precisely, Jews were. More than this, however, Harris's erasure of Jews in his discussion of chivalry indicates the Jews' problematic position in the Southern economy of races: in identifying violent chivalry as something that "goes with the white man's skin and . . . in some cases [can be found] among niggers," Harris marks Frank as a double outsider—as a Northerner excluded from the Southern community of white and black chivalric masculinity, and as a racial outsider, neither precisely "white" nor precisely "a nigger"—fit, certainly, to be a lynch victim, but never to be part of a lynching party. This imprecision itself constitutes the terrain upon which observers, in North and South, discussed and debated the case.

There was much about the trial and the surrounding spectacle that actually upheld the South's traditional social bifurcation along the lines of black and white. Conley testified that he "was willing to do anything to help Mr. Frank because he was a white man and my superintendent." "Mr. Frank, you are a white man and you done it," he later testified that he had exclaimed to the Jew. The emergent contest between Conley and Frank, too, had the effect at the time of pitting "black" against "white." For instance, once it was clear that someone other than Phagan had written the note found along with her body, the question became, who was that someone? Race seemed to many to hold the answer. The journalist C. P. Connelly was not alone when, in his *Truth about the Frank Case*, he argued that the note was "so idiotic that no white man of intelligence . . . would have conceived it." Indeed, Frank himself wrote from prison that it was "preposterous for any white man of average common sense to leave documentary evidence behind [in] any crimes." On the broader question of veracity, Frank's lawyers, for their part, denounced Conley as a "dirty, filthy, black, drunken, lying nigger"; and in implicating Conley they were not at all reluctant to evoke the mythology of the Negro rapist (an especially powerful complex of images in 1915, the year of D. W. Griffith's *Birth of a Nation*).[52]

The dyadic racial sensibility of black and white came into play, too, in response to the unusual circumstance of a "white" defendant's guilt being established by a "Negro" witness. One clergyman called the fairness of Frank's trial into question on this basis, remarking that he "wouldn't hang a yellow dog on James Conley's testimony, much less a white man." Even the radical Carey McWilliams would register suspicion years later: "For the word of a Negro to be given this weight in a murder prosecution against a white man in Georgia was, in itself, a rather remarkable manifestation of anti-Semitic prejudice."[53]

We need not lament that Conley's testimony was accepted without corroboration—a circumstance that merely represents his momentary ascent to the status of a full citizen in the courtroom—nor is it fruitful to reify the whiteness of the Jew by identifying Frank's conviction on Conley's testimony as an insult to that whiteness. Rather, we might take this extraordinary conviction as a sign of Frank's *contested* whiteness at the time, and explore more fully the layers of racial signification that defined the status of the Jew at that moment in Georgia. Like Edith Labue, whose indeterminate racial status would result in the not-guilty verdict in *Rollins v. Alabama,* Leo Frank was *inconclusively white.*

No one has examined the racial element of the Frank case as closely as Jeffrey Melnick in his recent study of Black-Jewish relations early in the century, and there is no improving upon his analysis. The racial Jewishness that enveloped Leo Frank, according to Melnick, was heavily freighted with the ideological baggage of region, class, and sexuality. In a Jim Crow setting, "Jews like Leo Frank were more likely to take up whiteness as a self-concept and mode of behavior than their Northern counterparts," but even so, Frank's whiteness was open to question once the charges had been leveled. Although one detective on the case had early referred to Frank as a "racial descendant of the carpet-baggers," thus marking the significance of the Jew's Northern origins in this melodrama of criminality, finally it was the charge of perversion that crystallized Frank's Jewishness as race in public discussion. This is not to say, along with Frank's attorney, that "if Frank hadn't been a Jew, there never would have been a prosecution against him."[54] (Indeed, as a salve to the Jewish exceptionalism that colors much of the scholarship on Frank, it is worth asking which elements of the Frank story would have remained unchanged if he had been Italian, say, rather than Jewish.) But Frank's Jewishness did lend certain suspicions a ready frame.

First of all, Frank "looked Jewish," and, as Melnick argues, his Jewishness "came to light" for public consumption via the press's descriptions of the *physical* markers of his perversity. As Tom Watson put it, Leo Frank's "face looked the part to perfection." The *Jeffersonian* luridly described "those bulging satyr eyes . . . the protruding fearfully sensual lips; and also the animal jaw." Even sympathetic reporters were apt to mention Frank's "high-bridged nose"; and the general press stressed his "bulging eyes" and "thick lips."[55] Such descriptions of Frank's physicality conjoined nineteenth- and early-twentieth-century assumptions of lechery as a Jewish racial trait. In *The Old World in the New* (1914), for instance, the sociologist Edward A. Ross had written of the Jew's penchant for cross-racial perversion—sparing the Jewess but pursuing the Gentile.[56]

Watson brought the full force of the stereotype to bear directly on the Frank case: "Here we have the typical young libertine Jew who is dreaded and detested by the city authorities of the North for the very reason that

Jews of this type have an utter contempt for law, and a ravenous appetite for the forbidden fruit—a lustful eagerness enhanced by the racial novelty of the girl of the uncircumcised."[57] Thus Frank's racial status as a Jew and his criminal status as a "pervert" were inseparable—and both were proven by his physiognomy.

The perversion charge may have saved Jim Conley's life and sealed Leo Frank's fate, Melnick argues, but the racial inflection of Jewishness-as-difference paradoxically united the two men as well—it "posited the public identities of Negro and Jew as equally divergent from normative whiteness." On the one hand, Rabbi Stephen Wise could object that "crimes against women are not typical of our race." Whether Wise was actively defining Jews racially here in order to highlight their counterpoise with "Negroes," as Melnick argues, or rather unself-consciously revealing his own assumptions about Jewishness-as-difference, Wise clearly was contrasting Frank with the Negro Jim Conley, for whose race, presumably, crimes against women *were* "typical."[58]

Someone like Tom Watson, on the other hand, could steer the Black-versus-Jew question of racially determined criminality in a very different direction. It was not just that Frank seemed to be under the legal protection of a "Hebrew cabal" from New York, nor that the Jew seemed to "expect extraordinary favors and immunities because of his race." Nor was it merely that "it was determined by the rich Jews that no aristocrat of their race should die for the death of a working-class Gentile."[59] In addition, Watson constructed a complex racial equation by which the "perverse" nature of the crime at once exonerated the Negro, incriminated the Jew, and proved the Jew to be the greater racial menace to boot. The crimes committed against Mary Phagan (couched rather vaguely under the apparent misnomer "sodomy") represented "[vices] not of robust negroes but of decadent white men," according to the *Jeffersonian*. "Sodomy is not the crime of nature, barbarism, or of lustful black brutes; it is the overripe fruit of civilization and is always indicative of a decaying society."[60] In Watson's worldview, then, the perversion of the Jew surfaced not only as a racial trait, but as a racial trait of *overcivilization*. In the web of significations that, for Watson, at once contained and explained the case, Frank's race became the site where his Jewish looks, his perverse behavior, his outsider status, and his threatening class position converged. As C. Vann Woodward rather economically put it in his classic study of Watson, Frank "was a Jew, a Northerner, [and] an employer of underpaid female labor."[61] He was thus the perfect villain to suit the needs of the postbellum, industrializing South, complete with its special regional sorrows, its class antagonisms, and its racially accented, chivalric mythologies of pure white womanhood and avenging white manhood. And, as Watson noted, Frank *looked* the part. (The pastor of Mary Phagan's church, for one, concurred: in the Jew he saw "a victim worthy to pay for the crime" of Mary Phagan's death—and "a Yankee Jew at that.")[62]

It is worth noting, in this connection, that though Tom Watson may have acted like a self-appointed, one-man anti-Semitic posse during 1914 and 1915, the circulation figures of his journal, the *Jeffersonian,* leapt from 25,000 to 87,000 during the period of the Frank case.[63] His rantings are more than a mere sideshow in the overall story of the Frank case; and his view of Frank is more than a mere oddity in the overall racial economy of pre–World War I Atlanta. Watson at one point warned Frank's defense team that they had "blown the breath of life into the monster of Race Hatred: AND THIS FRANKENSTEIN, *whom you created at such enormous expense,* WILL HUNT YOU DOWN." Indeed, it is impossible to understand or even to narrate the Frank case without reference to Frank's racial status—by which one cannot simply mean his whiteness, even if that does seem to be the likely option offered by the binary caste system of the New South. In the years before Mary Phagan's murder, Southern nativism had risen sharply in response to an influx of South and East European immigrants. The *Manufacturers' Record,* for instance, had bluntly announced, "The South will have human sewage under no consideration." Throughout the Frank case, observers from Stephen Wise to Tom Watson to incoming Governor Nat Harris remarked in various ways upon the slippage between the defendant's whiteness and his Jewishness; to many, it was his racial Jewishness that finally settled the case against him and exonerated the more "barbaric" Negro, Jim Conley. Following Governor Slaton's commutation of Frank's sentence, Slaton was burned in effigy as "King of the Jews, and Georgia's Traitor Forever"; and Jews themselves were warned out of Canton and boycotted in Marietta.[64]

Perhaps the most telling piece of racial commentary in the entire affair was the Marietta *Journal and Courier's* self-satisfied report, after the lynching, that "we are proud, indeed, to say that the body hanged for more than two hours amid a vast throng and no violence was done. Cobb county people are civilized. They are no barbarians."[65] This, it seems, is race thinking carried to its logical extreme (and, in American political culture, *only* race has consistently had the ideological power to turn a savage lynch mob into a haughty exemplar of "civilized" comportment).

However different in other respects, then, the New York draft riots, the New Orleans lynching, and the Leo Frank case all illustrate the mobilization of racial languages and logics to interpret the social order and to provide a basis for social action. The three episodes illustrate as well the extent to which racial identity is inseparable from contests over class and sexuality. In each case racial depictions of the Irish, Italians, and Jews overlapped with an existing discourse of American nativism, which set a racial standard for good citizenship. But, significantly, these episodes played out largely independent of the immigration question proper, and so they afford a glimpse of how *live* these racial distinctions were when it came not only to debating the issue of immigration, but also to the more general matter of simply understanding the workings of a heterogeneous society. The intellectual history, as it were, of American nativism offers an even more detailed portrait of the European immigrant through the lens of race, but it will be important to keep in mind that, as we have just seen, nativism in no way represents an isolated or anomalous ideological pocket in its constructions of race, classification, and the inherent inclinations and capacities of various populations.

Race and American Nativism

The shifting perception of racial difference *among* "free white persons" points up two critical but largely neglected dimensions of the history of American nativism: first, nativism was a response to the political crisis created by the 1790 naturalization law—the over-inclusivity of the category "white persons." Hence, second, the history of American nativism from the 1840s to the 1920s is largely the history of a fundamental revision of whiteness itself. The late nineteenth and early twentieth centuries' frankly racial depictions of European immigrants were not mere oddities—unjust but finally quaint or quirky conceptions of ethnic difference. Rather, the racialism expressed in simian caricatures, naturalistic novels, and acts of Congress are more fruitfully examined within the broader pattern of race-bound notions of "fitness for self-government" that had characterized American political culture since the framers first plumbed the "utopian depths" of experimentation with republican government.

Modern scholars are most comfortable discussing Poles, Greeks, or Italians as "ethnic" or "national" groups, and thus they tend to disparage and dismiss the lexicon of white races that characterized an earlier era. But this is anachronism. As Lothrop Stoddard put it in 1924, "Race is what people physically really are; Nationality is what people politically think they are." Race and nation are not synonymous, Stoddard cautioned, but "blood-kinship ('Race')" *is* "one of the strongest factors which can go to make up a nation." Hence when the Senate Commission on Immigration reported in 1911 that Poles are "darker than the Lithuanians" and "lighter than the average Russian," for instance, this was a statement of what the Poles "physically really are." (Along with this immutable physical trait, it turns out, in temperament Poles are "more high strung than their neighbors").[66]

Throughout the race-based, eugenically driven political debates that followed, Americans pressed long-standing racial idioms into the service of a familiar argument about what constitutes good material for citizenship. This was not a new departure "toward racism" but a continuation of republican tradition. At issue now was simply which "white persons" *truly* shared what an earlier generation had indiscriminately conceived of as—in James Fenimore Cooper's phrase—the "white man's gifts." The restrictive legislation of 1924 decisively segmented the community of "white persons" and ranked its disparate members—the arrival of desirable "Nordics" continued to be favored, whereas the numbers of problematic "Alpines" and "Mediterraneans" would be dramatically curtailed. But in the context of the late nineteenth century's scientific racialism, even earlier restrictions on "convicts, idiots, lunatics, and people likely to become public charges" (1882) and "people with physical or mental defects" (1907) rested upon racial distinctions, as the scientific probabilities for such conditions were themselves determined by a calculus of race.[67]

Beginning with the arrival of the Irish in the 1840s and throughout the great waves of East Europeans in the 1880s and after, then, popular nativist logic shifted toward a racial conception of immigrant "difference" and its significance to the republic: from the American Party's concerns about dubious "Papist" allegiances or unfair labor competition, to that veritable cult of Anglo-Saxonism known as the Immigration Restriction League, to the frankly eugenic nativists of the 1910s and 1920s, who saw the immigrant "not as a source of cheap or competitive labor, nor as one seeking asylum from foreign oppression, nor as a migrant hunting a less strenuous life, but as a parent of future-born American citizens"—so much "hereditary stuff" that would have to be compatible with "American ideals."[68]

The loudest voices in the organized nativism of the 1840s and 1850s harped upon matters of Catholicism and economics, not race. Most worried, for example, that Catholic immigrants would taint this polity of independent freemen, as one writer put it in an early nativist tract, because they would "obey their priests as demigods."[69] But race was not altogether absent even from this anti-Papist brand of American nativism. One American Party address entitled "To the Native and Naturalized Citizens of the United States" (1844) described national greatness in these terms: "By superior energy, and through the influence of more enlightened institutions, the Anglo-Saxon race acquired pre-eminence, and placed almost the whole country under the tutelage of Great Britain." The tract went on, also in racial terms, to discuss the meager prospects for the assimilation of Scots, Italians, and Germans.[70]

Concerning the "Papist," too, religion was sometimes seen as a function of race. As an article entitled "Romanism and the Irish Race" in the *North American Review* explained (1879), the gravest objection to Irish immigrants was their incapacity, as Catholics, to participate in a democracy: "A republican form of government implies freedom and self-reliance," traits that are "extinguished in Romanism, as flame goes out in carbonic acid." Familiar enough. But further, by this account the persistence of Irish Catholicism was inseparable from the issue of Celtic racial identity. "The Celtic nature requires something which is intense, real, and passionate," the piece explained; and this is why the Irish are so ill suited to Protestantism and so stubbornly unconvinced by its merits. The Catholicism of the Irish immigrants "has prevented a fusion [of blood]" with their Protestant hosts, and so race and belief have conspired to leave the Irish as an unmetabolized lump in the body politic—"separate in blood, separate in religion."[71]

Daniel Ullman, a Know-Nothing leader in New York, proved an avid follower of then-current scientific thought on race. The "question of races," he pronounced in "The Constitution of the United States," a speech delivered throughout New York in 1868, "is perhaps as important as any which concerns humanity." Striking the familiar, anti-Papist chord of earlier Know-Nothing rhetoric, Ullman did argue that "there must be a common religious sentiment, pervading the whole mass of the people, or all else is vain." Yet he paid far more attention and energy to the question of race. Citing such racialist luminaries of the day as Gobineau, Morton, Augustin Thierry, and Louis Agassiz, he told audiences that "the origin of nations, the elements which constitute the strength of nations, and the sources of the American Republic and its Constitution, are among the most important subjects of human inquiry." "Origins," "elements," and "sources," as it turned out, were all racial terms in this explication of American political genius. A republic "situated as is the United States, must become one of vast strength, if it be chiefly peopled by one dominant, leading race." And that race was defined not merely as "white" but as "the Anglo-Saxon branch of the Teutonic race of the Caucasian group."[72]

Much of this tract detailed a racial myth of the origins of American political institutions. By this account God had hidden the continent of North America from Europe's "civilized races" until they were properly prepared to undertake the bold experiment of self-government. The American republic thus represents the "crown" of all European history. Ullman went on to trace the genius of American constitution to the four racial "elements" of Britain: "The chief element was undoubtedly Germanic. Hence springs the inherent love of freedom of the Anglo-Saxons in England and America, which has been the hereditary characteristic of the Teutonic or Germanic race from the earliest period." Teutons found Britain peopled by Romans, Danes, and Normans; and from this union "proceed the institutions of England, and, in the main, of America."[73]

But racial greatness itself does not eliminate political peril; on the contrary, if history demonstrates the racial potential for occasional political genius, so does it indicate the ever-present threat of decline. Just as the most powerful empires "have drawn their energy from the life vigor imparted by one single, dominant race," so a heterogeneous society, constituting a mere "mixture of discordant races," "contains, within itself, the elements of weakness and final ruin." Thus Ullman urged that racial distinctions were particularly important for Americans, whose porous political culture allowed for ever-increasing racial diversity: "Proximate species of the same type may assimilate," he warned, but "distinct types, never." By way of tragic example, he pointed to the Austrian Empire, a mere "congeries of peoples" populated by "four of the seven races of Europe." On the question of racial diversity, Ullman concluded, "Let not America . . . exalt herself so high, as to presume that she can disregard, with impunity, the laws, which God has established . . . for the moral and physical government of nations."[74]

This interpretation of human history was no academic exercise. Americans' handling of racial questions had profound implications for the political experiment for which God had set aside the continent in the first place. For Ullman, as, indeed, for many of his compatriots, the matter at hand was no less than the fate of "self-government" as a viable political principle. Upon the broadening of the male franchise in the Jacksonian period, and in a rapidly industrializing United States, a constant tension existed between the necessity of huge numbers of immigrants as laborers on the one hand, and the menace posed by these same immigrants as ill-equipped citizens on the other. Antiradicalism (a kind of class vigilance) was one common response to these new conditions; nativism (a kind of race vigilance) was the other. The problematic white immigrant was central to both of these often intertwined discussions.

Thus Daniel Ullman was in good company (or at least a lot of it). "We speak of self-government as if it was . . . a grand triumph of political sagacity," cautioned the *North American Review*. "We all admit, that particular races, the Asiatics for instance, are not yet fit for it. We interpret their incapacity by assuming that they are not sufficiently advanced on the road to perfection. Quite possibly these peoples may never advance along that road, and have no need to advance."[75] The democratic experiment may be forever closed, in other words, to certain peoples inherently unfit for the arduous demands of political self-possession.

But whereas this author and many others were quick to point to non-European peoples, there were those who wondered whether all Europeans themselves would prove to be "fit for self-government." In an essay entitled simply "Democracy" (1884), James Russell Lowell pointed to the brief history of urban bossism and machine politics as proof of immigrants' permanent state of unfitness: "If universal suffrage has worked ill in our larger cities, as it certainly has," he wrote, "this has been mainly because the hands that wielded it were untrained to its use." There government is controlled by "the most ignorant and vicious of a population which has come to us from abroad, wholly unpracticed in self-government and incapable of assimilation by American habits and methods." Or again, as Francis Walker wrote in the *Atlantic Monthly* (1896), the newer immigrants represented "beaten men from beaten races" who "have none of the ideas and aptitudes which fit men to take up readily and easily the problem of self-care and self-government, such as belong to those who are descended from the tribes that met under the oak trees of old Germany to make laws and choose chieftains."[76]

The period between the first massive Irish migration of the 1840s and the triumph of racially engineered immigration restriction in the 1920s was thus marked by a profound ideological tension between established codes of whiteness as inclusive of all Europeans, and new, racialist revisions. The newly urgent question of European immigration prompted a redefinition of whiteness; and yet, within a shifting context of slavery and Emancipation, continued continental (and later trans-Pacific) expansionism, and anti-Chinese agitation, that definition was fraught with contradictions.

Questions of citizenship, fitness for self-government, and race were reopened at the legislative level in 1870, when Senator Charles Sumner introduced an amendment providing that "all acts of Congress relating to naturalization be . . . amended by striking the word 'white' wherever it occurs, so that in naturalization there still be no distinction of race or color." A senator from Oregon, where anti-Chinese sentiment was mounting, quickly added, "But this act shall not be construed to authorize the naturalization of persons born in the Chinese empire." Both the significance of Sumner's proposal and the ramifications of Western dissent were acknowledged and summed up in an amendment proposed by a third senator in jest, "Provided, that the provisions of this act shall not apply to persons born in Asia, Africa, or any of the islands of the Pacific, nor to Indians born in the wilderness. [Laughter]."[77]

Congressional jesting aside, the ensuing debate revealed the complex interplay between citizenship and race, and raised the issue of what, exactly, whiteness was taken to denote. Were certain peoples disqualified from the republic, for instance, by their color or by their alleged "heathendom"? Sumner himself announced that, in striking the word "white," he merely wanted to "bring our system in harmony with the Declaration of Independence and the Constitution of the United States." "The word 'white,' " he offered, "cannot be found in either of these great title-deeds of this Republic." To senators from the West, by contrast, the word "white" provided a critical bulwark against national decline. "Does the Declaration mean," one wanted to know, "that the Chinese coolies, that the Bushmen of South Africa, that the Hottentots, the Digger Indians, heathen, pagan, and cannibal, shall have equal political rights under this Government with citizens of the United States?" The implicit logic of this list is telling in its very confusion. "White," by implication here, is a designation that indicates not only color but degree of freedom (as against "coolies"), level of "civilization" (as against "cannibals"), and devotion to Christianity (as against "heathens" and "pagans"). Indeed, throughout the debate the senators opposing Sumner's amendment objected to Chinese immigration on the alternating grounds of "their pagan allegiances," their position as "slave labor in competition with free labor," and the frankly racialist view that "Mongolians . . . will never lose their identity as a peculiar and separate people."[78] According to one senator from Nevada, the Chinese had to be both "republicanized and Christianized" before they could safely become citizens—a possibility logically denied by the entangled threads of race, civilization, and religion.

As the impossibility of Asian citizenship was asserted and reasserted, this congressional debate itself demonstrated the alchemic effects of racial discourse. Rethinking the problem of naturalization *through* race, first of all, could only result in a highly limited, paradoxical, and ultimately mean-spirited brand of liberality at the very best. After the Senate hit upon the formula of extending the privileges of citizenship to "any person of the African race or of African descent," for instance, Senator Trumball spoke out on the Asians' behalf: "Is it proposed to deny the right of naturalization to the Chinaman, who is infinitely above the African in intelligence, in manhood, and in every respect?"[79] As long as no one challenged the core republican principle that not all peoples were capable of self-government, then such deprecations were inextricably woven into racially accented political discourse—even where that discourse was employed in the service of antiracism. As long as the core principle of "fitness for self-government" was intact, the argument for inclusion could only generate other exclusions; this or that group's asserted "fitness" for self-government could only be measured by *some* group's *un*fitness.

At the same time, the presence of racially marked Others reified and further united the "white persons" of the 1790 naturalization law. Inasmuch as no one was suggesting that citizenship actually be *revoked* from those who had already entered under the terms of 1790, any discussion of the total exclusion of certain groups—whether Africans, Asians, or both—tended tacitly to endorse the unifying logic of a single European race whose credentials for self-government were above reproach. "The people coming here from Europe are of our own race," argued a senator from Nevada. "They are of us, and assimilate rapidly, and aid in the development and progress of our country. Let them come . . . But how is it with these Asiatics?"[80] Sumner's hope of raising whiteness itself as a point of debate finally fell afoul of the very white supremacism that such a debate was meant to challenge.

From 1870, then, "free white persons" were joined by persons "of the African race or of African descent" in eligibility for citizenship. This deliberate exclusion of Asians paired with the legal difficulty of whiteness as a stable, meaningful category gave rise to a series of legal challenges, beginning with *Ah Yup* eight years after the debate over Sumner's proposal (1878), and culminating with the famous *Halladjian, Ozawa,* and *Thind* cases in the 1910s and 1920s (see Chapter 7). Throughout these years, as the naturalization law was continually challenged in the courts by those hoping to get in, and as immigration restriction was kept alive in the nation's editorial columns and in the halls of Congress by those hoping to keep still others out, whiteness itself was subject to a curious, competing set of assumptions and interpretations.

The main currents of this peculiar dynamic had already been discernible in the congressional discussion of 1870. Whiteness was so freighted with political meanings and moral judgments that common usage of the term itself hinted at the problematic character of certain groups that, by custom, had already been included. Given the popular connotations of the phrase "white man," that is, one might question its applicability to certain of the Europeans now washing ashore at Castle Garden. But as *the* tool of exclusion barring Asian citizenship, the category "white" proved self-sustaining: whiteness at once depended upon, and created political capital out of, a series of contrasts whose very terms reinforced the original assumptions undergirding whiteness in the first place. Thus in this period of volatile racial meanings, peoples such as Celts, Italians, Hebrews, and Slavs were becoming less and less white in debates over who should be allowed to disembark on American shores, and yet were becoming whiter and whiter in debates over who should be granted the full rights of citizenship. The discourse of immigration restriction favored a scheme of hierarchically ordered white races, that is, and found some of these sorely wanting in the characteristics required for self-government, whereas naturalization discourse discovered fundamental and unforgiving differences between the white races on the one hand, and the hordes of nonwhite Syrian, Turkish, Hindu, and Japanese claimants who were petitioning the courts for citizenship on the other.

An insightful, if vexed, exploration of these contradictions appeared in the *American Law Review* in 1894, as John Wigmore, a Northwestern University law professor, puzzled over both the basis and the implications of legal whiteness. Wigmore wondered whether the word "white" in the 1790 statute had properly referred to literal "color-quality," to "people of the original race-stock known as the 'Caucasian' or 'Aryan' race," or to "the European peoples and their colonial progeny." His particular interest was in unlocking the bar to naturalized citizenship for Japanese immigrants, and he found whiteness elastic enough to suit his needs. Southern Europeans were so dark, he averred, that they "can be termed 'white' not in the ordinary sense, but only in contrast with the African negro." This he felt true of "the Semites, the Balkan people, the Greeks, the Italians, and the Hispano-Portuguese in Europe and in Latin America"—all "white" by U.S. naturalization standards. If these and other "dark and swarthy Europeans" were "white" only in contrast with Africans, as was surely the case, he argued, then should not anyone else who contrasted with Africans—Japanese immigrants, for instance—qualify as "white"?[81]

Wigmore did concede that "Caucasian" or "Aryan" was probably the intended meaning of "white" in the law as it was conceived in 1790, but this, too, presented significant logical inconsistencies: "If [the Aryan race] includes as eligible the Slav, Celt, Scandinavian, Germanic, Pelasgic, and Italic stocks, whose claims to naturalization are undisputed . . . it also includes the Afghans, Persians, and pure Hindus, and other minor Asian stocks, whose claims . . . can hardly be said to be conceded." One group in particular confounded the logic of standing naturalization law, being at once decided outsiders to the proper category "Caucasian," and yet accepted—if begrudged—insiders to American citizenship: "The disposition of the Semitic peoples . . . especially the Hebrews, caps the climax; for [the category "Caucasian"] involves the exclusion of a whole race whose industrious workers are found in all states of the Union." Jews are not Caucasians. Hence although the term "white" in the 1790 code does seem to refer to "Caucasians," neither the *ex*clusion of Hindus nor the *in*clusion of Hebrews is supportable by that logic. The "systematic application of the term 'white' is attended with the greatest difficulty," Wigmore concluded. But clearly Japanese immigrants "could pass as Bulgarians or Spaniards" where literal color is concerned, and are therefore " 'white' enough to satisfy the statute" and hold "as good a claim to the color 'white' as the Southern European and Semitic peoples."[82]

Wigmore's device of casting "contrast with Africans" as the key to whiteness while dismantling the seeming fixities of the idea "Caucasian" conveys the central contradiction regarding the immigrating white races of the period: their own whiteness was questionable in regard to proper Americanism (whatever Wigmore's good intentions on behalf of Japanese immigrants, his 1894 audience could not have missed the restrictionist implications of his revising away the difference between Eastern Europeans and Asians); and yet they were rendered indelibly white by the presence of populations even more problematic than themselves.

The ascendent view among native-born Americans in the 1890s, even as John Wigmore was writing, was not that Japanese immigrants held "as good a claim to the color 'white' as the Southern European and Semitic peoples," and therefore ought to be granted citizenship, but rather, that Southern European, Semitic, and Slavic immigrants held as *poor* a claim to the color "white" as the Japanese, and therefore ought to be turned away at once. The racialism of this prevailing view of the newer European immigrants, its basis in republican logic, and its relationship to racialized assessments of Asians were all nicely embodied in another piece by Henry Cabot Lodge for the *North American Review* in 1891. After rehearsing the history of how the thirteen colonies had been founded by "people of the same stock" whose "community of race" contributed to the work of assimilation, Lodge went on to investigate the repercussions of the recent shift in the sending countries—particularly the "Slavic" countries of Eastern Europe. Quoting the U.S. consul at Budapest, Lodge announced that "these Slovacks are not a good acquisition for us to make, since they appear to have so many items in common with the Chinese." Not only would their presence in large numbers "interfere with a civilized laborer's earning a 'white' laborer's wage," but, indeed, representing "races most alien to the body of the American people," they would be "very difficult to assimilate" and hence "do not promise well for the standard of civilization of the United States."[83]

Lodge held this logic in common with other New England patricians, including Prescott F. Hall, Robert DeCourcy Ward, and John Fiske, who went on to found the Immigration Restriction League in 1893. The league crystallized around the issue of a literacy test for incoming aliens. Race was central to the league's conception of literacy from the beginning, and it became more prominent over time in its rhetoric of Americanism and civic requirements. From its founding in 1893 to World War I, the league moved steadily away from that vague set of prides and prejudices that Barbara Miller Solomon has called an "Anglo-Saxon Complex," and toward a fully eugenic program concerning questions of racial pedigree, national character, and the proper role of the state in tending the biological make-up of its population. Indeed, the historian Kenneth Ludmerer has traced the pedigree of the American eugenics movement to the Harvard class of 1889, a group that included some of the key figures of the Immigration Restriction League—Charles Warren in addition to Hall and Ward. By the 1910s league officials like Hall would not only embrace the term "eugenics" and the science it represented—that is, the *biological* engineering of the body politic—but would couch the entire discussion of the immigration question in a language of "desirable" versus "useless" races, the important national work of "breeding," and the statistical averages for this or that race's possessing this or that trait. But the eugenic implications of mere Anglo-Saxon prejudice had been evident in embryo even in 1891, when Henry Cabot Lodge voiced his concern over "races most alien to the body of the American people" and his ideas about which peoples would and which would not represent "a good acquisition for us to make."[84]

If the ideology of the eugenic standpoint emerged more or less logically and gradually from the mid-nineteenth-century scientific and political arguments regarding racial stocks and their inherent qualities, the *apparatus* of eugenics as a presence on the American scene rose rather dramatically after the turn of the century. In 1904 the Carnegie Institution put up money to open a Station for the Study of Evolution at Cold Spring Harbor, Long Island, under the direction of Charles Davenport. Davenport himself was among the enthusiastic supporters within the scientific community who felt that, to paraphrase the historian Daniel Kevles, "nationality" was primarily a function of "race," and "race" was the prime determinant of behavior. "The idea of a 'melting-pot' belongs to a pre-Mendelian age," Davenport wrote to one colleague, showing his hand on the immigration question. "Now we recognize that characters are inherited as units and do not readily break up." In the ensuing years, under Davenport's direction, the station at Cold Spring Harbor provided critical institutional focus to the eugenics movement, serving both as a major intellectual and material resource and as a dispenser of information and data.[85]

The influence of eugenics on legislation in the United States crested, of course, with the immigration act of 1924, whose provisions ensured that those new arrivals who were still allowed entry, in the self-congratulatory words of the immigration commissioner, once again "looked exactly like Americans." But such views of race and immigration had become fixed in the lexicon of the state as early as 1911. Most significant in this respect is volume nine of the Dillingham Commission's Report on Immigration, *A Dictionary of Races or Peoples*. In an attempted clarification of terms, the commission endorsed Blumenbach's five-tier scheme ("Caucasian, Mongolian, Ethiopian, Malay, and American"), yet also noted that "the bureau [of immigration] recognizes 45 races or peoples among immigrants coming to the United States, and of these 36 are indigenous to Europe."[86]

The phrase "races or peoples," used throughout the document, leaves plenty of room to wonder about this taxonomy of "difference." And indeed, in addressing the "popular looseness of the word ['race']" directly, the commission asserted that "race is determined by language in such phrases as 'the races of Europe,' but by physical qualities, such as color, hair, and shape of head, when we speak of 'the five great races' or grand divisions of mankind." Nonetheless, Europe's linguistic groups are irretrievably cast as racial groups throughout the *Dictionary,* so that even within the unifying construction of a grand "Caucasian" race, among European peoples difference itself is consistently defined as both biological in nature and extreme in degree. (Indeed, even the *Dictionary*'s definition of "Caucasian" is begrudging: it includes "all races, which, although dark in color or aberrant in other directions, are, when considered from all points of view, felt to be more like the white race than like any of the other four races.") Although the report insists that race is primarily a linguistic category and not a physical one when it comes to "the European races," nonetheless the Albanian "has one of the broadest heads not only of Europe but of the world"; "the weight of [the Bohemian's] brain is said to be greater than [that of] any other people in Europe"; modern Greeks are "broad-headed, broad-faced, and more heavily built, although perhaps no darker than the ancients"; "the 'Jewish nose,' and to a less degree other facial characteristics, are found well-nigh everywhere throughout the race"; and Poles are "darker than the Lithuanians" and "lighter than the average Russian."[87]

As ever, physical properties here are keyed to essential characterological, moral, and intellectual qualities: despite a tone of scientific detachment, the commission's *Dictionary of Races or Peoples* is fundamentally a hierarchical scale of human development and worth. Alongside its observations on Slavic, Iberic, Hebrew, and Celtic physicality, the *Dictionary* argues, for instance, that Bohemians are "the most advanced of all [the Slavs]"; "the savage manners of the last century are still met with amongst some Serbo-Croatians of to-day"; "the ancient Greeks were preeminent in philosophy and science, a position not generally accredited to the modern Greeks as a race . . . they compete with the Hebrew race as the best traders of the Orient"; "the Gypsy resents the restraint of a higher social organization . . . to him laws and statutes are persecutions to be evaded"; the South Italian is "an individualist having little adaptability to highly organized society"; Poles are "high strung"; Roumanians "compare favorably with the races of the Balkans, although some say that they are more backward"; Ruthenians are "less practical, solid, and persevering than their competitors of the north . . . but they often show a higher grade of intelligence and taste"; "Sicilians are vivid in imagination, affable, and benevolent, but excitable, superstitious, and revengeful"; and the Slav is "inequable or changeable in mood and in effort—now exalted, now depressed, melancholy, and fatalistic." Along with this "changeability," one observes "carelessness as to the business virtues of punctuality and often honesty."[88]

Although the *Dictionary* is not nearly as virulent in its racism as, say, Madison Grant's *Passing of the Great Race* (see below), nonetheless the political intent of this taxonomy of peoples is not far beneath the surface. Again and again, in various connections, the authors note the significance of the changing "source" and "character" of immigration to the United States. Italians, Hebrews, and Slavs now constitute the most numerous arrivals to American shores, and if their "difference" from old-stock Americans is cause enough for concern, their sheer numbers and the possibilities for their future numbers ought positively to sound a national alarm. Although never as blatant in its distaste for the newcomer as the adherents of "race suicide," the *Dictionary* announces an incipient but perhaps inevitable demographic apocalypse: "The immense capacity of the Italian race to populate other parts of the earth," for example, "is shown by the fact that they outnumber the Spanish race in Spanish Argentina and the Portuguese race in Brazil, a 'Portuguese' country."[89]

Such concerns over the biological powers of immigrants to effect a kind of conquest by procreation led to a heightened debate over the eugenic dimensions of immigration policy, and to an increasingly high profile for eugenic experts both in the popular presses and in congressional hearingrooms. The Immigration Restriction League now pressed the language of racial hygiene, arguing in one report submitted to the Dillingham Commission (under the subheading "Restriction Needed from a Eugenic Standpoint"), "We should see to it that the breeding of the human race in this country receives the attention which it so surely deserves." "A considerable proportion of the immigrants now coming," warned the league, "are from races and countries . . . which have not progressed, but have been backward, downtrodden, and relatively useless for centuries. If these immigrants 'have not had opportunities,' it is because their races have not made the opportunities." The secretary of the Executive Committee, Prescott Hall, added that the league opposed, not all immigration, but only that which "lowers the mental, moral, and physical average of our people." In this connection he noted ominously that of recent immigrants, "three-fifths were of the Slavic and Iberic races of southern and eastern Europe."[90]

Among the most important and popular expressions of the rising eugenic view of immigration was Madison Grant's *Passing of the Great Race,* an extended diatribe against the "pathetic and fatuous belief in the efficacy of American institutions" to absorb and transform diverse populations. The book first appeared in 1916, but achieved its peak popularity only in the early 1920s, undergoing successive editions in 1920 and 1921. The old-stock American's liberal immigration policies, in Grant's view, were tantamount to "suicidal ethics which are exterminating his own race." Grant took issue with Franz Boas and others who now emphasized the influence of environment and the potential for changes— even changes in physical characteristics—among newly arrived immigrant populations: what the melting pot (a biological, not a cultural, contrivance) really accomplishes, Grant argued, is best exemplified by "the racial mixture which we call Mexican, and which is now engaged in demonstrating its incapacity for self-government." Here, indeed, are the stakes of immigration policy, and the underlying peril of the "melting-pot" ideal. "Whether we like to admit it or not, the result of the mixture of two races, in the long run, gives us a race reverting to the more ancient, generalized and lower type. The cross between a white man and an Indian is an Indian; the cross between a white man and a negro is a negro; the cross between a white man and a Hindu is a Hindu; and the cross between any of the three European races and a Jew is a Jew."[91]

This combination of immutable racial traits and an ineluctable tendency toward decline among any multiracial crosses spelled danger indeed for the republic. The "new immigration" consisted largely of "the weak, the broken, and the mentally crippled of all races drawn from the lowest stratum of the Mediterranean basin and the Balkans, together with hordes of the wretched, submerged populations of the Polish Ghettos." As Grant saw it, in cities like New York "old stock" Americans were being "literally driven off the streets" by "swarms" of immigrants—primarily Polish Jews—who "adopt the language of the native American; they wear his clothes; they steal his name; and they are beginning to take his women, but they seldom adopt his religion or understand his ideals."[92]

In assessing the traits and the relative merits of the European races, Grant sketched out a three-tiered scheme of "Nordics," "Alpines," and "Mediterraneans." Predictably, he reserved harsh judgment for American blacks, who had become "a serious drag on civilization" from the moment "they were given the rights of citizenship and were incorporated in the body politic." But so salient are the differences among Nordics, Alpines, and Mediterraneans, that when Grant lumps them together at all, he does so only by the self-undermining phrase "so-called Caucasians." The term " 'Caucasian race' has ceased to have any meaning," he argued, except where it is used to contrast white populations with "Negroes," "Indians," or "Mongols."[93]

Grant's views on the hierarchy of whiteness are highly symptomatic; they not only influenced debates over immigration and restriction, but also influenced and reflected popular understanding of peoplehood and diversity. As Madison Grant and his counterparts at Cold Spring Harbor gained notoriety in the 1910s and early 1920s (due, in no small part, to the Dillingham Commission itself), the eugenic cast of the American immigration debate became more and more pronounced. During the hearings before the House Committee on Immigration and Naturalization in 1922, the prominent eugenicist Harry Laughlin explained, "Social inadequacy as an effect and racial degeneracy as a primary cause go hand in hand"; therefore he had undertaken to study "the relative soundness of recent and older immigrant stocks." Laughlin unabashedly referred to his research as "investigations into the biological or eugenical aspects of immigration," and in this spirit offered up to the committee a series of "racial" breakdowns (following the scheme of races in the Dillingham Commission's *Dictionary*) of various types of "social inadequacy" in the United States: feeblemindedness, insanity, criminality, epilepsy, tuberculosis, leprosy, inebriety, blindness, deafness, deformity, and a catch-all, "dependency." Amid his discussion of immigration as "a long-time national investment in hereditary traits," Laughlin, for one, was quite willing to refer to the proposed system of immigration quotas—the basis for an eventual scheme of "national origins quotas"—as "race quotas."[94]

If his testimony and the voluminous writing he submitted during the key period of debate helped to bring eugenic thinking into the mainstream of political discourse, his very presence before the committee and his ubiquitous writings mark the extent to which the eugenic view had already entered popular American thinking. Looking back with approval upon this legislative victory for the eugenics movement years later, Laughlin wrote, "Henceforth, after 1924, the immigrant to the United States was to be looked upon, not as a source of cheap or competitive labor, nor as one seeking asylum from foreign oppression, nor as a migrant hunting a less strenuous life, but as a parent of future-born American citizens. This meant that the hereditary stuff out of which future immigrants were made would have to be compatible racially with American ideals."[95]

The stakes of immigration restriction, as defined by the eugenically minded, ultimately determined the shape of the new legislation. The formula that was finally written into the Johnson Act—that is, a quota system based on 2 percent of each group's population according to the 1890 census—originally emerged in a Report of the Eugenics Committee of the United States Committee on Selective Immigration. That committee, chaired by none other than Madison Grant and including Congressman Albert Johnson of Washington (the president of the Eugenic Research Association, 1923–1924), argued that a formula based on the 1890 census rather than on a more recent one "would change the character of immigration, and hence of our future population, by bringing about a preponderance of immigration of the stock which originally settled this country." North and West Europeans, read the report, were of "higher intelligence" and hence provided "the best material for American citizenship." Although the authors of the report alleged that this was not a question of "superior" and "inferior" races, but merely a matter of admitting an "adaptable, helpful and homogenous element in our American national life," they did venture that their formula would "greatly reduce the number of immigrants of the lower grades of intelligence, and of immigrants who are making excessive contribution to our feeble-minded, insane, criminal, and other socially inadequate classes." Citing data from Yerkes's Army Intelligence Tests, the authors now poured the very old wine of fitness for self-government into the new bottle of eugenics: "Had mental tests been in operation, and had the 'inferior' and 'very inferior' immigrants been refused admission to the United States, over six million aliens now living in this country, free to vote, and to become the fathers and mothers of future Americans, would never have been admitted."[96]

Exact figures concerning the probable effects of the Johnson formula varied, but the principle was clear enough. These sample figures, entered in the *Congressional Record* during the debate, demonstrate the stakes involved in the racial make-up of continuing immigration according to the two formulas being considered, one based on group population percentages derived from the 1910 census, the other (eugenic) derived from the 1890 census:

Country of Origin	Current law	Senate bill (1910 census)	Johnson Act (1890 census)
Greece	3,063	2,042	100
Italy	42,057	28,038	3,889
Poland	30,979	20,652	8,872
Russia	24,405	16,270	1,792
Yugoslavia	6,426	4,284	735

N = immigrants per year under the competing plans

Later in the spring of 1924, at a convocation of the Second International Congress of Eugenics, Professor Henry Fairfield Osborn succinctly pronounced upon the Johnson Act's republican intent and its reliance upon hereditary, rather than environmental, principles of "difference." It is the sovereign right of the state "to safeguard the character and integrity of the race or races on which its future depends," he declared. And further, the political dictum that "all men are born with equal rights and duties has been confused with the political sophistry that all men are born with equal character and ability to govern themselves and others, and with the educational sophistry that education and environment will offset the handicap of heredity."[97]

If the system of "difference" governing the logic of the Johnson Act seems novel and the policy of "racial hygiene" seems distasteful from the standpoint of the late twentieth century, neither aspect was a point of much squeamishness at the time. Eugenicists were as frank in their laudatory assessments of the act's import as they were in their assertions as to the soundness of its core principles. Harry Laughlin, among the most visible experts called upon by Congress during the debates, explained the eugenic project of which the Johnson Act was a part in a later tract, *Immigration and Conquest*:

> Racially the American people, if they are to remain American, are to purge their existing family stocks of degeneracy, and are to encourage a high rate of reproduction by the best-endowed portions of their population, can successfully assimilate in the future many thousands of Northwestern European immigrants . . . But we can assimilate only a small fraction of this number of other white races; and of the colored races practically none.

Laughlin identified the act as an important "turning point" in immigration policy, in that it squarely set state policy on "a biological basis"; "the American people began to look upon immigration as the importation of human seed-stock." (Laughlin supplied not only much of the thinking behind the eugenic policy, but also its most vivid analogy: "In the rat world the record is not one of conquest by direct war and formal battle, but one by the quiet immigration—a few at a time—of members of the invading species, which established itself, reproduced at a high rate . . . [and] succeeded to the ownership of the invaded territory.")[98]

Other eugenicists were hardly more charitable toward the "new immigrants." Thurman Rice, in *Racial Hygiene* (1929), viewed them as "immigrants of unrelated blood," and argued that perhaps quotas—even under the eugenic formula of the 1924 legislation—were not enough: "Members of the Slavic or Alpine sub-race should be allowed to enter only in exceptional cases, since we now have all of this blood that we can absorb, and probably more than is good for us." On the fundamental, hereditary traits of the new immigration in general, Rice commented, "A man may be made physically clean for the moment by the use of soap, water, and disinfecting and delousing agents, but the habits of a lifetime which allowed him to become dirty and lousy, and those traits of a defective germ plasm which permitted him to be contented in remaining so, cannot be changed by soap and water, and disinfecting and delousing agents."[99]

Two points bear particular emphasis here. The first is that the eugenic view met vigorous opposition in this period from immigrants and natives alike. Eugenic outlooks on immigration and other social questions were in ascendence, but their hegemony was not without ruptures. During the congressional debate, for instance, one representative called Grant's *Passing of the Great Race* "as fine an example of dogmatic piffle as has ever been written," and lamented that the committee had granted so much time to the likes of Grant, Lothrop Stoddard, and Harry Laughlin, and so little to the cooler scientific voices of Franz Boas or Ernest Hooton. Another objected to the eugenicists' contention that their bill was not discriminatory: "If the bill does not discriminate against south and east Europeans, deliberately so, why the report of Dr. Laughlin, why all the scientific investigation under the Carnegie Foundation to prove that those races were inferior, socially and nationally; that they were inferior stock?" It should never be said to some Americans, he insisted, "You come from an inferior race. Your race is practically barred now from this country, and we today regret that we let you in." "That," he concluded, "is not the America I want to be a part of. [Applause]."[100]

Opposition to the proposed restriction bill was led in Congress by the New York delegation, and in particular by Fiorello LaGuardia, Nathan Perlman, and Samuel Dickstein; Dickstein's dealing with the Committee on Immigration had made it clear to him that its members "did not want anybody else in this country except Nordics." A series of popular rallies and demonstrations further manifested widespread opposition. Giving the lie to the public fiction of inferior and superior white races, Rabbi Stephen Wise told an immense audience at a Carnegie Hall rally, the "Nordic race" was no more than a convenient political invention, simply "devised to prove its [own] superiority, and in order to prove the inferiority of some of the great races of the earth which are unacceptable to the inventors of the Nordic."[101]

As had been the case in the nineteenth century, however, there was a troubling aspect to much of this opposition. Like earlier arguments on behalf of this or that group which left intact the core principle that the incapacities of *some* groups did indeed require their exclusion from the nation's political life, the opposition in 1924 embraced exclusion as an acceptable tradition in American politics. Like their forerunners, the dissidents of 1924 asked simply which groups were properly to be the target of exclusion. Representative Clancy of Michigan, for example, attacked the "fearful fallacy of chosen peoples and inferior peoples" with an argument that rested upon an implicit foundation of white supremacism: "The fearful fallacy is that one is made to rule and the other abominated," he objected, "all Caucasians and worshipping the same God." The question that had been posed overtly in 1870 now merely lingered between the lines: what of groups who were *not* "Caucasian" or did *not* worship the same God? Or again, a letter of protest by Max Kohler decried the *de facto* exclusion of Greeks, Italians, Poles, and Jews by this trickery of basing the immigration quotas on the 1890 census: "Will any thinking man dare to put these races among the relatively inferior races of the world?" he wanted to know, thereby endorsing the notion of racial superiority.[102]

Nowhere was this underside of the protest as clear as in the following exchange on the floor of Congress, when one representative led another through a catechism on the principles of self-government. "Is it the gentleman's idea," the questioner asked, "that the primary object of this bill is to discriminate against certain people?"

> *Mr. O'Connor of New York:* I believe that the committee and the proponents of this bill believe that, in order to preserve the ideals of this country, it is necessary to discriminate against certain races.
>
> *Mr. MacLafferty:* That is fairly put. Would you discriminate against Asiatic races?
>
> *Mr. O'Connor of New York:* I believe that is a well-founded tradition of America.
>
> *Mr. MacLafferty:* Is it discrimination?
>
> *Mr. O'Connor of New York:* It is.
>
> *Mr. MacLafferty:* Is it necessary?
>
> *Mr. O'Connor of New York:* It may be.
>
> *Mr. MacLafferty:* Is necessary discrimination ever justified?
>
> *Mr. O'Connor of New York:* Sometimes.
>
> *Mr. MacLafferty:* Very good.[103]

This brings us to the second critical point regarding the position of eugenic ideas in American political culture at this moment in the twentieth century: the triumph of eugenic logic in 1924 was not a political anomaly, the fleeting victory of so many cranks and crackpots. Although acceptance of eugenic premises was not universal—as is demonstrated by much of the congressional wrangling—neither had some mad eugenic fringe momentarily seized the reins of government. The terms of debate and the Johnson Act itself expressed a fear for the well-being of the republic and asserted a philosophy of "fitness for self-government" that were deeply embedded in American political culture, and that extended all the way back to the Revolutionary generation and its own naturalization law of 1790. The exclusionary logic of the 1924 legislation represented not a new deployment of race in American political culture, but merely a new refinement of how the races were to be defined for the purposes of discussing good citizenship. "Fitness for self-government" had been a concept intimately linked to race from the advent of the new nation, and the eugenicists almost certainly could not have won this battle had their program represented a complete departure from the tenets of inclusion and exclusion that had long characterized the nation's political conduct. They could not have won in 1924, that is, had their argument on behalf of "justifiable," "necessary discrimination" been a new idea under the sun.

Eugenicists probably could not have gained a hearing at all, moreover, had their views of racial hygiene violated the common assumptions of human diversity as "difference" to begin with. The Johnson Act did not invent the hierarchy of white races, but merely formalized a refined understanding of whiteness that had steadily gained currency since the early Celtic famine refugees had dragged themselves ashore in "Black 'Forty-Seven." The eugenic program behind the Johnson Act may have been bold in its positive use of the state, but it was founded upon an understanding of "difference" which was neither bold nor terribly unusual. Although it may be tempting in retrospect to identify the likes of Madison Grant, Lothrop Stoddard, Harry Laughlin, and Albert Johnson as extreme in their views, it is critical to recognize that figures far more central to American political and intellectual life shared many of their basic assumptions—Theodore Roosevelt, Calvin Coolidge, Edward A. Ross, Frederick Jackson Turner, W. E. B. Du Bois, and Charlotte Perkins Gilman are among them. Herbert Hoover's Committee on Social Trends could enthusiastically laud the immigration act as selecting "a physical type which closely resembles the prevailing stock in our country."[104]

Even more important than the compatibility of eugenic thought with accepted scientific wisdom was its firm rooting in notions of racial difference that had become familiar in a number of less rarified cultural venues as well. The Celts *were* Celtic during these years, and Hebrews *were* racially Hebrew. The Slavs were Slavic in ways that even Madison Grant's political enemies perceived. It was not just a handful at the margins who saw certain immigrants as racially distinct; nor did the eugenic view of white races emerge in a vacuum. The consensus on this point was impressive. In a Fourth of July oration at Narragansett Pier in 1906, for instance, Brander Matthews (then in a pro-immigrant phase) had repudiated those who were "willing enough to welcome Teuton and even Celt, [yet] see peril to our citizenship in granting it to Slav and to Scythian, with 'tiger passions, here to stretch their claws.' " Matthews went on, in a logic based no less upon race than the most virulent eugenic tract, to develop a passionate argument regarding the non–Anglo-Saxon immigrants' potential contribution to the republic. "It is true that the latest newcomers are not altogether Teutonic or even Celtic," he conceded; "they are Latin and Slav and Semitic . . . [But] the suave manner of the Italian may modify in time the careless discourtesy which discredits us now in the eyes of foreign visitors. The ardor of the Slav may quicken our appreciation of music and of the fine arts." Quoting the sociologist

Franklin Giddings to the same effect, he argued that "a mixture of elements not Anglo-Teuton 'will soften the emotional nature' and 'quicken the poetic and artistic nature' of the American people; gentler in our thoughts and feelings because of the Alpine strain . . . we shall find ourselves 'with a higher power to enjoy the beautiful things of life because of the Celtic and the Latin blood.' "[105]

During the latter decades of the nineteenth century and the early years of the twentieth, such racial depictions of white immigrant groups fully saturated American culture, providing the necessary ideological soil for the eugenicists' vision to triumph. As Thomas Gossett has argued, "No American writers have done more to publicize race theories and to glorify the Anglo-Saxons than have Frank Norris, Jack London, and Owen Wister." Literary naturalism was in large part defined by the very notions of race that drove the immigration debate. On the positive end is Wolf Larson in Jack London's *Sea Wolf* (1904), the very embodiment of regeneration and strenuous life. In a debate between Larson and Humphrey Van Weyden on Spencerian philosophy—a man should act for the benefit of himself, then his children, then his race—Larson declares flatly, "I cut out the race and children." And yet it is his race that sets him apart as an *Ubermensch*: "the face, with large features and strong lines, of the square order . . . The jaw, the chin, the brow rising to a goodly height and swelling heavily above the eyes . . . seemed to speak an immense vigor or virility of spirit"; "he is oppressed by the primal melancholy of the race"; he is akin to the "white-skinned, fair-haired savages" of old. At the negative end is the "old Jew" Zerkow, in Frank Norris's *McTeague* (1899): "He had the thin, eager cat-like lips of the covetous; eyes that had grown keen as those of a lynx from long searching amidst muck and debris; and claw-like, prehensile fingers—the fingers of a man who accumulates but never disburses. It was impossible to look at Zerkow and not know instantly that greed—inordinate, insatiable greed—was the dominant passion of the man." (Later, when Zerkow and Maria have a baby who soon dies, Norris describes the child as "a hybrid little being . . . combining in its puny little body the blood of the Hebrew, the Pole, and the Spaniard." Perhaps it was also because of their racial degeneracy that "neither Zerkow nor Maria was much affected by either the birth or the death.")[106]

Nor was it only naturalist writers like London and Norris who imbibed and popularized the racial truth of divisible whiteness. A character in Charles Chesnutt's *Marrow of Tradition* (1901) speaks comically of "de Angry-Saxon race—ez dey call deyse'ves nowadays"; and, later, noting the bearing of a certain Jewish merchant during the Charlotte race riot, Chesnutt muses, "A Jew—a God of Moses!—had so far forgotten twenty centuries of history as to join in the persecution of another oppressed race!" Although James Weldon Johnson's *Autobiography of an Ex-Colored Man* (1912) is founded upon the unforgiving cultural (though not biological) dyad of black-white, Johnson nonetheless remarks, "In the discussion of the race question the diplomacy of the Jew was something to be admired." The Jew "knew that to sanction Negro oppression would be to sanction Jewish oppression." With an essentialist flourish typical for the period, he added, "Long traditions and business instincts told him when in Rome to act as a Roman." In 1903 John R. Dos Passos heralded the coming of "The Anglo-Saxon Century," and traces of this view of a hierarchy of white races informed his son's *U.S.A.* trilogy years later.[107]

In the decades bracketing the eugenic triumph of the 1924 immigration act such conceptions of the white races and their "difference" had surfaced in the lurid reformist writings of figures like Jacob Riis; in political debate over an Anglo-Saxon alliance of the United States and Great Britain; in reviews of the (alarming) popularity of the exotic Rudolph Valentino; in critical discussions of "mongrelized" Jews like Irving Berlin and George Gershwin in the business of making "Negro" music; in the language of metropolitan dailies and their account of urban criminality; and even in the nationalist discussions of many immigrant groups themselves.[108]

In a 1921 contribution to the immigration debate carried (appropriately) in *Good Housekeeping,* Calvin Coolidge had remarked, "Biological laws tell us that certain divergent people will not mix or blend. The Nordics propagate themselves successfully. With the other races, the outcome shows deterioration on both sides." In June 1924 Coolidge issued his proclamation setting the terms of the new, eugenic immigration law into effect that summer, thus closing the debate and presaging the end of the most fractious period in the political history of whiteness in the United States, the period that had begun with the massive influx of undesirable "white persons" from Ireland and Germany in the 1840s.[109] In the decades following the 1924 legislation, the problem posed to the United States by the non-Nordic races of Europe would lose salience in public concern, to the extent, finally, that their perceived "difference" would cease to register as *racial* at all.

She'd said something perfectly casual about "the Jewish race." Phil had explained once or twice that the phrase was based on misconceptions which were completely disproved by modern anthropologists. But she'd said it—it was just habit. She wasn't fighting the scientists when they said there was no such thing. She knew perfectly well that the three great divisions of mankind were the Caucasian Race, the Mongoloid, the Negroid.

—Laura Z. Hobson, *Gentleman's Agreement* (1947)

[The Negro's] African ancestry and physical characteristics are fixed to his person much more ineffaceably than the yellow star is fixed to the Jew during the Nazi regime in Germany.

—Gunnar Myrdal, *An American Dilemma: The Negro Problem and Modern Democracy* (1944)

 3

Becoming Caucasian, 1924–1965

One San Francisco newspaper had argued in 1910 that Asian immigrants were taking the jobs of "Anglo-Saxons, Celts, Teutons, Slavs and members of other races who are part of the real population of the country."[1] The formulation is atypical. Most native comment that identified European groups as racially distinct Celts, Teutons, and Slavs did not number them among "the real population of the country"; and most native comment that did accept them as "the real population" depicted them not as racially distinct but as consanguine "whites."

In general a pattern of racially based, Anglo-Saxonist exclusivity dominated the years from 1840 to the 1920s, whereas a pattern of Caucasian unity gradually took its place in the 1920s and after. If "discrimination is a fool's economy," as *Education* declared in 1946, then certain coin became increasingly rare in the decades leading up to the electoral victory of the Celtic presidential hopeful John F. Kennedy.[2]

At the Second International Congress of Eugenics in 1924, Henry Fairfield Osborn had asserted that the motive of the eugenics movement was to "discover the virtues and the values of the minor divisions of the human species, as well as the needs of the major divisions, known as the Caucasian, the Mongolian, and the Negroid."[3] Between the 1920s and the 1960s concerns of "the major divisions" would so overwhelm the national consciousness that the "minor divisions," which had so preoccupied Americans during the period of massive European immigration, would lose their salience in American culture and disappear altogether as racially based differences. By the election of 1960 a Celt could become president, and though his religion might have been cause for concern in some quarters, his race never was. That same year, writing of the earlier waves of European immigrants to the United States, the historian Maldwyn Allen Jones could announce with supreme confidence, "In the middle of the twentieth century ethnic distinctions might still persist. But they were less sharp, less conspicuous than before and they were fading rapidly from view." That Euro-Americans' *racial* distinctions had already faded from view was a development so complete that it went unnoted.[4]

Indeed, between the mid-1920s and the end of World War II, "Caucasian" as a "natural" division of humanity became part of a popular national catechism. Scientists "apply the term 'race' only to the broadest subdivisions of mankind, Negro, Caucasian, Mongolian, Malayan, and Australian," explained a 1939 handbook for high school teachers. "ALL THESE SCIENTISTS AGREE THAT NO NATION CAN BE CALLED A RACE," the text emphasized, self-consciously undoing the notions of "Aryan" and "Semitic" integrity.[5] Even Harry Laughlin, distanced by ten years from the eugenic victory of the Johnson Act and its formula for staying the tide of undesirable Mediterraneans and Alpines, could cooly include in his "Specific Recommendations" to the Special Committee on Immigration and Alien Insane (1934): "That no immigrant be admitted, whether by quota or otherwise, who is not—First, a member of the white race"; and that, for the purposes of immigration law, "a white person be defined as one all of whose ancestors were members of the white or Caucasian race."[6]

By the 1930s and 1940s the logic and terminology of these "major divisions" had become part of the lexicon of both popular and high culture. The Los Angeles *Times* could write of "non-Caucasians' " property rights, and a human interest piece in the New Orleans *Times-Picayune* could casually describe kissing as "a Caucasian habit."[7] The term "Caucasian" would surface in a range of cultural productions, including James T. Farrell's *A World I Never Made,* Laura Z. Hobson's *Gentleman's*

Agreement, Sinclair Lewis's *Kingsblood Royal*, and Rogers and Hammerstein's *South Pacific*. Betraying the prevailing understanding of "difference" even as it popularized a liberal view of racial "tolerance," *South Pacific* preached that prejudice does not come naturally; rather, one has to be *taught* to hate "people whose eyes are oddly made / or people whose skin is a different shade." The consolidation of a unified whiteness was complete when the category "Caucasian" leapt from actual police blotters to television cop shows like *Dragnet*. Jack Webb's authoritative assertion that "the suspect is a Caucasian male" now replaced the longstanding formula of earlier pulp genres, in which the criminal underground had been a dark social terrain of not-exactly-white Others—the "Levantine" Joel Cairo in *The Maltese Falcon*, for instance.[8]

Again, this shift did not take place overnight, and residual traces of the scheme that had reigned between the 1840s and the 1920s persisted into the mid-twentieth century. As *Common Ground* reported in 1944, the Bank of America's lending restrictions in Fresno, California, "prohibit Armenians among other Asiatic and Oriental nationality groups . . . to own or occupy property" in certain sections unless employed as servants. Such policies, said the journal, are "sowing the seeds of future race riots." A year later the same publication noted that "many large companies won't hire anyone who looks or sounds Irish."[9] In his study of race and the Catholic parishes of the urban North, John McGreevy finds distinct European races persisting in popular, street-level thinking into the 1930s— just as Michael Denning discovers these races lingering in the lexicon of various Popular Front cultural formations. Indeed, as noted at the very outset, even the characters in Philip Roth's *Counterlife* could, some six decades after the Johnson Act, engage in heated debate over whether or not Jews were really "Caucasian."[10]

Nineteen twenty-four may be the high-water mark of the regime of Anglo-Saxon or Nordic supremacy, in other words, and not its proper closing date. But in "solving" the immigration problem, the Johnson Act laid the way for a redrawing of racial lines, and so that year does mark the beginning of the ascent of monolithic whiteness. Whether the critical decade is the 1930s (according to John McGreevy) or the 1940s (according to Michael Denning), the general trend between the 1920s and the 1960s is unmistakable.[11] As one Minnesota congressman would couch it in a characteristic plea for "tolerance," "if we try to act justly, we will alter our attitude toward not only the Negroes and other racial groups but also toward Jewish members of the white race as well." Oliver Cox was more systematic in articulating the distinction between anti-Semitism (an "unwillingness on the part of the dominant group to tolerate the beliefs or practices of a subordinate group") and race prejudice ("a social attitude propagated among the public by an exploiting class for the purpose of stigmatizing some group as inferior so the exploitation of either the group itself, or its resources, may be justified").[12] Such racial certainties—articulated on either side of the color line—tended more and more often to rest on some version of "the three great divisions of mankind . . . the Caucasian Race, the Mongoloid, the Negroid."[13] W. E. B. Du Bois would dream of a world beyond racism, and he would call it "transcaucasia"; George Schuyler would dedicate his scathing satire on the American color line, *Black No More* (1931), to "all Caucasians in the great republic who can trace their ancestry back ten generations and confidently assert that there are no Black leaves, twigs, limbs or branches on their family trees."[14]

What did "Caucasian" mean in the mid-twentieth century? What is the relationship between "white" on the one hand, and "Caucasian" on the other? Although the categories "white" and "Caucasian" may have overlapped almost entirely, the idea "Caucasian" did accomplish something that the more casual notion of whiteness could not: it brought the full authority of modern science to bear on white identity, and it did so in a way that challenged the scheme of hierarchically ordered white races which had itself been created and policed by the authority of modern science. The idea of a "Caucasian race" represents whiteness ratcheted up to a new epistemological realm of certainty. If the idea "white persons" has become so naturalized that we still speak of "whites" as if this grouping refers to a natural fact beyond dispute, then the idea "Caucasian" naturalizes both the grouping and the authority by which that grouping is comprehended. To speak of "Caucasians" is tacitly to footnote Blumenbach, Morton, Boas, Hooten, and Benedict. Among self-ascribed "Caucasians," the term not only lays claim to a consanguine whiteness, but evokes a scientific certainty regarding its boundaries and integrity. This was explicit in some of the early deployments of the term—in California's Order of Caucasians and Louisiana's Caucasian Clubs, for instance. It remains, though only implicitly, when the high scholarly diction of the "Caucasian race" crosses over into vernacular conversation. Among non-"Caucasians," by contrast, the term holds all whites—Mediterraneans, Celts, and Hebrews included—responsible for the reified social category created by and for white privilege. It was in this vein that Kelly

Miller decried the "haughty Caucasian," that William Monroe Trotter warned of "the Caucasian in our midst" after the Chicago riot of 1919, and that Rudolph Fisher noted the "Invasion of Harlem by the Caucasian" during the 1920s.[15]

When he found Jim Rollins not guilty of miscegenation because Rollins's Sicilian accomplice was inconclusively white, that Alabama judge in 1922 provided a good way of understanding racial distinctions such as "Mediterranean," "Hebrew," "Iberic," or "Slavic" as they operated through the early twentieth century. These groups represented a kind of provisional or probationary whiteness. To become "Caucasian" in the 1920s and after, then, was not simply to be "white" (in the way that Teague O'Regan, say, had been white in *Modern Chivalry*); it was to be *conclusively, certifiably, scientifically* white. "Caucasian" identity represents a whiteness discovered and apprehended by that regime of knowledge whose cultural authority is greatest.

Several circumstances conspired in the early and mid-twentieth century to heighten the premium on race as *color* and to erode the once-salient "differences" among the white races. Not least, the triumph of the eugenics movement in making the Johnson formula into law quickly reduced the threat posed by inferior white races to the body politic, and so decreased the political and social stakes that had kept such distinctions alive. With this dramatic decrease in the flow of new arrivals, moreover, the overall center of gravity of these immigrant populations shifted toward an American-born generation for whom the racial oppressions of the Old World—if significant grist for the plaintive songs and heroic stories of a group's subculture—were far less significant than American white privilege where immediate racial experience was concerned.[16]

The massive migrations of African-Americans from the rural South to the urban North and West between the 1910s and the 1940s, too, produced an entirely new racial alchemy in those sections. Mid-century civil rights agitation on the part of African-Americans—and particularly the protests against segregation in the military and discrimination in the defense industries around World War II—nationalized Jim Crow as *the* racial issue of American political discourse. Both the progressive and the regressive coalitions that formed around questions of segregation and desegregation solidified whiteness as a monolith of privilege; racial differences *within* the white community lost their salience, as they lost their reference to important power arrangements of the day. And finally, events in Nazi Germany, too, exerted a powerful influence on public opinion regarding the dangers of race thinking. As if by collective fiat, race was willfully erased among the so-called minor divisions of humanity; the culture-based notion of "ethnicity" was urgently and decisively proposed in its place; and the racial characteristics of Jewishness or Irishness or Greekness were emphatically revised away as a matter of sober, war-chastened "tolerance."[17]

In 1936 Margaret Mitchell described Scarlett O'Hara, who was to become the most famous Irishwoman in American history, as possessing "magnolia-white skin—that skin so prized by Southern women and so carefully guarded with bonnets, veils and mittens against hot Georgia suns."[18] The notion that Irishness, like other "ethnic" whitenesses, was a cultural trait rather than a visual racial cue became deeply embedded in the nation's political culture between the 1920s and the 1960s. By the time the Kerner Commission reported in 1968 that the United States consisted of "two societies—one white, one black, separate and unequal," this understanding of the nation's racial make-up had long become part of popular consciousness.[19]

The "Caucasian Family of Races"

The notion of a reforged, consanguine Caucasian race emerged even within the eugenic circles that had been so instrumental in policing the borders separating Nordics from non-Nordics in the years before 1924. Lothrop Stoddard's incendiary 1920 tract *The Rising Tide of Color against White World Supremacy* had predicted a war among the "primary" races of the world and had identified the "weakening" of the white race—through immigration and mongrelization, for example—as a bitter portent for this coming war. Stoddard's pan–white-supremacist logic proceeded, paradoxically, from a delineation of superior and inferior whites. He began by noting a decline in the Nordic population:

> Our country, originally settled almost exclusively by the Nordics, was toward the close of the nineteenth century invaded by hordes of immigrant Alpines and Mediterraneans, not to mention Asiatic elements like Levantines and Jews. As a result, the Nordic native American has been crowded out with amazing rapidity by the swarming, prolific aliens, and after two short generations he has in many of our urban areas become almost extinct . . . The melting-pot may mix, but does not melt. Each race-type, formed ages ago . . . is a stub-

bornly persistent entity. Each type possesses a special set of characters: not merely the physical characters visible to the naked eye, but
moral, intellectual, and spiritual characters as well.[20]

But despite the importance of these variegations in the "white race,"
whiteness itself is not without meaning—differences granted, there must
be *some* sense of a shared race solidarity, pride, and destiny among Nordics, Alpines, and even Mediterraneans. Summing up the perils faced by
the "white world" in the wake of the devastating "white civil war" that
was World War I, Stoddard pronounced, "The prospect is not a brilliant
one. Weakened and impoverished by Armageddon, handicapped by an
unconstructive peace, and facing internal Bolshevist disaffection . . . the
white world is ill-prepared to confront—the rising tide of color." The
Great War was as nothing compared with the coming Apocalypse, when
the "white" and "colored" worlds would collide, according to Stoddard.
Amid the "deluge" of peoples of color against the "dikes" of white political control, "the white man, like King Canute, seats himself upon the
tidal sands and bids the waves be stayed. He will be lucky if he escapes
merely with wet shoes."[21]

The renown of Stoddard's views was at once noted and extended in
F. Scott Fitzgerald's *Great Gatsby* (1925), when Tom Buchanan ranted
about the prospects for the white race: "Civilization is going to pieces . . .
Have you read 'The Rise of the Coloured Empires' by this man Goddard?" (Here Fitzgerald conflates Stoddard with H. H. Goddard, the ex-
pert on race and intelligence.) "The idea is," Buchanan continues, "if we
don't look out the white race will be—will be utterly submerged. It's all
scientific stuff; it's been proved." Although Stoddard, no less than Laughlin or Grant, held firmly to a biological ranking of the white races (in the
plural), this is indeed the deepest consequence of his argument: the reforging of an imperiled white *race* (in the singular). As Fitzgerald's Jordan
Baker put it in response to another of Buchanan's impassioned racial ti-
rades, this time on "intermarriage between black and white," "We're all
white here." (Significantly, the "we" subsumed under "all white here"
included the Hebrew Jimmy Gatz.)[22]

Stoddard's own refiguring of non-Nordics as fellow Caucasians became
clearer still in *Reforging America* (1927). Once the Johnson Act had been
passed, even so alarmist a thinker as Stoddard could take heart and re-
consider the stakes of the non-Nordic presence. He remained optimistic
despite "the serious consequences produced by [the 'new'] immigration,"

he now wrote, because "most of the immigrant stocks are racially not too remote for ultimate assimilation." Because the new immigrants represented an insignificant percentage of the nation's total "white" population, it now seemed likely that they could "be absorbed into the nation's blood" without altering America's "racial make-up" enough to "endanger the stability and continuity of our national life."

> But what is thus true of European immigrants, most of whom belong to some branch of the white racial group, most emphatically does not apply to non-white immigrants, like the Chinese, Japanese, or Mexicans; neither does it apply to the large resident negro element which has been a tragic anomaly from our earliest times. Here, ethnic differences are so great that "assimilation" in the racial sense is impossible.[23]

From the vantage point of post-1924, suddenly it seemed that the new immigrants were "so basically like us in blood, culture, and outlook that their eventual assimilation is only a matter of time." Indeed, the very point of *Reforging America* is firmly to establish the nation's political and social life along the color line (with "new immigrants" unambiguously on the "white" side), much as the South had done since the collapse of Reconstruction. In the tract's pivotal chapter, "Bi-racialism: The Key to Social Peace," Stoddard argued the "very real advantages to be gained by a separate race-life"—that is, by Southern-style segregation.[24]

This signals the waning of the paradigm that had produced the Johnson Act, and the emergence and consolidation of a new, binary racial arrangement that would come to dominate American political culture for the balance of the twentieth century. It is not just that thinkers like Stoddard turned their attention more and more to questions of "color," nor even that eugenics itself gradually passed from fashion and then from view over the succeeding decades. The patterns of racial reorganization evident in Stoddard's *Reforging America* were reflected in the broader developments within anthropology and sociology as well.

The treatment of race in the sciences underwent two fundamental changes in the years between the eugenic triumph of 1924 and the post–World War II period: culture eclipsed biology as the prime determinant of the social behavior of races, and "race relations" displaced characterology as the major field of racial inquiry. Both of these trends significantly revised "the race concept" in general, and had especially profound implications for the notion of "difference" as it applied to the white races of Europe and the United States.

Strictly biological understandings of race as the key to the diversity of humanity gave way to cultural and environmental explanations. The historian Elazar Barkan has meticulously tracked this shift in the intellectual underpinnings of race, summing up the overall trend as a "retreat from scientific racialism," a paradigmatic shift "from race to ethnicity." This was exemplified most starkly in anthropology, where the Boasian vision of environmentalism, culture, and human changeability gained primacy; it was reflected as well in the decline of the eugenic movement, and, as the Nazis' eugenic policies came to light in Europe, in a scramble among scholars like Julian Huxley, Ashley Montagu, and Ruth Benedict to eradicate race altogether as a measure of human capacity and thus as an instrument of state policy. A spate of books revising racial thinking thus appeared in the 1930s and 1940s, ranging from provocative explorations like Benedict's *Race: Science and Politics* (1940) to more strident repudiations such as Montagu's *Race: Man's Most Dangerous Myth* (1942).

There was certainly a precedent for rethinking race along these lines— Boas had been pushing an environmentalist model since the early part of the century. (Indeed, he had contributed his findings on the changeability of European races in the United States to the Dillingham Commission back in 1910, but Congress at the time had been far more interested in the views of the eugenicists.) But in the 1930s and 1940s, for transparent but compelling political reasons, there was a willful intellectual reorientation on the question of race and its portents. At a trickle in response to the racialist codes of fascist Italy and Germany, then in a torrent following revelations of the Nazi death camps, the academic community on both sides of the Atlantic produced feverish reevaluations of the race concept and its applications. In response to menacing trends in Germany and elsewhere, in *Patterns of Culture* (1934) Benedict declared, "The racial purist is a victim of mythology." Although she did not find race itself a baseless term, Benedict staunchly opposed any account of human "difference" that did not properly weigh the power of culture and environment.[25]

Written largely in response to the same developments in the fascist states of Europe, Huxley's *We Europeans* (1935) made an even stronger case for the eradication of race as an explanatory category. "One of the greatest enemies of science is pseudo-science," Huxley wrote. "A vast pseudo-science of 'racial biology' has been erected which serves to justify political ambitions, economic ends, social grudges, class prejudices." " 'Racial prob-lems' are among the urgent actualities of twentieth-century politics," he noted, later making direct reference to recent "pure Nordic" laws in Ger-many and other eugenic interventions of the state. But if one subjects the concept of race to cool analysis, "it turns out to be a pseudo-scientific rather than a scientific term . . . Its use implies an appeal to the accuracy and the prestige of science; but on investigation it turns out to have no precise or definable meaning." Huxley thus opted for the concept "ethnicity," which in his thinking combined the physical and genetic attributes of race with the environmental, social, cultural, and historical influences that accounted for the coherence and distinctness of human groups.[26]

Such politically driven revisions of "the race concept" became more urgent still as the fully horrific details of the fascist programs in Europe became known. In response to German and Italian state policies, for in-stance, a handbook for secondary school teachers (1939) pointed out that "Mussolini's effort to drive the Jews out of Italy is impossible, because not even the foremost anthropologist could tell exactly whose ancestry is free of Jewish blood."[27] Likewise, Benedict's popular pamphlet *The Races of Mankind* (1943) insisted, "Aryans, Jews, Italians are *not* races."[28]

A collection of Franz Boas's essays, *Race and Democratic Society* (1945), was emblematic of the self-conscious effort among social scientists to refashion the race concept, and to reverse the uses to which it was being put in behalf of rightist political agendas. As these collected works themselves attest, concern over the pernicious consequences of race think-ing did not spring full blown out of nowhere in the Nazi period. Boas had been skeptically interrogating the race concept for several decades. This particular collection includes not only essays from the 1930s and early 1940s, but also some works published as far back as the 1900s in venues as diverse as *Forum,* the *Christian Register, Yale Quarterly Review, The Nation,* and the New York *Evening Post.* This reissue, however, does bear unmistakable marks of its production in the Nazi years. "A new duty arises," Boas announced in his introduction. "No longer can we keep the search for truth a privilege of the scientist." He spelled out his reasons in direct references to Nazism in essays such as "The 'Aryans' " (1934), and enumerated what this "truth" might be in "The Jews" (1923), "Race: What Is It?" (1925), and "Race: Prejudice" (1937). This last essay pro-vides the keynote to the collection. Although the pieces range across a number of decades and hence track significant shifts in Boas's own thinking, here he offers his readers a bottom line: the biologist's assumption regarding the power of heredity "will not stand analysis"; mind, body, custom, and social behavior are all subject to the "plastic influence of environment," and therefore "man is a highly unstable animal." There is no foolproof way of "distinguishing one people as a whole from another people as a whole by mere physical appearance," yet "racial" thinking continues to hold sway—"the Nazis have driven this form of logic to its fanatical extreme," and "we are not free from these tendencies in the United States."[29]

Among those most set, with Boas, on overturning conventional race thinking in the United States was Ashley Montagu, the author of *Race: Man's Most Dangerous Myth* (1942). The very idea of race, he argued, had taken on "an exaggerated emotional content," and the very language that framed discussions of race lent them "a high emotional and a low rational, or reasonable, quality." Thus the term "race" ought to be dropped entirely, replaced by less loaded distinctions such as "divisions" for the major branches of mankind—Negroid, Australoid, Caucasian, and Mongoloid—and "ethnic group" for the minor divisions.[30]

Montagu developed this line tirelessly throughout the 1940s in a stream of essays for publications ranging from the New York *Times* to the *American Journal of Anthropology*. Typical was an essay for teachers, "What Every Child and Adult Should Know about 'Race,'" which appeared in a special "Race" issue of *Education* (1946). Here Montagu defined race as a mere "congeries of errors," an absolute misunderstanding of humanity and its diversity. And yet "the error of 'race' has already caused the death of millions of innocent human beings." Since children could only learn "the truth" about race by having adults explain it to them, Montagu interrogated common assumptions and presented his revision in a simple catechism. The conventional notion of race, he began, was that of a "prime determiner of all the important traits of body and soul, of character and personality," a "fixed and unchangeable part of the germ plasm." He went on to explain why this was unsound: conventional views assume inherited mental traits and ignore the power of environmental factors, for instance; just as individuals differ because of differing personal experience, "so will the members of ethnic groups differ from the members of other ethnic groups because of very real differences in social experience." In this context he makes his plea for a redefinition of "difference" itself, a revaluation of the currency of race:

Because the conventional stereotype of "race" is so erroneous, confusing, and productive of injustice and cruelties without number, and yet is so firmly established in the minds of most men, it were better to drop the term "race" altogether from the vocabulary. Some noncommital term like "ethnic group" should be used to designate human groups which differ from one another physically.[31]

This intellectual reworking of race reached its zenith in *The Race Concept* (1950, 1952), a series of statements hammered out by the world scientific community under the auspices of the United Nations Educational, Scientific, and Cultural Organization (UNESCO). Its major points had become familiar fare by 1950: humanity is characterized by an essential and undeniable unity, and such differences as exist are paltry; not heredity alone, but both heredity and environment are at play in creating these paltry differences; there is no demonstrated connection between cultural traits and racial traits; classifications vary, but most agree that there are three great races (Caucasian, Negroid, and Mongoloid); intelligence and psychology do not coincide with race; there is no evidence supporting genetic explanations of cultural difference; and there is no such thing as a "pure" race.

The statement's final points cut to the political issue of race, equality, and democracy: social equality as an ethical principle does not depend upon equality of endowment among diverse human beings; there is no evidence for the belief that groups differ in capacities for intellectual and emotional development; differences *within* a given race may outstrip differences *between* races; and there is no evidence that racial mixture is disadvantageous from a biological point of view.[32]

Again, the urgency of the UNESCO statement is easily traceable to then-recent state policies, especially in Nazi Germany. As one scholar noted in his commentary on the statement, "I think I am right in assuming that Unesco is primarily concerned to show that Jews are not specifically different from the other members of the communities in which they [live]." He went on to suggest that "Jews should be considered as belonging to the European group. The term 'Asiatics' . . . applied to the Jews, is misleading."[33] His comments capture a crucial element of the feverish postwar revision of "difference": the reification of humanity's "grand divisions" in an effort to expunge wherever possible its "lesser" divisions. The effort to prove that "Jews are not specifically different," in this instance, reflected a tacit distinction between "the European group" on the one hand and "Asiatics" on the other. In a more general sense, as scientists asserted over and over that "Aryans," "Jews," "Italians," "Nordics," and the like were not races, their myriad assertions themselves all buttressed an edifice founded upon three grand divisions of mankind—"Caucasian," "Mongoloid," and "Negroid"—whose differences by implication *were* racial.

This dynamic was fully explicit in much of the literature. Benedict's *Races of Mankind*, for instance, included a tricolored world map whose three broad regions corresponded to "Caucasian," "Mongoloid," and "Negroid" areas.[34] Thus as Huxley had noted in *We Europeans*, "Even where lip-service is rendered" to the abolition of race as a sound theoretical construct, "the terms employed (such as 'race' itself) carry far-reaching implications of a contrary nature."[35] Much of the antiracist work of the period was founded upon the very epistemology of race that it sought to dismantle. For the probationary whites who had immigrated to the United States before the eugenic restrictions of 1924, this was a deeply significant trend in mid-century race thinking.

This emergent pattern of revised racial distinctions was solidified by a second trend in the mid-century scholarship. At precisely the moment when the cataclysm in Nazi Germany suggested that race as a category of ascription best be abolished as far and as quickly as possible, so the historic fact of the Nazis' racial policies themselves—combined with increasing social tensions and escalating civil rights agitation on the home-front—demanded that race as a political force be further studied and better understood. Thus the growing body of literature questioning the objective standing of race in nature was joined by a second, also burgeoning scholarship that fortified the race concept by analyzing the social and political struggles among "races." Although often contrary in their implications—the one attempting to deny race, the other at least tacitly affirming it—these two distinct orientations could contend with each other even within a single work.

Whereas the first development in mid-century scholarship represented a thoroughgoing revision of "the race concept," this latter development represented a shift in the *locus* of scholarly inquiry. An interest in various kinds of typology and in discovering "essential" traits or the paths of development of this or that race—interests that had shaped the scholarship from Blumenbach on down—now gave way to the more immediate question of social relations. "Race relations" now came into its own as a field, from the Chicago school's sociological studies of urban cultural geography in the 1920s, to historical works like W. E. B. Du Bois's *Black Reconstruction* in the 1930s, to social analyses like Gunnar Myrdal's *American Dilemma* and Oliver Cox's *Caste, Race, and Class* in the 1940s. (Again, as an emblem of overlap, Franz Boas's 1945 compendium *Race and Democratic Society* embodies both impulses.)

"Race relations" was not altogether new, of course—the field dates back at least as far as Mary Roberts Coolidge's *Chinese Immigration* (1909), Ray Stannard Baker's *Following the Color Line* (1906), or W. E. B. Du Bois's *Philadelphia Negro* (1899). What was new among white scholars in this period (and thus to dominant disciplines and institutions) was a reversal in the presumed link between "race" and "race relations." In an earlier period, the categories of distinct races and the presumed moral-intellectual *content* of these distinctions were thought to govern the social and historical details that made up the story of "race relations." "Celtic" character *caused* impoverishment and frequent incarceration, that is; "Hebrew" character itself was the prime explanation for Jews' social ostracism; "Anglo-Saxon" character naturally led to world domination; and the history of slavery and the harsh life under Jim Crow were nicely explained by "the Negro character." In the 1930s and 1940s this link was dramatically reversed. Now, among writers as diverse as Robert Park, George Schuyler, Ashley Montagu, Gordon Allport, and Ruth Benedict, "race *relations*" required study, because social relations governed the presumed moral-intellectual content of racial distinctions, and race in and of itself held relatively little interest. The literature of race had thus dealt in a lexicon of "capacities," "traits," "characters," and "deficiencies." It had dealt, occasionally, in a lexicon of "genius," although far more often in a lexicon of "idiocy," "imbecilism," and "feeblemindedness." The rising literature of race relations, by contrast, dealt in a language of "equality," "justice," "democracy," "discrimination," and "prejudice."

In "The Nature of Race Relations" (1939), Robert Ezra Park defined the phrase itself as referring to "the relations existing between peoples distinguished by marks of racial descent, particularly when these racial differences enter into consciousness of the individuals and groups so distinguished, and by doing so determine in each case the individual's conception of himself as well as his status in the community." Further,

> anything that intensifies race consciousness; anything, particularly if it is a permanent physical trait, that increases an individual's visibility and by so doing makes more obvious his identity with a particular

ethnic unit or genetic group, tends to create and maintain the conditions under which race relations, as here defined, may be said to
exist. Race consciousness, therefore, is to be regarded as a phenomenon, like class or caste consciousness, that enforces social distances.
Race relations, in this sense, are not so much the relations that exist
between individuals of different races as between individuals conscious of those differences.[36]

The idea here is deceptive in its apparent simplicity: physical markers
generate race consciousness, and race consciousness in its turn influences
social relations. The content of race, then—the specific set of traits that
constitutes "blackness," for instance—is secondary to the social relations
created and maintained by the consciousness that such traits stir within
both those who possess them and those who do not.

Yet the passage conceals some vexing complexities which speak to the
social power of the scholarship on race in this period. First, Park writes
of "marks of racial descent" and "permanent physical traits" as if they
are independent of the eye of their beholder. But if physical traits can
generate consciousness, so can a consciousness of social distinctions generate an awareness of otherwise unnotable physical markers. When the
position of a particular "ethnic unit or genetic group" becomes socially
or politically important for one reason or another, its physical markers
and other "racial distinctions" are more likely to "enter into consciousness"—as they did in the 1850s, for instance, when Anglo-Saxons became
so adept at recognizing the distinct physiognomy of the newly arrived and
problematic Celts.

Second, inasmuch as race itself depends upon consciousness, a number
of things can generate such consciousness, not the least of which might
be an avalanche of scientific data on "the races" and a stream of goodwill
propaganda on their "relations." As Yehudi Webster argues and as Park's
own logic suggests, if race itself is highly unstable and experience is not
inherently racial but is in fact racial*ized* by consciousness, then "racialized
relations, not race relations, should be considered the object of study. And
the relations are racialized by social scientists themselves."[37] There is a
danger in overstating this case—as, indeed, I believe Webster has. The
social sciences did not create the social division between black and white;
writers like Park, Louis Wirth, and Lloyd Warner were remarking on the
impact of distinctions that predated modern sociology and that had long
been maintained by law, by real estate and housing policies, by employ-

ment practices, and by a range of segregated institutions from movie theaters and churches to labor unions and military units. Nonetheless, in
defining certain social relations as the proper object of study and in absolutely neglecting others, the disciplines devoted to "race relations" did
generate their own "races." And inasmuch as there was a broad consensus
on which relations were most important, for good or bad the populace
became racialized along certain lines and not others.

Which is to say, third, that the study of "social distances," as Park
defined it, quietly and by implication generated its own series of social
proximities: whatever these writings accomplished for the social relations
of people defined as "Negroid" and people defined as "Caucasian," they
worked a profound alchemy with the former groups of Slavs and Hebrews
and Celts and Mediterraneans and other probationary immigrant groups
now within the Caucasian fold. Although these works were not devoted
to defining the races, such studies did generate a race-making power of
their own, as certain categories of "difference" were naturalized by their
logic of opposition ("white" and "Negro," most significantly) while others
dropped away entirely. Typifying the dynamics of this approach to race,
for instance, was Ruth Benedict's antiracist objection in *Patterns of Culture* (1934), "We have come to the point where we entertain race prejudice
against our blood brothers the Irish."[38] The sentence quietly gathers the
Irish into the fold of presumed white readers, while the *even* implicit in
its logic—"we *even* entertain prejudice against the Irish," the line clearly
implies—expels some unnamed Others against whom prejudice may be
more understandable. The upshot of this feverish revision of race at mid-
century, then, was less a new understanding of the race concept itself than
merely a new pattern of races delineated along new lines.

Among the self-conscious popularizations of this new, post-Nazi racial
economy of "difference" was a public exhibit entitled "Races of Mankind" based on Benedict's pamphlet of the same name. Combining both
the "revision of race" and the "race relations" projects, the exhibit was
developed by the Cranbrook Institute of Science in 1943 and purchased
by the American Missionary Association as a traveling show for use by
any group "seeking to promote interracial understanding and goodwill
through the medium of visual education." The exhibit translated current
scientific thinking into easily digested pictorial and short-text panels,
matching in its bedrock assumptions the intellectual content of publications by the Council against Intolerance in America, or, later, the
UNESCO statements on "the race concept."

A quick stroll through the twenty-nine panels conveys both the ideology and the tone of the project.[39] The exhibit opened with a panel on the "races of mankind" emphasizing "the common origin of all races." Significantly, the opening mural featured "cut outs of Adam and Eve with yellow, white, and Negro children"—that is, children representing the three grand divisions of mankind, Mongoloid, Caucasian, and Negroid. The next several panels were devoted to the race concept itself—"What Is Race?" "Early Concepts of Race," "Physical Characters of the Human Races," "Why Are the Races Different?" The intent here was not necessarily to destabilize the fixities of race, but rather to call into question the degree of difference which race represented: "Each so-called race became functionally adapted to the region in which it found itself. So-called racial differences are superficial." After a brief discussion of which human differences do and which do not qualify as "racial," the exhibit moved on to celebrate the cornucopia of architectural, poetic, artistic, technological, and culinary achievements of the world's diverse peoples. Next came panels emphasizing the environmental determinants of racial difference in titles such as "It's Not in the Blood," "No Race Is Most Primitive," "No Race Is Mentally Superior," and "Races Persist—Cultures Change." (Panel 24, "Culture Is Not Inborn," demonstrated that "habits depend on environment" by depicting a "Chinese girl holding [a] Shirley Temple doll.") The closing two panels, "What Is an American?" and "Let Us Live at Peace," cut to the civic heart of the matter, summing up "the aim of the entire exhibit—to show that race is superficial—that with this knowledge we all will work towards a better and greater world civilization on the basis of democracy for all."

Central to this project—indeed, to the broader project of redrawing racial lines according to the three great divisions—were the ideas expressed in panels 7 through 10 of the exhibit:

Panel 7: Nationalities Are Not Races—The commonest mistake in all discussions of race is the confusion of nationality with race.

Panel 8: The Jews Are Not a Race—Jews are people who practice the religion of Judaism; they are represented in many racial groups.

Panel 9: Who Are the Aryans?—Ideal Aryan would be slender, long headed, blond, and virile, making references thereto by Hitler, Goering and Goebbels utterly ridiculous.

Panel 10: Composition of the American Negro—Shows him to be a descendant of the African Negro, American Indian, and white man.

Here again is proof of Huxley's dictum that, even when marshaled toward the aim of abolishing hierarchies of difference, racial categories inherently carry with them "far-reaching implications of a contrary nature"—a very real power to create and police boundaries. In the guise of a direct refutation of the racial logic of the Nazi program, the Johnson Act, and the "Negro problem" in the United States, this educational exhibit evaporated an earlier era's white races (panels 7, 8, and 9) and reproduced them simply as "the white man" (panel 10). And even if the intent of panel 10 is to destabilize any facile notions of reified blackness, the text nonetheless *does* reify blackness (and whiteness and Indianness) by taking as its genetic building-blocks "the African Negro, American Indian, and white man."

Similarly, the breakdown of races in Panel 18, "The Foods We Cultivate Are a Gift from All Peoples," demonstrates this refashioning of races:

1. African Negro (Black Race)
2. American Indian (Yellow Race)
3. West Asiatic (White Race)
4. South Asiatic (Yellow Race)
5. North European (White Race)
6. East Asiatic (Yellow Race)

The division of the "white race" into "North European" and "West Asiatic" is at the very crux of becoming "Caucasian" for, say, the Semite or the Armenian, just as the strained categorization of the American Indian as representing the "Yellow Race" conveys the urgency by which Benedict has organized the exhibit around humanity's "three great divisions."

The racial dynamic of the "three great divisions" gained power, moreover, by its replication and repetition throughout the culture—in films such as *South Pacific, Showboat, The Ten Commandments,* and the myriad Cold War westerns; in novels such as *Studs Lonigan, The Edge of Sadness,* and *The Changelings;* and in the racial terminology of print journalism. Interest in race was now largely an inquiry into "race relations," and "race relations" were defined almost exclusively by the divide separating black from white. Hence those who were not "Negroid" became "Caucasian" (and "Mongoloids," meanwhile, became largely invisible in serious civic discussion, making mostly minstrelized appearances as a foil for "Western" values in popular texts ranging from *South Pacific* and *Drums along the Mohawk* to comic books and *Gilligan's Island).*[40]

As ever, the transformations here were not instantaneous but glacial.

Even individual writers might demonstrate some inconsistency as one scheme gave way to the next. Benedict, among the chief popularizers of the new racial geography, could nonetheless lapse into a language of "Celts, Alpines, [and] Mediterraneans." In *Patterns of Culture,* within a span of ten pages she had slipped back and forth among terms like "Alpine sub-race," "Nordics," and "Mediterranean sub-group of the white race" on the one hand, and a less nuanced phraseology of "the white man" on the other.[41] Lloyd Warner and Leo Srole's *Social Systems of American Ethnic Groups* (1945), too, reflected an allegiance to both the waxing and the waning paradigms of difference. The authors defined "race" along the color line, yet one discovers thick traces of the older system of plural white races in their discussion of "ethnicity" and the prospects for assimilation. Thus "the people racially most like white 'old Americans' "—and therefore possessing the greatest chance for unhindered assimilation—"are other Caucasians." And yet, "the Caucasoid immigrant population has been divided into those who are largely like the present old-American stock and those who are least like them"—"light Caucasians" (like the South Irish and English Jews) and "dark Caucasians" (like Armenians, Sicilians, and the " 'dark skinned' Jews and Mohammedans of Europe").[42]

On the scale of assimilability, groups turn out to be predictably ordered according to their degree of deviation from a white Protestant norm, and the division of Caucasians into "light" and "dark" suspiciously coincides with the earlier scheme of distinct white races. Thus the purely cultural matter of assimilation is not entirely independent of race, even for those who have now become "Caucasians": "the light-skinned Jew who is not physically different and thereby not burdened with negatively evaluated racial traits" assimilates more easily than "his dark-skinned co-religionist," the dark Caucasian.[43]

But by the 1950s, if scholars might wonder about the persistence of ethnic subcultures among European groups, few seemed to think anymore that race had much to do with it. By the universality it tacitly bestowed, their silence on race underwrote the view of immigrants and their children and grandchildren as unquestionably Caucasian, and whiteness itself as the normative American condition.

E Pluribus Duo (I): American Politics in Black and White

When four Armenian immigrants petitioned to overturn a lower court's ruling that they did not qualify for citizenship as "free white persons," a

Circuit Court judge in Massachusetts ruled in their favor, citing, among other things, standing segregation statutes in the South whose formulas regarding whiteness and blackness set Armenians squarely on the white side of the divide.[44] The ruling in *In Re Halladjian* (1909) thus demonstrated most succinctly a pivotal principle: for certain groups, at certain moments, under certain conditions, Jim Crow whitened, and whitened decisively. (Du Bois captured this from the opposite side of the color line in *Dusk of Dawn*, when, at the end of a tortuous socratic dialogue exposing the impossible contradictions of the race concept, he offered the easy rule of thumb, "the black man is a person who must ride 'Jim Crow' in Georgia.")[45] This lesson was writ large in American politics in the 1940s. As questions of segregation and desegregation assumed new prominence, thus elevating to national significance the power of Jim Crow to create or enforce racial distinctions along strict, binary lines, a number of hitherto probationary white races became more decisively white.

In the logic and conduct of American politics, no less than in the social sciences, this mid-century revision of race had profound consequences. The dynamic relationship between the scientific revision of race and the changing political climate—particularly the race politics of World War II at home—generated three distinct developments. First, *ethnicity* was adopted to describe a new brand of "difference" whose basis was cultural; thus peoples still defined as racial groups were also tacitly marked by a degree of difference that was more than merely cultural. The faultlines dividing color from whiteness ("colored races" from "white ethnics") deepened. Second, ethnicity itself provided a paradigm for assimilation which erased race as a category of historical experience for European and some Near Eastern immigrants. Not only did these groups now belong to a unified Caucasian race, but race was deemed so irrelevant to who they were that it became something possessed only by "other" peoples. As Lillian Smith remarked, "It must seem to people watching us a strange and curious thing that when we in America study race relations we study the Negro—not the white man. No governor, no mayor, no President has ever appointed a committee to study the white man and race."[46]

Finally, the Cold War period witnessed a celebration of ethnic diversity as universalism in which conflations of "difference" and self-congratulation over the superior system of capitalist democracy were closely enmeshed, and the logic of this entire scheme was proved by a single anomaly: "the Negro." A complex system of races had given way to a strict scheme of black and white, which itself implied an absence of race on the white side and a presence of race on the black. The "ethnic" experience of European immigrant assimilation and mobility, meanwhile, became the standard against which blacks were measured—and found wanting.[47]

If a national politics of race based upon the simplified dyad of black and white had been visible even in the urban North earlier on—in the riots of 1919, in Stoddard's *Rising Tide of Color*, in *Birth of a Nation*, *The Jazz Singer*, and *Gone with the Wind*—this systemic, bifurcated understanding of the populace gained considerable credence in the 1940s. World War II heightened both the consciousness and the perceived stakes of that segregation, which Stoddard had euphemistically called "bi-racialism." On the one hand, as Alain Locke wrote, because of the jarring confluence of Nazi racial rhetoric from one side of the Atlantic and nationally embarrassing Jim Crow practices from the other, the war brought the race issue "around from a backyard domestic issue to front-porch exposure." On the other hand, as Louis Wirth put it, "given adverse economic circumstances, war, and propaganda, [ethnic and racial prejudices] can be aroused to white heat."[48] Many non-Nordic immigrants became full-fledged "whites" in precisely this social and political "heat" of wartime. In public discourse the plurality of former race questions was now totally eclipsed by the longstanding but singular "Negro Problem."

As had been true during World War I, the sacrifices made by African-Americans in the Second World War dramatically altered the racial climate on the homefront. The racial issues of the war itself, in this instance, went even one better than Woodrow Wilson's pious declarations in the 1910s concerning a world made "safe for democracy." As C. L. R. James wrote in the *Socialist Appeal* (1939), "The democracy I want to fight for, Hitler is not depriving me of."

> When Roosevelt and the other so-called lovers of "democracy" protested to Hitler against his treatment of the Jews, Hitler laughed scornfully and replied, "Look at how you treat the Negroes. I learned how to persecute Jews by studying the manner in which you Americans persecute Negroes." Roosevelt has no answer to that. Yet he will call on Negroes to go to war against Hitler.[49]

Even among the defense industries that assembled the engines of this war against fascism abroad, companies like Vultee Aircraft announced baldly that "only members of the Caucasian race will be employed in our plant."[50] One black schoolteacher from North Carolina queried Louis Adamic: "Can the people of the United States afford to criticize Germany for crushing the Jews when people in America will hang Negroes up trees and cut off parts of their bodies for souvenirs?" In 1944 a sixteen-year-old black student in Columbus, Ohio, won an essay contest on the theme "What to Do with Hitler after the War" by submitting the single sentence, "Put him in a black skin and let him live the rest of his life in America."[51]

The spirit of such arguments was manifest in A. Philip Randolph's March on Washington Movement, which secured (without actually marching) the establishment of a Fair Employment Practices Commission at the federal level; it was manifest in the Pittsburgh *Courier's* "Double V" campaign—victory against fascism abroad, victory against racism at home; and it was manifest in a spate of books, articles, and journals throughout the 1940s devoted (as *Survey Graphic* couched it in 1942) to "Color, Unfinished Business of Democracy."[52]

If continuing inequities and the wartime sacrifices of African-Americans brought white-black issues to center stage with a new urgency, the world political climate in the postwar years only added to that urgency. Pursuing the logic of the Nuremberg trials, argued the *Courier*, the American North was morally responsible for the lynchings in the American South, and no white American could dodge responsibility for anything that happened in Georgia or Tennessee. The question of national moral responsibility became especially sensitive during the Cold War, as the United States and the Soviet Union vied for the hearts and minds of the unaligned nations of the world. No one put this matter more forcefully than Fisk University President Charles Johnson, writing in the early Cold War chills of 1948. Commenting upon efforts by the United States to peddle its brand of democracy abroad, and the inexplicable failure "of the peoples of the world to rush up and buy our product as we took it for granted they would do," Johnson contended that the problem was "the breakdown of American democratic theory" on the issue of race. News of American race relations carries "to every corner of the world, two thirds of whose inhabitants are colored." Thus race

has become the scale on which democracy is being weighed in a world that is being relentlessly forced to choose between ideologies . . . It is my belief that some genuine act of democratic conviction at home such as repeal of the poll-tax, enactment of federal fair employment practice legislation, the elimination of segregation in the nation's Capital or the banning of segregation in our Armed Forces—

would do more to strengthen our cause than the threat of superior weapons. The time of proof has come, and race is the touchstone.[53]

Such views took firmer hold as the Cold War progressed. Even an amicus brief filed by the U.S. Justice Department in *Brown v. Board of Education* argued that desegregation was in the national interest because "the United States is trying to prove to the people of the world, of every nationality, race and color, that a free democracy is the most civilized and most secure form of government yet devised by man."[54]

In such a bifurcated racial climate, the whiteness of the former white races became more salient than the once-perceived differences among them. For those who were not encompassed by the one-fourth, one-eighth, or one-drop rules establishing how much "black blood" renders a person "black," ineluctably and irrefutably Jim Crow whitened. Nor was it simply the case that probationary whites became Caucasian purely through a regressive politics played out at the expense of nonwhites, like the Irish who had resisted the draft in 1863, insisting upon their privileges as "white men." Rather, progressive projects and coalitions, too, exerted a powerful influence in creating out of many races, two. As "bi-racialism" came to be widely identified as the overriding social problem facing the nation, even many of the solutions militated toward a racial dyad of black and white (see Chapter 8).

It lies beyond the scope of this chapter to chart the history of the early Civil Rights movement during World War II and after, but, as standard narratives most often take 1954 as the opening date of the modern movement, a quick refresher on the race politics of the 1940s may be useful.[55] In the wake of the Detroit race riot of 1943, Fisk University instituted a new journal with the self-explanatory title *A Monthly Summary of Events and Trends in Race Relations*. This eye-opening compendium presents a society fully racked by racial strife and increasingly obsessed with race problems and racial solutions even before the war had come to an end. Summarizing the ten-month period from March to December 1943, for instance, the journal recorded "242 major incidents involving Negro-white conflict in 47 cities" (46 percent in the South, 42 percent in the North, and 12 percent in the West). Southern conflict most frequently occurred "in relation to the armed forces, transportation, civil rights, and racial etiquette"; Northern incidents most often involved "housing, labor, and the police." In addition, the journal noted that more than 145 new interracial committees for unity had formed in 1943, "practically all" in the North.[56]

Certain items in *Race Relations* hint at the stakes of these developments for European immigrants and their children. Scanning the popular press accounts of the Detroit riot, the journal pointed out the "interminority conflicts involving, particularly, Negroes and Poles and Irish Catholics in such Northern cities as Detroit, Philadelphia, Chicago, and Buffalo." (Indeed, the two major convictions stemming from the Detroit violence were those of Aldo Trani, Italian, convicted of manslaughter in the death of a black man; and Aaron Fox, black, convicted of second-degree murder for killing an Italian.) Likewise, *Race Relations* noted the "interminority" character of a Chicago case in which a Jewish landlord had opened housing to black tenants, much to the displeasure of Italian residents. The blacks were driven out, and as the journal explained, "many of those who participated in the threats and abuse to the new Negro residents had been led to believe that a Jewish real estate man was attempting to cause the deterioration of an Italian neighborhood by deliberately introducing Negro residents." The journal did institute a section entitled "Jewish Scene" and a regular column on Japanese-Americans in 1945, and occasionally noted the social struggles of the white races—as when Frank Sinatra slugged a Hearst journalist for calling him a "dago." But typically the world of *Race Relations* was a world starkly depicted in black and white. This racial binarism reflected the nationalization of the race questions that had characterized the South for generations.[57]

From 1943 until the end of 1948, the staff of *Race Relations* monitored and reported myriad crises, outbreaks, protests, court battles, hostilities, and alliances among the races nationwide. The journal's pages present a dizzying staccato of race in social action. The overall tableau of *Race Relations* included an alarming rise in "race-angled" juvenile delinquency, as when a "free for all" erupted in Cambridge, Massachusetts, after "300 white youths (largely of Irish Catholic extraction)" marched into a black section looking for trouble; or when "forty to sixty Negro youths" on a Brooklyn trolley purposely sought "to annoy white passengers—in some cases going as far as robbery and assault." It included episodes of local insult and national response, such as the Kiwanis Club raffle in Ahoskie, North Carolina, whose first prize—a new Cadillac—was denied to the rightful winner, the tenant farmer Harvey Jones, on the simple grounds that as a "Negro" he was "ineligible." The nationwide outcry on Jones's behalf—including a "Cadillac for Jones Fund" sponsored by a New York

City radio station—forced the Kiwanis Club to reverse its initial decision. The tableau included major civil rights struggles, such as the desegregation of major league baseball, the desegregation of the Cotton Bowl (both on the field and in the stands), and the attempted desegregation of the University of Oklahoma Law School. And it included dramatic challenges to American racial custom in the court of world opinion, as when the National Association for the Advancement of Colored People (NAACP) took the case of African-Americans before the United Nations, noting that the new world organization's charter referred in five separate articles to the obligation of the international body to uphold basic human freedoms and rights.

Increasingly *Race Relations* also covered acts of white resistance. It reported a case of arson in Redwood City, California, that destroyed the home of a black veteran in a white neighborhood, and the more tragic case of a Fantana, California, family who were engulfed in the flames of a similar, racially motivated arson. It included a strike of white schoolchildren in Gary, Indiana, who refused to attend school with blacks, and the massive "sick leaves" mysteriously taken by white restaurant and hotel workers in Cincinnati during the NAACP convention there. And it included an escalating battle over housing in Chicago—a "restrictive covenant war." Covenants drawn up by local white homeowners' associations forbade the sale of property to blacks. In May and June 1946, bombs ripped through thirty-five homes belonging to black families in covenanted areas of Chicago. In the fall, "hysterical mobs of white persons of both sexes" demonstrated against the entrance of blacks in Fernwood Park Homes, an emergency veterans' housing project in southwest Chicago; only a riot detail of one thousand averted what, according to observers, threatened to become the city's worst riot since 1919.[58]

Against this backdrop, race moved dramatically toward the center of national political discussion in the war years and after, particularly in the wake of the 1943 riots. Several developments marked this shift in American politics: the debate over Jim Crow military and defense industry policies; the establishment of a Fair Employment Practices Commission; the emergence of "racial equality" (by which was not meant Nordics, Mediterraneans, and Alpines) as an issue in the 1944 presidential campaign; and the emergence of lynching, employment practices, and the poll tax as chief congressional issues in 1945. Both the Republicans and the Democrats took up civil rights questions and passed civil rights resolutions in their 1948 conventions, and it was the issue of race that divided the Democrats, prompting the third-party movement of Strom Thurmond and the Dixiecrats.

Indeed, already by the mid-1940s goodwill activists like Mary McLeod Bethune, Charles Johnson, Pearl Buck, Ralph Bunche, Ernesto Galarza, Robert Redfield, and Walter White had organized the American Council on Race Relations. In December 1946, Harry Truman issued Executive Order 9808, creating a Committee on Civil Rights at the federal level. The committee's recommendations, published toward the end of that year, may not have represented a "second abolition movement," as the *Richmond News* had it, but the report was sweeping in its recommendations. Its provisions included strengthening the machinery for the protection of civil rights by bolstering the Justice Department and the FBI, and establishing a standing Committee on Civil Rights in Congress; securing the right to safety through legislative measures such as antilynching legislation; securing the right to citizenship and its privileges by guaranteeing electoral participation and desegregating the armed forces; and securing the right to equality of opportunity by eliminating segregation, denying federal dollars to companies or agencies with discriminatory practices, passing a Fair Employment Practices Act, guaranteeing equal access to public accommodations, and eliminating discrimination in educational admissions, housing, health facilities, public services, transportation, and federal spending.[59]

Under the heading of "strengthening the right to citizenship," the committee also recommended a revision in standing naturalization law so as to do away with the one-hundred-fifty-year-old color qualification. Like so much in the committee report, this would have to wait. But perhaps the clearest indication of the shifting signification of race between 1924 and the 1950s was the congressional debate over precisely this point when it reappeared as part of the Walter and MacCarren immigration bills (1952). Although John Kennedy and others objected to continued restrictions on immigration from Eastern and Southern Europe, and although the phrase "Anglo-Saxon" surfaced from time to time in the debate, far and away the greatest "racial" issue identified in this discussion was the fate of aspiring "Negro" immigrants from the former colonies. Inasmuch as the proposed bills represented "racial quotas" or "racial discrimination," it was because they would "exclude Negroes by drastically reducing immigration from colonies in the Western Hemisphere," according to a newspaper ad taken out by more than seventy prominent liberals. Adam Clayton Powell, Jr., who emerged as the most vocal of the bill's opponents, decried various clauses devised to minimize the flow of nonwhite immigration. "The ancestry test smacks closely of the infamous Nuremberg laws of Hitler Germany," he protested; the bill discriminated against "would-be immigrants from Jamaica, Trinidad, and other colonies of the West Indies, most of whom are Negroes." Harking back to the Johnson Act, Powell chided his colleagues in the House:

> The 1924 law early achieved notoriety for the racist sentiments which engendered it and the Ku Klux Klan support which insured its passage. The McCarren-Walter bills perpetuate this obvious racist discrimination, and by doing so reaffirm a bias against Negro immigrants which should have been repudiated long ago.

The bill, in Powell's estimation, "sets up a Cape-Town–Washington D.C. axis."[60]

That "the Negro question" now dominated discussions of race even in the context of immigration quotas—in sharp contrast to the eugenics debates of the 1920s—dramatizes the extent to which American politics had come to be drawn in black and white. Well before *Brown v. Board of Education,* in other words, well before Rosa Parks's courageous stand in Montgomery and the sit-ins in Greensboro, a number of developments charted an increasing significance of race in national politics. Race itself no longer retained any salient distinctions among Madison Grant's Nordics, Alpines, and Mediterraneans—much less the thirty-six European races enumerated by the Dillingham Commission—but rather referred to the longstanding, simpler black-white dyad of the Jim Crow South. The liberalized immigration legislation of 1965—passed, as David Reimers points out, by the first U.S. Congress in which Roman Catholics constituted a plurality[61]—consecrated the earlier waves of European immigration by giving preference to those immigrants' relatives and so normalizing the presence of non–Anglo-Saxon white persons in the body politic.

E Pluribus Duo (II): American Culture in Black and White

"The Lord must have had His reasons for making some of us white and some of us black," muses Annie Johnson in *Imitation of Life* (1959). In sharp contrast to the fading cultural regime under which writers like Dashiel Hammett would depict a racial underworld of immigrant gangsters, under which Frank Norris and Jack London would depict a naturalistic universe menaced by racially degenerate villains, or under which

Hollywood could seize upon the Italian Rudolph Valentino to portray the racial exotic in a spectacle of Otherness, increasingly in the 1920s and afterward the landscape of American popular culture was peopled simply by blacks and whites. A sharp, bifurcated understanding of black and white increasingly gave form to the images and representations of American culture.

Again, it is important to underscore that this bifurcation was not an invention of the 1920s in the nation's popular culture or in its burgeoning visual culture. Thomas Edison's turn-of-the-century mocked battles between American soldiers and Filipino "savages" (filmed in New Jersey) were among the earliest popular films; and cultural productions such as the Midway Plaisance and the ethnographic exhibits of Chicago's Columbian Exposition (1893), too, presented an "ascending scale" of humanity that overtly enforced a pan–white-supremacist reading of world history.[62] Among the most influential white-over-black icons of American visual culture was *Birth of a Nation* (1915), D. W. Griffith's effort at galvanizing the nation by glorifying the white-supremacist bargain that had brought Reconstruction to a close in 1877. Despite occasional references to other racial systems of difference (to Americans' "Aryan birthright," for instance), the political logic and the visual economy of the film had rested upon the dualism of black and white.[63] The incarnation of the Ku Klux Klan, which rose up in the urban North in the film's wake, of course, endorsed a more nuanced reading of whiteness itself—far more so than that presented in Griffith's work. White Catholics and Jews hardly qualified for this brand of white supremacism. But as *Birth of a Nation* proved so popular even among urban immigrants, it must be numbered among the Progressive Era's transformative cultural icons. As Walter Benn Michaels boldly puts it, "White supremacy made possible the Americanization of the immigrant."[64]

An encyclopedic consideration of the black-white dyad in U.S. culture might run from *King Kong* and *Gone with the Wind*, to *Absolom, Absolom!, Studs Lonigan, Dragnet*, and *The Goldbergs*. I will focus on four works (or clusters of works) that in different ways illuminate the rivaling conceptions of race during these decades: Al Jolson's *Jazz Singer* (1927), which appropriates blackness to constitute Jews' whiteness; George Schuyler's satirical novel *Black No More* (1931), which documented the fluidity of "Nordic," "Anglo-Saxon," and "Caucasian" whiteness as part of an effort to dismantle established notions of immutable races; Laura Z. Hobson's *Gentleman's Agreement* (1947), which revised racial Jewishness by demonstrating the interchangeability of Jews and non-Jews, but which, ultimately, surrendered to its own rejected notions of stable, immutable Jewish racial identity; and finally, a group of urban dramas from the 1950s and early 1960s including *West Side Story* (1957, 1961) and *Corner Boy* (1957), in which adherence to the sharpening color line is the means of becoming "American" for a range of probationary "white persons"—the newly minted "white ethnics" of American social science. These texts reveal the power dynamics, the possibilities for resistance, the conscious strategies, and the unconscious assumptions attaching to the question of whiteness in the middle decades of the twentieth century. Taken together they lay bare the layers of interpretation that defined "difference" itself.

In American popular culture this reworking of racial "difference" and the emergence of a binary system were most clearly announced in Hollywood's first talkie, Al Jolson's *Jazz Singer* (1927). The film tells the story of a young Jewish man, the last of a long line of cantors, who renounces his traditional calling to become a jazz singer on the secular stage; who falls in love with a non-Jewish performer named Mary; and who is on the verge of hitting the big time. When his father the cantor takes ill on the holiest night of the year, Jakie Rabinowitz (now Jack Robin) must either renounce the stage and return to Orchard Street to sing the Kol Nidre for "his people," or forsake his people for his frivolous and individualistic success on the American stage. Melodramatic though it is, *The Jazz Singer* thus represents the question of assimilation perfectly posed, the immigrant family's clashing sensibilities perfectly scripted.

But this film of assimilation is not so much about cultural Americanization and the reweaving of tradition as it is, ultimately, about the whiteness of Jews. *The Jazz Singer* encapsulates the racial transformation of the Jews in the twentieth century in all its elements. Jolson's metamorphosis from Jakie Rabinowitz to the Americanized Jack Robin is predicated upon a literal racial redefinition, which is effected in its turn by the racial masquerade of the jazz singer's blackface routine. The film does mark "assimilation" in part by its attention to the imbibed spirit of New World popular culture, to the "Anglo-Saxon severity" of modern American clothing and styles, and to emergent patterns of desire and consumption ("Diamonds!" his mother exclaims upon opening a gift from Jack; "I got so much money, Mama, Rockefeller is jealous of me").[65] At bottom, however, it is not just that the immigrant becomes American by appropriating jazz and "singing nigger songs" in a German beergarden, as various residents of the Jewish ghetto put it in the original screenplay. Rather, it is that, paradoxically, by donning blackface the Hebrew becomes Caucasian.[66]

Jolson's blackface routine becomes the vehicle for a complex racial triangulation among Hebrews (Jakie's family and their congregation), African-Americans (literally absent but ubiquitously suggested by the blackface itself), and white Americans (embodied by Mary). The burnt cork at once masks Jewishness and accentuates whiteness: in playing black, the Jew becomes white. On the one hand, the blackness of the blackface distances or alienates Jakie from the Jewish community: according to title card 49, "Orchard Street would have had some difficulty in recognizing Jakie Rabinowitz of Beth-El choir under the burnt cork of Jack Robin." Or again, as his neighbor Yudelson exclaims in title card 143 as he beholds the jazz singer in full burnt-cork regalia, "It talks like Jakie, but it looks like a nigger."[67]

And what is being hidden here, precisely? Significantly, throughout the screenplay Jewishness is written in as a *visible* marker; and Jewishness as race is effaced only by the whiteness created by the blackface routine. One might guess reasonably enough that certain physical properties would be assigned to Jewishness in a screenplay of the 1920s, but various stage directions remove all doubt: Yudelson is "a tall, spare Hebrew with a straggly beard"; the theater "is filled with a fashionable throng and a generous sprinkling of Jewish types"; another scene features "a typical businessman of the Hebraic type"; at the front of the synagogue "there is a steady stream of people entering, Jews, old and young, bearded and clean-shaven, women in shawls and stylish street attire." (Other white races, too, are marked by their unmistakable physicality: among the earliest shots in the film is one labeled simply, "Close-up Italian"; and Dr. O'Shaughnessy is described as "a big husky, greyhaired Irishman.")[68] The blackface thus racially revises Jolson by masking his physical Jewishness—it renders him, as titles 49 and 143 note, unrecognizable as a Jew.

But this is only half of the transformation. The blackness of the blackface not only masks Jewish physicality but also unites Jack with Mary by casting the actor's whiteness in stark relief. The film self-consciously plays on the white-and-black contrasts inherent in the minstrel form—as when, in one scene backstage, "Jack wipes a white glove across his eyes, leaving a white streak across his face"—thus heightening the visual impact of Jolson's white skin.[69] The white streaking effect is important to Jakie's overall transformation, but it is especially important to his liaison with

Mary: it is this harshly juxtaposed black and white that emphasizes Robin's whiteness—that is, his racial consanguinity with Mary.

"Playing a romantic scene in blackface may be something of an experiment," warns one stage direction, and it goes on to offer the director an alternative way of shooting the scene. But playing the love scene *without* blackface is rather a different kind of experiment—an experiment in interracial romance—and the blackface thus solves at least as many problems socially as it creates logistically. As the blackface turns Jolson white, it erases the racial "difference" between Jakie and the *shikse,* and transforms Jewishness itself into a mere matter of culture and religion (which Jack can continue to embrace). In the final scene, as Jolson sings the Kol Nidre for "his people," an onlooker exclaims, "You are listening to the stage's greatest blackface comedian singing to his God" (in the final film version the title reads simply, "a jazz singer—singing to his God").[70]

Ultimately, then, the burnt cork serves not only to change the race of the Jew, but also to eradicate race from *Judaism:* one might embrace the Hebrew God without necessarily being a "Hebrew type." Not incidentally, finally, the film polices the very boundaries whose creation it depicts: the whiteness of Jews that the film announces in its internal logic is reinforced by the external logic of its Jim Crow casting. The absence of African-Americans from this production about jazz reiterates Jordan Baker's assertion in the presence of Jimmy Gatz, "We're all white here."

As Jeffrey Melnick has remarked, *The Jazz Singer* is a kind of "nostalgic valentine" which marks the decline of blackface minstrelsy as a cultural form. Although this first talking picture was in some sense the very high point of the form, it also marks the end of an era in which blackface would be among the most popular forms in urban culture. But it is worth noting that the age of minstrelsy roughly coincides with the age of problematic whiteness. It would be a mistake to venture that the minstrel tradition accomplished any one thing exclusively. Indeed, the act of blacking up is complex: it provided a visual idiom for projecting, disavowing, and yet appropriating certain traits presumed to be racial; it was a means of cultural theft and political protest; and it gave voice to antimodernism and to a raucous white republicanism, as scholars like Michael Rogin have demonstrated.[71] Nonetheless, laying claim to whiteness through a deployment of contrasting blackness was certainly one of the things this form accomplished, and its declining popularity in the 1930s and after may have had something to do with immigrants' diminishing need for a whitener. In any case, if Jakie Rabinowitz's use of blackface to make the transition from Hebrew to Caucasian merely replicates several decades of practice among vernacular theater performers of various backgrounds, in 1927 there was a difference: the transformation was about to take hold. From the vantage point of the late twentieth century, it is the visual cue to a racial Hebrewness that strikes us as most peculiar, not Jack and Mary's daring interracial romance.

Whereas the blackface and the visual racial economy of *The Jazz Singer* represent a strategy for claiming whiteness paired with an unself-conscious symptomatology of the distinctions and hierarchies still presumed *within* whiteness, George Schuyler's *Black No More* (1931) is a more meditative approach to race and races. *Black No More* is a biting satire of figures on all sides of the race question and on both sides of the color line. It is also a brilliant analysis of the fundamental position of race in American political economy and culture. The plot is propelled by the miraculous process invented by Dr. Junius Crookman, a "great and lucrative experiment of turning Negroes into Caucasians." As a result of his experimentation with a blanching skin disease that "both Negroes and Caucasians" may be susceptible to, Crookman comes up with a method by which "in three days the Negro becomes to all appearances a Caucasian." At a public unveiling of his invention, and as a powerful demonstration of his method's effects, Crookman points out "the most Nordic-looking person in the room" and explains that he is, in fact, Senegalese.[72] Virtually all of Harlem, it turns out, is eager to become Caucasian.

The story's central figure is the "Negro" Max Disher, who decides to become the "white" Matthew Fisher because, among other things, he wants to meet a certain white woman whom he has been able to admire only from afar. As Schuyler traces the career of this racial shape-shifter, he demonstrates the enormous stake that all kinds of people have in the racial status quo—not only outright white supremacists like the "Knights of Nordica" or the "Anglo-Saxon Association of America," but "Negro" leaders and cultural figures like "Santop Licorice" (Marcus Garvey), "Dr. Shakespeare Agamemnon Beard" (W. E. B. Du Bois), the leaders of "Dusky River Agricultural Institute" (Tuskegee), and Madam Sisseretta Blandish (Madam C. J. Walker). The erasure of racial distinction turns the nation upside down until, at last, "real" whites discover that Crookman's former "Negroes" tend now to be *whiter* than white, and so racial hierarchy is built anew on the inverse principle of dark-over-light.

Schuyler's twin themes throughout the novel are the unforgiving nature of the color line on the one hand, and the absolute social fabrication of race on the other. Once Dishman had become Caucasian, for instance, such were the imperatives of American life that "there was no other alternative than to seek his future among the Caucasians with whom he now rightfully belonged." One could scarcely turn back. Nor, given the realities of power and its disposition, would one necessarily want to: "At last he felt like an American citizen." (Indeed, following the reasoning of 1790, having become white, "an American citizen" is precisely what Dishman had at last become.) And yet for all the social and political certainties that go along with being either a "Negro" or a "Caucasian," Schuyler argues, neither category really makes any sense at all. Visual cues are notoriously unreliable, for instance, as there are

> plenty of Caucasians who have lips quite as thick and noses quite as broad as any of us. As a matter of fact there has been considerable exaggeration about the contrast between Caucasian and Negro features. The cartoonists and minstrel men have been responsible for it . . . many so-called Caucasians, particularly the Latins, Jews and South Irish, and frequently the most Nordic of peoples like the Swedes, show almost Negroid lips and noses.

Or again, even "blood" is dubious: genealogical statistics generated by a race "purity" law prove that more than fifty million "Anglo-Saxons" in fact have some measure of "black" blood.[73] It is this manufactured, arbitrary, *mistaken* quality of race, in fact, that gives such bite to Schuyler's observations on its primacy as an organizer of the nation's political and social life.

But though Schuyler was primarily concerned with the white-black color line, he had tremendous insight into the social relations on the white side of this divide as well. As the juxtaposition of the "Knights of Nordica," the "Anglo-Saxon Association of America," and Crookman's own experiment of "turning Negroes into Caucasians" suggests, Schuyler was keenly attuned to the vicissitudes of whiteness. Consider his very assertion, for example, that "many so-called Caucasians, particularly the Latins, Jews and South Irish, and frequently the most Nordic of peoples like the Swedes, show almost Negroid lips and noses." Here the self-undermining appellation "so-called Caucasians" has two distinct referents: the undergirding logic of the sentence seems to be that it is their "almost Negroid lips and noses" that call their "Caucasian" identity into question and render them "so-called Caucasians." There is no racial purity, and the lips and noses of these would-be "Caucasians" proclaim as much.

But Schuyler's division of the "Caucasian race," his assertion that suspect lips and noses are "particularly" found among "Latins, Jews and South Irish, and frequently the most Nordic of peoples like the Swedes," also gives the lie to the category "Caucasian" by evoking a series of counter-races whose salience had been so powerful in recent years. These peoples are "so-called Caucasians" not only because they may in fact be part "black," in other words, but because popular eugenic propaganda had so convincingly cast them as members of distinctive races.

Schuyler apprehended the shift that was just taking place in the reconsolidation of whiteness, and he drew upon the power of that observation to further his argument about the general fabrication of races—*all* races. These "Caucasians" were pulling a fast one, and Schuyler knew it more than a decade before Ruth Benedict, Ashley Montagu, and others had made "Caucasian, Negroid, and Mongoloid" the mantra of America's public discourse of "difference." Among the customers of Madame Sisseretta Blandish's beauty parlor were "two or three Jewish girls from downtown . . . [who] came up regularly to have their hair straightened because it wouldn't stand inspection in the Nordic world." Other references to racially subdivided whiteness include the depiction of one of Crookman's patients as an "ersatz Nordic"; a reference to the uptown businesses of "canny Hebrews"; the characterization of a German immigrant as a heavy "Teuton"; and mention of the popularly proclaimed virtues of "docile, contented, Anglo-Saxon labor."[74] By freezing this vision of racial difference at the very moment when such differences were melting away in the popular imagination, Schuyler rendered the core instability of race in accessible terms. If yesterday's "Nordics," "Latins," "Hebrews," "Teutons," and "Anglo-Saxons" could be today's "Caucasians," then how solid, after all, are the certainties that separate "Caucasian" from "Negro"? The novel is indeed about racial changeability, but not just the changeability of Crookman's imitation whites.

Schuyler not only depicts the superficial divisions among conceptual categories like "Anglo-Saxon," "Nordic," and "Hebrew," moreover; he explores the working of such distinctions in the power relations among these white peoples. The Knights of Nordica advance a pan–white-supremacist agenda, for example, as when one of their broadsides blares that "the racial integrity of the Caucasian Race is being threatened by the activities of a scientific black Beelzebub in New York." Schuyler identifies this kind of race allegiance in terms very similar to those used by Du Bois in his description of the "psychological wage" of whiteness: "As long as the ignorant white masses could be kept thinking of the menace of the Negro to Caucasian race purity and political control, they would give little thought to labor organization."[75]

The "Anglo-Saxon Association of America," by contrast, represented something else again: members "believe in white supremacy the same as [the Knights of Nordica] but they claim that Anglo-Saxons are the cream of the white race and should maintain the leadership in American social, economic and political life." This group corresponds more closely with the eugenic organizations of the 1910s and 1920s than with pan–white supremacism. Indeed, its leader, Arthur Snobbcraft (who, incidentally, is "suspiciously swarthy for an Anglo-Saxon"), advances a frankly eugenic program that not only distinguishes among the white races but is framed in the good old, time-honored republican logic of "fitness for self-government." He proposed "sterilization of the unfit, meaning Negroes, aliens, Jews and other riff raff, and he had an abiding hatred of democracy." His pet scheme was to pass a "genealogical law" disfranchising all people "of Negro or unknown ancestry," as "good citizens could not be made out of such material."[76]

Later, as political battlelines are drawn, Schuyler notes that Jews and Catholics seem ready to support the nativist candidate purely on the strength of his staunchly antiblack program. "In this they were but running true to form, however, as they had usually been on the side of white supremacy in the old days when there was a Negro population observable to the eye."[77] Thus *Black No More* captures the social-political stakes of the nation's white-over-black power relations, especially for marginal whites who stand to benefit from inclusion as "Caucasians"; and yet it also depicts the racial struggle *among* whites, and the potentially diverging patterns of inclusion and exclusion summoned by a conceptual category like "Anglo-Saxon." Schuyler's attention to problematic whitenesses and the power struggles attending them, then, adds a second dimension to his primary concern for problematic blackness: the public fiction of race itself, and its tremendous power to decide the fortunes and misfortunes of the populace. Like all races, the Caucasian race is a fabrication— a fact made tragic by the inflexibility of the color line and the profound social and political consequences at stake in the public caprice of classification.[78]

A decade and a half after the appearance of *Black No More*, Laura Z. Hobson's *Gentleman's Agreement* (1947) offered yet another meditation on whiteness and "difference." Like *Black No More*, this novel evokes a number of racial categories in motion and collision. Despite the transnational history of anti-Semitism that surely has inflected the Jewish experience in North America, Schuyler and Jolson's "Hebrews" nonetheless traveled the path of other white races through the historic vicissitudes from white, to non–Anglo-Saxon, to Caucasian. Hobson comments upon the last leg of this racial odyssey, from Semite or Hebrew to Caucasian, both consciously and unconsciously in *Gentleman's Agreement*.

Hobson was more interested in anti-Semitism than in Jewishness per se, but she could not write about the one without coming to some kind of understanding of the other; and in 1947 this meant taking up Jewishness as a race question. A Gentile journalist named Philip Green (played in the movie by Gregory Peck) is assigned a series on American anti-Semitism for a major news magazine. Looking for a fresh angle, he hits upon the idea of posing as a Jew—passing—and then writing an exposé of American anti-Semitism based on his own experience. "I Was Jewish for Six Months," this *tour de force* will be called. He actually does pull this off, and he finds out many interesting things along the way (not least, that most everyone he knows, including his fiancée, is anti-Semitic).

On its face, *Gentleman's Agreement* is unequivocal in its erasure of Jewish racial difference; indeed, whatever statement the novel seeks to make about Jewishness, and, finally, about justice, derives entirely from the central idea of *interchangeability*. Phil Green can experience anti-Semitism firsthand because he can pass as a Jew; and he can pass because, at bottom, there is no "difference" between Jews and Gentiles. (This, in turn, is what is so absurd about anti-Semitism, Hobson will have us conclude. What does it mean that a non-Jew can be the victim of Jew-hatred?)

But the text is at war with itself in a way that not only undermines Hobson's project of expunging racial Jewishness, but also wonderfully demonstrates the nature of racial categorization itself as ideology deeply entrenched. Hobson's novel offers a unique snapshot of the contest in the mid-twentieth century between a waning racial order that identified Jews as Semites or Hebrews, and the ascendant order by which their status as Caucasians would become more salient. Though clearly connected to a transnational history of Jewishness and anti-Semitism (it is no accident that the novel appears in the wake of the Holocaust), this contest nonetheless bears witness to shifting paradigms of race particular to the American context—shifts that at certain historical junctures also produced questions regarding the racial identity of Celts, Slavs, Mediterraneans,

and Iberics—categories that have faded from our visual lexicon as well
as from our racial vocabulary.

The pivotal moment in Hobson's political project is when Green first
decides that he could indeed pass as a Jew—that Jews and Gentiles are
essentially interchangeable. In the movie, Gregory Peck runs over and
checks himself out in the mirror. In the novel Green mentally scans his
own physiognomy to make sure that such an imposture would be believ-
able:

> He checked on himself in his mind's eye—tall, lanky; sure so was
> Dave [Goldman, his Jewish friend], so were a hell of a lot of guys
> who were Jewish. He had no accent or mannerisms that were Jew-
> ish—neither did lots of Jews, and anti-Semitism was hitting them just
> the same. His nose was straight—so was Dave's, so were a lot of
> other guys'. He had dark eyes, dark hair, a kind of sensitive look . . .
> Brother, it was a cinch.

When his son asks him about anti-Semitism and Jewishness ("What *are*
Jews anyhow?"), race is not in the lexicon with which Green is prepared
to deal with the question. Jewishness is a religion, period; "Oh, they talk
about the Jewish race, but never about the Catholic race or the Protestant
race."[79]

Later Hobson takes up the race question overtly, referring to the (non-
fictional) anthropologist Ernest Hooton's work on "the balderdash of race
and types." Or again, as his fiancée struggles with her own anti-Semitism,
she racializes and then quickly re-racializes Jews in her own thinking:
having slipped and used the phrase "the Jewish race," she scrambles to
correct herself: "She knew perfectly well that the three great divisions of
mankind were the Caucasian race, the Mongoloid, the Negroid. She remembered [Phil's] finger pointing out a phrase in a pamphlet written by
leading anthropologists. 'There is no Jewish race.' "[80] Hobson thus endorsed a system of difference not yet fully ascendant in 1947—a system
by which Jews are Caucasian rather than Hebrew or Semitic—and she
willfully sought to eradicate the vestiges of an older order based upon
white races and Anglo-Saxon supremacism.

In a social context like the United States, however, a politics of justice
based upon literal "sameness" is highly problematic. The ideological move
entailed by this revision of Jewishness is fraught with implications for
other racially defined groups. The broadest, most sweeping stakes of

Philip Green's project (and hence of Laura Z. Hobson's project) are summed up when Green poses the rhetorical question, "What the hell chance have we of getting decent with thirteen million Negroes if we can't lick the much easier business of anti-Semitism?" Here, by a kind of circular comment, the novel demonstrates its own political limitations: there *is* no chance of "getting decent" with everyone in this nation of nations if decency is predicated upon literal "sameness." And yet "sameness" itself is both constructed and arbitrary. The thing that makes anti-Semitism an "easier business" is Hobson's own decision to challenge the perceived "difference" dividing Anglo-Saxon from Hebrew while leaving intact that which divides "Caucasian" from "Negroid" from "Mongoloid." What makes anti-Semitism an "easier business," in short, is Hobson's unconscious endorsement of the color line. The social stakes of recasting the entire Jewish race as "Caucasian" were foreshadowed by the popular 1940s appellation "white Jews" as applied to those who, in the words of Green's secretary, were not "the kikey ones." Indeed, a conversation between Green and his mother about his boyhood friend Petey Alamacho (who was Mexican) overtly suggests that there are levels of "difference" whose bridging is less certain than in the case of the presumably consanguine Gentiles and Jews.[81]

Hence although the title is meant to refer to restrictive housing covenants in places like New Canaan, Connecticut, the most portentous "gentleman's agreement" here is *this* agreement to expose the constructedness of racial difference, then not to *un*think it, but simply to *re*think it as "color." What one cannot learn from this book about restrictive housing covenants is that in 1946, the year before the novel appeared, in the single city of Chicago in the months of May and June alone there were more than thirty residential bombings whose aim was not the expulsion of Jews by non-Jews, but the expulsion of "Negroes" by "Caucasians." The point is not simply that, by her silence on this bit of social context, Hobson misses an opportunity to take her critique further. More, by the particular ways in which the novel frames questions of "difference" and justice, it provides no moral syntax for commenting upon antiblack racism at all (other than simply to say that it represents the "tougher business" to which anti-Semitism is the "easier business"). Anti-Semitism is incomprehensible *primarily* because Jewish "difference" is called into question by an unreliable Jewish physicality. Wholly outside the novel's moral compass are cases where questions of "difference" and justice cannot be resolved by an argument of "sameness" indicated by literal interchangeability. Recast as biblical injunction, *Gentleman's Agreement* reads, "Do unto others—who could pass for you—as you would have others do unto you—if you could pass for them." This fairly captures the central tendency in American political culture from the 1920s to the 1960s: as race moved to the center of political discussion nationally, "difference" among the former white races diminished, race itself was recast as color, and race-as-difference was reified along the lines of what Hobson (after Hooten and Benedict and others) called the "three great divisions of mankind." American political life was *this* gentleman's agreement writ large.

In the novel itself, however, there is a second, countervailing current. We now know that the paradigm of racial difference that reified Caucasian unity won out. The nineteenth century's simian caricatures of Celts strike us as oddities; phrases like "the Jewish race," if not totally faded from our popular political lexicon, likely strike us, not as naturalized and invisible, but as noticeable and vaguely sinister. But as Hobson was writing in the 1940s, the residual scheme of distinct white races still had significant purchase on popular ideology and perception—Hobson's included. *Is* there such a thing as "looking Jewish"? Even Philip Green himself wonders. "Does Dave *look* Jewish? Yes, he supposed he did, now that he asked . . . Where was it, this Jewishness? . . . What makes people look or not look Jewish?" The most dramatic and telling passage, however, is Hobson's description of a guest at a cocktail party: "Lieberman was plump as well as short, middleaged, with the face of a Jew in a Nazi cartoon, the beaked nose, the blue jowls, and the curling black hair. Phil saw all of it, and the fine candid eyes."[82]

Despite a plot that turns on the presumption of interchangeability, it is this view of Jewish "difference" marked by a distinct Jewish physicality that silently gains the upper hand in the narrative. Despite Hobson's proposition of interchangeability, the remarkable fact is that in this novel, which is all about passing, the character who does all the passing *never actually passes*. That is, Phil Green's passing as a Jew depends upon his *telling* everyone that he is a Jew, and getting the rumor mill started ("I'm going to be Jewish, that's all. Just tell people I am, and see what happens"). Everyone *hears* that he is a Jew and believes it; but no one ever once (mis)takes him for one. The idea pivots on the same logic as a joke told of Michael Arlen, and quoted in the novel: when asked if he was "really" Armenian, Arlen answered, "Would anyone *say* he was Armenian if he wasn't Armenian?"[83] In 1947 in the United States, would a non-Jew ever claim to be Jewish? Phil Green's passing is predicated on his telling a lie that no one would ever have reason to question.

Not only do people not take him for Jewish until he announces that he is, but in fact they always comfortably assume that he *is not:* a cabdriver makes an anti-Semitic remark about the Jews on Park Avenue, comfortable in his assumption that Phil Green the passenger is not Jewish; a doctor makes an anti-Semitic remark about Jewish doctors who always overcharge, comfortable in his assumption that Phil Green the patient is not Jewish. Even when Green experiments by checking in at a restricted hotel in the country, he is about to be admitted until he raises a fuss about whether or not the hotel is in fact restricted, thereby arousing suspicions.[84] Green can volunteer to be outraged by anti-Semitism, in other words, but he cannot volunteer to be victimized by it.

The novel's "real" Jews, meanwhile, never need to announce it; their physiognomy always announces it for them. Lieberman looks like a Jew in a Nazi cartoon. Phil Green's friend Dave Goldman (who Green has decided he looks "just like") is verbally assaulted at a bar by a drunken soldier who doesn't like "yids"—precisely the kind of affront which Green is never subjected to in the course of his experimentation. And when Green inspects his new secretary, Elaine Wales, he notes that "high cheekbones made her seem Scandinavian, Slavic, something foreign and interesting." She turns out to be not Elaine Wales but Estelle Walovsky, a Jew who is passing. Foreign indeed.[85]

It is ultimately through Lieberman, a Jew distinctly marked by classically Jewish physicality, that Hobson attempts to resolve the question of racial Jewishness. "I have no religion," remarks Lieberman,

> so I am not Jewish by religion. Further, I am a scientist, so I must rely on science which tells me I am not Jewish by race since there's no such thing as a distinct Jewish race. As for ethnic group or Jewish type, we know I fit perfectly the Syrian or Turkish or Egyptian type— there's not even such a thing, anthropologically, as the Jewish type . . . I will go forth and state flatly, "I am not a Jew." . . . With this face that becomes not an evasion but a new principle.[86]

Here is Hobson's attempt to bring the warring elements of the narrative together—to suture the politics of interchangeability to her recognition of "difference" marked by Jewish physicality. There are two ways of looking at this "new principle" Hobson is groping for: if the New Principle is a politics of justice based not upon sameness but upon an acceptance of "difference," then it is a principle that the novel itself never adequately articulates; if the New Principle is a politics of unharassed *whiteness,* the novel articulates it all too well, regardless of Hobson's nobler intentions.

The dilemmas that Hobson sought to resolve and those that she unwittingly generated point to a fundamental dynamic of America's racially saturated political culture. *Gentleman's Agreement* is like a cultural videotape in which the fluidity of race and the collision of racial categories are captured in motion. By the logic of its "politics of sameness," the novel indicates the white-supremacist dynamic that was historically written into the racial odyssey from Hebrew (or Celt or Slav or Iberian or Levantine) to Caucasian. As we have seen, Hobson was scarcely alone in her tendency to expunge racial "difference" in one area in such a way as to leave it intact, unquestioned, unproblematic, and thus further naturalized elsewhere; this tacit, white-over-nonwhite dynamic in Hobson's liberal effort to rethink race was a staple of the social sciences. The novel demonstrates the ideological, constructed basis of a conception like "Caucasian," and it indicates the social and political capital inherent in the category. And finally, it suggests how that capital itself is contingent upon the category's seeming to be not ideologically constructed, but an irreducible fact of biology. Ultimately Hobson could not shake that conception of a racial Jewishness that posed so convincingly as a biological fact, just as we in our turn, a half-century later, have trouble shaking the conception of a Caucasian race that has so convincingly taken its place.

In the years after *Gentleman's Agreement* appeared, this cultural figure of the Caucasian ascended in a flourishing genre of urban realism that brought together some of the most salient political strands of the 1950s and 1960s—a changing urban geography, "ethnic" territoriality, housing discrimination, the fight for scarce resources, and, often, juvenile delinquency. Novels like Jo Sinclair's *The Changelings* (1955) and Edwin O'Connor's *Edge of Sadness* (1961) at once accepted and popularized the notion of "ethnic" difference as occupying an epistemological plane distinct from racial difference, even in their liberal attempts to question the bases of antagonisms rooted in racial thinking. "All that summer," begins *The Changelings,* "as no white people came to rent the empty, upstairs suites of the Valenti house or the Golden house, tension had mounted in the street. Only Negroes came."[87] Italian and Jew are here joined as consanguine "whites" in contrast to invading "Negroes"; and, later, it is the depth of the division between the black and the white races that renders Vincent and Clara's friendship across the color line so extraordinary.

In films like *Blackboard Jungle* (1955), too, an ethnic hodge-podge (Dadier, Katz, Murdock, Warnke) is made to stand for whiteness (and thus for Americanness). "I don't care if a boy's skin is black, yellow, or purple," says Warnke, the principal of this multi-ethnic high school. "He gets the same breaks, the same teaching, as any white boy."[88] Whiteness thus becomes the normative experience at the school; and in presenting its "lesson in democracy" through the relationship of a white teacher and his black student (Sidney Poitier), the film ultimately erases whatever distinctions are said to exist among the multi-ethnic group of whites themselves. In the teacher Dadier and Warnke's heated discussion of "what should not be said" in a democracy, for instance, the epithet "Mick" vanishes behind the veil of concern regarding the more explosive epithet "nigger"; and so Irish difference is rendered as no difference.

The tone and the logic of this kind of multi-ethnic pan-whiteness are matched and conveyed most succinctly in the opening stage direction of *West Side Story* (1957): "the Sharks are Puerto Ricans, the Jets an anthology of what is called 'American.' " This anthology, we come to find, consists chiefly of "Wops," "Micks," and "Polacks." Although the division between immigrant and native is not without significance in this conflict ("The mother of Tony was born in Poland; the father still goes to night school. Tony was born in America, so that makes him an American. But us? Foreigners!"), it is race that quietly confers rights and decides claims to national belonging. It is not necessarily the length of their residence in America that renders this rag-tag bunch of Wops, Micks, and Polacks "an anthology of what is called 'American,' " in other words. It is their whiteness, just as it is the Sharks' darkness that visibly marks them as national outsiders. Lieutenant Schrank refers to the Sharks as "half-breeds," then menaces: "Clear out, Spics. Sure; it's a free country and I ain't got the right. But it's a country with laws; and I can find the right. I got the badge, you got the skin." Or again, amid some quick banter between the rival gangs:

Anita: Will you let me pass?
Snowboy: She's too dark to pass.

Similarly, whereas Anita's Americanization is linked to consumption ("Automobile in America, / Chromium steel in America, / Wire-spoke wheel in America—/ Very big deal in America!") Maria's Americanization is both sexual and racial: in choosing the "Polack," the "Spic" will become "American." As in *The Changelings* and *Blackboard Jungle,* white "ethnicity" is deployed throughout *West Side Story* not so much as a marker of "difference," but as suggestive of mere variety in a way that consolidates whiteness and accentuates the distance between whiteness and its racial others.[89]

Perhaps most dramatically, in *Corner Boy* (1957) Herbert Simmons described the shifting cultural geography of a Midwestern city in these terms: "The black belt had spread ten miles in each direction in the last twenty years, and white families had fled, to avoid the plague further west and north, so that now the downtown district was almost completely surrounded by Negro communities. The Caucasians had to come alarming distances to go to work and shop." Among the "Caucasians" whom we meet straight away is Papaseppe Garveli. Much later, after Garveli's daughter, Georgia, has been killed in a car accident and rumors abound about her "interracial" affair with a black neighbor, Jake Adams, "on Peabody Avenue the gulf widened between the Garvelis and the [black] neighborhood . . . one thing was clear, the Garvelis were white, as white as all the white people in the world."[90]

As white as all the white people in the world. This was perhaps the fondest aspiration concealed behind the mask of the blackface minstrel; it was a certainty called into question by George Schuyler in his dismantling of race and races; and it was a biological fact secretly doubted by Laura Z. Hobson in her quiet distinction between "real" and "unreal" Jews despite a central trope of racial passing. But by the 1950s "as white as all the white people in the world" is indeed what the inferior European races—those genetic "bad investments" of Henry Cabot Lodge's day—had largely become, if not in socioeconomic status, then certainly in both scientific and popular thinking regarding the "natural divisions of mankind." In 1960 one of them would be elected president.

Looking back at an earlier era's race consciousness from the vantage point of the 1940s, Ruth Benedict wrote, "In all the American racist volumes there was an immediate political objective: revision of the immigration laws. The American temper had changed since the days when our motto was 'No distinction of race, creed, or color' and we offered an asylum for the oppressed."[91] And when, we ought to ask, was *that?* At the time that

Benedict was writing, the phrase "white persons" had been on the books for nearly a century and a half and still operated in naturalization law, although it had been modified by amended references to peoples of "African nativity and descent." Benedict's view typifies the liberal tendency to see turn-of-the-century racism as an anomaly rather than as a revision or an extension of the long-standing racial codes which had regulated citizenship since the first Congress took up the question in 1790. It is a tendency that rests upon a bedrock of Caucasian consanguinity among white peoples and upon a tacit acceptance of normative whiteness as the invisible marker of true citizenship. Only when "immigrant" means "European-American," and only when the immigrant experience is cast as an "ethnic" saga free of any racial valences, can the racism of the eugenics era of immigration restriction be seen as a departure from standard American practice.

Similarly, in *Race and Nationality in American Life* (1957), in tones now astonishing for their optimism, Oscar Handlin announced that Americans had "ceased to believe in race" after the 1930s. The "example of Europe" during the Nazi period, among other things, had "destroyed racism, the hate movements, and discrimination" in the United States; and "science, which created race as an intellectual concept, also helped destroy it. For it is the strength of science to contain within itself the means of its own redemption." Later in the same volume Handlin asked, "Is our belief in democracy coupled with the reservation that it is workable only in favored climes and in the hands of favored men, or is this a way of life open to all?" The question itself was not new; and (although Handlin merely posed it rhetorically) the answer is embedded in American history itself—in the "free white persons" clause of 1790, in slavery and the Black Codes, in miscegenation laws, in Indian wars and Chinese Exclusion, and in eugenically derived immigration quotas. "The national-origins quota system and segregation," Handlin continued,

> rest on totally false assumptions. They are the products of men who lost confidence. With their uneasy fears they sought refuge in a kind of withdrawal from the world about them, hoping for security in the purity of their own race. Out of the biased science of the early part of this century they drew the distorted notion of a fundamental difference between black and white, between old and new immigrants. From that notion there followed the idea that different groups of men enjoyed different capacities for becoming American citizens.[92]

This interpretation of race and racism as enjoying only a momentary reign in American political culture entails a rather remarkable erasure of the long history of race thinking across time: if Handlin's certainty that race thinking had been repudiated once and for all was perhaps a trifle premature, his positing an egalitarian "confidence" that had momentarily been "lost" in the early twentieth century is more problematic still. Unequivocal confidence in the fitness of all peoples for self-government, regardless of race, had been rare enough from the Revolutionary generation on down. But mid- to late-twentieth-century liberalism has demanded a certain amnesia regarding both the naturalization law of 1790 *and* the fact that today's Caucasians had ever been anything other than a single, biologically unified, and consanguine racial group. Liberalism's cherished myths of Golden-Door opportunity and the fundamental openness of American society require a repression of that racial odyssey in which various Teague O'Regans passed through several vicissitudes of whiteness from "bog-trotters" and "aborigines" to full-fledged "whites." And liberalism requires that we forget the extent to which that whiteness itself has been conferred or claimed largely as a result of confrontations with various versions of "de vile savage," who first marked, and later stressed, the "natural" boundaries of American citizenship.

HISTORY, RACE, AND PERCEPTION

If race is so mutable, then how is its instability registered at a single historical moment or in a single group's history? How is this instability manifest in social consciousness and in the political unconscious?

The chapters of part two explore the fluidity of race by focusing upon a rather narrow slice of time, 1877, and upon a single social group, Jews. The conflicting racial discourses in 1877 indicate the political character of race: civil strife over Negro rights in the South, anti-Chinese agitation and Indian Wars in the West, labor agitation and violence in the Midwest and East, reports of war in the Caucasus—each arena generated its own racial lexicon, invoked its own patterns of racial difference, introduced its own racially inscribed dramatis personae. A "Celt" among the uncivilized Molly Maguires in the Pennsylvania coal fields might easily number among the "Caucasians" on a New Orleans election day or amid the warfare on the Dakota plains. "Looking Jewish, Seeing Jews" next charts this racial instability as it has marked the social movement of a group whose character as a race apart was beyond question in the late nineteenth century, but was very much contested by the mid-twentieth.

These are matters of both conception and perception. "Anglo-Saxon," "Hebrew," "Celt," "Slav," "Mediterranean," "Caucasian"—such classifications are not a matter of nomenclature alone; indeed, racial differences are not only asserted or discussed but seen. The following chapters are meant not only to illustrate the changeable character of race, but also to trace the circuitry of race from the various historic encounters that generate this mode of ascribing "difference" to the uneven patterns of racial recognition which such encounters leave in their wake; and to the localized, even individualized experience of literally seeing, or not seeing, racial "difference" where such difference depends upon the play between social consciousness and literal vision. Whereas Chapter 4 focuses upon the power of history in the formation of race, Chapter 5 bears down more directly upon social consciousness and observable racial "fact"—upon the vagaries of race and the eye of the beholder.

Part one has sketched a succession from one racial paradigm to another across 175 years of American history; part two now examines the resulting discrepancies and the symptoms of uncertainty in the seeming fixity of race, as one regime gives way only imperfectly to the next. Competing discourses of race rise and fall in salience. Each is keyed to a different aspect of the unfolding national epic of encounter, conquest, enslavement and emancipation, and immigration; each offers a different version of the polity and its divisions; and each is subject to the concerns of the moment. One's view and interpretation of various real-life bodies, then—the bodies of Hebrews or of Celts or of Caucasians, for instance—is thus intimately aligned with one's comprehension of the body politic.

"Have you any objections to a foreigner?" [Mrs. Tristram] continued, addressing Newman. . .

"No Irish need apply," said Tristram.

Newman meditated awhile. "As a foreigner, no," he said at last; "I have no prejudices."

"My dear fellow, you have no suspicions!" cried Tristram. "You don't know what terrible customers these foreign women are; especially the 'magnificent' ones. How should you like a fair Circassian, with a dagger in her belt?"

Newman administered a vigorous slap to his knee. "I would marry a Japanese, if she pleased me," he affirmed.

"We had better confine ourselves to Europe," said Mrs. Tristram.

—Henry James, *The American* (1877)

 4

1877: The Instability of Race

Midway through *The American,* Valentin de Bellegard introduces his brother to James's prototypical American, remarking, "My brother is a great ethnologist." "An ethnologist? Ah," the American returns, "you collect negroes' skulls, and that sort of thing."[1] Although the reference to ethnology passes fleetingly as a textual oddity, James's concern throughout the novel is fundamentally "ethnological," and his ethnology is fundamentally racial. As the American makes his way through a maze of bewildering European social codes, he scans every face for clues as to proper bearing and deeper meaning. Likewise, as he seeks, then woos, and ultimately loses an aristocratic bride, the question of "pedigree"—his and hers—overwhelms the text. James becomes quietly preoccupied with race, and the narrative proceeds according to a kind of physiognomical surveillance by which every human face is made to tell. Of Lord Deepmere, for instance, the narrator remarks, "His physiognomy denoted great simplicity, a certain amount of brutishness, and a probable failure in the past to profit by rare educational advantages." ("Is he Irish?" Christopher Newman wants to know.)[2]

The racialist tensions within *The American*—the tension, for instance, between the sentiments "No Irish need apply" and "We had better confine ourselves to Europe" in Newman and the Tristrams' conversation about a suitable bride for the American—along with other cultural articulations from 1877, illuminate the instability of race as both an idiom of power and a category of perception. Not only do certain groups undergo a process of racial redefinition as shifting social and political circumstances require, but varying systems of "difference" can coexist and compete with one another at a given moment. One set of racial perceptions does not cleanly give way to the next. This was evident in the discussion of "Celtic" savagery and "Caucasian" entitlements during the draft riots of 1863; it was reflected in various court battles between the 1870s and the 1930s over who qualified as "free white persons" in naturalization law; and it was reflected in George Schuyler's deliberate dismantling of the Caucasian race in *Black No More* and in Laura Z. Hobson's conflicted view of racial Jewishness in *Gentleman's Agreement*.

There is nothing singular about the year 1877 when it comes to the discrepancy in racial classification, in other words. But given the problems of excavating archaic ways of seeing races, 1877 does provide an apt focal point for investigation. During that year race questions surfaced in every region of the country (and much of the wider world as well); the discourse of race addressed a range of pressing social and political questions; and the systems of race framing one debate did not necessarily suit the contours of the next. The Caucasians in one political context or in one locale might reappear, deeply divided, as Anglo-Saxons, Celts, and Hebrews in another.

Here is some of what was attracting racial attention in 1877: Reconstruction collapsed in the South, raising new questions about the relations among whites and blacks in an era of black Emancipation and the reintegration of the South into national political life. In the aftermath of Custer's demise the year before, the Great Sioux Wars ended with the defeat of the Minneconjou Sioux; Sitting Bull escaped to Canada, and Crazy Horse surrendered to federal troops. A vocal and often violent anti-Chinese movement coalesced in the West, particularly in California, where white workers decried the labor competition of "Mongolians" and insisted upon a "white man's republic." The East and Midwest, meanwhile, were wracked by labor unrest which raised questions in some quarters about the white immigrant working class itself. Members of the radical Irish Molly Maguires were on trial for murder in Pennsylvania; and reverberations of the Tweed scandal in New York continued to raise doubts about the Celtic proletariat there. Jewishness became a matter of intense debate following a Saratoga hotel's decision to bar Joseph Seligman, a prominent Jewish banker. A series of skirmishes (variously called "riots" and "raids") erupted between Mexicans and Americans along the nation's southwestern border. And, on the international scene, the Russo-Turkish war in the Caucasus ("the traditional cradle of the race," as *Harper's* put it) produced a rash of commentary on the "races of the Danube," while Henry Stanley's reports from Africa aroused tremendous popular enthusiasm for the white-over-black adventure of taming "the dark continent."[3]

In a discussion of the ideological power of travel writing as a genre, the sociologist Howard Winant has aptly noted, "We might usefully think of a racial *longue duree* in which the slow inscription of phenotypical signification took place upon the human body, in and through conquest and enslavement, to be sure, but also as an enormous act of expression, of narration."[4] As should be clear from this quick catalogue of the year's events, this glacial process has left in play multiple, contradictory racial understandings of who is who: competing "phenotypical significations" are etched upon the body (and the body politic) not only by the residual power of prior events and renewing acts of their cultural representation, but also by the untidiness of history itself.

A range of social, political, and economic encounters have been racially comprehended in U.S. history, and they carry, in their turn, a power to further define U.S. history in terms of race. These include European exploration (which generated and sustained a division between the white Christians of Europe and the nonwhite "heathens" of Africa, Asia, and the Americas); the conquest of North America (which similarly divided "white" rulers from subjugated "nonwhites," and "civilized" Europeans from "savage" Indians and "mongrelized" Mexicans); slavery and Emancipation (which divided white self-possessed citizens from black chattel, whites who were "fit" from blacks "unfit" for self-government); and immigration (which generated and sustained a division between those North and West Europeans who represented good material for citizenship from those South and East Europeans and Asians whose republican credentials were suspect).

Although these racial encounters do generally trace the nation's history as it unfolded across time in some semblance of succession, one phase never smoothly gave way to the next. Like any narrow sliver of time, then, the year 1877 is not simply a one-dimensional, static moment during the period of America's rapid industrialization. Rather, it embodies Winant's "slow inscription of phenotypical signification" in its entirety—European exploration (Stanley in Africa) *and* conquest (Miles and the Sioux, the Mexican border skirmishes) *and* slavery-Emancipation debates (the "redemption" of the South) *and* immigration (California's anti-Chinese agitation, the troubles with the Mollies, the flap over Seligman, the dramatic strike of "white" laborers in cities from Baltimore to St. Louis), all in the encompassing framework of capitalist development. And each of these historical stages, now contending at a single instant, produced its own particular patterns for seeing and understanding the world racially—its own racial mythologies, its own rivalries, and its own categories.

If race as a conceptual category is indeed a theory of history, then race as a *perceptual* category embodies that history in all its complexity and contradiction.[5] The racial conceptions of peoplehood generated during conquest—in California, say—may be partially effaced by secondary and tertiary inscriptions created by the anti-Chinese campaign or by the question of black-white segregation; but so may the initial inscription be reinforced by traditional narrations and ritual repetitions of the history of conquest, or rejuvenated by similar conquests in later periods. The "degenerate Mexicans" of 1840s imagery might become honorary "Caucasians" in the context of school segregation later in the century, only to be reinscribed as a dangerously shiftless and unassimilable element when Pancho Villa rides (or when intolerance of undocumented immigrants mounts in Pete Wilson's California).

Race is a palimpsest, a tablet whose most recent inscriptions only imperfectly cover those that had come before, and whose inscriptions can never be regarded as final. Contradictory racial identities come to coexist at the same moment in the same body in unstable combinations, as the specific histories that generated them linger in various cultural forms or in the social and political relationships that are their legacies. Thus it was, for instance, that Henry James drew his fateful racial line of exclusion both *within* and *around* Europe in his quest for a proper bride for the American: "No Irish need apply," "We had better confine ourselves to Europe."

Through the Lens of Race

Among the most telling snapshots of the complex, overlapping systems of racial differentiation at this moment is Charles Dudley Warner's two-volume sequence recounting his journey through northern Africa and the Near East, *Mummies and Moslems* (1876) and *In the Levant* (1877). Although Warner is now remembered almost exclusively for his collaboration with Mark Twain on *The Gilded Age,* his travel writings were widely read and frequently commented upon in the press at the time. Although the narrative is far removed from the American scene, Warner deployed a distinctly American—which is to say, racial—understanding of "difference," of the relationship among the world's peoples, of history and human progress, and of power, potentiality, and merit.

Warner's narrative is a rich, protracted musing on "difference." Like James's prototypical American, Warner himself is ceaselessly scanning the human landscape, and both *Mummies and Moslems* and *In the Levant* become not geographical travelogues merely, but physiognomical tours of the region's "shifting kaleidoscope of races, colors, and graceful attitudes."[6] Indeed, Warner's fascination with skin color, features, physiognomy, and body type is tireless, "such a display of bare legs and swarthy figures" does this part of the world offer up. "Look! that's an East Indian, that's a Greek, that's a Turk, that's a Syrian-Jew? No, he's Egyptian, the crooked nose is not uncommon to Egyptians."

> And what a cosmopolitan place [Alexandria] is. We meet Turks, Greeks, Copts, Egyptians, Nubians, Syrians, Armenians, Italians; tattered derweeshes, "weelies" or holy Moslems, nearly naked, presenting the appearance of men who have been buried a long time and recently dug up; Greek priests, Jews, Persian Parsees, Algerines, Hindoos, negroes from Darfoor, and flat-nosed blacks from beyond Khartoum.

"The complexions exhaust the possibilities of human color," Warner exclaims.[7]

Warner thus offers a remarkably unself-conscious portrait of an American racial sensibility. From the opening pages onward any discussion is apt to come to rest on the image of "a stalwart, wild-eyed son of the sand, coal-black," "a yellow-skinned, cunning-eyed conjurer," "a fat negress . . . whose jet face has taken an incredible polish; only the most accomplished bootblack could raise such a shine on a shoe," a "pathetic-eyed little Jew [who] makes me feel that I am oppressing his race," "a negro, who puts all the fervor of the tropics into his [praying] . . . his black skin shines with moisture; there is, too, in his swaying and bowing, an *abandon,* a laxity of muscles, and a sort of jerk that belong only to his sympathetic race," "a perfect Congo negro in features and texture of skin—lips protruding and nose absolutely level with his cheeks; as faithful and affectionate as a Newfoundland dog," "antic crews of Nubians whose ebony bodies shine in the sun," "a company of Arab acrobats and pyramid-builders, their swarthy bodies shining in the white sunlight," "sharp-faced Greeks, impudent Jews, fair-faced women from Bethlehem, sleek Armenians," "light-haired barbarians from the Caucasus, dark-skinned men and women from Moscow . . . simple, rude, honest, clumsy boors," or "[Albanian Gypsy women, who] preserve, in their swarthy complexions, burning black eyes, and jet black hair, the characteristics of some savage Oriental tribe . . . it was a wild beauty which woman sometimes shares with the panther."[8] Warner's judgment concerning Jerusalem fairly captures his overall assessment of the peoples encountered throughout his trek: "Now and then . . . we saw a good face, a noble countenance . . . but the most whom we met were debased, misbegotten, the remnants of sin, squalor, and bad living."[9]

Undergirding these observations all along is a tacit theory of history by which physical facts presumably reflect underlying principles and grand historical forces. The glistening dark skins, hooked noses, and jet black eyes of Africa and the Levant all offer eloquent, indisputable comment on larger themes of civilization, barbarism, and savagery. To be "debased" *is* to be "misbegotten," in Warner's view, and "begetting" always denotes lineage-as-race. Race thus provides the necessary legend for mapping human history, even as it provides the physical proof that, when it comes to questions of relative merit of the world's peoples, history does not lie. That the inhabitants of modern Egypt suffer from a profound social and cultural stasis, for example, is intimately related to the "facts" attending their lineage: "Here the mongrel subjects of the Khedive, a mixture of ancient Egyptian, conquering Arabian, subject Nubian, enslaved Soudan, inheritors of all civilizations and appropriators of none, kennel amid these historic ash-heaps, caring for neither their past nor their future." The modern Greeks, too, are but "mongrel inheritors of the ancient [Greek] soil," "unappreciative possessors" of the ruins of what was once a "splendid civilization."[10] There is perhaps no worse crime than to be a "mongrel"—or to be, in Warner's own recurring phrase, "hopelessly mixed"—but, conveniently, to be a mongrel entails its own harsh historical punishments.

Ultimately, all racial logic leads back to the United States. If Warner himself seems most interested in "Oriental" physiognomy as a reflection of "Oriental" debasement, the text continuously evokes narrator and reader as a collective Euro-American "we" whose own physiognomy and history are normalized through the constant measurement of Levantine and African "difference." Significantly, though, this "we" is itself unstable, sometimes "white," sometimes "Caucasian," sometimes "English." Warner renders the Levant *through* the multiple lenses of American racial thinking, in other words; and in doing so he recreates his ("white") narrator-reader as precisely the racial palimpsest which is a product of the race-inscribing process of American conquest, enslavement, emancipation, and immigration.

The central reference point in Warner's cosmology of "difference," not surprisingly, is the distinction between "civilization" on the one hand and "barbarism" or "savagery" on the other, always keyed to whiteness and its Others. Upon meeting a certain European on his travels, Warner comments, "We were civilized beings, met by chance in a barbarous place." He renders the rhythmic chant of Nubian oarsmen as a "weird, barbarous refrain." At a certain African marketplace "the crowd hustles about us in a troublesome manner, showing special curiosity about the ladies, as if they had rarely seen white women . . . we learn that the natives 'not like you.' The feeling is mutual, though it is discouraging to our pride to be despised by such barbarous half-clad folk."[11]

Layered atop this general concern for shades of skin color and shades of "civilization" is an attention to lineage—musings upon the relative authenticity, purity, or contamination of a given people, linked to their racial history (most often a history of decline) and to their current moral or social condition (usually a condition of abjection). Thus some dancers encountered in Egypt "claim to be an unmixed race of ancient lineage; but I suspect their blood is no purer than their morals. There is not much in Egypt that is *not* hopelessly mixed." The "Levantines" of Smyrna are "descendants of the marriage of Europeans with Greek and Jewish women . . . But the race is said to be not self-sustaining, and is yielding to the original types."[12] In this vein, as noted above, the population of modern Greece comes in for harsh treatment, as mongrelized squanderers of a rich tradition.

Another tier in Warner's ideological edifice consists of a web of exegesis by which the human spectacle of Africa and the Levant seems to exist solely for the comment it offers upon the United States—upon its innate superiority as a civilization, and upon the troubling inferiority of some of its inhabitants. Observing a group of Bedouin dancers, for instance, Warner remarks that "their eyes shine with animal wildness." "It seems to be precisely the dance of North American Indians," he concludes. On a group of Moslem mourners, again, "You would not see in farthest Nubia a more barbarous assemblage, and not so fierce an one. In the presence of these wild mourners the term 'gentler sex' has a ludicrous sound . . . most of them were flamingly ugly, and—to liken them to what they most resembled—physically and mentally the type of the North American squaws." On another encounter down the Nile, "This group composes as barbaric a picture as one can anywhere see. I need not have gone so far to see such a miserable group; I could have found one as wretched in Pigville (every city has its Pigville?). Yes, but this is characteristic of the country. These people are as good as anyone here."[13]

Peoples encountered along the way thus highlight the incomparable civilization of the United States by their stunning contrast to it, or they evoke the few truly unfortunate elements within the United States ("North American squaws," the people of "Pigville"). But in conjuring the image of America's "savages," the sight of the Bedouin or Moslem yet again redoubles the overall sense of U.S. superiority, for *here* in the region of the Nile such a wretched level of existence "is characteristic of the country." Warner looks upon Africa and the Levant with a racial gaze that is distinctly American, then offers up a narrative version of these regions as objective proof of the very "truths" of American life that had created his racial gaze in the first place.

Most telling in the present connection are Warner's remarks not about "squaws" or "savages" but about those populations who by custom (and law) were "white" in the United States. His brief reflection on the Irish in the United States as he observes a street scene in Cairo is symptomatic. After describing at some length the physique and the occupation of a *sais*—a "slender handsome black fellow, probably a Nubian," who runs before carriages in order to clear the way through the busy thoroughfares—he pauses to consider whether such a custom could be established back home. "If they could not be naturalized in Central Park," he muses, "it might fill some of the requirements of luxury to train a patriot from the Green Isle to run before the horses, in knee breeches, flourishing a shillalah. Faith, I think he would clear the way."[14] The turn of mind by which Warner so effortlessly moves from the body of the "Nubian" to the "patriot of the Green Isle" underscores the racial niche the Irish occupy in his thinking, just as the simplicity with which he "naturalizes" the Irish *in place of* the "Nubian" for duty in Central Park underscores his overarching sense that "whiteness" and "Americanness" are inextricably entwined.

As are "whiteness" and Christianity. This becomes clear in Warner's lengthy passages on the Jews of the Levant. Seeking a glimpse of "real Jews of the type that inhabited [Jerusalem] at the time of our Lord," for instance, Warner discovered that "the persons whom we are accustomed to call Jews . . . have the Assyrian features, the hook nose, dark hair and eyes, and not at all the faces of the fair-haired race from which our Savior is supposed to have sprung."[15] One member of the "tribe of Benjamin," as Warner identifies him, is "the most unpleasant human being I have ever encountered . . . a dark, corkscrew, stringy curl hanging down each side of his face, and the appearance of nasty effeminacy which this gives cannot be described." "If this is a specimen of the restoration of the Jews," he concludes, "they had better not be restored any more." Simply put, "we find it easier to feel that Christ was born in New England than in Judea."[16]

His mercurial assessment of Greeks, too, hints at the instability of whiteness within this overarching framework of "civilization" and "savagery." On the one hand, "it would puzzle one to say of what race the person calling himself a modern Greek is." Judging by "types of face" alone, modern Greeks' relation to ancient Athenians seemed "no stronger than that of Englishmen to the ancient Britons." (Here he goes on to pass judgment on their mongrelization.) But on the other hand, when the context shifts the Greek can stand in for an unalloyed white "purity" worthy of D. W. Griffith or Louisiana's White League. Upon meeting the Greek wife of a Syrian merchant, Warner gushes, "Her fair complexion was touched by the sun and radiant with health. Her blue eyes danced with the pleasure of living . . . After our long regimen of the hideous women of the Nile, plastered with dirt, soaked in oil, and hung with tawdry ornaments, it may be imagined how welcome was this vision of a woman, handsome, natural, and clean, with neither the shyness of an animal nor the brazenness of a Ghawazee."[17]

As the Irish, Jews, and Greeks pass through their vicissitudes in the kaleidoscopic racial setting of Africa and the Near East, so, too, do Warner's idealized, disembodied readers—his imagined community of narrative fellow-travelers. Who is the "we" constituted by the racial syntax of Warner's narrative? "In the vales of the Caucasus, we are taught," he remarks, "our race has attained its most perfect form; in other days its men were as renowned for strength and valor as its women for beauty."[18] Elsewhere, however, he finds local anti-English sentiment to be "rather humiliating to us Americans, who are, after all, almost blood-relations of the English; . . . we are often taken for *Inglese,* in the villages where few strangers go."[19] "We" refers, by turns, to men who are "white" and who are jealous of "our" white women; to Europeans and Euro-Americans *excluding Jews, Greeks, and Irish;* to "Caucasians" who find their perfect form attained "in the vales of the Caucasus"; or to those who are "almost blood-relatives" of the English and are often mistaken for "Inglese." Such discrepancies throughout *Mummies and Moslems* and *In the Levant* are not inconsistencies, exactly: they faithfully replicate the palimpsestic inscriptions of race upon both the body and the imagination in American culture at large, as year upon year of exploration, conquest, slavery, emancipation, and immigration has multiplied the meanings of race.

The Encounter with Africans on Two Continents

A satirical piece entitled "The Origin of Man, by Darwin" that appeared in *Harper's New Monthly Magazine* in September 1877 exposes the bedrock, white-over-nonwhite assumptions undergirding the various American schemes of "difference" and differentiation. In response to her daughter's lament that their family was different from everyone else in the "tribe," a chimpanzee mother explains with great portent that this "difference" is not a mark of shame but a badge of pride. "It is a distinction. We are a higher race," she explains. "We are advancing, my dear. *You are whiter than I am.*"[20] The crude Darwinism and the blatant white supremacism of this piece were common enough in far more serious venues. According to an early *Visitor's Guide* to the newly opened American Museum of Natural History, for instance, the text of the Hall of Mammals began with this brief lesson in biology: "In deference to Man's superior estate he may well be left free from classification. It is, however, well to observe in this connection some of the lower examples of the human race." Casing number one exhibited "the Australians, represented by several skeletons." (The next several cases contained gorillas, orang-outans, and gibbons.)[21] Anthropologists at the time likewise reported fresh research comparing the surfaces of the brain among the "Gorilla," "Chimpanzee," "Orang," "Bush-woman," and the "European."[22] And in a section entitled "The Races of Man," *Intermediate Geography* (1877), a text for grade school children, reported rather matter-of-factly that "the *white* race is superior to all others"; "the nations of western Europe, and their descendants in all parts of the world, are the most highly civilized."[23] The fundamental distinction between civilization-as-whiteness and savagery-as-nonwhiteness retained tremendous power, even centuries after the original encounter.

Americans in 1877 could vicariously participate in the original phase of encounter through heavily romantic popular accounts of white explorations around the globe—in the Caribbean and the Pacific, in South America, and particularly in Africa. In March the New York *Herald* recounted a fierce conflict between "natives" and "white men" aboard a New York schooner in the Congo. The violence ended when the agent of a Dutch trading house "and about ten other Europeans or white men, all well armed, came over with about a hundred Kroomen and drove the natives out of the ship."[24] Whereas scholars like David Spurr and Michael Hunt have illuminated the influence of race thinking on colonial power, I am most interested here in the secondary power of imperialism to generate and regenerate races themselves. If imperial power and imperial wealth were the work of such expeditions, the manufacture of "Europeans or white men" (as consanguine with one another and as superior to the rest) was the central ideological work of popular journalistic accounts of them.

In this vein Colonel C. Chaille Long's *Central Africa* promised to deliver the "naked truths of a naked people." As one reviewer noted of "the dismal repulsiveness of the people" described in Long's account, "The hope of evangelizing Africa which Livingstone had awakened is dimmed by reading of the barbaric hospitality of M'Tse."[25] Similarly, middle-class journals like *Atlantic Monthly* and *Harper's* took readers on periodic excursions to "Barbadoes," "Among the Atlantic Islands," or "Across Africa." Here readers learned, for example, that "the Barbadian negro is *sui generis;* there is nothing like him on earth, above it, or under it. He will lie, cheat, and steal beyond all comprehension. He is impudent to a degree hardly to be understood by an American"; the Azores are characterized by "spectacles of human degradation and misery"; and the "men of Manyuema" in Africa, "although endowed with many good qualities . . . are cannibals, and most filthy cannibals."[26]

The most avidly followed accounts of the era were the dispatches from Henry Stanley in Africa to the New York *Herald*. Here, under subheads such as "Stanley the First White Man on the Ubwari Hills," *Herald* readers could enjoy descriptions of the "impenetrably savage countries west of the Burton Gulf."[27] Though focusing primarily upon the geographical "mysteries" of the region, Stanley's accounts and other dispatches from the Congo did offer American readers access to the peoples of "dark Africa": in Stanley's case, a prolonged history of European attempts to dis-

cover the source of the Nile led to a meditation on the comparative epistemologies of Europeans and Africans, as he found himself so much at
the mercy of local knowledge. As Stanley explained, "native and Arab"
statements were "not to be understood, by any means, as conveying accurate and exact information. Even the most intelligent of Arabs, Wau-
guana, Wasawhili, and Central Africa natives, as if they were originally
taken out of the same matrix, have a prurient palate for exaggeration."
This discussion (which appeared under the telling subhead "Native Statements and Explorer's Facts") ended with the sober judgment, "The best
weapon an explorer can arm himself with is distrust."[28]

But distrust was decidedly *not* the "best weapon" an explorer might
carry, according to these same accounts—indeed, actual warfare and the
weapons required became the point of most dispatches. (The very page
of the *Herald* that contained Stanley's musings on European and African
regimes of knowledge also contained a spectacular report under the heading "New York Schooner Plundered and Burned by Savages on the Congo
River.") Stanley's dispatches later in the year dramatically raised the specter of "Terrible Tribes of Cannibals." Commenting upon Livingstone's
earlier confusion over whether a certain stretch of the Lualaba (Congo)
River had been the Nile, Stanley asserted that an explorer of Livingstone's
reputation "certainly wouldn't attempt the foolhardy feat of following it
in canoes, and risk becoming black man's meat," unless he had thought
it as grand a discovery as the Nile itself. The sensational prospect of
becoming "black man's meat" was among the recurring motifs in *Herald*
reportage. On the Wabroire tribe and the "warlike Bakusu," Stanley sur-
mised that "the approaches of a whole congress of bishops and missionaries could have no effect, except as native 'roast beef.'" Or again, the
Herald's favorite quotation attributed to Livingstone, "You may say there
are cannibals who will eat me. It may be true; but I have one comfort,
they cannot eat me before they kill me. Can they?"[29]

Cannibalism is but one recurring image in a broader theme of irrec-
oncilable human differences. As Stanley renders this "region of fable and
mystery—a continent of dwarfs and cannibals and gorillas" for readers
in Europe and the United States, his subtext becomes the tremendous gulf
separating whites from the rest of the world's peoples. This gulf is evoked
by the specter of cannibalism, and by the degree of immutable "difference" implied by the very language of description—the Wenya, for instance, are "singularly cowardly, but also singularly treacherous and
crafty." Further, when Stanley tallies the losses incurred by the expedition,

he reports, "Our losses in men are one European and thirty-four Wan-guana." (Here and elsewhere he launches into a prolonged obituary of that "one European.") Or again, "difference" is evoked by the Europeans' own "curious" appearance, reflected back to them in the "natives'" re-actions: "We were allowed to proceed without violence, more as strange curiosities than anything else," Stanley reports, perhaps because they had come from the direction of "wild lands whither the white people had never ventured before." In a later encounter with "ferocious savages," "the na-tives had never heard of white men . . . neither could they possibly un-derstand what advantage white men or black men could gain by attempt-ing to begin an acquaintance."[30] The impassable gulf separating white from black became starker still in November, under the *Herald* banner, "Desperate Encounters with Swarms of Cannibals . . . A Picture of Savage Warfare." "We soon became acquainted with the worst side of the na-tives," reported Stanley, "and they presently demonstrated their wild-ness." This was to be the explorers' "initiation to savage warfare": "They came to fight. The cruel faces, the loudly triumphant drums, the deafening horns, the launched spears, the swaying bodies, all proved it." Stanley's men defeated these tribes and then plundered their temple for ivory.[31]

The original phase of Winant's long-enduring process of racial inscrip-tion—exploration and encounter—left as its legacy certain social relations pertaining to slavery on the one hand and conquest on the other, and in the United States these social relations were now perpetually buttressed by the ideological framework of "civilization" and "savagery," whiteness and its Others. Popular accounts like Henry Stanley's thus participated in live questions of political economy in significant ways. It is not merely a passing curiosity, for instance, that the *Herald*'s rendition of Stanley's "Picture of Savage Warfare" was directly adjacent to an article on Sitting Bull and the Sioux Wars. Nor is it of small consequence that explorers' depictions of "darkest Africa" appeared at a moment when the question of Negro citizenship in the United States was so hotly contested. Within the context of contemporary American political culture, the unstated but obvious ideological portent in these travel accounts was their comment upon African-Americans' fitness for self-government, or the "proof" they offered of how much better off Africans were in America, centuries of slavery notwithstanding.

Domestically, the white-over-black dynamic of racial inscription that animated Stanley's African adventures was most pressing as the Recon-struction South rapidly became the *post*-Reconstruction South upon the withdrawal of Northern troops and amid a rising national rhetoric of conciliation and reunion. "With respect to the two distinct races whose peculiar relations to each other have brought upon us the deplorable complications and perplexities which exist in those [Southern] states," intoned Rutherford B. Hayes in his inaugural address in March, "[ours] must be a government which guards the interests of both races carefully and equally." "It is my earnest desire to regard and promote . . . the interests of the white and of the colored people, both equally," he reiterated, ". . . and to put forth my best efforts on behalf of a civil policy which will forever wipe out in our political affairs the color line and the distinctions between North and South."[32] As we now know, over time the effacement of "distinctions between North and South" was accomplished in part through a *perpetuation* of the "color line," despite Hayes's plea for "the united and harmonious efforts of both races."[33] Political alignment and conduct in the South in 1877, and the fractious contests over the region's political fate, demonstrate the power of the white-black dyad to frame social relations and to determine Americans' social imagination.

Among the more painstaking contemporary examinations of Reconstruction, its legacies for the Southern polity, and its collapse—and thus among the more complete accounts of race as the enduring organizing principle of the New South—was the 1877 congressional investigation of fraud in Louisiana's 1876 elections. The Democrat Tilden had won Louisiana by a margin of 80,831 to Hayes's 74,426 (even though Republicans claimed that "the excess colored over white voters in Louisiana is one thousand"), and so questions arose concerning the integrity of the election supervision and the real political freedom of the state's "colored" voters. As one legislator put it, "Long years of misgovernment, such as that which has existed in Louisiana, with the disorder growing out of the late war, left many reckless and evil-disposed persons in the State, who have little regard for the rights of white and still less for the rights of black men."[34] The binary logic of a polity thus divided into "white" and "black" would have a greater and greater purchase on the nation's political life from the post–Reconstruction era on; and obviously this was of no little consequence for those "whites" who, like Charles Dudley Warner's Jews, were said in other contexts to have "not at all the faces of the fair-haired race from which our Savior is supposed to have sprung."[35]

The majority and minority reports of the House Special Committee on the Louisiana Elections present a tapestry of election-time violence. Taken together, the reports testify to "whipping and other violence"; "intimidation"; acts of "unjustifiable mischief" (including whites' "firing several shots in the evening against a colored church"); the organization of rifle clubs; and the nightriding activities of white-supremacist "bulldozers" and "regulators" carrying out "bloody and cowardly massacres," "whipping, hanging, shooting, and driving off colored Republicans."[36]

More telling still, however, are these reports' competing, race-based theories of the workings of the Southern polity in the wake of the Civil War. Even more than the descriptions of racial violence contained within them, the reports' *interpretations* of that violence demonstrate the power of race in framing the political life of the post-Reconstruction South. The majority report, highly sympathetic with the Louisiana Democrats (and thus with the agenda of white supremacy), interpreted the election-time violence as either black assaults on white Democrats, or, more often, white Republicans' assaults on black Democrats. According to this version, blacks' initial postwar "delusion of '40 acres and a mule' " had given way to "stern realities"; and thus, quite rightly, through disenchantment and impatience many blacks were now simply "no longer Republicans." The villains of this story of intimidation, then, are white Republican leaders who claimed a "proprietary right in the vote of the colored man. They regarded him as a mere political machine of their own invention." Black voters had properly rebelled against such political subservence. In this scenario, recent violence could be attributed to a cynical and rapacious Republican party: "Prominent Republicans considered the killing of a black man in Louisiana as equivalent to fifty thousand dollars of a campaign fund for the party ... Every homicide in which a colored man chanced to be the victim was seized upon with avidity, telegraphed over the North, and reckoned as a substantial addition to their party strength." Thus the House committee held white—and some black—Republicans accountable for "intimidation" practiced against "the inoffensive colored man" who had merely tried to break a vicious, Reconstruction-era Republican monopoly.[37]

The committee's minority report, by contrast, set election-time violence in a context of white-supremacist resistance to the aims of Reconstruction, stressing white-supremacist terror for (Democratic) political purposes. The minority recalled the rise of the Knights of the White Camelia in 1868, and their "distinctly bloody and cowardly massacres of colored people ... for political purposes and political effect," violent antiblack outbreaks at Saint Landrey, Bossier, Caddo, Jefferson, and Saint Bernard resulting in more than seven hundred Negro deaths. It recounted as well the emergence of the "White League" in 1874, an association of white Democrats "united for the express purpose of asserting the superiority of the white race in political matters." In his appearance before the committee, one witness testified that pre-election terror was so intense that "the plan of these people was to get the colored people so badly cowed before the election that they would do anything that they told them."

> Q: Your idea is that on election day it was not necessary to have any intimidation?
> A: No, sir; I never saw a more quiet election.[38]

In substantiation of this interpretation, the minority recounted the dramatic rising of the White League in New Orleans, which had effectively driven the Reconstruction government out of the Capitol: "More than two thousand men answered the summons and fell into line of battle with the promptness and accuracy which only drill and experience in arms can give." This well-trained white army then went on to take over the city's chief political and military institutions, demonstrating "the deliberate and settled determination of the white people, acting in the name of democracy, not to permit the exercise of political power by the blacks." "Educated whites look upon negro citizenship as a badge of humiliation," argued this second report; others "find free negro labor in constant and damaging competition." Thus the terror surrounding Louisiana's election was plain in its motivations and obvious in its source. In response to the majority report's assertion that most of the violence had been carried out against black voters eager to defect from the Republican party, the minority flatly declared,

> Neither bribery, nor interest, nor soft words, nor condescension, nor proof of misrule by local officers, nor even violence, can shake the deep-rooted love of the liberated black man for the party whose greatest achievement was universal emancipation and universal citizenship . . . The instant he is let alone, the moment the load of fear is taken off, the moment he dare stand up in his own right and his own strength, free to think, free to act, and free to choose, that moment he stands up ready and willing to vote the Republican ticket. For the negro, although unlearned, is no fool.

Representative Charles Joyce of Vermont concluded that, "had the colored people in those parishes been left free to vote as they pleased, the

Republican majority would have reached at least fifteen hundred or two thousand upon the most liberal count for the Democratic ticket."[39]

Although the Democrats of the solid South most often employed the rhetoric of "white men's government," it is worth noting that the heightened, self-conscious diction of "Caucasian" identity and supremacy did cross over from scientific discourse into street-level, vernacular usage in parts of the South as early as the 1860s. As one Louisiana newspaper had framed the matter in 1868, "Inducements to negroes to vote, involving directly or indirectly a promise of future advancement, are pregnant with future disaster and disgrace. *The Caucasian needs not to kneel to any other race.*" In Louisiana itself the Knights of the White Camelia, a forerunner of the White League, drew upon both racial designations in its "Charge to Initiates." The order's

> main and fundamental object is the MAINTENANCE OF THE SUPREM-
> ACY OF THE WHITE RACE in this republic. History and physiology
> teach us that we belong to a race which nature has endowed with an
> evident superiority over all other races . . . And it is a remarkable
> fact that as a race of men is more remote from the Caucasian and
> approaches nearer the black African, the more fatally that stamp of
> inferiority is affixed to its sons, and irrevocably dooms them to eter-
> nal imperfectability and degradation.[40]

As the umbrella organization of the Knights of the White Camelia waned in 1869, many local groups changed their name to "Caucasian Clubs." As had been the case with New York's white coalition behind the banner of the *Weekly Caucasian* during the Civil War, the diversity of the region's "white persons" perhaps explains the political appeal of a scientifically based appellation like "Caucasian." Louisiana was, in one historian's words, "the most heterogeneous place in the South."[41] But whether "white" or "Caucasian," antiblack forces in the South—like the national debate about their reentry into national life—tended sharply to divide the polity into two races, neither more nor less, precisely after the fashion of Stanley's popular accounts of latter-day "encounters" with the African in "darkest Africa."

Frontier Encounters with Indians, Mexicans, and Asians

An organized police power is "clearly necessary in the Indian country and on the Mexican frontier," warned *Harper's* in a typical piece entitled "The

Regular Army." While whites sought to wrest any semblance of political liberty from the recently liberated blacks of the Southern states, legislators, cavalrymen, and the "white" settlers of various "frontier" communities in 1877 wrestled with the practical questions attending the tensions, skirmishes, and outright warfare between whites and nonwhites in the West. As a popular ballad from the era of the Mexican War had warned, "the savage is over the border, / the savage is over the border." This "savage" remained as important as the border itself in marking the compass of the American nation. Frontier contingencies combined with rhetorical indulgences to invest American nationalism with perpetual appeals to "civilization" and "savagery," to "white" conquest and the defeat of the (always dark) Other. The comprehension of frontier realities, like the comprehension of the post-Reconstruction South, rested upon a racial syntax of simple whiteness and its others.[42]

As one *Harper's* piece on the nation's newest frontier—Alaska—remarked, the Eskimo "is a very different fellow in most respects from the savage with whom we are all pretty well acquainted."[43] The combination of their presumed "savagery" and the extent to which "we are all pretty well acquainted" with them renders "savages" important figures in the ideology of American nationalism and narratives of national belonging. By both their geographical position along the (white) republic's frontiers, and their ethnological position somewhere beneath the capacity for civilization, "savages" mark precisely the point where the American polity leaves off and the realm of degeneracy and chaos begins. Indeed, the "savages'" only redemption lies in their approximating whiteness itself—tribes may be suffered within our national boundaries, so long as they can "live like white men," as one 1877 treaty put it.[44]

As the Forty-fourth Congress considered an Indian Appropriation Bill concerning "contingent expenses of the Indian Department" and "treaty stipulations with various Indian tribes," debate repeatedly fell to the question of what "barbarous" or "savage" peoples *need,* and hence their comparison with "whites." As Senator Bogy of Missouri asked with unconcealed contempt, "What do these [Osage] Indians want? They have their ponies, their guns, their ammunition. Was it liquors or oysters or what?" He later asserted, "A white man, a hunter, could make a living in that country at any time under any circumstances." Later in the same debate, federal spending on the Osages pivoted on a heated exchange over whether Osages were in fact "the wealthiest community upon this continent, whether white, black, or any other color," or whether "it is nonsense to talk about their being a civilized tribe . . . They are wild as almost any Indians." "There is not a full-blooded Indian among them who wears white men's clothes," asserted one legislator; "they are in a state of barbarism." (But the Pawnees, he did have to concede, "are well advanced for Indians.")[45]

Similarly, one treaty which Congress took under discussion provided that the Sioux "may eventually become self-supporting and acquire the arts of civilized life." To that end, five Sioux delegates were to visit Indian Territory, and if they liked it, the tribe would move there within a year. "The Government may provide for them in the selection of a country suitable for a permanent home, where they may live like white men," the treaty read, although one senator did object to establishing these "wild Indians" where they might threaten slightly more "civilized" tribes who were "assimilating as near as their nature will admit to [the habits] of their white brethren."[46]

Security along the Mexican border represented yet another "frontier" concern of the Forty-fourth Congress. In August an armed band broke into a Starr City, Texas, jail to release two Mexican prisoners, killing the jailor and his wife. For the Texas delegation this was clearly a racial issue. These bandits were "of Mexican blood," observed Congressman Maxie; "perhaps there is not within the broad limits of civilized nations a more accursed population." "We know that the people over there are aliens to us in blood, aliens to us in their social habits and political education, aliens to us in every sense of the word." In response the Texans wanted a greater military appropriation on the part of Congress: "True economy tells us, in dealing with Mexicans and Indians, who respect nothing but visible physical power, place enough of that power in sight, overawe them and thus prevent war." Recent events offered the most persuasive argument imaginable, as far as the Texans were concerned, and they did not hesitate to lay the corpses of the white martyrs of Little Bighorn at the doorstep of Congress itself: "Had the Indian frontier been defended properly . . . there would have been no massacre of General Custer and his men . . . These men [Indian or Mexican savages] fear power, and it is all they do fear." Later in this discussion of military necessity, Maxie implored his colleagues to "give ample protection from the tomahawk of the savage" by placing military personnel "along the entire Indian line, wherever they are needed for protection of the frontiersmen, their wives and their children."[47] Most interesting is the conflation of Mexicans with Indians— and the powerful ideological effect this blanket notion of savagery has in homogenizing the imagined community of a white, "civilized" United States.

The Chinese Question in California and the West led Congress still further into a consideration of the legacies of conquest and the social relations of encounter. As scholars like Stuart Creighton Miller and Su-cheng Chan have argued, imperialism itself is the proper context within which the history of Chinese immigration must be situated and understood. Ideologically, white Americans came to "know" the Chinese through the images and reports provided by the missionaries, merchants, and diplomats engaged in the early "opening" of the "Orient." Materially, migration was encouraged and made possible by the dislocations in Asia associated with an increasing Western economic presence, by the new steam routes and the accessibility of travel, and by American continental expansionism and the industrialization of the West—particularly the rise of the railroad, the single largest employer of Chinese labor.[48] As ever, the presence of a sizable nonwhite population raised concerns over the workings of the self-governing republic and the boundaries of the polity.

On February 28, 1877, the House received the "Report of the Joint Special Committee to Investigate Chinese Immigration." The document is at once a reaffirmation of the 1790 principle that republican institutions require a "white" polity, and an endorsement of popular labor arguments for the primacy of "white" interests in the marketplace. In its uneven rhetoric of race the document moves from a competition between "Chinese" and "whites" to one between "Asiatics" and "Caucasians." The report's authority thus comes finally to rest upon the principle of "Caucasian" superiority.

The report begins with standard assertions of the economic yellow peril and its menacing implications for "white" laborers: Chinese workers "have reduced wages to what would be starvation prices for white men and women," "there is a lack of employment for whites," unabated Chinese immigration threatens to "degrade all white working people to the abject condition of a servile class." It then goes on to assert that, economics aside, "the safety of republican institutions requires that the exercise of the franchise shall be only by those who have a love and appreciation for our institutions, and this rule excludes the great mass of the Chinese from the ballot as a necessary measure for public safety." As discussion moves to the political demands of a smoothly functioning republic, the appellation "Chinese" quietly gives way to the ethnological category

"Mongolian": "The Mongolian race seems to have no desire for progress and to have no conception of representative and free institutions."

> Testimony was further taken upon the question of any radical differences existing between the Asiatic and Caucasian races, and in the evidence will be found much valuable information upon this point peculiarly interesting to the ethnologist. The deduction from the testimony taken by the committee on this point would seem to be that there is not sufficient brain capacity in the Chinese to furnish motive power for self-government. Upon the point of morals, there is no Aryan or European race which is not far superior to the Chinese as a class.[49]

As Alexander Saxton has documented, many anti-Chinese agitators in California and elsewhere were Irish, including one of the movement's most vocal leaders, Dennis Kearney. Thus even sympathetic treatments of Chinese immigrants in the popular press tended to embody their own brand of nativism. The *Argonaut*, for instance, would later decry "the refuse and sweeping of Europe, the ignorant, brutal, idle off-scourings of civilization, [who] meet weekly upon the Sand Lot in San Francisco, to determine whether respectable, industrious foreign-born citizens and native-born Americans shall be permitted to treat Chinese humanely and employ them in business ventures, or unite with this idle and worthless foreign gang in driving them into the sea."[50] Another observer of West Coast politics later recalled:

> There appeared on the scene [in Seattle] an Irish agitator from California, who proceeded to harangue the laboring people, and to organize them into lodges of the Knights of Labor . . . We had turned loose on us one wild Irishman, and out of his communistic heart has sprung a phantom whose shadow has darkened the whole Northwest coast, and whose tread has made our whole young city shake with terror. The mayor of Tacoma . . . is a German liquor-dealer, who can only make the blindest stagger toward speaking the English language. His family is yet in Germany, and all his money not spent on beer or anti-Chinese demonstrations goes back to the Fatherland.[51]

Hence the rhetoric and visual lexicon of pan–white supremacy had a particular appeal in the political culture of the West from the 1870s onward. According to an 1870 tract by John Swinton, for instance, "the ground of race" was among the chief reasons for opposing Asian immigration. Race, by this account, "is at once the beginning of history and the summing up of history." "The people of the United States are of the white European race, the Japhetic stock, from which have sprung the Germanic, Celtic, and Latin varieties—all immediately related to each other by historical terms . . . the life, genius, and power of the American republic is with the European race."[52] Although Swinton did not refer to "Caucasians," he did lay the groundwork for a scientific, racial discussion of the immigration question that would pit "Mongolians" (a term he did use) against "white Europeans"—this latter constituting one consanguine "stock" encompassing a number of "varieties." The central question in the ensuing debate over Chinese immigration, then, was "blood," as when ex-Governor Horatio Seymour of New York told a rally of anti-Chinese workers, "Europeans do not overthrow our customs, religion, or civilization. They do not bring here any strange blood."[53] An *Atlantic Monthly* piece in 1871, too, worried that in recent years "while the rate of Caucasian immigration was decreasing, that of the Mongolian was increasing . . . the steady gain of the percentage of the latter over the former was not an auspicious portent."[54] The "Caucasian race" was a construction that crossed well into the popular, even in cases where it was a term of sardonic opprobrium, as when, in "Wan Lee, the Pagan," Bret Harte wrote that the boy delighted to walk to school with a certain classmate and to carry her books, "a service always fraught with danger to him from the little hands of his Caucasian Christian brothers."[55]

By April 1877 the anti-Chinese movement was rising to high tide, and the press was abuzz with the emergence of a new secret political order in San Francisco, The Order of Caucasians, whose professed aim was to "drive Chinese out of California." The order represented but a late development in a fierce campaign that had been mounting among California's "white" workers since early in the 1870s. As the order's byzantine by-laws announced, "Each camp and every individual Caucasian, and every encampment, pledges to each and every merchant, manufacturer, and trader, traveler, mechanic, and laborer . . . all their combined influence, power, advertisement, and patronage; and shall oppose to annihilation by every manner and means within the thin gauze of the law all others." This pledge amounted to the "bounden and solemn duty" of every Caucasian to "pursue and injure" two classes of "enemies": class A (persons who hire or rent to "Mongolians" or who "countenance their

be achieved. The Huguenots in England and the United States who have intermingled with the Saxon stock have developed some of the finest race qualities to be found on either continent.[62]

Racial conceptions of peoplehood also typically framed popular discussion of the Russo-Turkish War, "the contest that shakes the historic Danube and echoes among the Caucasus and around the traditional cradle of the race." Indeed, it was probably this conflict's *racial* portent that fueled popular interest in it in the first place. Ethnological accounts of the region included Eugene Scuyler's *Turkistan,* presenting "a people whose character and civilization is but little known to Anglo-Saxon people." (Scuyler identified and charted thirteen "races" of Turkey: Turks, Circassians, Armenians, Jews, Gypsies, foreigners, and six subraces of Arabs.) *Harper's* tracked a heated anthropological debate over the relationship between Europeans and Turkey's "Sarmatae" peoples (were the Sarmatae "Aryans" or "Sclavs"?), and greeted a new volume on the racial "resume of the Russian people" (whose "stocks" were said to include "Lithuanians, Sclaves, Germans, Greeco-Roumanians, Iranians, Iberians, Caucasians, Finns, Turks, Mongolians, etc.").[63]

Popular concern over the outcome of the war likewise hung on racial hopes, fears, and aspirations. The *Nation* identified Russia as a crucial "civilizing agent" in the region, for example; and in a piece for the *Atlantic Monthly,* "The Races of the Danube," John Fiske identified the Mussulman Tartars as the most dangerous kind of racial spoilers—"a race politically unteachable and intellectually incurious, which has contributed absolutely nothing to the common weal of mankind," even while it has thwarted "the normal development of a more worthy community." In the service of his interpretation of current events along the Danube, Fiske offered a "comprehensive view" of European history—a kind of racial big bang, by which all of European history began with the clash of "two very different races," "Aryans" and "Iberians." It was owing to the mixture of these "strongly contrasting races that the peoples of Europe present such marked varieties of complexion."[64]

Nor were such assessments of racial variegation within whiteness limited to armchair ethnologists among the contributors to *Harper's, Atlantic Monthly,* or the *North American Review.* In July 1877, in what was to become a momentary cause célèbre in the popular press, the (Hilton) Grand Union Hotel in Saratoga Springs barred Joseph Seligman, a Bavarian Jewish immigrant who had risen to prominence in American bank-

ing. Carey McWilliams has called this the first major act of overt anti-
Semitism in American history, and both he and John Higham have
stressed the economic foundations of the perceptible rise in anti-Semitism
in 1877 and after. Jewish elites had begun to challenge traditional "status
hierarchies" in Gilded Age America, this argument runs, and so various
social exclusions of the type Seligman suffered at Saratoga represent a
concerted effort on the part of Gentile elites to reassert their social pre-
rogatives. The period's shifting economic circumstances and rivalries represent the material base for what Higham calls "discriminatory" (as distinct from "ideological") anti-Semitism.[65]

Whatever its basis in economics, however, Higham and McWilliams
have occluded the extent to which popular reportage and discussion of
the clash at Saratoga drew upon a language and a logic of race. Hilton
himself initially explained his rejection of Seligman on the grounds of
Jews' "vulgar ostentation," "puffed up vanity," "overweening display of
condition," and "lack of those considerate civilities appreciated by good
American society."[66] The *Commercial Advertiser* cast this as a simple
question of black and white: invoking the Civil Rights Act passed two
years before, this journal wanted to know, "Has the hotel-keeper the authority of law to exclude from his bed and board whom he pleases? Have
the colored population rights that the white man [that is, the Jew] has
not?"[67]

But the Jew's "ostentation" and lack of "civility" were themselves
widely interpreted as racial traits; and popular discussion of the affair
from the outset more often than not cast this as a drama of racial significance. In a rather supercilious summary of the popular response to the
affair, the *Nation* remarked that, though Seligman's "influence on the
attitude of the American people on race questions is admitted on all hands
to be very small," nonetheless sympathizers in some quarters had elevated
the affair to "a question of whether the Jewish race 'had no rights under
the constitution.' " An unfortunate and silly inflation, in this journal's
view. But despite the *Nation's* lament that this teapot had generated such
a tempest, for the magazine the question *was,* at bottom, a decidedly racial
one: the Jews' "tendency to gaudiness in dress or ornament we suspect
has its roots deeper than modern history goes, and testifies to the purity
of the race and the freshness with which its eye still retains the Oriental
passion for brilliancy of costume, though the effect in our climate is barbaric and coarse, instead of being . . . picturesque."[68]

This was not an idiosyncratic reading. The *Daily Graphic* argued that "the average American Jew can hardly be recognized in a company by anything save a cast of features which nothing but centuries of intermarriage with other races will change." (Despite this journal's fundamental sympathy with Seligman, the piece did contend that the verb "Jewed" was well earned by "the excessive sharpness of that race in business transactions.")[69] The *Evening Post,* too, put forward a philo-Semitic, but nonetheless racial, argument: recalling the tremendous bloodshed occasioned by the proscription of the Negroes, a race widely held to be inferior, this journal now asked, will Americans "tolerate the proscription of a race whose equality with the foremost races . . . is nowhere disputed?"[70]

Under the headline "No Jews Need Apply" (a direct reference to another European pariah group, the Irish), the New York *Tribune* rather weakly asserted that the only "dignified and sensible" response of those who "feel they have been insulted at the Grand Union on account of their race or religion is to withdraw quietly."[71] Thus leaving open the question of the basis of Jewish exclusion—a matter of *either* race or religion, precisely as was the case with the social doctrine of "No Irish Need Apply"— the *Tribune* in its initial coverage redoubled Anglo-Saxon hegemony by simply wishing that the pariah would be "dignified" and disappear. But this interpretation shifted overnight, and the *Tribune* went on to give the fullest racial interpretation of the episode extant. "Ostracism of a Race," the *Tribune* now called the affair (June 21); "Excluded Hebrews Indignant." Hilton's actions were a "direct insult to the Jewish race," according to one editorial; and in a man-in-the-street interview, one interviewee compared social even-handedness with Jews to "the employment of Chinese labor . . . or the cultivation of Southern lands by negroes." The *Tribune* elaborated a week later, under the banner "Not a Question of Religion": "Religion had nothing whatsoever to do with the subject"; "we presume a Christian Hebrew is as obnoxious to Mr. Hilton as one of Jewish belief."

> Social distinctions of race and color are bound to exist here as elsewhere . . . While politically all such distinctions may be ignored, they cannot be socially. Half the nation spent its blood and treasure to give freedom to the Negro, but it has left him to win his own social equality . . . Prejudices of race forbid equally the free social intercourse of Teuton, Latin, and Mongolian. It does not argue the superiority of either to recognize that the natural affinity between the Anglo-Saxon and the Hebrew is extremely weak. Nature is to blame

primarily, though peculiarities of different civilizations and different tendencies of distinct systems of education have increased this dislike between the two races.[72]

Under the headline "Race Prejudice," *Harper's Weekly* conveyed most succinctly both the distinctness and the affinity-in-whiteness of the Anglo-Saxon and the Hebrew. "There are undoubtedly disagreeable Hebrews or Jews, as there are disagreeable people of all other races"; and yet the exclusion at Saratoga was "monstrous." At least Hilton's "monstrous" act of race prejudice had the "good effect of showing how sincere and universal is the protest against the indulgence of a race prejudice against white skins. We beg to remind the protestants that a race prejudice against black skins is quite as despicable."[73]

Nor were Jews the only victims of "race prejudice against white skins" during the summer of 1877. Amid a trial of several members of the Irish Molly Maguires for murder in Pennsylvania, the New York *Tribune* opined, "The Mollies belong to a race with a more wholesome and probably unreasonable terror of law than any other. It has, unfortunately, been whipped into them for centuries. The cunning of resistance has been whipped into them, too." Then, borrowing language typical of the American discourse on the Indian Wars, the journal mused, "If the Pennsylvanians intend to civilize them by terror, it will need other and more wholesome slaughters than that of last week to do it. Is there no other way to civilize them?" The *Tribune* went on to advocate missionary activity among the Mollies in order to "humanize" them.[74] Indeed, in *The Molly Maguires* (1877), the first book-length study of the organization, F. P. Dewees grounded the troubles in Pennsylvania in a much longer history of unrest between "the Anglo-Saxon race" (which had kept the aim of constitutional freedom in view ever since the Magna Charta) and the "Celt" (who remained ever unsympathetic to such ideals).[75]

As Richard Slotkin has amply documented, the rhetoric of "civilization" and "savagery" likewise framed discussion of the great railroad strike that spread from Baltimore and Pittsburgh to St. Louis and New York in July. To urban elites, as Slotkin puts it, this outbreak of labor agitation was a case of Indian Wars coming "home" to the metropolis. Slotkin treats this as a matter of pure metaphor, noting that in this instance "the working-class 'hostiles' were predominantly white and largely American-born." "Thus," he argues, "the race war and Indian war provided a language for interpreting the class struggles attendant on the development of industry and served the ideological function of linking striking workers with racial aliens and primitive savages." For the urban elites of this account, "perhaps the savage-striker metaphor was literally true, and neither tribesman nor workingman was truly capable of self-government."[76]

Slotkin's analysis thus rests on various notions of metaphor and metanym, upon rhetorical conflations of class and race, underlying ideological "linkages" between radicalism and savagery, or "associations" of alien class ideologies with "biological-ethnic alienness." But given the extent to which many American-born observers did believe that the emergent, conscious, and militant working class literally was a class of foreigners, this literally *was* a "race war." Although the language of "civilization" and "savagery" has indeed been deployed metaphorically to great effect in American culture (and no one has revealed this as thoroughly as Slotkin himself), there is a second, absolutely literal dimension to these racial interpretations of the 1877 strike and of the unfitness of the strikers for self-government. If the myth of the frontier was among the cultural forms authorizing immigrants' whiteness in the latter phases of America's long-enduring period of racial inscription, these immigrants nonetheless did embody a kind of "savagery" that was neither rhetorical nor metaphorical.

Much of Slotkin's own evidence points in this direction. E. L. Godkin's *Nation* remarked upon the "vast additions . . . to our population" who "carry in their very blood traditions which give universal suffrage an air of menace to many of the things which civilized men hold most dear." It is not merely a metaphor, but race itself, that links the notions of "vast additions" to the population via immigration, traditions carried in the "very blood" of these peoples, and the resulting "menace" to the ideals of "civilized men." Godkin's plea for a restriction on universal suffrage is thus an early expression on the eugenic theme of degenerate races and their unfitness for self-government. Godkin had elsewhere decried a regimen of philanthropy toward the Indians that would "debauch white men of any race; no wonder it debauches savages."[77] That "white men" were divisible into so many distinct "races" was fundamental to his worldview, and so contiguous questions of "blood," "civilization," and the degree of "menace" immigrants posed to free institutions were linked by far more than mere metaphor.

As *Harper's Weekly* put it, again in reference to the unnamed European races presumed to be behind the labor agitation along the B & O Railroad, "What is the difference between civilization and barbarism, between America and Central Africa, but law, and the redress of grievances . . . by prescribed legal methods?" "The country has learned the necessity of a thorough and efficient local armed organization. The strikers have learned the hopeless folly of struggling against the unconquerable instinct of a race."[78] The *Daily Graphic* similarly argued for an enhanced militia, since the railroad capitalists had not been successful "in implanting in the breasts of the inferior race sentiments of respect and gratitude."[79] "We shall make a dreadful mistake," the New York *Tribune* chimed in,

> . . . if we allow ourselves to be deceived as to the real character of a good many of the lower classes in our large cities, in the coal and iron towns, and on the lines of railway. In becoming the refuge for the oppressed of all nations our country accepted a noble mission, but that mission has its perils and difficulties. The oppressed are not always the virtuous. We have taken into our body politic the refuse of the Paris Commune, incendiaries from Berlin and Tipperary, some hundreds of thousands of European agitators, who are always at war with every form of government thus far known among civilized nations.[80]

Here Anglo-Saxondom trumped mere whiteness in laying claim to civilization and to racial supremacy. And by its violation of "civilized" standards of conduct, conversely, immigrant radicalism offered incontrovertible proof of the immigrants' troubling racial pedigree. Like the Molly Maguires in Pennsylvania, Joseph Seligman at Saratoga Springs, Fiske's races of the Danube, or the French art students so reviled in *Harper's*, the strikers of 1877 were in whiteness but not of it, so to say. Their presence in the republic was doubly troubling from a racial standpoint: if their essential racial inferiority as non–Anglo-Saxons posed difficulties for the workings of a free republic, then their whiteness gave that inferiority as wide a field as possible to wreak real havoc. Godkin's ruminations on the "air of menace" attending "universal suffrage" in this context of mass immigration put the problem most succinctly: whiteness may have been indispensable in dividing the fit from the unfit in the earlier stages of the nation's history—in dividing civilized Europeans from savage Indians and blacks or degenerate Mexicans and mestizos—but in the era of mass migration whiteness was no longer a guarantee of civilization at all.

To return, briefly, to Henry James and *The American*: early on Mrs. Tristram refers to Christopher Newman as "the great Western Barbarian." "I am not a barbarian, by a good deal," objects Newman; "I am very much the reverse. I have seen barbarians; I know what they are." "I don't mean that you are a Comanche chief, or that you wear a blanket and feathers," returns Mrs. Tristram. "There are different shades."[81] As it unfolds, *The American* turns out to be precisely about these "different shades"—both the figurative shades of barbarism and civilization (or overcivilization) that define national character, and the literal shades of physiognomy perceived as race—just as American political culture itself was increasingly fixing upon the different shades of barbarism and civilization among "free white persons," and the different shades of a theretofore undifferentiated whiteness.

James's ethnological interest is announced in the opening paragraphs, when we are told that the American's "physiognomy would have sufficiently indicated that he was a shrewd and capable fellow"; he is a "powerful specimen of an American," having "a very well-formed head, with a shapely, symmetrical balance of the frontal and occipital development." By contrast, Valintin de Bellegard, for instance, "was a foreigner to his fingertips," although "there was something in his physiognomy which seemed to cast a sort of aerial bridge over the impassable gulf produced by difference of race." (Valintin's brother, too, was a familiar type despite his Gallic racial origins: he "looked much like an Englishman.") From the outset the novel moves along the twin tracks of race as a force in history ("Old trees have crooked branches . . . old races have odd secrets") and physiognomy as the key to social interpretation ("Mademoiselle Noemie's jealous votary was a tall robust young man with a thick nose, a prominent blue eye, a Germanic physiognomy").[82]

This ethnological and physiognomical quality unites *The American* with many other narrative productions of the moment—Warner's *In the Levant; Harper's* sketches on Alaskan mining, Barbadian travel, and French art; *Tribune* and *Nation* editorials on Hilton's anti-Semitism and the B & O strike; congressional reports on Louisiana polling practices and Chinese immigration. Flowing from precisely this racial consciousness, James's competing cautions regarding the proper bride for the American—"No Irish Need Apply" and the "Let us confine ourselves to Europe"—likewise capture a contradiction which lay at the heart of American political culture, not just in 1877, but for several decades to come. European identities became increasingly racialized in the context of immigration, labor struggle, and continuous scientific inquiry into human typologies and difference; and so the pan-white, *Herrenvolk* egalitarianism of "Let us confine ourselves to Europe" clashed with the rising sentiment, "No Irish Need Apply." Both palimpsestic inscriptions remained discernible for some time.

The discrepancy in racial usages such as "white," "Celt," and "Caucasian," then, do not denote a mere sloppiness or imprecision in the language of race; such contradictions do not in every case represent insignificant choices among interchangeable synonyms. Rather, they reflect the contending racial schemes in the air at a given moment and the multiplicity of available categories that the culture has generated and is capable of sustaining. In unpacking the ideology of race and its power in American life, in other words, we are on surest ground if we conclude, not that, because "Caucasian" and "Anglo-Saxon" can coincide, the distinctions between them are trifling, but rather, that their coexistence signifies the unceasing tendency of the culture to suggest race in perception and to etch race on bodies. We are better off not passing over such unstable categories as mere inconsistencies in usage, but investigating them for the fossilized power relationships embedded within them. The inherent instability of race becomes plain when a figure walks out of one context and into another—imagine the pariah Joseph Seligman on a Louisiana election day, or think of the Molly Maguires striking out West and joining The Order of Caucasians in San Francisco.

Culture, as a creature of history, destabilizes race by layering different conceptual schemes atop one another in response to shifting social and political circumstances. The palimpsest of race maps the terrain of ascription, perception, and subjectivity for a number of immigrant groups whose "American experience" has scarcely been recounted as a *racial* experience at all.

The Jew can be unknown in his Jewishness. He is not wholly what he is. One hopes, one waits. His actions, his behavior are the final determinant. He is a white man, and, apart from some rather debatable characteristics, he can sometimes go unnoticed . . . One has only not to be a nigger. Granted, the Jews are harassed—what am I thinking of? They are hunted down, exterminated, cremated. But these are little family quarrels.

—Frantz Fanon, *Black Skin, White Masks* (1952)

I like the idea of having a Jewish officer—what's his name, Jacobs—in Burma. See that you get a good clean-cut American type for Jacobs.

—Jack Warner's casting instructions for *Objective Burma* (1945)

 5

Looking Jewish, Seeing Jews

When Johann Blumenbach sat down to delineate *The Natural Varieties of Man* in 1775, he lighted upon the "racial face" of the Jews as the most powerful example of "the unadulterated countenance of nations." The principle of stable racial types was illustrated "above all [by] the nation of the Jews, who, under every climate, remain the same as far as the fundamental configuration of face goes, remarkable for a racial character almost universal, which can be distinguished at the first glance even by those little skilled in physiognomy."[1]

The racial character of Jewishness in the New World ebbed and flowed over time. The saga of Jewishness-as-difference in North America properly begins as early as 1654, when Peter Stuyvesant wrote to the Amsterdam Chamber of the Dutch West India Company that Christian settlers in New Amsterdam had "deemed it useful to require [Jews] in a friendly way to depart." Stuyvesant went on to pray "that the deceitful race,—such hateful enemies and blasphemers of the name of Christ,—be not allowed further to infect and trouble this new colony."[2] In the early republic Jewishness was most often taken up as a matter not of racial difference marked by physicality, but of religious difference marked by a stubborn and benighted failure to see Truth. Jews were "un-Christian," as in the laws limiting the right of office-holding in Maryland; they were "infidels" in more heated rhetoric. Then, like other non–Anglo-Saxon immigrants who entered under the terms of the 1790 naturalization law, Jews were increasingly seen as a racial group (in their case as Orientals, Semites, or Hebrews) in the mid to late nineteenth century—particularly as the demographics of immigration tilted away from German and other West European Jews, and toward the Yiddish-speaking Jews of Eastern Europe. Finally, again like other non–Anglo-Saxon immigrants, Jews gradually became Caucasians over the course of the twentieth century.

Thus anti-Semitism and the racial odyssey of Jews in the United States are neither wholly divisible from nor wholly dependent upon the history of whiteness and its vicissitudes in American political culture. When Henry James writes, "There were thousands of little chairs and almost as many little Jews; and there was music in the open rotunda, over which Jews wagged their big noses," it is useful to know that he is drawing upon a long European tradition of anti-Jewish imagery buttressed by arrangements of institutional power and political custom. It is also useful to know, however, that James's sensibilities could be as easily unsettled by a gang of Italian "ditchers" or a variety of other immigrant arrivals. After a visit to "the terrible little Ellis Island" in 1906, James ventured that the sight would bring "a new chill in [the] heart" of any long-standing American, as if he had "seen a ghost in his supposedly safe old house." American natives, he wrote, had been reduced to a state of "*unsettled possession*" of their own country; and it was not the Jew alone, but the "inconceivable alien" in general, who had him so worried.[3]

Yet as with Irish immigrants, who came ashore already carrying the cultural and political baggage of Saxon oppression, the Jews' version of becoming Caucasian cannot be understood apart from their particular history of special sorrows in the ghettos of Eastern Europe, apart from the deep history of anti-Semitism in Western culture, apart from anti-Semitic stereotypes that date back well before the European arrival on North American shores, or apart, finally and most obviously, from the historic cataclysm of the Holocaust.

The thick traces of this history and the Jewish discomfort with it are nicely captured in the exchange with which this study opened, a scene from *The Counterlife* in which two of Philip Roth's characters argue over whether or not Jews are Caucasian. In an era when religious orthodoxy has been eroded by the tides of secularization, and when race has been rendered unspeakable by the atrocities in Nazi Germany, what does Jewishness consist in? This is a point of no small disagreement, even as the twentieth century comes to a close. On the one hand, in a short story like "My Jewish Face" (1990), the Jewish writer Melanie Kaye/Kantrowitz can depict the recognition and public acknowledgment of one's own "Jewish face" as a powerful sign of cultural resistance or political maturation. In popular, street-level conversation among Jewish insiders, too, a common joke has it that so-and-so "doesn't look like a Jew—he looks like *two* Jews." And yet on the other hand, as Roth's Nathan Zuckerman uneasily remarks, "Some nasty superstitions always tend to crop up when people talk about a Jewish race." The touchiness of the very question of Jewish visibility in the late twentieth century denotes the searing and complicated history of "the Jewish race."[4]

My interest in physicality here has primarily to do with the relationship between race as a conceptual category and race as a perceptual category. From a historical standpoint, looking Jewish (or Irish or Levantine or Italian or Cape Verdean) is not terribly interesting in and of itself. But there is a dynamic relationship between visible "difference" on the one hand, and deep social and political meaning on the other. Recall Charles Dudley Warner's peculiar but telling description of his encounter with a group of Moslem mourners in *In the Levant*:

> You would not see in farthest Nubia a more barbarous assemblage, and not so fierce an one. In the presence of these wild mourners the term 'gentler sex' has a ludicrous sound . . . most of them were flamingly ugly, and—*to liken them to what they most resembled*—physically and mentally the type of the North American squaws.[5]

The emphasized phrase here signals a double task of first "recognizing" (that is, *assigning*) resemblance and then, second, reifying that resemblance by "likening" the two disparate objects of perception. The phrase "to liken them to what they most resembled" does not merely represent an awkward rendering on Warner's part, but conveys the crucial cognitive work of racial perception. Warner interpolates a group of actual Moslem mourners into his own, preexisting conception of "barbarism" and "wildness"—a conception that is evidently inflected by notions of "ugliness" and "womanliness," and that already comprises "Nubians" and "North American squaws." This cognitive act of "likening," of course, silently entails other, equally portentous acts of "differentiating."

Here, then, is a rudimentary model for thinking about the complex interplay between social distinctions and racial perceptions. Like Irishness, Italianness, Greekness, and other probationary whitenesses, visible Jewishness in American culture between the mid-nineteenth and mid-twentieth centuries represented a complex process of social value *become* perception: social and political meanings attached to Jewishness generate a kind of physiognomical surveillance that renders Jewishness itself discernible as a particular pattern of physical traits (skin color, nose shape, hair color and texture, and the like)—what Blumenbach called "the fundamental configuration of face." The visible markers may then be interpreted as outer signs of an essential, immutable, inner moral-intellectual character; and that character, in its turn—attested to by physical "difference"—is summoned up to explain the social value attached to Jewishness in the first place. The circuit is ineluctable. Race is social value become perception; Jewishness seen is social value naturalized and so enforced.

This is not to say that people all "really" look alike; rather, it is to argue that those physical differences which register in the consciousness as *"difference"* are keyed to particular social and historical circumstances. (We might all agree that Daniel Patrick Moynihan "looks Irish," for instance; but unlike our predecessors, we at the turn of the twenty-first century are not likely to note his Irishness first thing.) Thus a writer defending the "better" Jews (what a later generation would tellingly call "white Jews") in the *North American Review* in 1891 could collapse the distinction between behavior and physicality, arguing that "among cultured Jews the racial features are generally less strongly defined." (When Jews are of the "better" type, that is, the observing eye need not scout their Jewishness.)[6] That same year, meanwhile, in *The Witch of Prague*, the novelist Marion Crawford could thoroughly fuse physicality and inner character in his portrait of Jewish evil. In the Jewish quarter one encountered

> throngs of gowned men, crooked, bearded, filthy, vulture-eyed . . . hook-nosed and loose-lipped, grasping fat purses, in lean fingers, shaking greasy curls that straggled out under caps of greasy fur, glancing to the left and right with quick, gleaming looks that pierced the gloom like fitful flashes of lightening . . . a writhing mass of humanity, intoxicated by the smell of gold, mad for its possession, half hysteric with fear of losing it, timid, yet dangerous, poisoned to the core by the sweet sting of money, terrible in intelligence, vile in heart,

contemptible in body, irresistible in the unity of their greed—the Jews of Prague.⁷

Nor, indeed, have conceptions of a racial Jewishness necessarily been confined to negative depictions. The point is a critical one. As I have argued elsewhere, Yiddish writers like Abraham Cahan and Morris Winchevsky were as quick as their non-Jewish contemporaries to assign a distinctly racial integrity to Jewishness and Jews. Racial perceptions of Jewishness are not simply a subject for the annals of anti-Semitism, in other words; nor does racial ascription necessarily denote a negative assessment of a given group in every case. Among the secularized Jews of the *haskala,* or Jewish enlightenment, responses to "the Jewish Question" (such as Zionism, or bundist Yiddish socialism) rested solidly upon *racial* notions of a unified Jewish "peoplehood." In the sciences, too, it was not only the virulent Madison Grants and the Lothrop Stoddards, but Jewish scientists like Maurice Fishberg and Joseph Jacobs, who advanced the scholarly idea of Jewish racial purity.⁸ (Nor, for that matter, were Jewish versions of Jewish racial difference in every instance *positive,* either: as the *American Hebrew* remarked in response to the immigrant waves from further east in Europe [1894], the acculturated German Jew "is closer to the christian sentiment around him than to the Judaism of these miserable darkened Hebrews.")⁹

Thus the history of racial Jewishness is not merely the history of anti-Semitism; it encompasses the ways in which both Jews and non-Jews have construed Jewishness—and the ways in which they have *seen* it—over time. It encompasses not only arguments, like Madison Grant's, that "the mixture of a European and a Jew is a Jew," or the view of Jews as "mud people"—the progenitors of all nonwhites—which circulates in far right theology in the 1990s.¹⁰ It also comprises the race pride of a Morris Winchevsky or a Leon Kobrin, and the social forces under whose influence such conceptions of peoplehood have largely given way. By 1950 Ludwig Lewisohn could assert that "no sane man regards Jewish characteristics as 'racial.' "¹¹ And yet as late as the 1970s Raphael Patai would still be trying to dispel "the myth of the Jewish race"; and later still Philip Roth would be wincing at the "nasty superstitions" attached to racial Jewishness.

A few remarks on the strategy of the present inquiry are in order. The definition of "Jewishness" under investigation here is quite narrow. Surely religion and culture can figure prominently in the ascription of Jewishness by Jews or non-Jews, anti-Semites or philo-Semites. This discussion does not seek to exhaust Jewishness in all of its dimensions or in its full range of possibilities; rather, it investigates strictly ethnoracial conceptions and perceptions of Jewishness (answers to the question, is Jewishness a parcel of biological, heritable traits?). Such conceptions, and the inevitable debates over them, have been central to some Jews themselves as they pondered their common destiny irrespective of religious devotion, and to non-Jews wrestling with questions of immigration, intergroup relations, and the smooth functioning of the polity. I begin by sketching the emergence of a visible, physical—biological—Jewishness in common American understanding during the period preceding the mid-twentieth century. This history loosely parallels the chronology laid out for whiteness in general in part one, although in the case of Jews World War II will present a sharper turning point than 1924 in the final transformation toward Caucasian whiteness. The investigation ends, then, with a close reading of Arthur Miller's *Focus* (1945), a sustained inquiry into the properties of Jewishness rendered at precisely that post-Nazi moment—like *Gentleman's Agreement*—when "racial" Jewishness was still a live, yet a newly intolerable, conception.

"Are Jews white?" asks Sander Gilman. The question gets at the fundamental instability of Jewishness as racial difference, but so does its wording fundamentally misstate the contours of whiteness in American political culture.[12] From 1790 onward Jews were indeed "white" by the most significant measures of that appellation: they could enter the country and become naturalized citizens. Given the shades of meaning attaching to various racial classifications, given the nuances involved as whiteness slips off toward Semitic or Hebrew and back again toward Caucasian, the question is not *are* they white, nor even how white are they, but how have they been both white and Other? What have been the historical terms of their probationary whiteness?

Jews in American Culture

The idea of a unique Jewish physicality or Jewish "blood" was not new to nineteenth-century America. As James Shapiro has recently argued, theology heavily influenced early modern conceptions of both racial and national difference in Europe, and so the alien Jew figured prominently in European discussion as early as the sixteenth century. In 1590 Andrew Willet argued that "Jews have never been grafted onto the stock of other people." In 1604 the Spaniard Prudencio de Sandoval combined a proto-racialist argument of hereditary Jewish evil with a kind of racialism-by-association with the other Other, the Negro: "Who can deny that in the descendants of the Jews there persists and endures the evil inclination of their ancient ingratitude and lack of understanding, just as in Negroes [there persists] the inseparability of their blackness?" Such ideas evidently crossed the Atlantic early on in the settlement of the New World, assuming even more directly racialist overtones in Increase Mather's comments on the "blood" of nations and the purity of the Jews in 1669:

> The providence of God hath suffered other nations to have their blood mixed very much, as you know it is with our own nation: there is a mixture of British, Roman, Saxon, Danish, [and] Norman blood. But as for the body of the Jewish nation, it is far otherwise. Let an English family live in Spain for five or six hundred years successively, and they will become Spaniards. But though a Jewish family live in Spain a thousand years, they do not degenerate into Spaniards (for the most part).[13]

Until the second half of the nineteenth century, however, it was generally not their "blood" but their religion that marked the Jews as a people apart. The Jew was the perpetual "Historical Outsider," in Frederic Jaher's phrase, whose perceived difference derived above all from "Christian hostility." The Jew's difference was primarily cast in terms of the "infidel" or the "blasphemer" (one Jacob Lambrozo was indicted in Maryland for denouncing Jesus as a "necromancer," for example), and discussion was occasionally infused with a dose of long-standing European rumor (such as the twelfth-century "blood libel" that Jews needed Christian blood for certain holiday fêtes) or stereotypes of Jews as well-poisoners and usurers. Although the popular view of Jews was "amply negative" in the colonies, by Jaher's account, it was far better there than in Europe; and their status was characterized by a general state of toleration disrupted only by occasional anti-Semitic outbursts, as when the New York Assembly disfranchised them in 1737, or when Savannah freeholders resisted the expansion of a Jewish cemetery in 1770.[14]

These religiously grounded ideas about the Jewish alien could occasionally take on a racialist cast in the new nation, just as they had in early modern Europe. In a rabid denunciation of the Jacobin propensities of the Democratic Society in 1795, for instance, one Federalist publisher asserted that the democrats would be "easily known by their physiognomy"; they seem to be "of the tribe of Shylock: they have that leering underlook and malicious grin."[15] But generally Jews remained "free [though unchristian] white persons" in the early republic, and the overt depictions of the Jew as a racial Other rose sharply only in the second half of the nineteenth century, particularly in the decades after what John Higham has called "a mild flurry of ideological anti-Semitism" during the Civil War. Now it was not only that Jews could be known in their greed (or their Jacobinism or their infidelism or their treachery) by their physiognomy, but that their physiognomy itself was significant—denoting, as it did, their essential unassimilability to the republic. Only now did the "Israelitish nose" stand for something in and of itself—not greed, or usury, or infidelism, or well-poisoning, but simply "difference." Only now was the dark Jew equated with "mongrelization," that catch-all term for "unfitness" in American political culture.[16] Thus a century after Johann Blumenbach introduced as scientific fact the remarkable stability of the Jews when it came to "the fundamental configuration of face," the New York Sun offered this vernacular explanation of "why the Jews are kept apart" (1893):

> Other races of men lose their identity by migration and by intermarrying with different peoples, with the result that their peculiar characteristics and physiognomies are lost in the mess. The Jewish face and character remain the same as they were in the days of PHARAOH. Everybody can distinguish the Jewish features in the most ancient carvings and representations, for they are the same as those seen at this day. Usually a Jew is recognizable as such by sight. In whatever country he is, his race is always conspicuous . . . After a few generations other immigrants to this country lose their race identity and become Americans only. Generally the Jews retain theirs undiminished, so that it is observable by all men.[17]

Others, as we have seen, strongly contested the blithe assertion that "other immigrants to this country lose their race identity," but the Sun was nonetheless expressing a point of impressive consensus on the unassimilability of the Jews.

This intensifying perception of a distinctly racial Jewishness coincided with two entangling developments between the 1850s and the early twentieth century: the rise of the racial sciences, and the rise of what John Higham has called "discriminatory" (as opposed to "ideological") anti-Semitism.[18] Popular accounts of the racial Otherness of Jews, that is, at once framed, and were framed by, a scientific discourse of race on the one hand, and a set of social practices (including hiring and admissions patterns, and the barring of Jews from certain Saratoga resorts) on the other. This coincidence of scientific racialism, discriminatory practice, and the popular expression of racial Jewishness attests to the centrality of race as an organizer of American social life. It also attests to the similarity between the Jewish odyssey from white to Hebrew and, say, the Irish odyssey from white to Celt. Despite its capacity to absorb and adapt unique, long-standing anti-Semitic notions of Jewish greed and the like, the racial ideology encompassing Jewishness in the United States in the latter half of the nineteenth century did set Jews on a social trajectory similar to that traveled by many other probationary "white persons." The full texture of anti-Semitism in this country thus combined strains of an international phenomenon of Jew-hatred with the mutability of American whiteness.[19]

The rise of races and phenotypes in scientific discourse, as described earlier, was a creature of the age of European expansionism and exploration. Non-European races were "discovered" and became "known" through the technologies of conquest; then scientific accounts of these races, in their turn, justified and explained colonial domination and slavery. But Jews received a fair amount of attention even in this context, in part because of the mutual accommodations of scientific and religious understandings of genesis (or Genesis) and "difference," and in part because, as somewhat anomalous Europeans, Jews put stress upon the ideas of consanguinity and race which undergirded emergent European nationalisms. Just as the alien Jew raised questions as to who could or could not be truly "English" in Shakespeare's England, so romantic nationalisms of the nineteenth century had to come to terms with the anomalous Jew in any effort to theorize and police the "imagined community" of the nation. As one scholar puts it, science itself was "often either motivated by or soon annexed to political causes."[20] Just as the plunder of exploration and slavery formed the context within which Africans became "known" to Western science, so Jewish emancipation, debates over citizenship, and the emergence of modern nationalism formed the context within which science comprehended "the Jewish race." Were "Jewish traits" properly attributed to social isolation, environment, or immutable character? Could Jews be compatriots of non-Jews? Could they be redeemed as Europeans?

Thus from the outset scientific writings on Jews in Europe tended to focus upon questions of assimilation, most often emphasizing the race's stubborn immutability—which is to say, its unassimilability. As Gobineau wrote in his essay *Sur l'Inegalite des Races Humaines,* the "Jewish type" has remained much the same over the centuries; "the modifications it has undergone . . . have never been enough, in any country or latitude, to change the general character of the race. The warlike Rechabites of the Arabian desert, the peaceful Portuguese, French, German, and Polish Jews—they all look alike . . . The Semitic face looks exactly the same as it appears on the Egyptian paintings of three or four thousand years ago."[21] The Jews may be incorporated, but they will forever be Jews. In *Races of Man* (1850), Robert Knox similarly noted Jews' essential physicality, leaving little doubt as to the further question of racial merit:

> Brow marked with furrows or prominent points of bone, or with both; high cheek-bones; a sloping and disproportioned chin; and elongated, projecting mouth, which at the angles threatens every moment to reach the temples; a large, massive, club-shaped, hooked nose, three or four times larger than suits the face—these are features which stamp the African character of the Jew, his muzzle-shaped mouth and face removing him from certain other races . . . Thus it is that the Jewish face never can [be], and never is, perfectly beautiful.[22]

The presumed immutability of the Jews became a staple of American science by mid-century as well, even though slavery and the question of Negro citizenship still dominated racial discussion. In *Types of Mankind* (1855) Josiah Nott remarked that the "well-marked Israelitish features are never beheld out of that race"; "The complexion may be bleached or tanned . . . but the Jewish features stand unalterably through all climates." In *Natural History of the Human Races* (1869) John Jeffries, too, argued that "the Jews have preserved their family type unimpaired; and though they number over five million souls, each individual retains the full impress of his primitive typical ancestors."[23] And of course we have already seen where these "observations" on Jewish racial integrity tended in the age of eugenics.

In this connection the British scholar Joseph Jacobs deserves special attention. A Jew himself, Jacobs was, as he announced in the preface to *Studies in Jewish Statistics* (1891), "inclined to support the long-standing belief in the substantial purity of the Jewish race."[24] For Jacobs, according to the historian John Efron, Jewish race science represented "a new form of Jewish self-defense" and his own work a new genre of political resistance, "the scientific apologia." But if aimed toward the redemption, rather than the renunciation, of racial Jewishness, Jacobs's work rests upon the same logic of "difference" as the most virulent of his anti-Semitic contemporaries. Indeed, it is in Jacobs's work perhaps above all that we glimpse the depth of "difference" associated with Jewish racial identity in this period. "Even more in Jewesses than in Jews," he wrote, "we can see that cast of face in which the racial so dominates the individual that whereas of other countenances we say, 'That is a kind, a sad, a cruel, or a tender face,' of this our first thought is, 'That is a Jewish face.' . . . Even the negroes of Surinam, when they see a European and a Jew approaching, do not say, 'Here are two whites,' but, 'Here is a white and a Jew.' "[25]

Just as earlier scientific approaches to the righteousness of slavery (the work of Josiah Nott and John Van Evrie, for instance) had seized upon the degeneracy of the "mulatto" as proof of the unbridgeable divide separating black from white, so Jacobs went into great detail on the "infertility of mixed marriages" between Jews and non-Jews, on the basis of statistics kept in Prussia and Bavaria between 1875 and 1881. The variance in fecundity, according to Jacobs, was an average of 4.41 children for Jewish-Jewish marriages to 1.65 for Jewish-Gentile marriages in Prussia; and 4.7 to 1.1 in Bavaria. He also charted various physical characteristics of Jews and non-Jews in different regions, including the color of eyes, hair, and skin. (Only 65.4 percent of Austrian Jews had "white" skin, he found, as compared with more than 80 percent of the Gentiles.)[26]

Like conceptions of Anglo-Saxon, Celtic, or Teutonic racial character, scientific observations on the Hebrew passed from the rarified discourse of ethnological journals into the American vernacular and the American visual lexicon of race as well. Racial depiction did not necessarily entail a negative judgment; racially accented declarations of *philo*-Semitism were common enough. William Cullen Bryant lamented that Edwin Booth's rendering of Shylock, for instance, failed to do justice to "the grandeurs of the Jewish race." He later sang of "the wonderful working of the soul of the Hebrew."[27] James Russell Lowell, in an ambivalent twist, couched highly sympathetic remarks on Jewishness in a language of physicality and character, but also drew upon the common, anti-Semitic imagery of his day. "All share in government of the world was denied for centuries to perhaps the ablest, certainly the most tenacious, race that ever lived in it," he wrote compassionately in "Democracy" (1884), ". . . a race in which ability seems as natural and hereditary as the curve of their noses . . . We drove them into a corner, but they had their revenge . . . They made their corner the counter and banking house of the world, and thence they rule it and us with the ignoble scepter of finance."[28] Lowell's respect for "perhaps the ablest" race is the basis for an indictment of Christian political conduct, and particularly its lamentable exclusions. Even if blame lies at the doorstep of Christians, however, the Jewish "revenge" Lowell envisions taps the popular currents of nineteenth-century anti-Semitism.

More positive a view still, yet no less racial, is Oliver Wendell Holmes's philo-Semitic paean "At the Pantomime" (1874):

> Amidst the throng the pageant drew
> Were gathered Hebrews, not a few,
> Black bearded, swarthy,—at their side
> Dark, jewelled women, orient-eyed.
>
> . . . . .
>
> Next on my left a breathing form
> Wedged up against me, close and warm;
> The beak that crowned the bistred face
> Betrayed the mould of Abraham's race,—
> That coal-black hair, that smoke-brown hue,—
> Ah, cursed, unbelieving Jew!
> I started, shuddering, to the right,
> And squeezed—a second Israelite!

Over the course of ten stanzas the narrator has a change of heart, and as he recognizes his Hebrew neighbors as distant kinsmen of Jesus Christ, his racial hatred gives way to racial glorification:

> Thou couldst scorn the peerless blood
> That flows unmingled from the flood,—
> Thy scutcheon spotted with the stains
> Of Norman thieves and pirate Danes!
> The New World's foundling, in thy pride
> Scowl on the Hebrew at thy side,
> And lo! the very semblance there
> The Lord of Glory deigned to wear!

Holmes concludes, perhaps with as much self-congratulation as contrition, "Peace be upon thee, Israel!"[29]

In *The Ambivalent Image*, her study of Jews in American cultural imagery, Louise Mayo has amassed an invaluable compendium of racial figures of Jewishness across time. Although Mayo's project did not entail theorizing the relationship between racial Jewishness and the American social order, her work supports the trajectory of Anglo-Saxondom and its Others sketched out above. Racial depictions of Jews would become most urgent, of course, as immigration figures climbed in the decades following Russia's May Laws of 1881. Nonetheless, as Mayo has so nicely laid bare in her cultural excavations, Hebrews appeared as a counterpoint to Anglo-Saxons in American cultural representation long before actual Hebrews began to disembark in huge numbers at Castle Garden and Ellis Island toward the end of the century. This seems part of the reflex toward an Anglo-supremacist exclusivity beginning in the 1840s. Thus in the cosmos of American popular literature, for instance, George Lippard could remark in *Quaker City* (1844), "Jew was written on his face as though he had fallen asleep for three thousand years at the building of the Temple"; in Peter Hamilton Meyers's *The Miser's Heir* (1854), a certain character's "features . . . proclaim him a Jew"; and in J. Richter Jones's *Quaker Soldier* (1866), a Jew is characterized by the "hereditary habits of his race."[30] By the early twentieth century a Jewish group could organize a grassroots boycott of certain New York theaters, protesting their "scurrilous and debasing impersonations of the Hebrew type." Judge Hugo Pam, the leader of the boycott, argued that the theater was fostering "race prejudice" because so many theater goers "get their impressions of the race from the stage Jew." (Significantly, this group took its cue from Irish activists, who, Pam said, had succeeded in eliminating "stage lampoons of the Celtic race" from popular theater.)[31]

Racial depictions of Jewishness circulated not only in cultural productions themselves, but also in cultural commentary, as when *Harper's Weekly* reported that the audience of the Yiddish theater was "remarkably strange in appearance to an Anglo-Saxon," or when *Bookman* reviewed Abraham Cahan's *Yekl* as a penetrating look at the Yiddish immigrant's "racial weakness." William Dean Howells, too, discussed Cahan's novella in racial terms, identifying Cahan as a "Hebrew" and his ghetto sketches as "so foreign to our race and civilization."[32]

Wherever "difference" was cast as race, certainly, the weight of the culture in general tended most often toward negative depiction. Nativist discussion of immigration restriction in the 1890s and the eugenics movement of the earlier twentieth century, of course, stated Jewish difference most boldly. Sounding the familiar chord of race and republicanism, Henry Cabot Lodge warned that Jews "lack the nobler abilities which enable a people to rule and administer and to display that social efficiency in war, peace, and government without which all else is vain." The *Illustrated American* was blunter still, crying in 1894 that "the inroad of the hungry Semitic barbarian is a positive calamity." In a piece on immigration and anarchism, the New York *Times,* too, lamented the arrival of "unwashed, ignorant, unkempt, childish semi-savages," and remarked upon the "hatchet-faced, sallow, rat-eyed young men of the Russian Jewish colony." In response to Franz Boas's innovative argument that in fact no biological chasm did separate new immigrants from America's "old stock," Lothrop Stoddard dismissed his views as "the desperate attempt of a Jew to pass himself off as 'white.' "[33]

Franz Boas's argument notwithstanding, increasingly in the years after the Russian May Laws and the pogroms of 1881, Jews, too, embraced race as a basis for unity. This was particularly true among some Zionists and freethinkers for whom religion had ceased meaningfully to explain their ties to the "folk." The "Jewish Question" as it was posed during the period of pogroms in the East and the Dreyfus Affair in the West generated new secular and political notions of Jewish peoplehood in response. It was in this period, for instance, that Joseph Jacobs began his forays into Jewish race science in Europe. And, as John Efron has amply documented, the *racial* individuality of the Jews as a people was of particular interest within the budding Zionist movement. Aron Sandler's *Anthropologie und Zionismus* (1904), for instance, mobilized the scientific language of a distinct racial genius in order to press the necessity of a Jewish territory where that genius could properly take root and develop.[34]

Indeed, a much longer tradition entwined Jewish nationalism with Jewish racialism. The proto-Zionist Moses Hess, in *Rome and Jerusalem* (1862), had flatly announced that "Jewish noses cannot be reformed, nor black, curly, Jewish hair be turned through baptism or combing into smooth hair. The Jewish race is a primal one, which had reproduced itself in its integrity despite climatic influences . . . The Jewish type is indestructible."[35] The American proto-Zionist Emma Lazarus, too, wrote in *Epistle to the Hebrews* (1887) that Judaism was emphatically *both* a race and a religion. She rhapsodized over the Jews' "fusion of Oriental genius with Occidental enterprise and energy," "the fire of our Oriental blood," and "the deeper lights and shadows of [Jews'] Oriental temperament." She lamented that Jews in America tended to be condemned "as a race" for failings of a single individual. At once demonstrating her own commitment to racialism, yet marking the extent to which race was a contested concept, she lamented the Jews' lack of unanimity on their own racial status: "A race whose members are recognized at a glance, whatever be their color, complexion, costume or language, yet who dispute the cardinal fact as to whether they are a race, cannot easily be brought into unanimity upon more doubtful propositions," she sighed.[36]

In the 1890s and early 1900s immigrant writers in the United States like Abraham Cahan, Leon Kobrin, Abraham Liessen [Abraham Wald], and Bernard Gorin also lighted upon race both as a way of understanding their own secular Jewishness and as a way of couching their (socialist) appeals to the Yiddish masses. And even as late as the 1920s and 1930s a literature of Jewish assimilation toyed with race in its exploration of Jewish destiny in the New World.[37] "What of today and of America?" asked Ludwig Lewisohn. "Were the Jews Germans? Are they Americans? . . . I am not talking about citizenship and passports or external loyalties. What are the inner facts?"[38]

The Island Within (1928), an immigrant saga tracing several generations of a German-Jewish family from Germany in the mid-nineteenth century to the United States in the early twentieth, is Lewisohn's exploration of precisely these "inner facts." "How was it," the novel's young hero, Arthur, wants to know, "that, before they went to school, always and always, as far back as the awakening of consciousness, the children knew that they were Jews? . . . There was in the house no visible symbol of religion and of race." What does Jewishness consist in? What is its basis, especially in the crucible of a transnational history in which questions of national belonging are so vexed?

Arthur vows to understand. Along the way in this ethnoracial *Bildungsroman*, he takes up anthropology and studies the "variableness of racial types" (but later discovers, to his distaste, that his professor rather undemocratically believes in "fixed qualitative racial differences," and so he searches elsewhere). A neighbor, Mrs. Goldman, provides a simple formula: "Jews always have been Jews and they always will be." The tautology actually foreshadows Arthur's own resolution at the end of the novel.[39]

Throughout the quest, race is central both to Arthur's crisis and to its resolution; for him it becomes a measure of his own alienation. He first registers the degree of his assimilation when he discovers that his own father "looks Jewish" to him: "His father's profile under the hat, pale and unwontedly sorrowful, looked immemorially Jewish . . . Arthur realized instantly that this perception of his was itself an un-Jewish one and showed how he had grown up to view his very parents slightly from without and how, indeed, in all thoughts and discussions, he treated the Jews as objects of his discourse." Some two hundred pages later, after a good deal of soul-searching and after many tortured conversations on the subject of Jewishness, Arthur discovers and reclaims his own "island within"—his own immutable, unshakable Jewishness. "You didn't know you were going to resurrect the Jew in you?" asks his Gentile wife, Elizabeth. He responds, "You're quite right . . . But really I didn't even have to resurrect the Jew. I just put away a pretense." Thus eternal Jewishness (what a generation of Yiddish speakers had called *dos pintele yid*, "the quintessence of the Jew"), if racially ambiguous, does have distinctly racial connotations. "It's kind of an argument, isn't it, against mixed marriages?" asks Elizabeth. "I'm afraid it is."[40]

In *I Am a Woman—and a Jew* (1926), Leah Morton [Elizabeth Stern], too, recounted her marriage to a non-Jew, her foray into the world of social work, her secularization, and her eventual re-embrace of Jewishness (if not exactly of Judaism), all in the terms of her relationship to the "race." The authenticity of this narrative has recently been questioned; but it is nonetheless significant that this public embrace of her Jewish identity—however real or imagined—is cast in the thoroughly racial terms of the period's public discourse of Jewishness as difference.[41] Of New York's Bohemia, she wrote, "They were frankly Jewish. They had Jewish names, Jewish faces and the psychology of the Jew." Upon her first taste of public life in the settlement house movement, Leah came to realize that "here, in this office, I was not a girl representing a race. I was not a Jewish maiden responsible to a race, as at home." This fairly conveys Morton's own version of that Jewish immutability so stressed by writers from Knox and Gobineau to Jacobs and Cahan. "Was there a Jewish 'race'?" she asks. "Scientists were taking sides, saying, yes, or no, as they decided. What did it matter to us who were Jews? There was a Jewish people, something that belonged to us, so unchanging that we could not destroy it." The biological basis of that "something that belonged to us," in Morton's estimation, finally comes through when she discovers and embraces "all that we, who are Jews, 'part Jews' or 'all Jews' share." This is Morton's version of the "island within": "We Jews are alike. We have the same intensities, the sensitiveness, poetry, bitterness, sorrow, the same humor, the same memories. The memories are not those we can bring forth from our minds: they are centuries old and are written in our features, in the cells of our brain."[42]

This, then, was the vision of difference that the blackface of an Al

Jolson or an Eddie Cantor sought to efface. *The Jazz Singer* marks the
beginning of the drift by which American Jews became racial Caucasians
and illustrates Frantz Fanon's contention that, when it comes to race-
hatred or race-acceptance, "one has only not to be a nigger."[43] As with
all racial transformations, the next leg of the Jews' odyssey—the cultural
trek from Hebrew to Caucasian—would be a gradual affair, glacial rather
than catastrophic. A new paradigm was in ascendance in the 1920s and
after; perhaps nothing demonstrates so well the power of that paradigm
in redefining Jews as the odd, archaic ring that so much of the material
in the foregoing pages now has. Whether it is Leah Morton writing
proudly of the features and the brain cells of the eternal Jew, or Lothrop
Stoddard commenting upon the slim prospects of Franz Boas's passing
himself off as "white," these commentators from the mid-nineteenth century to the early twentieth were clearly speaking from a racial consciousness not our own.

Arthur Miller's *Focus*

Jews did not disappear from racial view overnight in the mid-1920s, nor
had racial Jewishness vanished completely even by the 1940s. An *Atlantic
Monthly* piece entitled "The Jewish Problem in America" (1941) could
still assert that the Jew had become European "only in residence; by nature he did not become an Occidental; he could not possibly have done
so." Comparing Jews to another problematic "Oriental" group, Armenians, this writer went on to wonder "whether [differences] can be faded
out by association, *miscegenation,* or other means of composition."[44]
When Nazi policy began to make news in the 1930s and early 1940s,
too, headlines in journals like the *Baltimore Sun* and the *Detroit Free
Press* revealed the extent to which Americans and Germans shared a common lexicon of racial Jewishness: American papers unself-consciously reported upon the Nazis' "steps to solve [the] race problem," "laws restrict-
ing [the] rights of Hebrews," and the "persecution of members of the
Jewish race." Hearst papers remarked upon the "extermination of an ancient and cultured race," while the Allentown (Pennsylvania) *Chronicle
and News* commented upon Jews' inability to assimilate with "any other
race."[45]

   World War II and the revelations of the horrors of Nazi Germany were
in fact part of what catapulted American Hebrews into the community
of Caucasians in the mid-twentieth century. As mentioned in Chapter 3,

the feverish and self-conscious revision of "the Jewish race" was at the very heart of the scientific project to rethink the "race concept" in general—the racial devastation in Germany, that is, was largely responsible for the mid-century ascendance of "ethnicity."

Changes wrought in the U.S. social order by the war itself and by the early Cold War, too, helped to speed the alchemy by which Hebrews became Caucasian. From A. Phillip Randolph's threatened march on Washington, to African-Americans' campaign for Double Victory, to the major parties' civil rights planks in 1944 and the rise of the Dixiecrats in 1948, the steady but certain ascendance of Jim Crow as *the* pressing political issue of the day brought the ineluctable logic of the South's white-black binary into play with new force in national life. Postwar prosperity and postindustrial shifts in the economy, too, tended to disperse Jews geographically, either to outlying suburbs or toward sunbelt cities like Los Angeles and Miami—in either case, to places where whiteness itself eclipsed Jewishness in racial salience. As scholars like Deborah Dash Moore and Karen Brodkin Sacks have written, Jews became simply "white or Anglo" in the regional racial schemes of the sunbelt; and racially tilted policies like the GI Bill of Rights and the Federal Housing Authority's "whites only" approach to suburban housing loans re-created Jews in their new regime of racial homogenization. Nikhil Singh has rightly called the postwar suburban boom a case of "state sponsored apartheid"; its hardening of race along exclusive and unforgiving lines of color held tremendous portent for Jews and other white races.[46] And finally, ironically, if racialism had historically been an important component of Zionism, the establishment of a Jewish state ultimately had the opposite effect of whitening the Jews in cultural representations of all sorts: America's client state in the Middle East became, of ideological necessity and by the imperatives of American nationalism, a *white* client state. This revision was popularized not only in mainstream journalism, but in Technicolor extravaganzas on Middle Eastern history like *The Ten Commandments* and *Exodus*.[47]

Given these many historical changes, and given the dawning horror of Nazi Germany and the overtly racial state policy that was its basis, it is not surprising that the 1940s produced a profound revision in the taxonomy of the world's races. Among nonscientific intellectuals, the revision included, most notably, Laura Z. Hobson's *Gentleman's Agreement* (1947) and Arthur Miller's *Focus* (1945). Both of these novels took up Jewishness-as-difference in the racial terms of physiognomy or visibility.

Both novels self-consciously undermined that notion of stable Jewish physicality by plot devices of mistaken or assumed identity and racial interchangeability: both involved central characters who, although Gentile in fact, "looked Jewish" and so discovered the social cost attached to that physiognomical circumstance.

Focus, Miller's second novel, shares a good deal with the spirit of *Gentleman's Agreement,* but this work more thoroughly disentangles the skein of race and perception. *Focus* is perhaps the most thoroughgoing meditation ever produced on the questions of American justice and Jewish racial difference—on "looking Jewish." The novel is a brilliant piece of social commentary, at once a psychological study of the dynamics of hatred and desire, and a nuanced exploration of Jewish "difference." In this novel Jewish physicality is a dual phenomenon of "appearing" and "seeing." The plot turns on the fate of an anti-Semitic Milquetoast named Newman who, because he happens to "look Jewish," himself becomes the victim of anti-Semitism. He loses his job; he runs afoul of the local Christian Front; his house is vandalized; he is assaulted. Ultimately Newman embraces his fate as an honorary Jew, thus literally becoming a "new man"—a newly minted social Jew and a newly converted racial liberal.

The plot device at the center of this ironic turn of events is a creation of wry genius: Newman, a corporate personnel officer whose job it is to screen prospective employees (that is, to discriminate) slips up and hires someone who appears to be a Jew. Reprimanded by his boss and rattled by this rare mistake on his part, he gets a new pair of glasses so that he might be more discriminating in the future. But if the new glasses help Newman to see Jews, they also happen to make him look Jewish. "Since you got the glasses," remarks an affable neighbor, "you got to admit you do look a little Hebey." Even his mother confirms his worst suspicions: "you almost look like a Jew."[48]

Despite the whimsicality of its plot construction, *Focus* offers a profound analysis of anti-Semitism as an instrument of economic and political power. (In this respect *Focus* has more in common with Carey McWilliams's *Mask for Privilege* than with *Gentleman's Agreement.*) Miller addresses the *work* of anti-Semitism from the standpoint of political economy through the character of Finkelstein, a Jew in Newman's neighborhood who witnesses Newman's victimization at the hands of the (mistaken) Christian Front. According to Finkelstein, "the Jew" is not so much the *object* of anti-Semitism as its mode of operation. The object of Jew-hatred, that is, is an allocation of economic and social resources based upon a spontaneous popular allegiance to anti-Semitic leadership and a web of discriminatory practices. "What the hell can [the Christian Front] get out of the Jews?" he asks Newman.

> "There's a hundred and thirty million people in this country and a couple million is Jews. It's you they want, not me. I'm . . . I'm," he started to stutter in his fury, "I'm chicken feed, I'm nothin'. All I'm good for is they can point to me and everybody else will give them their brains and their money, and then they will have the country. It's a trick, it's a racket."[49]

Miller demonstrates the principle in action by the string of misfortunes Newman suffers (and thus, the string of *fortunes* some unnamed "non-Jew" enjoys) as a result of his looking Jewish.

Finkelstein has evidently come to his own understanding of anti-Semitism by way of an East European parable he recalled while visiting his father's grave. The parable, an eight-page story-within-the-story, involves a Jewish peddler in Poland named Itzik. After a fearsome uprising in which the serfs have murdered their overseer and plundered a certain baron's estate, the baron ingeniously lures Itzik into a position not only to recover the riches for him, but to dampen the dangerous fervor of the rebellious serfs: "I am changing my policy," he tells a naïve and uninformed Itzik, "and will allow you to sell your wares among the peasants." Itzik enters the gates of the manor, and indeed for his meager wares he finds ready buyers, who pay with the money they have earlier stolen from the estate. Soon enough Itzik is predictably stripped of the million Kroner after the baron's army has wracked the peddler's village and destroyed his family in a horrific pogrom. Thus does Itzik function as a "middleman" not only in the East European economy, but in its *political* economy; the Jewish merchant is a living buffer between the grasping Gentile nobility and the exploited Gentile peasantry. "From that day onward Itzik the peddler was insane."[50]

The story had puzzled Finkelstein as a child, and his father had offered no interpretation. As he ponders the tale at his father's graveside, however, he is struck not so much by the diabolism with which the baron has diverted the wrath of the serfs by offering up Itzik and his wares, as by the tragic willingness with which Itzik has allowed himself to be scripted in on the baron's terms, first as an errand-boy and finally as a scapegoat. The meaning of the story, Finkelstein now concludes, "was that this Itzik should never have allowed himself to accept a role that was not his, a role that the baron had created for him." "They are not going to make an Itzik out of me," he resolves.[51]

The parable of Itzik gathers its force when, on his way out of the cemetery where his father is buried, Finkelstein discovers a headstone that has been toppled by hoodlums and defaced with a yellow swastika. "In America *noch*" [In America yet], Finkelstein thinks, thus bringing European and American history to unbearable proximity, both by the literal sense of the sentence and by its poignant bilingualism. The toppled gravestone and the swastika, indeed, symbolize the occasion for *Focus* itself, just as Finkelstein's resolve never to be made "an Itzik" condenses the sense of the novel to its purest form. The tale of Itzik in Poland provides the deep genealogy of that "racket" which Finkelstein deems anti-Semitism; the stone and the swastika are the immediate, concrete emblems of that racket and its contemporary sway.[52]

This sociopolitical dimension of "being made an Itzik" has its psychological analogues as well; and the two dimensions of anti-Semitism will come together over the course of the novel in Miller's treatment of the ways in which the social category "Jew" becomes aligned with the visual category "Jew." Layered atop this foundation of political exploitation, in Miller's scheme, is a superstructure of Jew-hatred deriving in large part from a psychology of *self*-hatred. If the motive for anti-Semitic practice is largely economic, in other words, the venom of anti-Semitic belief is largely psychological.

Miller develops this most clearly in a scene involving Newman's interview with an applicant named Gertrude Hart when he is still working in the personnel office. Newman's mistaken hire, Miss Kapp (whom he now refers to matter-of-factly as "Kapinsky"), has been fired; Newman now has his new glasses, and he is eager to prove himself and his sharpness of vision by hiring the "perfect girl"—someone whose visual credentials as a Gentile are above reproach. In this frame of mind he scrutinizes Gertrude Hart, whom he takes to be a Jew. But as a result of this scrutiny on his part he also thinks he discerns her scrutinizing *him*. Miss Hart seems to be taking him for a Jew, and his uneasy posture under her suspicious gaze leads Newman into the house of mirrors of his own hatreds and fears. He cannot bring himself to rebut her unspoken racial accusation, and in his own embarrassment and discomfiture—his acquiescent *imposture*—he feels her eyes actually transforming him into a Jew, for "to him Jew had always meant impostor": "poor Jews pretended they were poorer than they were, the rich richer . . . Their houses smelled, and when they did not it was only because they wanted to seem like gentiles. For him, whatever they did that was pleasing was never done naturally, but out of a desire to ingratiate themselves . . . And when he encountered an open-handed Jew . . . in the Jew's open-handedness he saw only trickery or self-display. Pretenders, impostors. Always." Under Gertrude Hart's gaze Newman comes to feel the impostor, which is to say, he comes to feel the Jew.[53]

This passage is a compelling study of the hatred that can attach to race—virtually no piece of evidence is enough to reverse its course. What follows is a stunning treatment of the complex processes of projection, ascription, and reification, as the anti-Semite contemplates one whom he supposes to be "the Jew" and slowly recognizes the desire he feels for her.

> He was sitting there in the guilt of the fact that the evil nature of the Jews and their numberless deceits, especially their sensuous lust for women—of which fact he had daily proof in the dark folds of their eyes and their swarthy skin—all were the reflections of his own desires with which he had invested them . . . her eyes had made a Jew of him; and his monstrous desire was holding back his denial.

As he continues to scan her face he pegs her racially, first as looking "almost Irish," but he then notices a "Hebrew dip to the nose," and he can finally conclude comfortably, "She had the vitriol of the Hebrews . . . and their lack of taste."[54]

For Arthur Miller the manner in which a particular class of people comes to "look Jewish" is crucial to the internal dynamic of anti-Semitism. Like Hobson, Miller could not take up the question of Jewishness and justice without taking up the elusive problem of Jewishness-as-difference itself. But whereas Hobson would interrogate the static category "Jews" under an epistemological regime of race and "difference," Miller investigates racial Jewishness itself as a dynamic *process* that is set in motion, in part, by the conventions of an anti-Semitism whose purpose is not hatred but profit. The novel thus aims primarily to illumine the complex relationship between appearance and vision, between the physiognomy of the Jew and the eye of the beholder. Gertrude's "eyes made a Jew of [Newman]" in their first interview. "You ought to have more sense than to make a Jew out of me," Newman objects to his neighbor, Fred. "No one makes a Jew out of me and gets away with it," Gertrude later tells Newman.[55] This drumming on the theme of "making a Jew out of me" by acts of perception and social intercourse lends a second dimension to

Finkelstein's notion of "making an Itzik of me" by acts of political coercion. In order to be exploited as an Itzik on the American scene the Jew must first be seen and known; but it is the seeing and knowing themselves that render the Jew racially Jewish.

Miller introduces the relationship between essential "difference" and social modes of perception when Newman first examines himself in the mirror with his new glasses on: "In the mirror in his bathroom, the bathroom he had used for nearly seven years, he was looking at what might very properly be called the face of a Jew. A Jew, in effect, had gotten into his bathroom." Newman's own preconceived notion of Jewish physicality is reflected back to him as Jewishness. It is not that now his face merely looks Jewish; in looking like the face of a Jew, it "might very properly be called the face of a Jew." The anti-Semitic gaze and the Semitic physiognomy meet at the mirror's surface to produce a "Jew" where before there had been none. That Jew is now loose in Newman's house.[56]

Although there seems an optical trickery at work in his newly discovered visual Jewishness—"He took the glasses off and slowly put them on again to observe the distortion"—Newman's torrent of associations confounds the notions of objectivity and subjectivity, revealing his presumptive "Jewishness" as a complicated interplay of physicality and character:

> He tried his smile. It was the smile of one who is forced to pose before a camera, but he held it and it was no longer his smile. Under such bulbous eyes it was a grin, and his teeth which had always been irregular now seemed to insult the smile and warped it into a cunning, insincere mockery of a smile, an expression whose attempt at simulating joy was belied, in his opinion, by the Semitic prominence of his nose, the bulging set of his eyes, the listening posture of his ears. His face was drawn forward, he fancied, like the face of a fish.[57]

By a density of description and a confusion of logic this passage renders two distinct recitations at once: the account of Newman's own unhappiness to find himself a Jew, and an account of Newman's presuppositions about Jewishness, now reflected back to him as physiognomical facts in his own Jewish face. The extent to which Newman is "making a Jew of himself" is indicated in the first two lines quoted here, where "his smile" becomes "no longer his smile" as Newman "forces" himself to "pose." In Newman's worldview, as we come to find, "being forced" and "posing" are the chief conditions marking the Jew's movement in the social world. As he stands smiling before the mirror under the harsh command of his own inspection, he literally *becomes* someone who "is forced" and who "poses"—a Jew. This recognition of his own Jewish posture, then, comes back to Newman as observable fact. Although the presence of the anti-Semitic gaze is marked throughout the passage by phrases like "seemed," "in his opinion," and "he fancied," Newman registers only the observable facts of a "cunning, insincere mockery of a smile," a "Semitic" nose, "bulbous" eyes, "listening" ears—the "face of a fish." This physiognomical condition, and the state it represents, "belie" the pretense of "joy." There *can* be no joy for the Jew; and indeed, for Newman there *is* no joy *as* a Jew—a fact he sees as plainly as the nose on his face.

Similarly, when Newman loses a job opportunity because of his Semitic appearance, he muses over the way in which he has been artificially but nonetheless irretrievably interpolated as a racial Jew. "Is it possible . . . that Mr. Stevens looked at me and thought me untrustworthy, or grasping, or loud because of my face?" he wonders. His reflection on this injustice stirs an inchoate protest against a regime of social perception that renders individuals so utterly knowable by their outward appearance. For the moment, however, Newman's capacity for protest is limited by his own stubborn adherence to that very regime.

> *He* was not his face. Nobody had a right to dismiss him like that because of his face. Nobody! He was *him,* a human being with a certain definite history and he was not this face which looked like it had grown out of another alien and dirty history.

On the one hand, back when he was working in the personnel office, "no proof, no documents, no words could have changed the shape of a face that he himself suspected," and hence he now understands as well as anyone the power of racial suspicions to generate their own racial objects. And yet, on the other hand, even as he is beginning to recognize the process by which racial Jews are created, he still does not recognize the Jewish race as a creation of that process. Rather, Jews are products of an "alien and dirty history."[58]

The latter half of this equation will ultimately shift for Newman; the Jews' history comes to seem neither alien nor dirty, as his own victimization as a Jew forces the realization that racial "Jewishness" is not the stable essence he had always supposed, but a highly unstable categorical convention based upon certain social practices and ways of seeing. By the novel's end Newman the sometime anti-Semite could perhaps say of the Jews, after Theodore Herzl, "We are one people—our enemies have made us one without our consent."⁵⁹ Unlike Herzl, however, Newman could note that not all those who had been rendered members in this unified Jewish people had originally been Jews in fact. The Jews, according to the bottom-line definition in Newman's evolving cosmos, are people who are treated in a particular way, socially and politically; and anyone so treated is "in effect" a Jew. "Jewish" identity is thus unhinged from any stable notions of race—*anybody* can turn out to be Jewish—but neither can Jewishness be entirely uncoupled from the question of looking and being seen a certain racially charged way.

The twin themes of political and psychological Jewishness ("making an Itzik" and "making a Jew") converge in the ironic early history of Newman and Gertrude Hart. In his capacity as personnel officer, Newman has refused to hire Gertrude because she looked Jewish, because she seemed to take him for a Jew, because he experienced a monstrous desire for her, because his desire for her (a Jewess) was indeed monstrous, and because in his very monstrousness he in fact became the Jew she took him to be. After Newman himself has lost his job, their paths cross again in another interview at a second firm—this time he is the Jewish-looking applicant and she is working in the personnel office. Gertrude understands that Newman had taken her for a Jew, and she comments simply that he must have been looking at her "cockeyed" before. Her remark causes Newman to focus upon Gertrude's changeability and upon his own vision:

> It was like seeing a face in a movie change and dissolve, taking on a new character and yet remaining the same face . . . Her eyes in which he had detected that mocking secretiveness were now simply the darkened eyes of a woman who had done a lot of crying. And yet they were the same eyes. Her nose . . . it occurred to him that the Irish often had a dip in their noses, and he thought now that it became her well . . . As a Jewess she had seemed vitriolic and pushy and he had hated himself even as he was drawn fearfully to her, but now he no longer feared her.

Once again later on, after the two are married, Newman changes Gertrude back and forth from Jewish to Gentile, like a Nekar cube or a figure-ground puzzle, by sheer effort of mind: "There she was . . . , Jewish. Now he changed her back again . . . Here she was, Gertrude, his wife, gentile, as easily understandable as his own mother."⁶⁰

Like other works that interrogate conventional notions of "difference" only by mobilizing the very categories they seek to undermine

(*Pudd'nhead Wilson* and *Black No More*, for instance), *Focus* refuses to sit completely still for analysis. *Is* there such a thing as a Jewish race, by this account? Miller does define anti-Semitism as a peculiar brand of madness—"People were in asylums for being afraid that the sky would fall, and here were millions walking around as insane as anyone could be who feared the shape of a human face." And yet that "shape of a human face" is so fundamental to the phenomenon of anti-Semitism as Miller sees it that one cannot dispense with the notion of race and races in unraveling the complexities involved either in "making Jews" or "making Itziks" in the American social order. Race is a self-sustaining feature of the social landscape, and no less so in its moments of self-collapse. Newman—like Phil Green in *Gentleman's Agreement*—can make a muddle of the notion of a Jewish race by "looking Jewish" without in fact *being* Jewish. But "looking Jewish" is the baseline reality that Newman must approximate in order to call into question the idea of Jewish physicality; and so just as Phil Green proves the racial basis of Jewishness by failing to pass, so Newman reifies the Jewish "look" by assuming it. (Nor are Jews alone among white races in *Focus:* when Newman makes his report against the Christian Front, the beat cop whom he deals with has a "broad Irish face.")[61]

At bottom *Focus* and *Gentleman's Agreement* are predicated on the same assumption of interchangeability, and subject to the same limitations of that assumption. Just as the Gentile Green can volunteer to be victimized by anti-Semitism (or so, at least, would Hobson like to think), so the Gentile Newman can be *in*voluntarily victimized by it. But the way in which both works are structured by the Jewish "look" is symptomatic of their production amid the historic flux of stable Semitic racial character and newly consolidated Caucasian whiteness: that there *is* in fact such a thing as "looking Jewish" is, paradoxically, precisely why Green cannot pass and why Newman can.

Finally, it is less the theme of mistaken identity than Newman's dramatic decision simply to go ahead and be a Jew that aligns Miller's novel with *Gentleman's Agreement*. Newman turns out not to be Philip Green's inverted double, but Professor Lieberman's. Whereas Lieberman is a Jew marked by classically Jewish physiognomy who goes forth to proclaim, "I am *not* a Jew," Newman is a *non*-Jew marked by classically Jewish physiognomy who goes forth to proclaim, "I *am* a Jew"—a reverse variation on Lieberman's "new principle." By setting the more radical shape-shifter at the center of his work, Miller thus makes *Focus* a novel less about Jewishness than about social conscience and justice generally—a theme embodied as well in the character of Finkelstein.

It is worth pausing, in closing, to consider the nexus established here between justice and race, especially in the mid-1940s, the era of the March on Washington Movement and the Fair Employment Practices Committee (FEPC), the campaign for Double Victory, Chicago's housing covenant wars, and early federal promises "to secure these rights" for American Negroes. Miller could not write about race and justice in 1945 and avoid the question of the color line. If, as Carey McWilliams had it, anti-Semitism had been a "mask for privilege" in the decades before the 1940s, then the racial revision of Jewishness into Caucasian whiteness would become the invisible mask of *Jewish* privilege in the decades *after* the 1940s. (Jews, for instance, would move in next door to Gentiles in the suburban neighborhoods that Federal Housing Authority policy so vigilantly preserved for members of "the same social and racial classes." If Jewishness never faded altogether as a social distinction, it did fade considerably in these years as a *racial* one.)[62] No less than Laura Z. Hobson's disquieting assertion of equality based upon literal interchangeability, *Focus,* by its revision of racial Jewishness, raises the question of the relationship between real justice and real "difference."

The novel offers but fleeting commentary on the meaning of the sharpening American color line for the prospect of Jewish racial identity. After the Christian Front had vandalized his property by strewing garbage across his lawn, Newman stood "white and clean in his pajamas on the porch, [staring] down the stoop at the glistening of some wet food leavings that were scattered in the grass." The reference to Newman's whiteness here could be, like the logic of justice based upon sameness that governs *Gentleman's Agreement,* a protest against the unjust treatment, not of a citizen or neighbor, but of a specifically *white* citizen and neighbor. But if so, this seems Newman's sentiment, not Arthur Miller's. Later, as Newman reflects upon his alienation from his own (lily-white) neighborhood, he recalls an earlier evening when a Puerto Rican maid had been accosted on his street, and no one had come to her aid.

> She could have been murdered, clubbed to death out here that night. No one would have dared outdoors to help, to even say she was a human being. Because all of them watching from their windows knew she was not white.
>
> But he was white. A white man, a neighbor. He *belonged* here. Or

did he? Undoubtedly they all knew the rumor by now. Newman is a Jew.[63]

The compelling indeterminacy here—"He belonged here. Or did he?"—may mark the ambiguous racial status of the Jewish pariah in 1945, but it also signals Miller's refusal to take refuge in whiteness. The novel's notable silence on the African-American presence and on antiblack racism as a phenomenon related in some way to anti-Semitism does leave lingering questions about the overall politics of race envisioned here. Yet this treatment still does not seek to efface the physicality of the white races; nor does Miller lay claim to a simpler, self-assured whiteness. In this respect *Focus* represents a more progressive political impulse than either of the dominant approaches to the Jewish race in more recent decades—that is, scientific rebuttals to racially inflected anti-Semitism, like Raphael Patai and Jennifer Wing's *Myth of the Jewish Race* (1975), or politically spirited disavowals of whiteness and white privilege, like Michael Lerner's "Jews Are Not White" (1993).[64] In other words, Miller neither reifies race by arguing the biogenetic specifics of Jewishness nor dodges the issue of white privilege that surely undergirds the history of Jews in the United States. Rather, he locates the phenomenon of race in the eye of the beholder—in disparate acts of perception engendered by the contingencies of political economy and power relations.

Newman's racial conversion or awakening at the end of *Focus,* indeed, represents one of the few models extant for a truly progressive politics based upon the deconstruction of race: it is a progressive politics on the coalition model (see Chapter 8), and yet it is coalition rooted not in a reification of categories, but in a recognition of their logical nonsense. When questioning Newman in the wake of the Christian Front's assault, a policeman asks him to name all the Jews in the neighborhood.

"There are the Finkelsteins on the corner . . ."
"Just them and yourself?" interrupted the policeman.
"Yes. Just them and myself."[65]

Newman recognizes his own Jewishness as a product of the perception of others, and he decides to band together with others so perceived. *This* is a solidarity uniquely attuned to race, not as a biological bond, but as a historical process; it is a solidarity founded upon a keen understanding of race, perception, and the vicissitudes of whiteness—the cultural and historical contingencies of looking Jewish and seeing Jews.

*   *   *

In Saratoga in 1877 Joseph Seligman discovered just how racially distant were the Hebrew and the Anglo-Saxon, even if contemporary circumstances in the frontier West and the Reconstruction South pulled for a homogenized political whiteness. Across the latter half of the nineteenth century Jews, by common consensus, did represent a distinct race; but by the mid-twentieth such certainties had evaporated. Miller and Hobson could now toy with and undermine notions of distinct Jewish racial character, though the older view still left traces on their work. If the core concern for "fitness for self-government" determined the broad patterns of racial perception over time in the United States from 1790 to the 1840s to the post-1924 period, these instances of racial instability and indeterminacy reveal the social, political, and psychological circuitry by which history has divided the polity along racial lines that, paradoxically, can be as unforgiving as they are unreliable. The racial contradictions of 1877 and the racial odyssey of American Jews from "white persons" to "Hebrews" to "Caucasians" illustrate how historical circumstance, politically driven categorization, and the eye of the beholder all conspire to create distinctions of race that are nonetheless experienced as *natural* phenomena, above history and beyond question.

The Celtic physiognomy and "black-tinted" skin. "Outward Bound," T. H. Maguire, lithograph, 1854, after a painting by T. Nichol. © Collection of the New-York Historical Society.

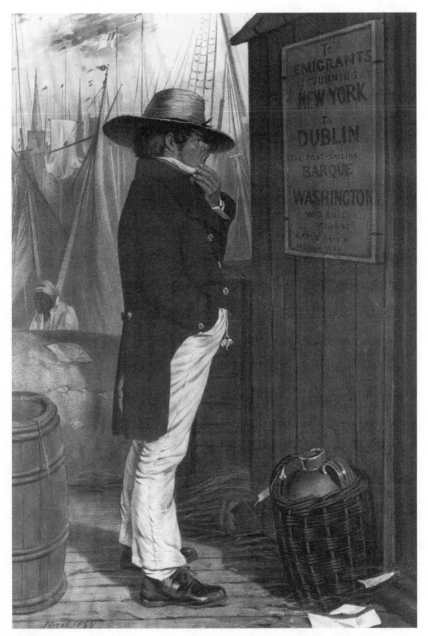

The Celt partially whitened. "Homeward Bound," T. H. Maguire, lithograph, 1854, after a painting by T. Nichol. © Collection of the New-York Historical Society.

THE IGNORANT VOTE—HONORS ARE EASY.

Racially charged portraits of the two leading threats to the Republic, the Negro and the Celt. *Harper's Weekly,* 1876.

A.D. 1877.

APPLE LADY. "It ain't no use you're comin' here, Moses Levy; you must buy your peanuts summers else in future. I ain't no objection to you personally; but, in the commercial sense of the word, me guests don't like it."

Jewishness as "difference." In this satire of Hilton's policy at Saratoga, Moses Levy's expulsion is intimately related to his distinct physiognomy. *Harper's Weekly,* 1877.

"Italian Street Musicians and Their Masters." Racialized physicality matches demonic Italian brutality, as a young boy is punished for failing to bring home as much money as expected from his day's work. *Frank Leslie's Illustrated*, 1878. © Collection of the New-York Historical Society.

Stanley in Africa. Popularized depictions of blackness and savagery underwrote an ideology of united, consanguine whiteness. *Harper's Weekly,* 1878.

Demographic apocalypse in the 1890s: "Unrestricted Immigration and Its Results—
A Possible Curiosity of the Twentieth Century, The Last Yankee." *Frank Leslie's
Illustrated*, 1896.

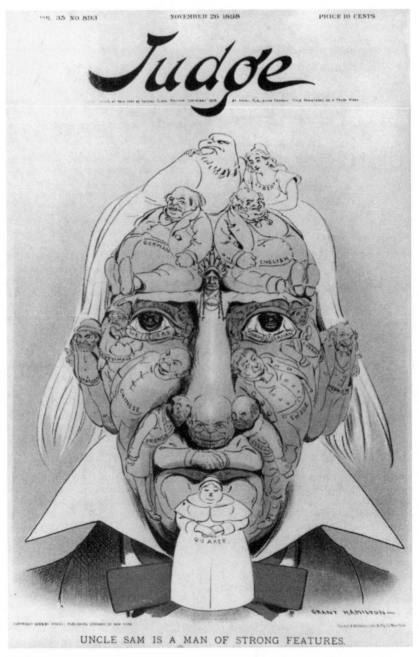

VOL. 35 NO 893   NOVEMBER 26 1898   PRICE 10 CENTS

Judge

GRANT HAMILTON —

UNCLE SAM IS A MAN OF STRONG FEATURES.

"Uncle Sam is a man of strong features." The racial make-up of the United States as depicted in *Judge*, 1898.

White yet Other—Other yet white. Rudolph Valentino menaces Agnes Ayres in *The Sheik*, Famous Players, 1921.

The birth of "ethnicity": cookie-cutter depictions of the peoples of Europe contrast sharply with an earlier era's graphic conventions of physiognomy, race, and descent. *Detroit Free Press,* 1941.

In donning the black, the Hebrew becomes Caucasian: Al Jolson, "unrecognizable as a Jew," in *The Jazz Singer,* Warner, 1927.

CLERK. "I am very sorry, but my orders are —"
TOURIST. "Yesh, yesh, I know all about your orters; but how voz it dot you knowed I vozn't a Ghristian?"

Failing to pass (1): marked by an unmistakable physiognomy, a Jewish registrant is denied entry to a restricted hotel. *Harper's Weekly*, 1877.

Failing to pass (2): marked by an unmistakable physiognomy, Phil Green (Gregory Peck) is granted entry to a restricted resort, until he arouses suspicions by asking about the hotel's policy of restriction. *Gentleman's Agreement*, Fox Studios, 1947.

At left, the Sharks ("too dark to pass"); at right, the Jets ("an anthology of what is called American"). *West Side Story,* United Artists, 1963.

THE MANUFACTURE OF CAUCASIANS

If it was not a foregone conclusion that the hierarchically ordered white races ever would become a single, consanguine race of Caucasians in popular estimation, then what circumstances account for the transformation? What are some of the social, political, and cultural forces that moved the white races so decisively in the direction of "Caucasian" whiteness?

The chapters of part three examine three critical areas in this reforging of a unified whiteness. American imperialism conferred its benefits by a logic of pan–white supremacy, even if it was carried out under the banner of "Anglo-Saxon" entitlement; naturalization case law upheld the logic of the "free white persons" clause of 1790 just as agitation for immigration restriction was challenging the notion of white consanguinity; and civil rights politics eclipsed the lingering divisions among the white races as it pressed an agenda of racial justice defined by the binary logic of the Jim Crow South. In each case a powerful counterlogic of white-over-black, of color/not-color, mitigated for non–Anglo-Saxons the effects of narrowly conceived Anglo-Saxon supremacism, revising the subordinate position that the regime of Anglo-Saxondom had reserved for these "inferior" white races.

Hence though conceptions of racial "difference" and hierarchy among the peoples of Europe were ascendant between the 1840s and the 1920s, the discourse of empire and the conservative racial logic of naturalization law stabilized and kept afloat the otherwise battered notion of monolithic, indivisible whiteness. Similarly, in the decades following the 1924 immigration legislation, emergent civil rights agitation—a new politics of black and white—was among the social and political phenomena that hastened the reunification of whiteness or papered over its presumed faultlines.

These chapters exhaust neither the social practices contributing to the reconsolidation and ideological survival of "Caucasian" whiteness, nor the sites at which such whiteness was constructed and maintained. Others might include cultural forms like segregated baseball and integrated boxing, the legal and medical discourses of sexuality and "miscegenation," or the Jim Crow practices of labor unions and real estate brokers. Rather, the chapters that follow point up a few of the ways in which American political culture reconciled competing racial schemes for dividing the polity; and it suggests some of the reasons that the racial "sameness" of today's so-called white ethnics was one outcome of this competition.

We too, even though we are not Anglo-Saxons, believe in "manifest destiny" and—we add for the benefit of the nativists—"manifest destiny" also believes in us.

—Julius Frobel, *Aus America* (1857)

Probably the majority of Americans would prefer to be excused from loading this country with another "negro problem." We may swallow a small black morsel like Hawaii; but if we must expand largely, our acquisitions should be civilized Caucasian communities, such as can adapt to our democratic system. Barbarian dominions can never be amalgamated with the American republic, and we want no such satrapies.

—*Catholic Citizen,* 1898

 6

The Crucible of Empire

In Edgar Allan Poe's *Narrative of A. Gordon Pym* (1838) the line manager aboard ship, Dirk Peters, undergoes a transformation much like Teague O'Regan's metamorphosis from "bog-trotter" to "white" ambassador in Brackenridge's *Modern Chivalry*. Peters is first introduced as "the son of an Indian squaw of the tribe of Upsorokas," "one of the most purely ferocious-looking men I ever beheld." Pym further marks him racially and phrenologically, noting an indentation on the crown of his head "like that on the head of most Negroes." He is described as a "hybrid" whose own racially mixed identity and whose lusty stories of the South Pacific entice the mutinous crew with visions of a sexual pleasure more luring than the monetary profits of a whaling voyage. Ultimately, however, this adventure whitens the line manager: once they find themselves amidst a "savage" people whose "complexion was a jet black, with thick and long woolly hair," Pym regards himself and Peters as "the only living white men upon the island."[1]

The volatility of race in American culture has derived in part from the effects of expansionism into territories peopled, as in Pym's narrative, by "savages." For the *Catholic Citizen* in 1898, to cite a case, it was partly by juxtaposition to the "small black morsel" of Hawaii that the Celtic community in the United States became so comfortably "Caucasian." As the sociologist Howard Winant has observed, "Just as the noise of the big bang still resonates through the universe, so the overdetermined construction of world 'civilization' as a product of the rise of Europe and the subjugation of the rest of us still defines the race concept."[2] In racial figurations in the United States, this historic rise of "European civilization" was compressed, as it were, and tortuously convoluted, in the years between the 1840s and the 1920s. During that time, continual expansion and conquest pulled for a unified collectivity of European "white men," monolithic and supreme, even while nativism and the immigration question fractured that whiteness into its component—"superior" and "inferior"—parts.

In the preface to *Warpath and Bivouac,* his 1890 account of the "stirring events" of the Plains Indian Wars a decade and a half earlier, John Finerty noted, "Stories of Indian warfare . . . have ever been popular with people of all nations, and more particularly with the American people, to whom such warfare is rendered familiar both by tradition and experience."[3] Finerty here indicated a powerful subterranean current in American political culture: the self-renewing quality of American expansionism, both as a periodic reality and as a perpetually narrated (and thus ever-present) past. The "experience" and the "tradition" are fused in such a way that to be "American" is in some sense to locate oneself on a map whose coordinates are determined by a national narrative whose chief themes (in Finerty's rendition, though one might as easily cite Francis Parkman, George Bancroft, John Fiske, Theodore Roosevelt, or Frederick Jackson Turner) include "advancing our banner in the wilderness of the West," "subduing the savage and sanguinary tribes that so long barred the path of progress in our Territories," braving the "terrors of fiendish torture and mutilation in case of capture by the savages," exposing oneself to "the most cunning and merciless of all existing human races"—all for "the extension of our peaceful borders."[4]

That the "savage" resides at the borders of our imagined national community has textured American political life from the Indian Wars to the Gulf War: debates over actual policies regarding actual "savages" work a kind of homogenizing magic on the homefront, just as experience itself—as soldier, nurse, or captive—casts the racial character of citizenship in stark relief. For most Americans it is not Finerty's "experience" but his "tradition" that exerts its force. American national history is narrated in such a way—Americans receive their historical sense of place in such a way—that citizenship itself interpolates "the American" as the antithesis of that "savage" on the border. For African-, Latino-, and Asian-Americans this has been a matter of some consternation and conflict. For members of the probationary white races of the nineteenth and early twentieth centuries—John Finerty included—it was a matter of some moment. As one German immigrant announced in the late 1850s, "We too, even though we are not Anglo-Saxons, believe in 'manifest destiny.' " And, he added portentously for the benefit of the nativists, " 'manifest destiny' also believes in us."[5]

Expansionism and Public Debate

The history of nineteenth-century American expansionism had a racial contradiction at its core: while U.S. conquests across North America and the Pacific at once enacted and reinforced a principle of *white* supremacy, between at least the 1840s and the early twentieth century they were carried out under an ideological banner of *Anglo-Saxon* supremacy. This is not a question of mere semantics. Senator Albert Beveridge of Indiana, for example, was among the most outspoken enthusiasts for "Anglo-Saxon" expansion: in his famous "March of the Flag" (1898) he lauded "the Anglo-Saxon impulse" whose "watchword [in Jefferson's time] and whose watchword throughout the world today is 'Forward!' " The notion of an ever-advancing Anglo-Saxondom was attached to a specific phenotype as well. Reviewing the army of advance ("these thoroughbred soldiers from the plantations of the South, [and] from the plains and valleys and farms of the west"), Beveridge fixed upon a distinctly racial male aesthetic:

> The fine line is everywhere. The nose is straight, the mouth is sensitive and delicate. There are very few bulldog jaws. There is, instead, the steel-trap jaw of the lion. The whole face and figure is the face and figure of the thoroughbred fighter, who has always been the fine-featured, delicate-nostriled, thin-eared, and generally clean-cut featured man.[6]

In lingering upon the physiognomical details of the American soldier, Beveridge was distinguishing the Anglo-Saxon not merely from the Malay and Negrito enemy of the moment, but also from the many non–Anglo-Saxon elements within U.S. borders.[7]

The designation "Anglo-Saxon" had crossed over from scientific discourse into American vernacular in the 1840s, within a context of *both* Mexican conquest in the West and Celtic immigration in the East. As a racialist unit of meaning, then, "Anglo-Saxon" performed two distinct, exclusionary functions within the reigning ideology of American nationalism: it separated racially "pure" Americans from "mongrelized" and "degenerate" Mexicans on one front; and it divided virtuous, self-governing Anglo-Saxon citizens from pathetic Celtic newcomers on another. But, as street-level social practices and legal codes (laws governing citizenship, voting, jury service, and officeholding, for example) included even those problematic Celts within the ranks of the conquerors, "Anglo-Saxondom" itself was an unstable and hotly contested terrain. The "Anglo-Saxon" mission of subduing the continent and reaching across the Pacific thus both destabilized and shored up immigrants' whiteness: it excluded them (as the wrong kind of citizens) from the glories of national destiny, and yet conferred upon them (as citizens nonetheless) the fruits of white-supremacist conquest.

Simple whiteness was not always foremost on the minds of those who discussed and debated expansionist policy. As Reginald Horsman has argued, the idea of Anglo-Saxon racial integrity existed in high discourse on "liberty" and "law" even as early as the Revolutionary generation; that enlightenment vision gradually became "an ideology of continental, hemispheric, and even racial destiny for a particular chosen people" in the nineteenth century. Increasingly by mid-century "our nation" referred to an "Anglo-Saxon" people; and in the context of Texan annexation and the war with Mexico, "our national destiny" referred to a distinctly racial agenda.[8] Thus in the 1840s James Buchanan could remark of Texas's independence from Mexico and eventual annexation to the United States, "The Anglo-Saxon blood could never be subdued by anything that claimed Mexican origin." The *Southern Quarterly Review* chimed in on "the imperial Anglo-Saxon race, whose mission on earth is like that of the Jews in Canaan, 'to subdue the land and possess it.' " John O'Sullivan (the *Democratic Review* editor who coined the phrase "Manifest Destiny") observed of California, "The irresistible army of Anglo-Saxon emigration has begun to pour down upon it, armed with the plough and the rifle, and marking its trail with schools and colleges, courts and representative halls, mills and meeting houses." James Gordon Bennett, too, added his voice to this Anglo-Saxonist chorus in the New York *Herald:* "Assigned to the dominion of republicanism on this continent, the pioneers of Anglo-Saxon civilization and Anglo-Saxon free institutions, now seek distant territories ... The arms of the republic ... must soon embrace the whole hemisphere."[9]

This conception of Anglo-Saxon peoplehood and genius was still at play later in the century, when Hawaii, Cuba, the Philippines, Puerto Rico, and Samoa succeeded Mexico as the territories in question. Most outspoken in this regard was Josiah Strong, who predicted in the 1880s that the world was about "to enter upon a new stage of its history—the final competition of races for which the Anglo-Saxon is being schooled. If I do not read amiss, this powerful race will move down upon Mexico, down upon Central and South America, out upon the islands of the sea, over upon Africa and beyond." "Is there any room for reasonable doubt," Strong asked elsewhere, "that this race ... is destined to dispossess many weaker races, assimilate others, and mold the remainder, until ... it has Anglo-Saxonized mankind?"[10]

Politicians like Albert Beveridge and Theodore Roosevelt, too, inclined to such Anglo-Saxon rhapsody; and in 1898, New York's *Irish World* took note of the "Anglo-Maniac Chorus" attending the Spanish-Cuban-American War and the prospect of an Anglo-American entente. It included one clergyman who identified England as "bone of our bone, flesh of our flesh," and another who identified Anglo-Saxons as "the one great race to whom God has given the endowment to civilize the world." It also included Reverend Thomas Dixon, whose understanding of proper American sentiment regarding English-Russian tensions rested on the belief that "the Slav and the Anglo-Saxon have nothing in common."[11]

The peculiar status of many immigrants as both supreme whites and non–Anglo-Saxon Others is readily apparent in the response to imperialism registered in the immigrant press around the time of the Spanish-Cuban-American and Philippine-American Wars. On the one hand, in the context of Asian penetration and the labor migrations it threatened to generate, even a socialist journal like the Yiddish *Abend Blatt* could easily speak of "the Caucasian *[koikazish]*, white race."[12] Similarly, in a piece introducing its readers to the Philippine Islands in 1898, the *Abend Blatt* would offer a racial portrait of the archipelago, broken down into "Malays" (some of whom are "mixed together with a Chinese element"), "Negritos," "Tagalogs" ("they are built well, but we wouldn't regard them as very beautiful, because they have high cheekbones, flat noses, thick lips"), and "Igolots" (who "look very dirty and savage"). Another ethnological catalogue entitled "The Wild Tribes of the Philippines" noted that "the wild Indians" remained "in the same state of savagery that the Spaniards found them in."[13] This was a judgment shared by journals like the *Catholic Citizen* and the *Irish American*. According to the latter, most Filipinos "are in a state of barbarism but little removed from their condition at the time when Columbus revealed America to the eyes of Europe, and gave to Spain the opening of an empire."[14]

On the other hand, however, immigrant editors (and especially Celts) were quite sensitive to the narrow racial patriotism of Anglo-Saxondom, and to its troubling historical erasures. As T. St. John Gaffney remarked,

> The "Anglo-Saxon race," which, according to the best informed ethnical students, is but one-tenth of the population of this country, is accredited with a much larger portion of the upbuilding of this Republic than it deserves . . . The moment a Teuton or a Celt achieves fame in the world of letters, art, or professional life, the moment he wins a victory on land or sea, he is hailed as a new product of "Anglo-Saxon" civilization! But if he winds up in the police court in the morning, he is regarded simply as a drunken German or Irishman.[15]

Wherever these commentators came down on the question of Filipino rights or the prospect of Philippine sovereignty, they did protest an ascendant American brand of Anglo-Saxon supremacism. "Shall we add 10,000,000 Malays . . . and set out to 'civilize' them by means of lynching and Ku-Kluxism for the benefit of a new brood of Carpet-Baggers?" asked James Jeffrey Roche in the Boston *Pilot*. "Or is it not about time to halt the mad career of Anglo-Saxonizing the world?" Patrick Ford's *Irish World* complained of a public school curriculum that taught "each rising generation of Irish, German, French, Scandinavian, Polish, Italian and other children that they were the descendants of a class of commercial marauders in England styling themselves the great 'Anglo-Saxon race.' "[16]

Nor, again, were these merely rhetorical flights of racial fancy. The notion of a racial distinction between Anglo-Saxons and Others gave shape to much immigrant commentary on world affairs at this moment. As a Boston *Pilot* piece on European rivalries in Samoa declared, "If this is to be an 'Anglo-Saxon' war [German immigrants] will beg to be excused. They are quite right. They are not Anglo-Saxons."[17] "You are not of the self same race / Nor blood of the self same clan," the *Irish World* proclaimed in a poem protesting Anglo-Saxon grandiosity. "But Celt and

Teuton face to face / Talk back to you man to man."[18] Elsewhere, in response to popular talk of an Anglo-American alliance and "patriotism of race," Patrick Ford urged "a coming together of Americans of all races and antecedents in opposition to the Anglicized set who would emasculate the virility of American nationality and reduce it to a British colony . . . The one enemy of the honor of the Republic on American soil . . . is the presumptuous and intolerant Anglo-Saxon."[19] A letter-writer to the *Irish World,* signing "Celto-Teutonic," advocated an alliance of Irish and German immigrants to combat "the virus of Anglo-mania"; and another to the Boston *Transcript* chided, "Possibly when the Celt grows stupid and muddy-brained he may grow British"; in the meantime he is able "to love America and despise Britain simultaneously."[20]

But if the language and logic of an "Anglo-Saxon mission" in the Pacific complicated the political location of these "free white persons" who happened not to be Anglo-Saxons, the white-over-nonwhite dynamic of the imperialist project did exert tremendous ideological pull. Even while the *Irish American* decried the sorry example of "Saxon Civilization" in the Soudan (John Bull is "the same brutal savage, today, that he was when he burned the French heroine, Joan of Arc"), on the very same page the editor could castigate the "Filipino Banditti," blithely arguing that "powder and lead . . . are the only arguments that will bring such savages to their senses."[21]

The extent to which even non–Anglo-Saxon immigrants could participate in the festival of racial self-aggrandizement attending trans-Pacific expansion became clear enough in the pro-imperialist arguments of various immigrant journals. The orthodox *Yiddishes Tageblatt* tacitly positioned the Jews of the Lower East Side as natural allies of the Anglo-Saxons in its rendering of the conflict in Manila: "The Filipino revolutionaries are half wild men about whom every barbaric action can be believed." In letters to the editor many of the *Tageblatt*'s readers responded with their own renditions of the "wild, uncivilized," or "half wild" Filipinos, or assertions that the Philippines was a "wild country of mulattoes." Echoing the editor's view that the Filipinos were like the Levites who so misguidedly revolted against the wiser guidance of Moses, one letter-writer declared that the rebellious Filipinos were "like a sick child who will not take the medicine the doctor prescribed."[22]

Kuryer Polski, a Polish journal in Milwaukee, too, identified the Filipinos as a "half savage people," comparing their prospect of independence to the "negro republic of Hayti" (where, by this account, whites were murdered in the most terrible manner, where every moment gave birth to a new revolutionary government, where each new dictator murdered a thousand opponents, and where corruption reigned). Under these circumstances, to be a protectorate of the United States would be "beneficial." Whereas some might have sympathized with the Philippine independence movement on the basis of its parallels with the case of partitioned Poland (as, indeed, *Kuryer Polski* had early on), the editor Michael Kruszka ultimately naturalized his pro-expansionist sympathies in most pithy fashion: "In regard to civilization, the Polish nation stands higher beyond comparison than the Filipinos."[23] Imperialism, then, fostered a pan-European, pan-white political sensibility that countervailed the otherwise divisive logic of Anglo-Saxon supremacy dominating other arenas of public discourse.

Often, paradoxically, it was not imperialism but *anti*-imperialism that rested upon the more virulently racialist logic of civilization, sovereignty, and self-government. There was good precedent for this. In the era of the War with Mexico, the *Democratic Review* had asserted that the "very virtues of the Anglo-Saxon race made their political union with the degraded Mexican-Spanish impossible." On the floor of the Senate one southerner had worried aloud that the nation would be "compelled to receive not merely the white citizens of California and New Mexico, but the peons, negroes, and Indians of all sorts, the wild tribe of Comanches, the bug-and-lizard-eating 'Diggers,' and other half-monkey savages in those countries as *equal citizens of the United States*."[24] As Christopher Lasch has shown, American anti-imperialism in the 1890s, too, most often reflected not sympathy with the Filipino independence movement, but a racial fear for the republic should Emilio Aguinaldo and his "savage" followers gain entrance to the halls of self-government via annexation. For prominent anti-imperialists like "Pitchfork" Ben Tillman of South Carolina, in other words, their patent inferiority was reason enough to let the Filipinos alone.[25]

The Yiddish *Abend Blatt,* echoing the anticoolie arguments of the 1870s, worried about the possibility of Filipinos' gaining American citizenship, competing with American workers, or even attaining employment as scabs. The discussion was cast in an ethnological account of the half-Filipino, half-Chinese "mixtures" *[mishlungen],* and of the Malays themselves: "how many long years," Philip Krantz wanted to know, would it take to make them over into "intelligent people"?[26] A writer in the Polish *Dziennik Chicagoski* likewise worried that the Philippine "Malays" *[malajczycy]* would have the right to come to the United States in search of work: "The inhabitants of these islands, Malays, numbering over eight million, are a nation which, in respect to their manner of life, differ very little from the Chinese."[27] This was perhaps the strongest analogy possible in America's late-nineteenth-century racial lexicon: whatever was being said of Indians, African-Americans, and European immigrants, in the wake of the Chinese Exclusion Act the notion that *this* particular group was uniquely unsuited to the rigors of American citizenship was the nearest thing contemporary discourse offered to a settled national will.

Humphrey Desmond's *Catholic Citizen* was most outspoken in its racialist anti-imperialism. By Desmond's reckoning in late 1898, if the United States annexed the Philippines, then the "unripe fruit of victory" in the war with Spain would finally have to include "barbarism," "Chinese emigration," "Malay citizenship," "miscegenation," and "a general transformation of our democratic system."[28] The *Catholic Citizen*'s reasoning is worth examining in some detail: this Catholic, largely immigrant and second-generation journal reproduced in its anti-imperialism precisely the racialist-republicanist arguments that characterized the immigration restriction movement. "The inhabitants of the Philippine Islands include . . . Kanakas and Malays who are half civilized and in rebellion; canny Chinese and shrewd Japanese and—in the interior—thousands of naked negritos, wild and untamed as the red aborigines," the journal announced in the fall of 1898. "How can a system of self-government be extended to such a people?"[29] By displacing the standard concern for a non–Anglo-Saxon Other with a concern for an Asiatic Other in its rhetoric of self-government, the *Catholic Citizen* illustrated the alchemy that imperialism could work upon the maligned European immigrant. "The successful working of the American system," wrote Desmond,

> demands a civilized Caucasian people and an educated democracy. In the southern states the black population hamper and clog the working of the American system of government . . . The annexation to this country of nine million native Malays residing in the Philippine Islands—many of them savages, and most of them illiterate—is a proposition that is full of danger . . . If we expect to amalgamate these millions, so utterly foreign to us in race and civilization, why should we exclude the Chinese?[30]

Later in the year, in a manifesto entitled "Why We Don't Want the Philippines," Desmond explained, "It means that American citizenship is to be diluted by an infusion of Malay citizenship, and that American democracy is to stand the test of working itself out among inferior peoples." (Interestingly, Desmond went on to quote an *obiter dictum* from the *Dred Scott* decision regarding the federal right to establish or maintain colonies. Although this is quite a separate issue, given the substance of his argument against "Malay citizenship" and "inferior peoples," it is not surprising that *Dred Scott* came to Desmond's mind.)[31] Desmond's outlook on Pacific expansion affords a dramatic view of that ideological magic by which imperialism could reinvent the *Catholic Citizen*'s readership as an unquestioned part of "a civilized Caucasian people and an educated democracy." Unlike writers such as James Jeffrey Roche, who tended to regard such racialist republicanism as a slander against the Filipinos (as it was against the Irish in America and against the Irish in Ireland), Desmond embraced the exclusionary logic of *racial* "fitness for self-government," but neatly folded his polyglot, non–Anglo-Saxon readership—as "Caucasians"—into the racial ranks of the "fit."

Even for writers like Roche, however, whose sympathies were with the Filipinos and whose enmity was directed against the "Anglo-Saxons," the imperialism debate had an inexorable power to redraw racial lines along strict color lines. His poem "The White Wolf's Cry," for instance, is a self-critical lament for the political misdeeds of a nation of marauders "whose skin—like the leper's—is white!"[32] Although the anti-imperialism that derived from his Irish nationalism allowed Roche to cross racial lines in his empathy for the Filipinos, these sympathies whitened him and his compatriots nonetheless. In response to the Boston *Evening Record*'s remark that "the 'brown man,' be he American Negro, Filipino, dervish or Chinese, is going to the wall with a velocity that is appalling, and yet, what has he done?" Roche asked sarcastically, "Hasn't he done enough to deserve extermination, in being born black, yellow or brown?"[33] Or again, "Where is this madness of foreign conquest to end," Roche asked,

> and how many drops of American and other blood must be shed in order to attain the result of civilizing the Asiatics and conferring on them such blessings as other red and black men enjoy under the beneficent rule of the superior race, here at home in the land of the free? We have accounted, in part, to Heaven for our treatment of the black man. We have yet to account for our treatment of the red man. With such unsettled and halfsettled accounts to our debit, it would seem to be foolish to open another with the brown man.[34]

Symptomatic of the inexorable whiteness of Roche's anti-imperialism was his response when Senator George Frisbee Hoar remarked that the Filipinos were "aliens in race and religion." "The United States has no national religion," wrote Roche. "The Fathers of our country were too wise for that."[35] The lapse was an unusual one for Roche; but his tacit acceptance of the *racial* dimension of Hoar's comment hints at his underlying acknowledgment that there was in fact a "national race"—not Anglo-Saxon, but white. Even if the historical record reads like so many debits which "we" must pay and so many sins for which "we" must atone, atonement itself reinforces a pan-white "we" which, given the division between Celts and Anglo-Saxons in the 1890s, could not at all be taken for granted.

As the *Irish American* remarked regarding the prospect of U.S. annexation of Samoa, such a project "is altogether antagonistic to the American idea of union—aside from the fact that the people of these islands are of a race altogether distinct from those composing the population of the United States."[36] The key here resides in the phrases "altogether distinct" and "those [races] composing the population." There is "difference," and then there is *"difference."* In 1898 even the maligned Celt could endorse the bottom-line proposition that race reliably defined legitimate participation in national political life. Howard Winant's racializing "big bang," resonating throughout the turn-of-the-century polity in the form of the imperialism question and its attention to "civilization" and "savagery," underwrote the unifying concept of "free white persons" even at a moment when the notion of unity-in-whiteness was under such vigorous assault by the Immigration Restriction League and the incipient eugenics movement. Although in such violent disagreement on the imperialism question itself, immigrant expansionists like Khasriel Sarasohn and anti-imperialists like James Jeffrey Roche, Humphrey Desmond, and Stefan Barszczewski quietly implied their kinship with one another and even with Anglo-Saxons in a reified whiteness constituted by its contrast to the "savage" on the border.

Narrating the Nation

During the debate in early 1899 over the proper disposition of Spain's former colonies, the *Yiddishes Tageblatt*, Sarasohn's influential orthodox daily, was optimistic about the assimilation of the Philippines: "The United States, which was able to educate the Indian and the Negro, will also be able to educate the Filipino."[37] This Eurocentric formulation of a "United States" standing in opposition to both "the Indian" and "the Negro" indicates the influence of empire in the racial formation of "white" Europeans. It is not simply that the Philippine question posited yet another "savage" on the border whose presence influenced the racial dynamics within U.S. boundaries. Standard narratives of American history had already provided racial roles for the various actors in this drama: "the Filipino" stands in for "the Indian" and "the Negro," uncivilized groups who can be *in* the United States but never *of* it; the nation itself, meanwhile, becomes a monolith of civilization which is by implication "white." Not least, the Semitic readers of the *Tageblatt* silently gather into this fold of a monolithic European community. Not just the Philippine issue per se, but the whole weight of European expansion is brought to bear on the definitions of peoplehood that surfaced at this imperialist moment.

If the slippage between expansionism's "Anglo-Saxon" mission and its "white" supremacism destabilized the relationship among the white races, a powerful stabilizing counterforce was at hand in popular conceptions of American history itself: quite aside from the national romances of a James Fenimore Cooper, standard historical narratives emphasized a pan-European conquest of an otherwise "savage" continent. From the Whig historians on down, both popular and academic versions of U.S. history ratified the logic of the 1790 naturalization law and its emphasis upon a polity of "free white persons." As one *Federal Textbook on Citizenship Training* (1924) announced in "Our Nation / Lesson 1": "Our nation is made up of many millions of people who have come from every land. We have not always had people from so many countries making their home here. Until almost 1500 A.D. very little was known about this part of the world, because people were then afraid to travel very far out upon the unknown sea."[38] A peculiar convolution is at work here: the nation consists of a "we" who lay timeless claim to the land ("We have not always had people from so many countries . . ."), and yet this "we" can only be conceived to have arrived on American shores on some kind of journey from Europe. This is an awesome combination, and it provides a particularly powerful "lesson" with which to begin "training" aspiring American citizens. Europe's natural, God-given claim to North America is fundamental to the very idea of the nation, just as "Americanness" is naturalized as Europeanness-in-migration.

Horace Kallen, the nation's foremost theorist of pluralism, unselfconsciously remarked upon the power of precisely this kind of history lesson. Professing that the moral education of the Passover seder and the story of Egyptian bondage had a profound effect on him, Kallen went on:

The textbook story of the Declaration of Independence came upon me, nurtured upon the deliverance from Egypt and the bondage in exile, like the clangor of trumpets, like a sudden light. What a resounding battle cry of freedom! And then, what an invincible march of Democracy to triumph over every enemy—over the English king, over the American Indian, over the uncivilized Mexican, over the champions of slavery betraying American freedom, over everything, to the very day of the history lesson![39]

The inclusion of "the American Indian" and "the uncivilized Mexican" in this catalogue of "Democracy's" vanquished Others says more than Kallen might have liked about American citizenship and the limits of pluralism. This pride in the legacy of conquest is integral to American nationalism and national belonging; and it is a pride constantly regenerated not only in the perpetually expansive spirit of actual state policy, but in the less formal and more pervasive telling of the tale.

Racialism was among the theoretical mainsprings of much American historiography in the nineteenth and early twentieth centuries. (Without the clue of race, wrote Henry Adams, "history was a nursery tale.")[40] Theodore Roosevelt's *Winning of the West* (1889–1896) opened with a deep past of "Germanic Wanderings," "Frankish and Visigothic invasions," and infusions of "Celtic" blood, all in order properly to situate the sturdy stock who eventually conquered North America.[41] Frederick Jackson Turner's "Significance of the Frontier in American History" (1893) was a self-conscious reworking of the "germ theory" of history that had emphasized "Germanic origins." His thesis depicted a revised "social evolution" in which "the wilderness masters the colonist."[42]

A generation earlier, Francis Parkman's *Conspiracy of Pontiac* (1851), too, had proceeded from certain racial verities: "Nature has stamped the Indian with a hard and stern physiognomy. Ambition, revenge, envy, jealousy, are his ruling passions . . . A wild love of liberty, an utter intolerance of control, lie at the basis of his character, and fire his whole existence." Asserting that the Indian's intellect is "as peculiar as his moral organization," Parkman went on to link Indians' bleak fate to their racial essence:

Some races of men seem moulded in wax, soft and melting, at once plastic and feeble. Some races, like some metals, combine the greatest flexibility with the greatest strength. But the Indian is hewn out of rock . . . Races of inferior energy have possessed a powerful expansion and assimilation to which he is a stranger; and it is this fixed

and rigid quality which has proved his ruin. He will not learn the
arts of civilization, and he and his forest must perish together.[43]

More than its grounding in up-to-the-minute racial thought, the very
narrative line of American historiography holds a formidable racial-
ideological power. In the opening paragraph of *A Larger History of the
United States* (1886), Thomas Wentworth Higginson reflected upon his
experience sailing up "some great Southern river" during the Civil War:
"I was for the first time enabled to picture to myself the American Continent as its first European visitor saw it."[44] Higginson here identifies the
essential gaze of American historiography. ("We may imagine how Columbus felt," he wrote in *Young Folks' History of the United States*
[1876], "when, at daybreak, he was rowed ashore, with waving banners,
and to the sound of music, and when he stepped upon the beach where
no European had ever before landed!")[45] American history becomes a
grand romance of arrival, settlement, conquest, and expansion, all against
the backdrop of a mysterious, mute, and "savage" land.

The narrative customarily begins with an "encounter" distinctly viewed
from the European side. Francis Parkman opens *The Conspiracy of Pontiac* with the rapt observation, "Primitive America, with her savage scen-
ery and savage men, opens to the imagination a boundless world, un-
matched in wild sublimity."[46] Turner's famous essay on the frontier
identifies American history as "the history of the colonization of the Great
West. The existence of an area of free land, its continuous recession, and
the advance of American settlement westward, explain American development."[47] Roosevelt's opening gambit in *The Winning of the West* is to
define "the spread of the English-speaking peoples over the world's waste
spaces" as the "most striking feature in the world's history."[48] And the
Yiddish writer Abraham Cahan announces in the opening of his two-
volume *Historie fun die fereynigte shtaaten* (1910–1912), "The history
of the present day American peoples begins not in America, but in Europe."[49]

Such beginnings, of course, are the product of a fierce teleology. The
narrative arc of Parkman's *Pontiac,* to take just one, ends with "The Death
of Pontiac": "Neither mound nor tablet marked the burial place of Pontiac. For a mausoleum, a city has risen above the forest hero; and the race
whom he hated with such burning rancor trample with unceasing foot-
steps over his forgotten grave."[50] This triumphant narrative line is standard fare. In *A Book of American Explorers* (1877), Higginson remarked

that explorers' narratives had always seemed to him "as interesting as
'Robinson Crusoe,' and indeed . . . very much like it."[51] Under Higginson's pen American history itself becomes pure romance—and starkly
racial romance at that. "Who were the very first men and women that
ever trod the soil of North America?" he asks in *Young Folks' History.*
"Of what race were they, of what color, of what size?" Higginson's earliest
European arrivals find the Atlantic coast "occupied by roving tribes of
men very unlike Europeans in aspect. They were of a copper-color, with
high cheekbones, small black eyes, and straight black hair." The Indians
may not have been "commonly equal to the Europeans in bodily
strength," but still "their endurance was wonderful." Within the first
twenty-five pages, building upon this initial, racial encounter, Higginson's
narrative has already indicated its trajectory along the same line as Parkman's *Pontiac:*

> When first visited by Europeans, the Indians were said to be already
> diminishing in number, through war and pestilence . . . At first they
> were disposed to be friendly with the white men; but quarrels soon
> arose, each side being partly to blame. The savages often burned
> villages, carried away captives, and laid whole regions to waste . . .
> to this day some of the western settlements of the United States live
> in constant fear of attack from Indian tribes. But this race is passing
> away . . . Only those tribes will survive which have adopted, in part,
> the habits of civilization.[52]

Higginson's outlook is not pan-European at every turn. The maturing
nation has succeeded in its mission in spite of "the annual arrival of many
thousand immigrants, wholly untrained in republican institutions," for
instance; nor was it a mere slip by which, in *Larger History,* Higginson
wrote of the "modern American [who] makes a pilgrimage . . . to the
English village church *at whose altars his ancestors once ministered.*" But
the prevailing enmities in the epic of American history finally eclipse intra-
European rivalries and render them but moot distinctions. The powerful
enmity of "white man" and "Indian" culminates, for Higginson, in "The
Great Western March" that is the glory of American history—"the crowning pride of an American citizen, that the States of the Union are spread
from the Atlantic to the Pacific." He revels in "the great transfer of population" from east to west along the turnpike of the Mohawk Valley and
the National Road farther south, and applauds the U.S. Census, which

has documented this romantic triumph. "Progress" itself is measured by the "depth of the strip of civilization" from the Atlantic inland.[53]

Thus, on one level, the historiography of American expansion *justifies* American expansion by a combined logic of race, righteousness, and civilization. The United States won lands from the Indians, according to Roosevelt's *Winning of the West*, "as much by treaty as by war" and paid "many times what we would have paid any civilized people whose claim was as vague and shadowy as theirs." But, by Roosevelt's reckoning in one of the most remarkable passages in American historiography, this magnanimity is immaterial: precisely *how* whites came to possess the land—whether by treaty or by conquest—did not matter, "so long as the land was won."

> All men of sane and wholesome thought must dismiss with impatient contempt the plea that these continents should be reserved for the use of scattered savage tribes, whose life was but a few degrees less meaningless, squalid, and ferocious than that of the wild beasts with whom they held joint ownership . . . The most ultimately righteous of all wars is a war with savages, though it is apt to be also the most terrible and inhuman. The rude, fierce settler who drives the savage from the land lays all civilized mankind under a debt to him. American and Indian, Boer and Zulu, Cossack and Tartar, New Zealander and Maori,—in each case the victor . . . has laid deep the foundations for the future greatness of a mighty people.[54]

Roosevelt's epic song of the "race-important work" of the pioneers brings out the full meaning of the axiom "History is written by the victors." The dynamic relationship between actual policy-making and this kind of historical narrative is nowhere so clearly delineated as in Roosevelt's 1900 Foreword to *The Winning of the West*. "In the year 1898 the United States finished the work begun over a century before by the backwoodsman, and drove the Spaniard outright from the western world," writes the hero of San Juan Hill. He goes on to applaud the most recent burst of expansionist enthusiasm, to describe in Darwinian terms "the vigor and prowess shown by our fighting men" and the nation's "lift toward mighty things," and to scorn the "shortsighted and timid" people who had opposed wars for "the advance of American civilization at the cost of savagery."[55]

The depth of expansionism as an ideological foundation for American national belonging is illustrated by John Finerty's *Warpath and Bivouac*

(1893), a memoir of his experiences during the plains wars of the 1870s. Finerty, an Irish nationalist who throughout the last quarter of the nineteenth century had more than his share of troubles with "Anglo-Saxons" on both sides of the Atlantic, could nonetheless join the Anglo-Saxon with considerable enthusiasm when it came to confronting the Indians of the northern plains. By his account "the white man's government" had signed a treaty favorable to Sitting Bull, sparing most of the Black Hills region from "the daring, restless, and acquisitive Caucasian race." But soon the rumors of gold "fired the Caucasian heart with the spirit of adventure and exploration," and in the months and years immediately following George Custer's Black Hills expedition of 1874, nothing could stop "the encroachments of that terrible white race before which all other races of mankind, from Thibet to Hindostan, and from Algiers to Zululand, have gone down." That "terrible white race," he went on to elaborate, included among others "the Australian miner," "the worried and worn city clerks of London, Liverpool, New York, or Chicago," "the stout English yeoman," "the sturdy Scotchman," "the light-hearted Irishman," and "the daring mine-delvers of Wales and of Cornwall"—varied elements that, in other contexts, decidedly did not make up an indivisible race, either "terrible" or otherwise.[56]

The rank and file of the United States Army, as Finerty recalled it, were largely "either of Irish or German birth or parentage, but there was also a fair-sized contingent of what may be called Anglo-Americans." But Anglo and Celt and Teuton were melted down in this "demon-peopled land," so that though a large proportion of the rank and file was made up of "the never war-absent Irish . . . and of Germans, whose slow bravery solidifies the Celtic ardor with Yankee coolness," it is their unifying whiteness that remains at the fore of Finerty's consciousness and his narrative.[57]

But this western setting, the stage of national expansion, forged "Caucasians" in opposition to an implacable Indian enemy. For Finerty, coyotes are *next to the Indians* the pest of the plains"; he asserts that "the average Indian" is still "the same mysterious, untamable, barbaric, unreasonable, childish, superstitious, treacherous, thievish, murderous creature . . . that he has been since first Columbus set eyes upon him at San Salvador." Thus "nothing better illustrated the dauntless spirit of the Caucasian race than to see . . . a log cabin inhabited by some daring whites, who were prepared to risk all their worldly interests against the Wild Sioux at the muzzles of their long and deadly rifles." Indeed, so taken is Finerty by his own sense of whiteness that, by his account, even the wildlife are apt to comment on his racial identity: "Dozens of American eagles rose majestically from the rocks and soared proudly above us, screaming with all their might, for, doubtless, they had never seen white men before."[58]

Even Finerty's (rare) pleas for justice posit an unbridgeable "difference" between the Indian and the Caucasian, rather than their common humanity:

> We of the Caucasian race must confess, however reluctantly, that even the red Indian has some rights on the soil which bore him that the whites are bound to respect. The Indians have their vicious qualities, many of them borrowed, it is sad to be obliged to admit, from their invaders . . . Their misfortunes have been many, their crimes innumerable, but the honor of the American nation demands that this mysterious, indomitable, and interesting people should be protected against those of the white race who would not, if they could, leave an Indian a single rod of his native land, except for the purpose of sepulture.[59]

As with Dirk Peters, John Finerty's own status as a "Caucasian" emerges amid the violent clash between Euro-Americans and "savages." And like *Pontiac, A Young Folks' History,* and *Winning of the West,* Finerty's treatment of the plains wars of the 1870s interpolates an imagined American citizen for whom national belonging itself is predicated upon an emotional-ideological participation in "subduing the savage and sanguinary tribes that so long barred the path of progress."[60]

William McKinley termed his policy of imperialism in the Philippines "benevolent assimilation." The phrase is wonderfully suggestive not only of the power of paternalism to mask violent social and political realities, but also of the affinities in American discourse between subject peoples abroad and immigrants at home—problem populations whose "difference" stood in the way of successful republican citizenship. Racial discourse in both cases rendered "assimilation" as urgent as it was doubtful. Republican ideology provided the terms by which racial Others were understood, and yet so was republicanism constituted by boundaries of public virtue marked off by those same Others. If racial notions of a superior Anglo-Saxon peoplehood promoted "large policies" abroad, so did they generate anxieties about the fate of a free republic that had taken on too many "undesirable" elements.

In this context of expansion and immigration, census-taking in the United States took on a peculiar sense of drama. A tension existed in nineteenth-century thinking on the question of how the continent was to be peopled. The grandeur of the narrative of conquest, by which the continent was to be inhabited by triumphant Europeans, was increasingly tinged by anxieties regarding the arriving throngs of precisely the wrong Europeans. The census held the key to both stories; and thus otherwise dry statistics and demographic data became the stuff of true romance (for Thomas Wentworth Higginson), tragedy (for Frederick Jackson Turner), or gothic horror (for eugenicists).

In a rhapsodic piece entitled "The Great Western March" (1886), Higginson identified the peopling of the continent (by Europeans) as the "crowning pride" of every American citizen. "The newly published volumes of the United States Census for 1880 give . . . the panorama of this vast westward march," he wrote.

> The successive centres for the United States are here exhibited on a chart with a precision as great, and an impressiveness to the imagination as vast, as when astronomers represent for us the successive positions of a planet. Like the shadow thrown by the hand of some great clock, this inevitable point advances year by year across the continent, sometimes four miles a year, sometimes eight miles, but always advancing. And with this striking summary the census report gives us a series of successive representations on colored charts, at ten year intervals, of the gradual expansion and filling in of population over the whole territory of the United States. No romance is so fascinating as the thought suggested by these silent sheets, each line and tint representing the unspoken sacrifices and fatigues of thousands of nameless men and women.[61]

Turner, for his part, would see this not as a matter of romance but, in the wake of the 1890 census announcing the "close" of the frontier, as a matter of no little discomfort. "The free lands are gone," he wrote in 1896, "the continent is crossed, and all this push and energy is turning into channels of agitation . . . the conditions of a settled society are being reached with suddenness and with confusion."[62] By the first decade of the twentieth century he had begun to worry that "classes are becoming alarmingly distinct," and this drama of population took a decidedly racial turn. Breaking down the arrivals of 1907 "by physical type," Turner found that "one-quarter of them were of the Mediterranean race, one-quarter of the Slavic race, one-eighth Jewish, and only one-sixth of the Alpine, and one-sixth of the Teutonic."[63]

The combination of urbanization and the changing racial make-up of the United States took the luster off of Higginson's romance of the "westward march." The eugenic thinking of the 1910s and 1920s echoed Turner's misgivings, but now in gothic-horrific tones. Recall the congressional eugenics committee's assertion, for instance, that "had mental tests been in operation, and had the 'inferior' and 'very inferior' immigrants been refused admission to the United States, over six million aliens now living in this country, free to vote, and to become the fathers and mothers of future Americans, would never have been admitted."[64] Having successfully conquered the continent, the nation now risked conquest by the immigrant.

But conquest of the continent and conquests across national boundaries proved a more powerful influence on the racial imagination than the prospective biological conquest of the nation by the immigrant. Like the discourse of naturalization law, which, as we shall see, upheld the racial logic of the "free white persons" of 1790, discourses of nationhood, savagery, and civilization throughout this period also gathered European immigrants—however grudgingly—into the community of European conquerors. The manufacture and maintenance of "Caucasian" whiteness depended in part, as Humphrey Desmond had it in 1898, upon national encounters with "barbarian dominions" even more problematic than the immigrants themselves—from constant (and constantly narrated) contact with "black morsels" like the nations of the plains, Mexico, Hawaii, Samoa, Cuba, Puerto Rico, or the Philippines.[65] Like the fictional Teague O'Regan and Dirk Peters before them, non–Anglo-Saxon immigrants thus attained racial parity with the nation's Anglo-Saxon stewards partly in a domestic crucible of empire-building whose white-supremacist heat melted down the distinction between "superior" and "inferior" whites.

7

Naturalization and the Courts

In handing down his decision on the petition for citizenship filed in 1914 by a Syrian immigrant named George Dow, a South Carolina judge complained that "to make the words 'white person' conform to any racial classification" is to plunge oneself into a "Serbonian bog."[1] A century and a quarter after the words "free white persons" had been written into the nation's naturalization law, their vagueness continued to generate contests over inclusion and exclusion in the polity. If the elasticity of the words continued to give hope to aspiring immigrants from Syria, India, Turkey, the Pacific, Mexico, Afghanistan, Japan, China, and the Philippines, this ambiguity was also a ready-made cudgel with which restrictionist judges might beat back these claimants. As the judge in *Dow* concluded, for instance, the framers of the original naturalization law "neither expected nor desired" immigration from anywhere on the globe but Europe—"certainly not from Syria."[2] A Syrian, therefore, must not be "white." This much was plain even to one mired in a "Serbonian bog."

The frankness with which the courts asserted the relationship between race on the one hand and "fitness for self-government" on the other is striking. If boundaries were ever in dispute, largely untouched and unquestioned was the core principle that only certain peoples were sound candidates for good citizenship. At once articulating and sustaining the prejudices of the lawmakers of 1790, one judge explained in 1921:

It is obvious that the objection on the part of congress [to admitting Asians to citizenship] is not due to color, as color, but only to color as an evidence of a type of civilization which it characterizes. The yellow or brown racial color is the hallmark of Oriental despotisms ... It was deemed that the subjects of these despotisms, with their fixed and ingrained pride in the type of their civilization . . . were not fitted and suited to make for the success of a republican form of Government. Hence they were denied citizenship.

"The more homogenous the parts," such reasoning ran, "the more perfect the union."[3] Thus it was not merely *citizenship* that was at issue in these cases but whiteness itself—its boundaries and its good republican substance.

Historically the courts had more than just an academic interest in whiteness. As the legal scholar Cheryl Harris has argued, race had been central to early Anglo-American legal conceptions of property. In the legal customs governing slavery, most notably, race alone separated people who could *own* property (whites) from those who could *be* property (blacks). Further, as European settlers sought to gain control of lands occupied but not legally "possessed" by American Indians, issues of deed, title, and rightful claim were also racialized along an axis of white-nonwhite. Since reigning notions of "liberty" itself were intimately related to "the pursuit of property," moreover, such racial conceptions of property rights brought race to the very core of American political culture. Whiteness itself, Harris argues, became such a social asset as to constitute a tangible *thing*— property—and the courts have historically regarded it and protected it as precisely that. W. E. B. Du Bois's "wage" of whiteness, then, is more than just an apt metaphor; it quite literally describes one dimension of the nation's social reality. Notions of possession, property as the signifier of a citizen's "stake in society," and *self*-possession all converge in race.[4]

The historian Michael O'Malley has advanced a similar argument, although cast in somewhat different terms. Tracing the intimate links between "specie" and "species" in the moral-political syntax of American debates in the late nineteenth century, O'Malley notes a kindred logic at work in assigning "value" either to peoples (especially freed slaves) or to currencies, and an identical anxiety in some quarters over the instability of "intrinsic" value in the face of "artificial" coinage. In this scheme, for instance, counterfeiting and racial passing both represent threats to stable systems of value. And the Reconstruction-era state encroached on long-standing principles of intrinsic, unarguable economic and social value in both areas by its simultaneous experiments in issuing paper monies in the economic sphere and "coining" Negro citizens in the political. O'Malley focuses upon the question of blackness in this complex equation; but between the lines of his comments clearly lies an appreciation of whiteness as value in nineteenth-century social and political relations.[5]

This intrinsic value was precisely what was at stake in the naturalization cases that came before the courts in the 1870s and after, as petitioners from around the globe laid claim not only to citizenship, but to whiteness of the sort specified by the 1790 naturalization law, which still governed matters of inclusion and exclusion. A few aspects of this contest within the courts are worth underscoring at the outset. First, in defending both the border of national belonging and the border of certifiable racial whiteness, the courts gave legal, codified form to a complex of popular, street-level prejudices on the one hand and learned, scientific judgments on the other. These rulings drew upon a number of different sources in wildly inconsistent fashion, but the power of the courts' decisions—like the power of race generally—resided in their withholding or extending favor *seemingly* by a fixed logic of natural, biological fact. There were, however, no "facts," as a District Court judge in Oregon discovered in sorting out the case of Bhagat Singh Thind (1920). This judge finally granted Thind citizenship, noting that although there were precedents running in both directions, those against the petitioner were "not in line with the greater weight of authority."[6] The courts thus *created* authority, even in their feverish search for it.

Second, it is one of the paradoxes of legal logic that between the 1870s and the 1920s the courts consolidated and defended the idea "Caucasian" in their naturalization decisions just as popular and congressional debate over immigration itself was producing a contrary notion of Anglo-Saxon supremacy and Celtic, Hebrew, Slavic, and Mediterranean degeneracy. As portentous as these decisions were for petitioners who were either denied or admitted to citizenship, these cases shored up the whiteness of Europe's probationary white races by inflating the difference between the insiders and the outsiders of 1790, and at a time when the weight of so much other cultural authority was tending in the opposite direction. The bids for citizenship on the part of Chinese, Indian, Armenian, Syrian, or Filipino petitioners, in other words, were *part* of what kept the probationary white races from Europe white. Faced with the task of defining Syrian racial status, for instance, the judge in *Dow* could comfortably pronounce, "The broad fact remains that the European peoples taken as a whole are the fair-skinned or light complexioned races of the world, and form the peoples generally referred to as 'white,' and so classed since classification based on complexion was adopted."[7] Like the nation's frontier warfare and its perpetual narrations, then, these legal skirmishes along the borders of naturalized citizenship staked out a brand of monolithic whiteness which corroborated the reasoning of 1790 precisely in a period when that reasoning was undergoing massive revision.

The Legal Epistemology of Race

Whiteness, as defined by the courts, was a very slippery substance. Indeed, its very indeterminacy rendered it impossible for some to attain. As one California judge rather arrogantly put it in 1928, "What ethnologists, anthropologists, and other so-called scientists may speculate and conjecture in respect to races and origins may interest the curious and convince the credulous, but it is of no moment in arriving at the intent of Congress in the [naturalization] statute aforesaid." All anyone really needed to know about Feroz Din, the Afghan immigrant whose admissibility to citizenship was at issue in this case, was that "he is readily distinguishable from 'white' persons."[8] No further explanation was required.

The indeterminacy of whiteness did raise problems for the courts, however, as most judges were eager to explain how a certain petitioner might be "readily distinguishable from 'white' persons." Between the 1870s and the 1920s the courts thus generated their own epistemology of race, a way of *knowing* that drew from scientific doctrine, from popular understanding, from historical reasoning as to this or that group's place in world events, from "commonsense" notions of color, from geographic conceptions of the world's peoples, and from legal precedent itself. Of course the very process here threatened to shatter the commonsense understanding of race as a system of natural demarcations: that a judge could decide on the spot whether or not a Syrian was "white," for instance, was evidence of the most concrete kind that race was a social convention, not a biological fact. But such an admission was intolerable. Just as this string of cases betrays the extent to which race functioned as an ideological tool in the allocation of social and political privilege, so does the language of these rulings demonstrate the requirement that ideology disguise itself as something else. Vested with all the authority in the world, the courts continually appealed to some "neutral" basis for arriving at judgments of racial demarcation. Rulings on the meaning of "free white persons" thus erected a fragile—though finally unassailable—edifice of authority regarding race itself.[9]

In the nation's legal epistemology of race, the "Caucasian race" traces its origins to *In re Ah Yup* (1878), "the first application made by a native Chinaman for naturalization" in the United States. Circuit Court Judge Sawyer's ruling in the case set an important precedent; as it was recalled and repeated over the years in response to a cavalcade of petitioners for naturalized citizenship, Sawyer's reasoning in the matter single-handedly established "Caucasians" as a legally recognized racial group. The terms of the initial naturalization law had been muddied in 1870, when post– Civil War legislation had made provisions for "aliens of African nativity, and . . . persons of African descent" without reiterating the initial language regarding "free white persons." A subsequent amendment in 1875 read, "The provisions of this title apply to aliens being free white persons, and to aliens of African nativity, and to persons of African descent." The question put before the court in *Ah Yup*, then, was whether a person of the "Mongolian race" qualified as a "white person." By what measure was white *white?*

Judge Sawyer was sensitive to the complexities here. "The words 'white person,'" he opined,

> . . . constitute a very indefinite description of a class of persons, where none can be said to be literally white, and those called white may be found of every shade from the lightest blonde to the most swarthy brunette. But these words in this country, at least, have undoubtedly acquired a well settled meaning in common popular speech, and they are constantly used in the sense so acquired in the literature of the country, as well as in common parlance. As ordinarily used everywhere in the United States, one would scarcely fail to understand that the party employing the words "white person" would intend a person of the Caucasian race.[10]

Sawyer went on to cite Blumenbach (indirectly, via *Webster's Dictionary*) and his five-tiered scheme of races: "Caucasian" ("or white race," in Sawyer's words, comprising "the greater part of European nations and those of western Asia"), "Mongolian," "Ethiopian," "American," and "Malay." He discussed the competing scientific schemes offered by Linnaeus, Buffon, and Cuvier to demonstrate the disagreement within the scientific community, but pointed out that "no one includes the white, or

Caucasian, with the Mongolian or yellow race; and no one of those classifications recognizing color as one of the distinguishing characteristics
includes the Mongolian in the white or whitish race."[11]

Sawyer's construction would leave some room for questions: what is
meant by "whitish," for instance? What is meant by the assertion that
"the greater part of European nations" was included under the term "Caucasian"? These would be taken up in response to various suits over the
next several decades. But two issues were settled authoritatively in Sawyer's decision, and *Ah Yup* exerted considerable force on later decisions
when it came to these key issues: first, this decision reified "the Caucasian
race" not simply as a schematic convention, but as a meaningful legal and
scientific concept that clarified the vague phrase "free white persons." "I
find nothing in the history of the country," Sawyer declared, "in common
or scientific usage, or in legislative proceedings, to indicate that congress
intended to include in the term 'white person' any other than an individual
of the Caucasian race." (Here was a concept with some reach: decades
later, in 1910, an Oregon court ruled that a certain Chinese husband was
obligated to buy his Norwegian wife "Caucasian foods" rather than "rice,
chop suey and noodles.")[12] Second, having established "Caucasian" peoplehood as a self-evident and natural fact, Sawyer left no question as to
the relationship between alleged Caucasians and alleged Mongolians: noting that in 1870 Congress had revised the naturalization code by adding
"African nativity" and "African descent" rather than striking the qualification "white," Sawyer concluded that "whatever latitudinarian construction might otherwise have been given to the term 'white person,' it
is entirely clear that congress intended by this legislation to exclude Mongolians from the right of naturalization."[13]

Thus Sawyer cited several authorities in handing down this ruling on
whiteness, including science, congressional intent, and, not least, "common" understanding. In the naturalization cases that followed in the wake
of *Ah Yup,* Sawyer himself would be numbered among these various authorities. In the case of Frank Camille (1880), a Canadian immigrant of
"half white and half Indian blood," an Oregon Circuit Court cited Sawyer's definition of "white person" in denying the application.[14] In the Utah
case of a petitioner simply referred to as Kanaka Nian (1889), a Hawaiian
"of Malayan or Mongolian complexion," the court drew upon both Sawyer and Blumenbach in arguing that there was no basis for classing Ha-
waiians among "Caucasians."[15] And in the New York case of the Burmese
immigrant San C. Po (1894), the court first evoked literal color ("in color

he is a dark yellow"), but then rested upon the precedents of *Kanaka Nian, Camille,* and *Ah Yup* in holding that "white" really referred to the scientific classification "Caucasian" and that, scientifically considered, "the Burmese are Malays."[16]

Judge Sawyer's reasoning did not lose its purchase entirely on legal interpretations of whiteness for many years, but several cases between the 1890s and the 1910s did cloud the seeming ethnological clarity by which *Ah Yup, Camille, Kanaka Nian,* and *Po* had been decided. A Texas court in 1897, for instance, departed from the ethnological reasoning of *Ah Yup* in granting the application of Ricardo Rodriguez, ruling that "whatever may be the status of the applicant viewed solely from the standpoint of the ethnologist, he is embraced within the spirit and intent of our laws upon naturalization."[17]

The *Rodriguez* case raised some vexing questions. "As to color," the case noted, Rodriguez "may be classed with the copper colored or red men"—another race whose status was left in doubt by laws naming only "white persons" and persons of "African" nativity or descent. Thus the question before the court was precisely what it had been nineteen years earlier in the case of *Ah Yup:* could the petitioner be construed as "white"? A brief on behalf of the petitioner brought into question one of the keynotes of the *Ah Yup* decision, and so opened debate on a point that had been settled in the courts since 1878. "The term 'Caucasian,' " the counsel A. M. Paschal argued,

> is now abandoned by all acknowledged writers on ethnology as too restricted a term to embrace all those races who first peopled and flourished on the shores of the Mediterranean, and [are] erroneously supposed to be a pure Caucasian stock. The term now applied is "Mediterraneans." These are now scattered over the whole world, and, as a species, have no equal, physically or mentally.[18]

As to the question of assimilability, Paschal found the "Mongolians" obviously wanting, and so acceded to that bit of exclusionary reasoning in the *Ah Yup* decision. The question, though, was whether or not the idea "Caucasian" was the proper tool for arriving at systems of inclusion and exclusion. Paschal had no question as to the civic capabilities of Ricardo Rodriguez.

Briefs for the opposition stressed whiteness as a phenotype, and elaborated upon the inner qualities that physiognomy allegedly revealed. One brief noted rather straightforwardly that Rodriguez could not possibly be "white," since "the applicant has dark eyes, straight, black hair, chocolate brown skin, and high cheek bones." A second brief appealed to the racial history of U.S. debate over the Mexicans' fitness for self-government. Attorney T. J. McMinn invoked the Texas Declaration of Independence, which had characterized the Mexicans as "unfit to be free." He cited Sam Houston's remark "I have no confidence in them," and John C. Calhoun's caustic "They cannot govern themselves. Shall they govern us?"[19]

The court finally brushed aside both the commentary on phenotypes and the anti-Mexican declarations of earlier Texas patriots. According to the 1836 Texas constitution, "all persons (Africans, descendants of Africans, and Indians excepted) who were residing in Texas on the day of the declaration of independence" became *de jure* citizens upon the constitution's adoption.[20] The status of the Mexican in relation to the prototypical "free white person" of the 1790 law remained unclear, and the court made no effort to sort this out; but Mexicans had been singled out in much relevant legislation for inclusion. If exclusivity was a critical principle in the workings of the free republic, the category "Caucasian" was not in every case the appropriate tool for determining the boundaries. Thus, in extending the domain of "free white persons," *Rodriguez* identified a logic by which nonracial considerations (in this case, the history of Mexico and Texas) could supersede both ethnological authority and popular conventions of describing skin color.[21]

More vexed still was the Massachusetts case of *In re Halladjian* (1909). As in *Rodriguez,* the court here arrived at a construction of "white" that was inclusive enough to grant the application of the petitioners—in this case four Armenian immigrants. Unlike *Rodriguez,* however, *Halladjian* met the question of race head on. Remarkably ambitious in its scope, this ruling not only attempted to pinpoint the intent of the 1790 naturalization law and its wording, but in doing so addressed specific ethnological questions of racial taxonomy. Drawing upon an impressive array of colonial usages of the word "white," the court held, first, that the word "white" was *not* synonymous with "European," but was used to classify the inhabitants and to include all persons not otherwise classified. This argument was sweeping in and of itself: because Armenians had never been singled out and named for exclusion, we must presume their admissibility to citizenship; and the terms of their inclusion could only be the phrase "free white persons." "White" must be read as an *inclusive* category, not an exclusive one.[22]

But the ruling went even further, maintaining that there was in fact no "white" race as a distinctive class, nor a "yellow" race that comprised all the peoples of Asia. Hence "free white persons" included Armenians born in Asiatic Turkey and on the west side of the Bosphorus. *Halladjian* thus rendered a legal definition of race itself:

> The term "race" primarily means an ethnical stock; a great division of mankind having in common certain distinguishing physical peculiarities, and thus constituting a *comprehensive class appearing to be derived from a distinct primitive source.* A second definition is a tribal or national stock; a division or subdivision of one of the great racial stocks of mankind, distinguished by minor peculiarities. The word "race" connotes descent.[23]

The ruling thus imported into naturalization law the racial scheme that would shape the Dillingham Commission on Immigration, and yet in doing so it countered restrictionist arguments as to "tribal or national stocks" and their fitness for citizenship. Whereas arguments for immigration restriction tended to stress considerable differences among "tribal or national stocks," *Halladjian* identified this as merely a secondary definition of race and, further still, rendered the "peculiarities" of such races "minor."[24] This approach to legal whiteness was conservative in that it upheld the 1790 construction of "white persons" that had allowed for the massive immigration of many European races.

It is worth examining the reasoning in the *Halladjian* decision in more detail for its contribution to the legal epistemology of race in the early twentieth century. Although a lower court had identified the petitioners as "Armenian by race," the first resort to physical description seemed to favor their admissibility: "I find that all were white persons in appearance, not darker in complexion than some persons of North European descent traceable for generations. Their complexion was lighter than that of many south Italians and Portuguese." As such "borderline" cases had not before made their way into the courts, this court faced a novel task: the petitioners are "neither Chinamen nor Africans of any sort, and the court has here to decide whether they are white or not." The interference of a court clerk, who (rather imprecisely) urged the district attorney to "oppose the granting of naturalization to Hindoos or East Indians," signaled the prejudices surrounding this case.[25]

The court gave many reasons for ruling on the Armenians' borderline whiteness. The heart of the United States' argument for exclusion was the contention that " 'white' is the equivalent of 'European,' and is used to

'describe the variations of domicile or origin which are so closely associated with the mental development of a people.' " The court dispatched
with this contention in quick order. Addressing the question of the alleged
integrity of the "European" race and the ancillary argument that Armenians were racially "Asiatic," the court noted, first, that geography was
rarely an essential or reliable factor in racial classification: "we speak of
the Anglo-Saxon race, the Teutonic, the Celtic, the Slavonic, the Caucasian, the Mongolian, the Hebrew, the [N]egro, more commonly than of
the Swiss race, the Austrian, the Spanish, or the Egyptian." European
peoples are not "unmixed," moreover, and therefore there is no "European race" in a unified sense. Second, the court similarly challenged the
contention that the petitioners belonged to the "Asiatic race": "They are
no darker than many west Europeans, and they resemble the Chinese in
feature no more than they resemble the American aborigines." The average man would understand Armenians to be white. The court rounded
out this segment of the decision by citing the authority of intellectual
tradition in matters racial, and, in so doing, returning to the realm of
scientific authority with which this discussion had begun: "Armenians
have always been classified in the white or Caucasian race, and not in the
yellow or Mongolian"; scientists such as Cuvier had "expressly included
Armenians as well as Hindoos, in the Caucasian race."[26]

　　Had the court stopped right here, this would have been as complete a
discussion of the matter as was typical in cases of this sort. From this
scientific discussion, however, the decision went on at great length to locate the established meaning of whiteness within American legal history
and within the functioning of the state as well. The syntax is telling: this
highly "liberal" ruling on the admissibility of Armenian immigrants is
thoroughly grounded in the very history of white supremacism that the
fact of racial indeterminacy *might* have been deployed to subvert. The
court offered a long litany of colonial usages of "white" in census data to
demonstrate that in the context of the times, "white" simply meant everyone who was neither "Negro" nor "Indian"—the only other racial designations specified in state documents of the era.[27]

　　The court went further still to defend its construction of "white persons" by invoking the authority of various segregation statutes from the
Jim Crow South and West (including Arkansas, Florida, Virginia, Ken-
tucky, and Oklahoma). In this body of statutory law, the court noted,
anyone not legally "black" was legally "white": "A statute in Arkansas

requires separate accommodation for 'the white and African races,' and provides that all persons not visibly African 'shall be deemed to belong to the white race.' " The Oklahoma constitution, too, specified that, "whenever in this Constitution and laws of this state the words 'colored' or 'colored person,' 'negro,' or 'negro race' are used, the same shall be construed to mean to apply to all persons of African descent. The term 'white race' shall include all other persons." Thus was Jim Crow invoked in the name of a liberalized naturalization code. Like the creators of this fretwork of segregation codes, the framers of the naturalization law of 1790 neither cared nor knew about Turks and Armenians; but the original census shows that, to them, everyone but Negroes and Indians constituted "white persons."[28]

Although *Halladjian* was far from the last word on the subject, this case did represent the bottom line in some important respects. As I will argue at greater length below, the *Halladjian* decision more than any other reveals the dual working of the legal construction of "white persons" as both a bulwark against undesirable Others without *and* a great crucible minimizing the perceived "difference" among the varied peoples and races within.

But the extent to which outright confusion persisted in matters of legal whiteness was manifest within a year. Notwithstanding the contention—cited in *Halladjian*—that "the average man in the street . . . would find no difficulty in assigning to the yellow race a Turk or Syrian with as much ease as he would bestow that designation on a Chinaman or a Korean," the court in *In re Mudarri* (1910), confronted with a petitioner who was "a Syrian by race," maintained: "The older writers on ethnology are substantially agreed that Syrians are to be classed as of the Caucasian or white race." "This court," moreover, "has long admitted Syrians to citizenship."[29] Although firmly settled in its own construction of Syrian racial identity, the court in *Mudarri* did call for a revision of existing codes to clarify the racial categories: "What may be called for want of a better name the Caucasian-Mongolian classification [meaning Armenians and Syrians] is not now held to be valid by any considerable body of ethnologists." More directly still, "The court greatly hopes that an amendment of the statutes will make quite clear the meaning of the word 'white' in section 2169."[30] Perhaps most striking about this "great hope" is that it is the first expression of its kind on the record, despite the tortuous logic by which whiteness had been contested and defended since *Ah Yup* in 1878. Here, at last, is an acknowledgement of epistemological crisis.

Legalized Racialisms, Racialized Legalisms

Clearly, then, knowledge of whiteness did not derive from any objective assessment of disinvested fact. The degree to which this is so is illustrated nowhere better than in a pair of federal cases from the early 1920s, the petitions of Takao Ozawa (1922) and Bhagat Singh Thind (1923). Taken together, the cases demonstrate how race has served as a powerful instrument for jealously guarding privilege rather than as a neutral, coolly biological basis for understanding the relationship among the world's peoples. Takao Ozawa, an immigrant from Japan, petitioned for U.S. citizenship in October 1922. His case was built on an assault on the principle that the qualification of "whiteness" *necessarily* excluded the Japanese from naturalized citizenship. This petition argued, first, that the spirit of the 1875 naturalization act that had extended citizenship to "Africans" was *in*clusive, not exclusive; indeed, the Chinese Exclusion Act had been passed and periodically renewed without mention of Japanese immigrants.

Second, certain precedents (most notably *Halladjian*) had held that "white," in the literal 1790 construction of the term, referred to anyone not black—"a person without negro blood." Third, the long history of U.S. expansionism and annexation had already brought into the national fold "vast numbers of members of races not Caucasian, including many Mongolians," most recently in Hawaii and Puerto Rico, for example. And fourth, "The Japanese are 'free.' They, or at least the dominant strains, are 'white persons,' speaking an Aryan tongue and having Caucasian root stocks; a superior class, fit for citizenship. They are assimilable." The petitioner Takao Ozawa himself was held up as sterling evidence of this last contention. Even a narrow insistence upon whiteness, in other words, would admit the likes of Ozawa, who was as white as any white person by any meaningful construction of that term.[31]

The U.S. counterargument, by contrast, rested upon a geographical, Eurocentric assumption of what "white" had to have meant in 1790:

> The men who settled this country were white men from Europe and the men who fought the Revolutionary War, framed the Constitution and established the Government, were white men from Europe and their descendants. They were eager for more of their kind to come, and it was to men of their own kind that they held out the opportunity for citizenship in the new nation.

As it had exclusively been "European immigration which was desired and expected" among the Revolutionary generation, whiteness was not meant to be inclusive. Citizenship "could only be obtained by those to whom it was given, and the men of 1790 gave it only to those whom they knew and regarded as worthy to share it with them, men of their own type, white men."[32]

In deciding the merits of these arguments, the court in *Ozawa* at once demonstrated the inadequacy of racial whiteness as a stable system of demarcation *and* insisted upon continued demarcation along racial lines. "[Color] differs greatly among persons of the same race," the opinion read,

> even among Anglo-Saxons, ranging by imperceptible gradations from the fair blond to the swarthy brunette, the latter being darker than many of the lighter hued persons of the brown or yellow races. Hence to adopt the color test alone would result in a confused over-lapping of races and a gradual merging of one into the other, without any practical line of separation.[33]

And yet courts since *Ah Yup* "in an almost unbroken line, have held that the words 'white person' were meant to indicate only a person of what is popularly known as the Caucasian race." Such a construction would tend undoubtedly to raise disputes among some borderline cases, such as Syrians or Armenians, the court conceded; but the appellant in this case "is clearly of a race which is not Caucasian and therefore belongs entirely outside the zone [of dispute] on the negative side." Thus grounding its ruling in the authority of precedent and "popular" racial understanding, the court in *Ozawa* articulated three principles of import to the legal construction of whiteness. First, the term "white person" applies only to those who would have been recognized as racially white in 1790— that is, to "Caucasians." Second, this construction establishes a zone on one side of which are those undoubtedly eligible, and on the other undoubtedly ineligible, for citizenship; questionable cases within the zone itself must be determined as they arise. But third, Japanese immigrants, who are "clearly" not "Caucasian," cannot become citizens of the United States.[34] You may indeed be "white," in other words, but you are not "Caucasian."

In early 1923, only a few months after the *Ozawa* decision had been handed down, a ruling in the United States' appeal in the case of Bhagat

Singh Thind made almost comic nonsense of the authority by which Ozawa had been excluded. Thind, recall, had been granted citizenship in 1920 by a District Court in Oregon on the grounds that, though there were precedents running in both directions, those against the petitioner were "not in line with the greater weight of authority."[35] The United States sued to reverse this decision on the whiteness of the "Hindu," and indeed won precisely such a reversal in *U.S. v. Thind*. If the court in *Ozawa* relied primarily upon the scientific concept of the "Caucasian," the court in *U.S. v. Thind* ruled that "Caucasian" was a bankrupt concept and that science itself was a bankrupt authority in matters racial. Not the scientist but the "average" man could best be counted on to determine whiteness. "It may be true that the blond Scandinavian and the brown Hindu have a common ancestor in the dim reaches of antiquity," this opinion read, "but the average man knows perfectly well that there are unmistakable and profound differences between them to-day."

> The word "Caucasian" is in scarcely better repute [than "Aryan"] . . . [and] has come to include far more than the unscientific mind suspects . . . it includes not only the Hindu, but some of the Polynesians . . . the Hamites of Africa, upon the Caucasic cast of their features, though in color they range from brown to black. We venture to think that the average well-informed white American would learn with some degree of astonishment that the race to which he belongs is made up of such heterogeneous elements.[36]

You may indeed be "Caucasian," in other words, but you are not "white."

The *Ozawa* and *Thind* decisions demonstrate the ultimate function of race as an ideological tool and whiteness as property whose value was to be protected. As the court suggested in *Ozawa,* race is a *"practical line of separation,"* not a natural one; and in social, economic, and political practice, separation is hierarchy. What would most "astonish" the average white person about the diminution of the "unmistakable and profound differences" between whites and Hindus, to take the language of the *Thind* decision, would be his or her own loss of standing as a result.

This principle of property-in-whiteness was upheld in less known cases as well. When another Syrian, Faras Shahid, petitioned for citizenship in South Carolina (1913), the court observed that "in color, he is about that of walnut, or somewhat darker than is the usual mulatto of one half mixed blood between the white and the negro races." Such an assessment did not bode well in South Carolina. The case quickly boiled down to the simple but explosive question of race and hierarchy—whether "a very dark brown, almost black, inhabitant of India is entitled to *rank* as a white person, because of a possible or hypothetical infusion of white blood 30 or 40 centuries old." The court was confounded by the scientific aspects of racial designation, and the seeming contradictions. "What is the race or color of the modern inhabitant of Syria is impossible to say," the court confessed. Far easier, evidently, was the task of saying what the modern inhabitant of Syria was *not:* he or she was not "white."[37] As far as the court was concerned, the bar to whiteness of South Carolinians who had one, but only one, demonstrably white parent was decisive. Would it not be terribly inconsistent, the judge wondered, to deny property-in-whiteness to people of mixed parentage but to grant it to peoples—like Syrians—whose white parentage was merely theoretical? Thus was the superstructure of white supremacism—in the form of Jim Crow statutes and miscegenation laws—enlisted to protect South Carolinian whiteness from potential taint-by-naturalization.

More direct in its articulation of property-in-whiteness (and more egregious) was another South Carolina judge's reasoning in 1914. This judge, too, invoked Southern regional custom in portioning out whiteness in the case of George Dow. He did not stop with contemporary custom, however, but rather looked all the way back to the mentality of the slave-holding states of the 1790s.

> The average citizen of the states was at that time firmly convinced of the superiority of his own white European race over the rest of the world, whether red, yellow, brown, or black. He had enslaved many of the American Indians on that ground. He would have enslaved a Moor, a Bedouin, a Syrian, a Turk, or an East Indian of sufficiently dark complexion with equal readiness on the same plea if he could have caught him.[38]

The first Congress could not have intended that the likes of George Dow be protected in his "pursuit of property," that is, because to them he would have *been* property. Though slavery had been abolished, its logic remained suitable for framing naturalization decisions, just as Jim Crow had been summoned by another court in admitting the Armenian Halladjian.

The presumptions attached to property-in-whiteness did not necessarily work against a petitioner, however. Tom Ellis, a "Turkish subject" also identified as "Syrian," petitioned a court in Oregon in 1910. As the District Court judge viewed him, "ethnologically he is of the Semitic stock, a markedly white type of the race." This judge did not elaborate what he meant by the word "white," but he did spend some time puzzling over what the first Congress must have meant by it. If by "white persons" the drafters of the 1790 law had intended "Europeans," the judge opined, "it might have been far better expressed than to use the simple term 'white.'"

> Not having been so expressed or particularized, the most reasonable inference would be that the word "white," ethnologically speaking, was intended to be applied in its popular sense to denote at least the members of the white or Caucasian race of people. If there be ambiguity and doubt, it is better to resolve that doubt in favor of the Caucasian possessed of the highest qualities which go to make an excellent citizen, as the applicant appears to be . . . If the word "white" in its popular sense is of too broad a signification, as applied to persons deemed suitable to become citizens of the United States, the remedy is easily at hand by an amendment of the law.[39]

This decision is remarkable in several respects. Liberal though the decision appears to be, it nonetheless derives from a kind of pretzel logic whose very twists are defined by white supremacism. The matter before the court was whether or not Tom Ellis was a member of the "white" race, and what, precisely, "white" might be taken to mean. Since there was no compelling basis for interpreting the term so narrowly as to mean "European," the court reasoned, it must refer to "the members of the *white or Caucasian race of people*"—it must mean the very thing whose meaning was in question, in other words. White meant white. Should doubts arise as to "whiteness," these could safely be resolved in the petitioner's favor, so long as the petitioner was "Caucasian." Hence it is no small matter that Ellis was described early on as "a markedly white type" of the Semitic race—this casual observation (interpretation), indeed, turned out to be the basis for rendering a decision in his favor. Just as it boded ill for Faras Shahid that he appeared "somewhat darker than is the usual mulatto," so Ellis's whiteness was indispensable in proving that he was in fact a "white person."

In identifying Ellis as a "markedly white type," the judge appears to have intended Ellis's literal color, but he could have been referring to any of a number of things, and he was likely referring to much more than he knew—Ellis's social bearing, his proficiency in English, his dress, his manner, his style, his demeanor, perhaps his class. In any case his reference to Ellis as markedly "white" and his inference that Ellis was a "white person" were very closely aligned. Ellis did not appear to the court to be the kind of person who should be excluded, therefore he could not be the kind of person who *must* be excluded. To fail to grant him citizenship would have been to do injury to Ellis's property-in-whiteness. Standing naturalization law might be too inclusive, it is true. But it was not for the courts to devalue the property-in-whiteness of any "Caucasian possessed of the highest qualities which go to make an excellent citizen."

Property-in-whiteness was a principle clearly recognized not only by those in power, moreover, but also by the petitioners themselves. Claimants in this long string of suits for citizenship never assailed the core premise that whiteness was a reasonable prerequisite for republican citizenship; nor did they suggest that such exclusivity was ill-founded. Rather, they uniformly argued that their rightful share in whiteness was being denied them. As contentious as this legal history was, in other words, combatants generally respected the value of whiteness, and in laying claim to its title they did nothing to challenge property-in-whiteness itself.

This underlying consensus is nowhere more apparent than in the case of George Dow, the Syrian whose case had led one South Carolina judge into a "Serbonian bog." In 1913 a lower court had relied upon a purely geographic definition of whiteness ("white" = "European") to deny Dow's admissibility to citizenship. A lower court had also debunked the idea of the "Caucasian" race, not in the process of pointing up the problem in the United States naturalization law, but in the process of exposing a central flaw in this petitioner's reasoning. The judge cited Huxley's remarks on Blumenbach to demonstrate the whimsicality of the category "Caucasian"—science's "oddest myth"—then went on to reason: "If there be no such race as the 'Caucasian race,' and the term Caucasian be incorrect as properly describing the white races, then the [petitioner's] whole argument based upon the Syrian being one of a Caucasian race falls to the ground."[40] Here, no less than in *Ozawa* and *Thind,* is race deployed as a blunt instrument of arrogant power.

An enraged Syrian community next appealed the decision (1914), protesting not so much the denial of the right to citizenship as the denial of a position in the "white race," and its attendant implication of inferiority to American blacks. Did not the case of "Semitic" Jews settle the matter in their favor? This 1915 appeal did yield a more liberal interpretation of "white persons," and Dow was finally admitted. The higher court now cited the Dillingham Commission's *Dictionary of Races and Peoples,* which had asserted that Syrians "belong to the Semitic branch of the Caucasian race, thus widely differing from their rulers, the Turks, who are in origin Mongolian." The court also cited the "more liberal construction" of whiteness that had characterized rulings like *Halladjian* and *Ellis.*[41]

Similarly, in *U.S. v. Cartozian* (1925) an Oregon court, adopting the three-tiered scheme of European races favored by writers like Madison Grant and Lothrop Stoddard, ruled that Tatos O. Cartozian and his Armenian compatriots were "Alpines" and therefore European—certainly not the most desirable of the European races, but not the least, either. Cartozian's counsel had called Franz Boas, who testified as to "the European origin of the Armenians and their migration into Asia Minor." "It would be utterly impossible," Boas declared, "to classify them as not belonging to the white race." The court dismissed the U.S. complaint against Cartozian, holding that Armenians "are white persons within the common usage of the term, and amalgamate readily with other white people."[42] (The verb "amalgamate" is worth pausing over: it conjures the literal "consanguinity" among races mandated by a web of miscegenation codes whose very *raison d'être* was the protection of both white property and whiteness-*as*-property.)

That same year in Michigan the United States sued John Mohammad Ali, a "high-caste Hindu or Arabian," to revoke his citizenship. Ali's argument, too, is interesting for its acceptance of a bedrock racist principle: his ancestors were Arabs who had invaded India and "kept their Arabian blood-line clear and pure by intermarriage within the family," he claimed. Like Homer Plessy, like George Dow and the South Carolina Syrian community, like the Armenians who had requested the aid of Franz Boas, John Mohammad Ali seemed comfortable enough with the principle of exclusion on racial grounds—it was simply *his* exclusion on racial grounds that bothered him. (Whereas the court had been swayed by Cartozian's argument, Ali's exclusion stood: "his skin is certainly not white," this court ruled; "the most that could be claimed by him . . . would be membership in the Caucasian race." In the wake of the *Thind* decision, however, this "manifestly would avail him nothing.")[43] Thus did the racialized legalisms and the legalistic racialisms of both claimants and the courts conspire to protect property-in-whiteness and the core principle of "whites' " supreme claim to fitness for self-government.

Presumed Caucasian

Between the 1870s and the 1920s the courts succeeded in normalizing and reinforcing the notion of a unified community of "white persons" that the 1790 law had articulated and decades of naturalization practice had established. Just as anxieties over the fate of the Anglo-Saxon republic in the face of an onslaught of inferior white races dominated popular discussion, the courts were busy minimizing the "difference" among these peoples by the very language they used to interpret the phrase "white persons." Thus whereas for some the phrase "white persons" became the instrument of exclusion, for others it became a powerful crucible whose exclusions based upon distinctions of color blurred other potentially divisive physical distinctions. This, indeed, is the melting pot.

A Washington state court remarked in *Yamashita* (1902), "Whether the classification according to color is technically scientific or natural is not a proper subject of inquiry here. From its existence co-extensively with the formation of the American republic, it must be taken to express a settled national will."[44] Vigorous eugenic arguments against the qualifications of certain "white persons" and the inconsistency of the courts themselves in deciding the presumably simpler matter of who was and who was not white belie the contention that the national will actually was "settled" on this matter. But if the courts could not determine the "national will," they could in fact *create* it. Among the more portentous effects of this decades-long struggle over "Caucasian" identity in the courts was the normalization of unified whiteness. The fact that Hebrews, Celts, Slavs, Mediterraneans, Alpines, Iberics, or Latins had traditionally entered the polity under the legal banner "white persons" must, at any rate, demonstrate a matter of "settled national will." By the logic of the courts, everyone who had been admitted to citizenship as "white persons" became indispensable evidence of the *meaning* of the phrase "white persons," and they were thus cordoned off, logically, from those who had been excluded. The courts' endorsement of the traditional interpretations of the 1790 law cemented whiteness for the probationary white races; and again, problematic Europeans owed their inclusion to the exclusion of others.

This principle was articulated explicitly at various points. The decision in *Halladjian*, for instance, singled out "Hebrews" as an especially vexing instance when it came to making sense of the laws and practices around naturalization. Hebrews, remarked the court, as a group racially "pure," represented an "extraordinary exception" in U.S. policy: they have sought

> with unusual strictness to maintain that purity [of the blood] for 2,000 years at the least . . . both Hebrew history and an approximation to general type show that the Hebrews are a true race, if a true race can be found widely distributed for many centuries. Their origin is Asiatic . . . If "the aboriginal peoples of Asia" are excluded from naturalization, as urged by the United States, it is hard to find a loophole for admitting the Hebrew.[45]

The court advanced these observations in service of the *inclusionary* argument that there was no unified "European race" (and hence no ethnological bar to the admittance of Armenians). Nonetheless, the tension admitted here between prevailing ethnological wisdom and traditional naturalization practices indicates the stakes involved in "Hebrews' " continued ability to lay claim to the status of "white persons." For the court in *Halladjian,* "Hebrews" represented the exception proving the inclusionary possibilities inhering in the term "white persons"; by implication, however, "Hebrews" in this discussion also became the exception proving the general rule of monolithic "whiteness." For instance, what becomes of problematic "Slavs" in this formulation? They slip silently into whiteness. The significance of such reasoning is unmistakable in the context of an insurgent and increasingly influential eugenic movement.

The question of ethnological "white races" and their relationship to the legal concept "white persons" was taken up even more forcefully the next year, in reference to the United States' case against the Parsee (Syrian) immigrant Bhicaji Franyi Balsara (1910). In response to the United States' contention that the phrase "free white persons" must be construed to mean what it did in 1790, the court remarked,

> No immigration being then known except from England, Ireland, Scotland, Wales, Germany, Sweden, France, and Holland, Congress must be taken to have intended aliens coming from those countries only. The consequence of this argument, viz., that Russians, Poles, Italians, Greeks, and others, who had not theretofore immigrated, are to be excluded, is so absurd that the government extends the intention of Congress to all Europeans.[46]

"If a Hebrew . . . had applied for naturalization in 1790," the court opined, "we cannot believe he would have been excluded on the ground that he was not a white person." Congress must have had "principally in mind the exclusion of Africans, whether slave or free, and Indians," and not Parsees like the petitioner Balsara.[47] Similarly, in denying the petition of Albert Henry Young, an immigrant of half German and half Japanese descent (1912), a Federal Court in Washington state offered that "Caucasian" referred to "all European races around the Mediterranean Sea, whether they are considered as 'fair whites' or 'dark whites,' as classified by Huxley, and notwithstanding that certain of the southern and eastern European races are technically classified as of Mongolian or Tartar origin."[48] This comment did establish the whiteness of certain problematic European immigrants, even if it did not explain it.

Similarly, a Pennsylvania court detailed the various inclusions and exclusions inhering in whiteness in its ruling against the "Hindu" Sadar Bhagwab Singh (1917). The legal concept "white persons" had expanded over the decades to include many whom the framers could not possibly have imagined in 1790, explained the court. It had come to include "Spaniards and Portuguese, and later the Italian peoples, and broadly the Latin race"; "Hungarians, Poles, Russians, and many divisions of the Slavic race"; and "Hebrews, who have always been recognized as a distinct race." This was painted as a process of some begrudgement, but ever more liberal all the same. The court did find, however, that Congress and the courts had never made provision for "the race of people commonly known as Hindus." "White," then, as intended by Congress, must primarily be understood to connote a geographical class, "those who were like unto themselves in blood, previous social and political environment, laws, usages, customs, and traditions, what has been called the geographical test."[49] "Hindus" did not pass this test. Significantly, according to the ruling in *Singh,* many other groups did.

In a similar rendering of "Hindu" racial identity in *United States v. Ali* (1925), a Michigan court ruled that a "high-caste Hindu or Arabian [is] not [a] 'white person' within Naturalization law." Again, in arguing the unassimilability of the Hindu, the court pronounced rather sweepingly and unproblematically on certain other groups whose assimilability was very much in question: "The children of European parentage quickly merge into the mass of our population and lose the distinctive marks of their European origin, while the children born in this country of Hindu parents retain indefinitely the evidence of their ancestry." This is an especially striking assertion for 1925, a year after the Johnson Act had passed Congress on precisely the logic that "children of European parentage" *would not* "lose the distinctive marks" of their origin or "quickly merge into the mass of our population."[50]

In *Morrison v. California,* a case involving "conspiracy" to violate the state's alien land law in 1934, the court upheld the logic of *Ozawa* in defining the precise meaning of the terms "white" and "Caucasian": " 'White persons' within the meaning of the statute are members of the Caucasian race, as Caucasian is defined in the understanding of the mass of men."[51] This casual blending of the scientific authority of "Caucasian" with the populist appeal to "the understanding of the mass of men" signals the end of an era in the legal battles over whiteness. The unconflicted tone suggests that the meaning behind the volatile phrase "white persons" had indeed become "a matter of settled national will." Indeed, only a handful of cases made their way through the courts between 1935 and the elimination of the phrase "white persons" in naturalization law in the early 1950s.[52]

The rather peculiar divorce case of *Delavigne v. Delavigne* (1975) provides an apt coda to this long, contentious history of whiteness-in-dispute. Having lost custody of his children, the husband in a divorce suit now claimed that males, as a class, constituted the social and legal equivalent of a "race," and that therefore the courts' favoritism toward women in custody cases was tantamount to "racial discrimination." The court responded by blowing the dust off of Blumenbach's schematic in *Natural Varieties of Mankind* and offering a latter-day lecture on the five divisions of mankind, "based on ancestry, with relatively unchanging characteristics, now usually referred to as the black, brown, red, white, and yellow races."[53] Although the case called only for a broad definition of race itself, and not for any close distinctions among the races, still the court's easy reversion to the taxonomy of the 1790s indicates the extent to which Caucasian whiteness had become an unproblematic concept both in street-level vernacular and in the courts after a period of fractious and heated contest.

It is worth noting here that it was in response to a civil rights claim, of all things, that the court reflexively resorted to Blumenbach's scheme in *Delavigne.* Civil rights logic has been crucial to the twentieth-century chapter of this racial saga. Like the reverberating big bang of American expansionism and the subtle alchemy of American naturalization law, as we shall see, civil rights agitation around questions of Jim Crow in the

1930s and after has quietly but decisively ratified the racial logic of white-over-color, helping so many immigrant Hebrews, Letts, Celts, and Mediterraneans to become the Caucasians of our modern-day visual and conceptual lexicon.

There is no one "race question" for the North and another for the South. There is a national question, and it concerns the integration of the Negro into our entire national community. But it concerns much more than the Negro; it concerns the integration of all the minority racial groups: the Mexican, the Oriental, the American Indian.

—John LaFarge, *The Race Question and the Negro* (1944)

The word *race* should be used sparingly. There really is no Slavic, Italian, Jewish, or Scandinavian race. Such differences as exist among people are due, in the main, to different environment, history and experience.

—Louis Adamic, *From Many Lands* (1939)

 8

The Dawning Civil Rights Era

In an address at Howard University, FDR announced that his social policy would proceed upon the conviction that "among American citizens there should be no forgotten men and no forgotten races."[1] The irony here is twofold. First, African-Americans were indeed "forgotten" by much New Deal legislation—the Federal Housing Authority's pro-segregation mortgage loan program, for instance—and blacks did not benefit from government largesse in proportion to their increasing importance to the New Deal coalition, notwithstanding the ascendance of civil rights in the nation's political life through five administrations, from Roosevelt to Johnson.[2]

Second, in part *because of* the centrality of "Negro-white" relations beginning with the New Deal, many other races were forgotten, too, though not at all in the sense that FDR intended in his Howard address: the problematic Letts, Finns, Hebrews, Slavs, and Greeks of 1924 became ever more "white" as the politics of segregation overwhelmed the national agenda. Thus by the 1950s what was "forgotten" was that these groups had ever *been* distinct races in the first place. The white ethnic revival of the 1960s and 1970s may have been a backlash-creature of the modern civil rights movement; but "white ethnicity" itself, much earlier on, was in part the creation of a newly invigorated black-white social dichotomy.

"Race politics" can only proceed from a racialized sense of the social order—an understanding that this or that race shall work toward this or that aim. In this sense the nation's first naturalization law, in 1790, represented "race politics" *par excellence,* as did its drastic revision in 1924. The former proceeded from an assumption that only "white persons" were truly fit for the rigors of republican self-government; the latter, from a revised estimation that, whoops, only Nordics were fit after all. But race politics itself also holds the power to generate a racial order of its own: the political mobilization of individuals and groups around a racially posed question can itself exert influence upon existing patterns of race-consciousness and racial salience.

A significant strand of twentieth-century American political life, then, is the story of how "race politics" ceased to concern the white races of Europe and came to refer exclusively to black-white relations and the struggle over Negro civil rights. Not only the regressive impulse among some whites to take economic and political refuge in whiteness, that is, but the progressive activities associated with civil rights struggle, too, are part of what ultimately rendered the varied white races "Caucasian." From the Communist Party's assault on "white chauvinism" and Father John LaFarge's Catholic Interracial Council in the 1930s, to Louis Adamic's Common Council for American Unity in the 1940s, progressive coalition-building around the "Negro Question" contributed to the re-forging of an undifferentiated racial whiteness.

Indeed, from the standpoint of racial epistemology, political coalition itself implies pre-existing, static, and self-evident social entities coming together with a singleness of purpose. As the "Negro Question" steadily eclipsed every other race question on the national agenda between the 1930s and the 1950s, the interracial coalitions that formed—on the left and in labor unions, within churches, and within the Democratic party—increasingly assumed a racially unvariegated group of whites to be precisely such a pre-existing, static, and self-evident entity. When James Ford testified to the Mayor's Commission on the Harlem Riot in 1935 that "the Negro people are treated like dogs in New York city," his chief "white" villains included a mayor named La Guardia and a beat cop named Zabitinski.[3] Such, indeed, was the nature of white power and privilege. But racial liberals who responded to the crisis and the call for a new politics of Negro civil rights, too, most often endorsed some version of Father

John LaFarge's contention that "minority racial groups" included only the "Negro," "Mexican," "Oriental," and "American Indian"; or Louis Adamic's caution, "The word *race* should be used sparingly. There really is no Slavic, Italian, Jewish, or Scandinavian race."[4] While pervasive patterns of racism themselves signified a degree of racial awareness among whites *as* whites, the emergent race politics of the 1930s and after dramatically heightened the salience of "Caucasian" identity by imploring whites to dwell upon their whiteness and to work toward the eradication of its unjust privileges.

Left and White

During the Popular Front period of the American left, it was broadly accepted that racism and fascism were aligned, and that any progressive movement would necessarily take an active stand against racism in all of its manifestations. Such a view had been in gestation within the Communist Party since the 1920s. In the years between 1928 and 1935 interracial activity became increasingly important in Party affairs, gradually escalating as a campaign behind the banner "Black and White, Unite and Fight!" From the "Black Belt Thesis" on Negro "national" rights that was advanced at the Sixth World Congress of the Comintern in 1928, to CP involvement in the trial of the Scottsboro boys, the in-Party struggle against "white chauvinism" throughout the 1930s and 1940s, and the Party's response to the Italian invasion of Ethiopia, the Communist Party was at the cutting edge of white agitation for Negro rights. "White members went around in a tizzy," recalled one Party publicist. "They had to check every figure of speech they used . . . They had to reexamine all the conventional attitudes of white life."[5] The very notion of "white life" was itself an innovation among the diverse peoples who made up the CP in cities like New York and Chicago. In noisily galvanizing a bi-racial coalition around the proposition that working-class struggle and Negro liberation were naturally aligned, the Party quietly remade the European immigrants within its ranks—whether Jewish, Italian, Finnish, or Irish—as a monolithic body of white workers.

Precedents to the CP's involvement in the Negro struggle date as far back as Cyril Briggs's African Blood Brotherhood (ABB). Founded in 1919, the ABB was a "race" organization emphasizing race pride, self-defense, and self-determination for blacks, but also drawn to the anticolonialism of the Bolshevik Revolution. Briggs, Richard Moore, and others later sought out the Communist Party in Harlem, when the ABB itself could neither compete with nor adequately influence the Garvey movement.[6] The Communists were receptive. In *The Negro Industrial Proletariat of America* (1928), James Ford noted the appearance of a "new type of Negro worker" and called for an interracial council and a new approach to race questions, as blacks emerged as a newly significant presence on the Northern, urban, industrial scene. According to Ford, "the labor movement is beginning to deal with a different type of Negro attitude towards the problem of colored and white workers . . . a class-conscious, aggressive, thinking type . . . that has studied and gone into the [relations] between colored and white workers."[7]

The "Black Belt Thesis," adopted by the Comintern in 1928, marked the full-scale entry of the Communist Party into race politics.[8] The thesis rested upon Stalin's definition of a "nation" as "a historically evolved, stable community of language, territory, economic life, and psychological make-up manifested in a community of culture."[9] As James Allen summarized the thesis in *Negro Liberation* (1932), since blacks outnumbered whites in a broad geographical swath stretching from the southern border of Maryland to the Mississippi delta, in this area "the Negro has been evolving as a nation." Blacks' proper participation in the international working-class struggle, therefore, was dependent upon their first attaining nationhood (or at least getting the chance to *entertain* it) and breaking the chains which shackled their national will: "Before a people can have equal rights with other peoples of the world, it must have the right itself to determine its relations with other nations. We can in no sense speak of the Negro people having achieved full equal rights until it has won the right of self-determination." This most basic right included the right to "set up a new political entity" in the majority area of the black belt, and to decide upon separation or political federation to the United States.[10]

Throughout the period that the thesis found favor, the Party continued to define the Negro struggle as "a phase of the class struggle of the American working class . . . a class struggle which assumes nationalist form." The bottom line, as the *Daily Worker* explained in 1931, was that "the natural differences between people are magnified, distorted, and emphasized beyond all measure by the white ruling class in order to cover up the really fundamental, important and decisive differences between those who labor and those who live on the surplus labor of the toiling masses."[11] Thus there existed "the closest connection between the struggles and demands of the Negro people and the struggles and demands of the labor and progressive movements." It is not that race and class exploitation represent two distinct phenomena; rather, "the Negroes are an extra-exploited and extra-oppressed people," and to fail to recognize this is simply "to capitulate to white chauvinism."[12]

Among the most revolutionary elements in the Party's approach was the insistence that "the white workers incorporate into their own trade union or political program and activities the vital demands of the Negro."[13] A Resolution of the Communist International in 1930 held that "it is the duty of the *white* workers to march at the head of this struggle [for the equal rights of Negroes] . . . white workers must boldly jump at the throat of the 100% bandits who strike a Negro in the face. This struggle will be the real test of international solidarity of the American white workers." The Party's presidential platform in 1932 incorporated a plank for "equal rights for the Negroes and self-determination for the Black Belt," and black Party member James Ford received the vice presidential nomination. By 1934 Party Secretary Earl Browder could identify "the liberation of the Negro people" as one of the "chief tasks of the Communist Party, which has come sharply to the front of our practical work."[14]

The Party assumed its highest profile in such "practical work" in the early 1930s, in defense of the Scottsboro boys, nine black youths falsely accused of raping two white women aboard a freight train in Alabama. The International Labor Defense handled the case (wresting control in a widely publicized contest with the NAACP); and the series of appeals became a focal point of Party mobilization both North and South in ensuing years. As ever, the need for Negro Liberation, as demonstrated by the "legal lynching" of the Scottsboro boys, bore directly upon broader questions of capitalist rule. Reviewing the long, violent history of race relations in the post-Reconstruction South in a pamphlet titled *Smash the Scottsboro Lynch Verdict!*, James Allen explained, "Once the white masses are convinced [that "Negroes are no good"], it becomes all the easier for the ruling class to prevent unity between the black and white masses in their struggle against exploitation and oppression." He exhorted white workers to "march, protest! Demand that Negroes be guaranteed their right to sit on juries, to vote, to hold office, to enjoy equal rights! Struggle against Jim-Crowism, lynching, persecution! White workers, dissociate yourselves from the lynch law policy of the ruling class, by being the first to strike out for Negro rights! Demand the release of the Scottsboro boys!"[15]

And protest they did. As the historian James Goodman has written of an early letter-writing campaign to Alabama officials:

Postcards, letters, and petitions from Communists, and mail from organizations that smelled radical or foreign or red, far outnumbered all others. And most of the letters began something like this: "We the members of the Anti-Imperialist League"; "We the members of the Young Communist League"; "We the League of Struggle for Negro Rights"; "We the members of the Lithuanian Working Women's Alliance"; "We the Ukrainian Labor Temple"; "We the Frederick Douglass Interracial Forum"; "We the Karl Marx Pioneer Troops"; "We the Vegetarian Workers' Club"; "We" the "Russian," "Finnish," "Scandinavian," "Croatian," "Hungarian," "Socialist," and "Jewish" toilers. Or worse, "We 900 white and colored workers assembled in a mass meeting in Kansas City . . ."[16]

In the context of the Black Belt Thesis and this kind of race-based social protest, a broad struggle against "white chauvinism" *within* Party circles developed and became one of the centerpieces of Party race policy in the 1930s and 1940s. As Harry Haywood recalled, "The mass entrance of Blacks into the revolutionary movement flushed out hitherto hidden areas of white chauvinism . . . white supremacist attitudes in their crudest form had cropped up in a number of the language clubs and cooperatives." A Lithuanian club in Chicago refused to serve black delegates, for instance; a Russian cooperative restaurant in Gary refused to hire black workers. Others in the Party resisted the call to work for racial justice, shunting all such projects onto the new League of Struggle for Negro Rights instead. Indeed, "the list of white racist manifestations was long and growing."[17] Haywood, along with Cyril Briggs and Maud White [Katz], took the issue straight to the Politburo in the form of a document listing "various forms of white chauvinism." The result, according to Haywood, was "a renewed campaign throughout the Party against white chauvinism and for unity of Black and white workers . . . A campaign of enlightenment resulted which was tied to organizational and disciplinary measures against those guilty of racist acts. A number of expulsions took place."[18]

Throughout the 1930s and 1940s, then, the *Daily Worker,* the *Communist,* and a slew of Party pamphlets spelled out the requirements of this antiracist campaign and elaborated its theoretical underpinnings. "Sections of the white workers have benefited indirectly from the superexploitation of the Negroes," wrote James Allen in *Negro Liberation.* By their "privileged position as compared with the Negro workers," many whites had become "polluted by white chauvinism." The "poison of white chauvinism," as George Blake called it, corresponded to the Great-Russian chauvinism in the U.S.S.R. (as theorized by Stalin), and it threatened the International in precisely the same way. From a theoretical standpoint, white workers had to overcome their own racism as a reactionary tendency that hobbled working-class unity and ultimately served the ruling classes; from a strategic standpoint, they had to demonstrate their racial egalitarianism in order to make a bi-racial coalition of workers possible. Blacks' "deep distrust against *all* whites has been nurtured by the prevailing atmosphere of 'white superiority' which reaches even into the labor movement," wrote Allen. Another Party pamphlet exhorted in 1932, "We must, as Bolsheviks, have a keen political nose for . . . hidden chauvinism, drag it out into the open and liquidate it." This campaign was sustained on into the 1940s, when it dovetailed with the fight against fascism. White chauvinism had developed into "a fascist ideology and a fascist weapon," wrote Blake. Thus, the fight against intra-Party racism "is a vital part of the fight against fascism."[19]

One of the most spectacular efforts to discover white chauvinism and "drag it out into the open and liquidate it" was the in-Party trial of August Yokinen, a Finnish immigrant in Harlem whose chauvinist acts indicated "views that are detrimental to the interests of the working class."[20] Yokinen, the caretaker of a Finnish Club in Harlem, was accused of (and confessed to) standing idly by while several whites harassed, pushed, and tried to expel three black workers who had come to a club dance. When confronted by Party leaders about their failure to intervene on the blacks' behalf, other Finnish Communists quickly admitted their mistake and recognized the bourgeois implications of their chauvinism, according to *Race Hatred on Trial,* the most popular in-Party account. "*All except Yokinen.* He more or less justified the chauvinist policy followed at the dance." Yokinen argued that, "if the Negroes came into the club and into the pool room, they would soon be coming into the bathroom, and . . . he for one, did not wish to bathe with Negroes." By his attitudes, the Party charged, Yokinen had allowed himself to become "a phonograph for the capitalists"; "he was giving expression to views that undermine the confidence of the Negro masses in the Communist Party and in the revolutionary white working class."[21]

Coming directly on the heels of Haywood, Briggs, and White's complaint to the Politburo, the incident became an irresistible opportunity concretely to demonstrate—for the sake of its own membership and for the wider bourgeois world—the Communist Party's commitment to the principle of racial justice. "Yokinen Mass Trial Sunday," announced the *Daily Worker;* "White Chauvinism Must Be Rooted Out." The public, in-Party "trial" of August Yokinen for "white chauvinism" would step up the Party's campaign "to smash this color line of the slave owners and unite the working class."[22]

In a hall "dotted with placards such as 'Race Inferiority Is a White Ruling Class Lie,'" Yokinen was tried "before 1500 white and Negro workers" on March 1, 1931.[23] Prosecutor Clarence Hathaway (the editor of the *Daily Worker*) used the trial as a platform for articulating the Party line on Negro liberation and class struggle, including a nutshell rendition of the Black Belt Thesis. "When white workers show the slightest race-superiority tendencies in working-class meetings, or in the shops and factories," he cautioned, "they actually become the agents of the bourgeoisie."[24] Speaking for the defense, Richard Moore (a black activist who had come into the Party by way of the African Blood Brotherhood) did not refute the charges; indeed, he reiterated much of Hathaway's theorizing. Rather, he merely argued that the punishment Hathaway had called for—expulsion from the Party—was too harsh. In a widely quoted, dramatic speech, Moore averred, "I would rather have my head severed from my body by the capitalist lynchers than to be expelled in disgrace from the Communist International."[25]

Finally, in a prepared statement which an interpreter translated from Finnish, Yokinen himself admitted "having been under the influence of white chauvinist ideology in my activities in connection with the Finnish Workers' Club." Joining Hathaway and Moore in elaborating the stakes of overcoming chauvinism, Yokinen explained, "American imperialism uses the artificial separation of the workers into groups to further split them from each other by spreading its vicious doctrines of race and national prejudices and by playing the Negro and the foreign born and American white workers all against each other."[26] Upon deliberation, a jury of fourteen then expelled Yokinen from the Party for a period of six months, during which time he was to work actively to combat white chauvinism both within and without the Finnish Club, to work for Negro rights, and to educate his compatriots on the importance of racial egalitarianism. (In a bizarre footnote to the whole affair, immigration authorities seized Yokinen the next day and sought to deport him for his membership in a party that "advocated the overthrow of the U.S. government."

The International Labor Defense took up his case and the CP staged several mass demonstrations on his behalf.)[27]

Although the Communists earned some skepticism among African-Americans as to what they could finally deliver in the way of "Negro liberation," the Party did stand out among white organizations for its analysis of racial oppression and for its extraordinary introspection on "white chauvinism" at a time when most unions were still Jim Crow and Congress refused even antilynching legislation. In the wake of another "white chauvinism" trial in Milwaukee in 1933, the *Chicago Defender* asked, "Is there any other political, religious, or civic organization in the country that would go to such lengths to prove itself not unfriendly to us? Is there any other group in the country that would not applaud the sentiments as expressed by the man who was ousted in this instance?" As St. Clair Drake and Horace Cayton wrote in *Black Metropolis,*

> What other party since Reconstruction days had ever run a Negro for vice president of the United States? And who had ever put Negroes in a position where they led white men as well as black? Every time a black communist appeared on the platform, or his picture appeared in the newspaper, Negroes were proud; and no stories of "atheistic Reds" or "alien Communists" could nullify the fact that here were people who accepted Negroes as complete equals and asked other white men to do so.[28]

Indeed, it was not only the intrigue of an American Party tribunal on the Moscow model, but the astonishing novelty of a white group's investigating its own racism, that prompted the New York *Times* to give August Yokinen's "white chauvinism" trial front-page coverage.[29] Among predominantly white groups, the Communist Party was decades ahead when it came to investigating antiblack racism.

But the racial syntax of the Yokinen trial begins to hint at the homogenous "white" racial identity that the Negro Question was helping to enforce. Yokinen himself defied the simplest binary social outlook when he remarked upon the "vicious doctrines" that played "the Negro and the foreign born and American white workers all against each other"; but he nonetheless characterized these as "vicious doctrines of race and national prejudices," thereby articulating two distinct planes of "difference." As the Party's pamphlet *Race Hatred on Trial* put it, "As a foreign born worker, [Yokinen] realized that he was being divided off by the ruling class from the other white workers, in the same way as the workers were being divided on race lines."[30] Despite an overall framework in which race itself represented merely an artificial, ruling-class scheme of division, phrases like "the other white workers" and "divided on race lines" are symptomatic of the racial assumptions of "difference" underlying this progressive effort at bi-racial coalition.

Recall, for instance, the *Daily Worker*'s reference to "natural differences" ("the natural differences between people are magnified, distorted, and emphasized beyond all measure by the white ruling class"). "We have on the one hand the *natural question* [that is, race]—the fight for equal rights of the Negroes with the whites," the journal explained, "and on the other hand we have the struggle of the working class, in which Negroes are included."[31] Although the CP was not at all interested in theorizing the epistemological status of race beyond its contribution to capitalist hegemony and working-class disorder, the Party's definition of "nations" and "minorities" did set African-Americans on a plane of social significance far removed from any other group on the American scene. The CP's deracination of European immigrants thus became plain in its denial of their existence as "national entities." As James Allen wrote in *Negro Liberation*,

> If a group of people has only some of the characteristics noted [in Stalin's definition] it is not a nation. Thus, it would be incorrect to consider the Jews in the United States a national entity . . . nor can the numerous immigrant groups constitute national minorities who are gradually being amalgamated with the American people, just as other groups before them have gone into the melting pot from which has emerged the American nation.[32]

Allen's reference to "amalgamation" suggests the distinctly racial basis of his thinking on the national question, even if, like other communist theorists, he shied away from the explicit language of "race" and "races." Although "blackness" and "whiteness" as relevant categories derive from social and legal practices (like poll taxes and lynching) rather than from biological differences in Allen's scheme, still it is a reified, amalgamated racial whiteness that evaporates the Europeans' prior nationalities and unites immigrant Americans as not-black. If the "natural differences" between white and black workers are exaggerated and exploited by the ruling class, nonetheless there *are* no "natural differences" among white workers themselves.

Throughout the CP's campaign for racial justice there were fleeting glimmers of a contrary racial logic of plural "white races" as opposed to a consolidated "white race." The *Daily Worker* could argue that "the bosses will make every effort to exaggerate the antagonisms between black and white, between foreign born and white, between foreign born and black," for example. James Ford could assert that "anti-Semitism and Negrophobia . . . stem from the same source"; and Benjamin Davis, Jr., might refer to "Jim Crow, anti-Semitism and all other forms of racial discrimination." As Mark Naison has noted, too, many Jewish immigrants were drawn to the CP's position on the Negro Question precisely because it "represented an analogue of the bolsheviks' war on antisemitism."[33] Such formulations echo other progressive assessments of the race-based, "natural alliance" of African-Americans and Jews—for instance, one rabbi's 1919 sermon entitled "The Jew, Who Knows What Race Prejudice Is, Can Plead for His Stricken Brother."[34]

In general, however, the tendency was toward homogenization and consolidation of whiteness. "White workers must stand in the forefront of the struggle for Negro rights and against white chauvinism," Earl Browder implored at the time; and, as Harvard Sitkoff has noted in retrospect, a "galaxy of first- and second-generation immigrants assumed leadership positions in the struggle for racial equality" in this period.[35] Harry Haywood marks the Yokinen trial as "a breakthrough in understanding the importance of the struggle of the Afro-American people," and recalls Yokinen himself going on to become "a familiar and popular figure on the streets of Harlem, in demonstrations of the unemployed, for the Scottsboro boys and against the Jim Crow policies of a local cafeteria."[36] "White chauvinism . . . is not confined to drawing the color line in Jim Crow fashion," remarked the Party spokesperson Israel Amter on the eve of Yokinen's trial. "It has crept into the Communist Party, made up of both whites and Negroes."[37] In a context where "Nordic" supremacy still animated public discussion in certain arenas and where a popular, eugenically derived racial understanding still identified more than forty distinct races (Ugro-Finns among them), this racial lexicon of only two races— "white and Negro"—was as powerful as Jim Crow itself when it came to the matter of assessing (that is, assigning) "difference."

Common Ground

In 1947 John Caswell Smith, Jr., a black social worker and officer of Boston's Urban League, was invited to lead a series of discussions on race relations among the students of the Hudson Shore Labor School in New York, a body comprising "whites and Negroes (from both South and North), several religious faiths and at least a half-dozen nationality group-ings." During a session in which Smith and his students were attempting to break down and assess the implications of the idea of "group charac-teristics," one student, "a veteran whose parents were born in Greece," offered: "Well, you take me. I'm a Greek. Anyone can tell I'm a Greek!" Smith addressed another of the students:

> "Sue," I asked, "did you know Mike is a Greek?"
> She flushed. "Well, no. I . . ."
> ". . . We were talking about races and you tell me about Greeks. Are Greeks a race of people?" There was not a unanimous agreement . . . "Race," we decided, meant some reference to one of the three great groups of mankind: Mongoloid, Negroid, Caucasoid. Under-standable frowns of confusion spread over some faces, but nothing was said.[38]

Although Smith's account is unusual for its straightforward rendering of the confusion attending race and difference during this period of flux, his seminar's decision that "race" must refer to "the three great groups of mankind" was not at all unusual. It was ratified by myriad progressive groups—and by the culture at large—as the "Negro Question" loomed in popular discussion well before the mobilization of the modern civil rights movement.

Communists may have taken the lead on the race question among pre-dominantly white organizations, but as Harvard Sitkoff has so amply documented, by the Popular Front era the CP was hardly alone in pushing the Negro Question toward the center of the national agenda. The Federal Council of Churches instituted Race Relations Sunday in 1932; and the first Catholic Interracial Council was formed in 1934 behind Father John LaFarge, with branches in Detroit, Chicago, Los Angeles, St. Louis, Phila-delphia, Washington, Brooklyn, Kansas City, and San Antonio. The coun-cil carried out protest activities, promoted curricular changes, fought for fair employment practices and the opening of hospitals to "Negro and all non-Caucasian physicians and nurses"; and its *Friendship House News* offered homilies on how "Christians must love the Negro," or giving "Ad-vice to white Catholics when Negroes move into your area."[39] Eleanor Roosevelt publically championed black rights and privately importuned her husband to incorporate principles of racial justice in the New Deal.

Socialists abandoned their long-held contention that racial oppression was strictly an economic by-product of capitalism, and now took up the cudgel against lynching and Jim Crow.[40]

By 1935 the New York *Times* was announcing, "100 Unions Pledge Fight for Negroes," and the trade union movement under both the AFL and the CIO umbrellas now "moved to eradicate race prejudice and discrimination from the ranks of organized labor." As for electoral politics, *Time* magazine noted, "In no election since 1860 have politicians been so Negro-minded as in 1936." One Southern Democrat complained, "It is perfectly obvious that the so-called Democratic party of the North is now the negro party."[41] And during World War II, Fisk University's *Summary of Events and Trends in Race Relations* could note the appearance of "over two hundred organizations . . . with programs directed toward the relieving of racial tensions and the general improvement of race relations in the United States." The American Council on Race Relations was established as a clearing house to coordinate the activities of these myriad local, regional, and national groups.[42]

Hence while bigots like Senator John Rankin were railing against the "Kikes" who were trying to "mongrelize the nation," and while others, like the Greek veteran in Smith's discussion group, were clinging to racialized identity as their own birthright, the weight of American culture was steadily and inexorably reducing the polity to a simple dyad of black and white—a scheme in which the former white races vanished into whiteness, and in which, so far as public discussion went, American Indians, Filipinos, Pacific Islanders, and Mexican and Asian immigrants and their children vanished altogether. By the civil rights era library shelves were filling up with books bearing titles like *White and Black: Test of a Nation; Crisis in Black and White; Confrontation: Black and White; Black Families in White America; Race Riots in Black and White; Black and White: A Study of U.S. Racial Attitudes Today; Black Children, White Dreams; Beyond Black and White; Assertive Black, Puzzled White; Black and White Self Esteem;* and *White Justice, Black Experience.*[43]

Carey McWilliams, an architect of the "nation of nations" tradition in American social thought, stands out for his refusal to lose sight of the overall complexity of the American mosaic and for his refusal to make "race" identical with "the Negro" in American political life. Unlike Gunnar Myrdal and other social scientists, who would effectively expel from consideration those pegged neither as "white" nor as "black," McWilliams demonstrated a keen sensitivity to the complex racial tableau in

America, including "The Non-Vanishing Indian," "The Long-Suffering Chinese," "The Forgotten Mexican," "Our Japanese Hostages," "The Puerto Ricans and Other Islanders," and Filipinos, "The Little Brown Brothers," as he catalogued them in *Brothers under the Skin* (1942).[44]

But even so, "color" and the "color line" had become for McWilliams the primary organizer in thinking about American diversity. Indeed, if he carefully eschewed the simplicity of black-and-white, he did depict the political landscape in a binary of color/not-color that consolidated whiteness itself. While the "racial question" had once referred to "the 'new immigrant' from Southeastern Europe, the fellow with the brachycephalic skull," he noted, European immigrants had never posed "a serious long-range minority problem"; "no firmly entrenched caste system [had] developed." By 1942 "Joe, Vince, and Dominic DiMaggio . . . are, I should say, pretty typical Americans in every sense of the word." "Race" in the United States had become "a crisis about *color.*" This view is enforced in *Brothers under the Skin* by statistics regarding the "colored minority peoples in the United States" and the "white" and "colored" populations of the Western Hemisphere; by statistics on world population, broken down into "Continents Predominantly White" and "Continents Predominantly Non-White"; and by discussions of Jim Crow practices in the army and in the defense industries, the Red Cross's segregation of blood, and Virginia's "race registration act" of 1930.[45] For McWilliams, in other words, the salience of distinct white races was dependent upon the social practices that might be said to buttress them, and so patterns of bigotry and institutional racism now marked the extent to which whiteness had been consolidated and its internal differences erased.

Another of the leading racial liberals of the period, and a close associate of Carey McWilliams, was Louis Adamic, a Slovenian writer whose interest in the "patterns of diversity" in America led him to confront questions of "difference" in several volumes in the 1930s and 1940s. "America is only beginning," he wrote in 1938, "and every beginning is somewhat of a mess." What made this particular beginning such a mess, in Adamic's view, was the nation's failure to meet the challenges of its own remarkable diversity. In the main Slovenians "don't think much of the Croatians," he noted, "and *vice versa.* Many of the Czechs don't like the Slovaks. Few Germans think anything of the Slavs. Most of the non-Jewish immigrant groups are more or less anti-Semitic. The Jews scorn the Hunkies, but have this in common with them: they both stick up their noses at the Negro." Adamic went on to attribute these mutual animosities to "the fact that each of the groups knows no more of the others than old-stock Americans know about immigrants as a whole." The problem may be "immense," he allowed; "but, clearly, [it is] a problem of education."[46]

This passage represents the kernel of what would later become the Common Council for American Unity, a coalition dedicated to just such "education." The central problem as Adamic saw it was that old-stock Americans tended to view virtually everyone else as a menace to the historic "pattern of the country," when, in fact, "diversity itself is the pattern." Only when Americans recognized that Americanness resides precisely in the country's unique status as a "nation of nations" could its loftiest ideals be realized. The unofficial slogan of Adamic's Common Council for American Unity was "Let's make America safe for differences"; and the council's journal, *Common Ground* (along with Adamic's own published volumes), represented an effort to render such differences themselves intelligible, and to bring to light the largely suppressed "contributions" which every non–Anglo-Saxon group had made to American political, cultural, and artistic life.[47]

As an immigrant himself, Adamic assigned primacy in this project to the problem of "anti-alienism" and to the national embrace of America's foreign-born populations. Although the Common Council and *Common Ground* did ultimately take up the Negro Question with some vigor, Adamic initially launched the project with his lecture "Ellis Island and Plymouth Rock," a prolonged meditation on the status of the "non–Anglo-Saxon" immigrant in the United States, which he delivered "before about a hundred audiences all over the United States" in 1939 and 1940.[48] Adamic was also deeply involved in the vexing racial vicissitudes of non–Anglo-Saxondom in America. Much like Laura Z. Hobson at around the same time, for instance, Adamic was erratic in his application of "racial difference," invoking at one moment a community of "whites," at the next the specter of racial Anglo-Saxonism. "This Crisis Is an Opportunity" (1940) is typical. Having lamented the social barbs endured by those "whose names sound 'foreign' or who 'look Jewish' or 'Italian,' " for instance, and having lamented that racism "forces into their respective corners of disadvantage the Indians and the Negro, Oriental, and Jewish Americans," Adamic went on to sing of a potential alliance that unified whiteness and erased nonwhites from the picture:

> We need to work toward a synthesis of the old stock and the new immigrant America, of the Mayflower and the steerage, of Plymouth

Rock and Jamestown and Ellis Island, of the Liberty Bell and the Statue of Liberty, of the New England wilderness [!] and the slums of modern industrial cities, of the American Revolution and the industrial revolution.[49]

Elsewhere Adamic demonstrated even more forcefully his own difficulty in integrating peoples of color into the structure of his thinking on American diversity. In 1938 he proposed "a great educational-cultural work" whose aims included "to reach almost everybody in this country with the fact that socially and culturally the United States, as it stands today, is an extension not only of the British Isles and the Netherlands but, more or less, all of Europe."[50] (He later amended this with the clause "and parts of Asia and Africa.")[51] The racial syntax of *Nation of Nations* (1944), too, suggests the disparity Adamic assigned to the status of white immigrant identity and African-American identity. The study unfolds in thirteen chapters, twelve of which are structured along the identical lines of "Americans from Italy," "Americans from France," "Americans from Poland," "Americans from Yugoslavia," and so on. Chapter 8 is conspicuous for its alternative structure: "Negro Americans." Here blackness is a totalizing state of being, and whiteness is at once unified and rendered invisible in a narrative structure that identifies not race, but geographical movement and bi-continental history, as the foundational elements of disparate immigrant identities. The common ground upon which immigrants and their children stand, in other words, consists of their common experience with geographical relocation and persecution. It is a common racial experience in that race evidently has so little to do with it—as is highlighted by contrast with that group who *might* have been called "Americans from Africa."

The fate of African-Americans, like the fate of the new immigrants, will finally depend upon "the country's ability to discard the idea that it is exclusively White, Protestant and Anglo-Saxon." But this prevailing national idea wreaks even more havoc for blacks than for immigrants, Adamic notes, as "many new immigrant groups are anti-Negro as a psychological compensation for their own inferiority status under the White-Protestant-Anglo-Saxon concept . . . It is a *Herrenvolk* concept—a main ingredient of the dynamite laying loose about the country."[52] Still, for Adamic the social and cultural inclusion of new immigrants takes precedence over the inclusion of blacks, if only because—since they are "white"—it ought to be easier:

We have . . . about thirteen million Negroes, . . . a rather special and acute problem, possibly destined to be the ultimate and most severe test of our forming culture, of our pretensions to democracy—a test which the country will be able to meet, I feel, only if the white elements soon begin to solve the problems among themselves.

The whites number about 115,000,000. Slightly over half of them are Anglo-Saxons, or think they are.[53]

Like McWilliams, Adamic increasingly acknowledged the dualism of color/whiteness as the most significant division within the polity; yet unlike the Californian, he continued to focus primarily upon the social dynamics on the "white" side of this chasm. Indeed, *My America, From Many Lands,* and *Nation of Nations* roughly hint at the transformation of "Anglo-Saxons" themselves from a "racial" group to the "ethnic" group WASPs (White Anglo-Saxon Protestants, an appellation that would emerge only later). Thus Adamic's energetic but conflicted analysis of "difference" and the American design exhibits traces of a number of schemes which by now are familiar. Whereas the CP had unified workers' whiteness by denying their status as nationality groups (in contrast to African-Americans), Adamic unified immigrants' whiteness by *insisting* upon their status as nationality groups (in contrast to African-Americans). For Adamic, the recapitulated saga of arrival, settlement, and "contribution" to the nation of nations coded immigrant diversity as racial sameness. The chief obstacle to immigrants' full inclusion in American life was Anglo-Saxon arrogance. Since Anglo-Saxon arrogance was also responsible for generating immigrants' "anti-Negro" sentiments, to work for immigrant inclusion ultimately *was* to work for African-American inclusion, though the distinct two-step approach to the problem marked the clear levels of "difference" in the two cases.

Thus McWilliams and Adamic had each arrived at their view of a consolidated whiteness via different routes—McWilliams by way of a pragmatic recognition that the racial "difference" of the white races had lost its salience as an obstacle to national participation; Adamic by way of a more personalized, common bond with those whose "difference" on the American scene derived from a geographical saga, not a racial one. Nonetheless, this overall trend toward "Caucasian" racial sameness in their thinking was mirrored throughout the pages of *Common Ground,* the quarterly published by the Common Council for American Unity between 1940 and 1949. As spelled out in its masthead, the mission of the journal, which was edited first by Adamic and then by Margaret Anderson, with an advisory board that included Van Wyck Brooks, Pearl Buck, Langston Hughes, Alvin Johnson, Thomas Mann, and Lin Yutang, was to foster "unity and mutual understanding," to "further an appreciation of what each group has contributed to America," "to overcome intolerance and discrimination because of foreign birth or descent, race or nationality," and "to help the foreign-born and their children solve their special problems of adjustment."

Although it would be an oversimplification to trace the ideological movement in *Common Ground* in strictly linear terms, still, the journal's pages do mark the rising concern with black-white relations and the related evaporation of white races. This development was sometimes dramatic and plain, as in John Caswell Smith's essay on the Hudson Shore Labor School cited earlier. In addition to that group's "deciding" that "race meant reference to one of the three great groups of mankind" (rather than, say, to Greeks), Smith went on to explain that "to be Jewish was to be a member of a religious group, not a 'race,' and . . . one could not tell 'Jewishness' simply by looking at a person, any more than you could tell 'Baptistness' in this way."[54] Or again, in a *Common Ground* sketch on "tolerance," Lois Margaret Hamvas described the effect that the African-American presence at her college had on her and her Jewish friend Hannah: "If Hannah and I were really close friends, it was because we had completely forgotten that we were Jewish or not-Jewish. But we could never forget about Barbara [who was black]."[55]

Elsewhere the shift was less explicit, but overall the journal's commentary on diversity developed along the two distinct paths of "race," which was chiefly political (coverage of Jim Crow, the Detroit riot, and the rising black protest movement), and "nationality," which was primarily cultural (human interest pieces, short stories, and autobiographical sketches demonstrating the local color, as it were, of various immigrant enclaves and cultures). The number that appeared in the wake of the Detroit riot (Autumn 1943) powerfully announced the ascendent meaning of race both in liberal political culture at large and in the ideology of the journal itself. The number included a piece entitled "Race Tensions: Second Phase," in which Carey McWilliams charted the intractable problems attending "color" in the United States and explored some of the strident protest movements that were galvanizing in response. It then continued with essays by George Sanchez on "Pachucos in the making," Louis Martin on "the prelude to disaster" in Detroit, Marjorie McKenzie on "Negro-white" relations in the South, Margaret Walker on "growing out of the shadow"—an autobiographical piece on "what it means to be black in America"—and Lillian Smith on the segregated South, "where the relationship of the two races has become so intertwined with hate and love and fear and guilt and poverty and greed, with churches and with lynchings, with attraction and repulsion that it has taken on the ambivalent qualities . . . of a terrible and terrifying illness."[56]

By the mid-1940s "race," in the lexicon of *Common Ground,* was reserved for pieces like Marie Syrkin's "Jim Crow in the Classroom" or for pieces on black-white conflict by Langston Hughes or Louella MacFarlane. Steadily disappearing over the course of the decade were Louis Adamic's worries, voiced in the initial number (Autumn 1940), about the "anti-alienism" directed against people "who 'look Jewish' or 'Italian.' "[57]

Marjorie Berkowitz's poem "To the Negro" (1949) captures both the ideology of the racial coalition model (from the "Caucasian" side) and a rising protest sensibility that seizes upon its own whiteness even as it aligns itself with blackness. "There are those who give you sympathy," but that is such a "smug small thing," she intones.

> I give you something of another kind.
> I give you my anger.
> . . . . .
> My anger scoring its mark against the cancer of hate
> comes from an outraged soul whose eyes burn and whose face
>   reddens
> as the dignity of man is humiliated.
> I offer it to you to add to your own until the anger
> of men shall rise to such heights that indignities
> we now suffer will be crushed and your smooth brown skin
> will be no more than smooth brown skin.[58]

Here is the racialized and racializing thrust of mid-century American liberalism rendered as an aesthetic. Berkowitz insists upon an egalitarian principle and puts forward a universalizing notion of pan–human dignity. And yet so does she make a fetish of skin color. The whiteness of the speaker and the blackness of her object are strangely and unnecessarily accented: the whiteness behind the "reddened" face is essential to the anger as it is depicted here, just as the "smoothness" of the "smooth brown skin" denotes a lingering attention to difference, suggesting that perhaps this skin is indeed something *more* than mere skin. The "I" and the "you" of the poem are united in rage, perhaps; but the markers of color bespeak coalition, not kinship. This is an understanding of unity fundamentally different from that posed by, for instance, the 1919 sermon "The Jew, Who Knows What Race Prejudice Is, Can Plead for His Stricken Brother." It is liberalism-from-whiteness; and, where white liberalism reigned at all in the next several decades, it was largely this particular variety. Thus did the progressive impulse within the noncommunist left contribute to the broader trend toward the invention of "ethnicity" and the racial revision of diverse Caucasians now aligned in defense of "the Negro."

Sinclair Lewis's *Kingsblood Royal*

Carey McWilliams's approach to the politics of diversity represents one major road not taken in the struggles of the 1930s–1960s. If McWilliams was quick to join the consensus on a reified "Caucasian" racial identity for the erstwhile white races, his sensitivity to the extraordinary range of peoples and traditions on the American scene was nonetheless atypical. His *Brothers under the Skin* offered perhaps a distinctly Californian view of the complexity of the human mosaic called America and of the depth of race in structuring every relationship in American history. His view was quickly and decisively eclipsed by a simpler racial dyad in which whiteness represented the "normal" state of the American and "the Negro" represented the single racial problem to be solved. The appearance of Gunnar Myrdal's *American Dilemma* in 1944 marked the beginning of the end. All others outside this black-and-white model—the non*black* nonwhites catalogued chapter by chapter in *Brothers under the Skin*—effectively disappeared from public discussion of race, power, and social policy. Even the 1960s never fully produced a broad-based coalition or a revisionist history of the kind suggested by McWilliams's racial logic.

But if we have yet to discover what a coalition politics on the McWilliams model might look like, still less do we know about the possibilities of another of the common intellectual threads of the era—what today is called the "deconstruction" of race itself. It is a somewhat perplexing fact of American intellectual history that notions of the cultural construction of race that have begun to receive a hearing in recent years were in fact quite commonplace five decades ago. Writers like Ashley Montagu, Brewton Barry, and George Schuyler, as we have seen, argued that race was but a modern superstition. One routinely encounters the word "race" undermined by surrounding quotation marks in material from the 1940s (as in the 1990s), in a way that was quite rare in the 1950s, 1960s, and 1970s. Even Louis Adamic would remark in *Nation of Nations,* "I use 'Negro' and 'White' . . . for lack of other words." "Inexact descriptions of color-as-color, they represent color-as-a-race-symbol, a thing full of mischief not only in America but internationally." He went on to note, with irony, "Come summertime many Caucasian Americans go to great trouble and expense to be darker than are many Negroes whom they bar from bathing beaches."[59]

Among the most thorough efforts in this lost intellectual tradition was Sinclair Lewis's *Kingsblood Royal* (1947), advertised at the time as "the story of a man who resigns from the white race."[60] Like Schuyler's *Black No More, Kingsblood Royal* dismantles the race concept by underscoring the logical absurdities of what one character calls "that barbaric psychology" of the one-drop rule. Neil Kingsblood, an unremarkable middle-American racist from a smallish city in Minnesota, undergoes a dramatic moral transformation when, on a genealogical hunt in the local archives for a hypothetical royal ancestor, he discovers that he has a black ancestor, and that hence he and his descendants are "legally one hundred percent Negro" themselves.

"When a man is born a Negro at thirty-one," remarks the narrator, "he needs a family." Kingsblood's soul-searching takes him not only into unsuspected regions of his own heart, but also across the tracks into unfamiliar parts of town. Some surprises await him in both regions. The bulk of the novel—at once a social satire and a psychological study—deals with Kingsblood's attempts to discover "the right course for a person whom God had made white but whom the legislative enactments of the God-fearing States of the Union had made black." Sophie Concord, an African-American nurse who has befriended the newly black Kingsblood, supplies the novel's ultimate moral code, nicely rendered in a single sentence. In response to Kingsblood's essentialist and overdone enthusiasm as "a real member of the race" and his earnest appreciation for Negroes and the bravery "they" demonstrate, Sophie gently chides, "My benevolent but sophomoric friend, there isn't any They among human beings, only We!"[61]

"Only We," indeed: Kingsblood's late-blooming blackness after long years of unquestioned whiteness not only makes a mockery of his neighbors' racist denunciations (they had, after all, been friends and even admirers of this "Negro" for some time), but also calls into question *their* whiteness and the very notion of stable races. This is a critique not of "race relations" or of "prejudice," in other words, but of race itself as nothing more than "theoretical kinship."[62]

Lewis demolishes "difference" only after carefully establishing it in the first place—not least, after establishing it in Neil Kingsblood's own world-view in the days before his startling self-discovery. Although he likes to boast an untarnished liberalism on Race Questions ("I haven't any prejudices against any race. After all, I was in the War Against Prejudice"), he does tend to trip over the underbrush of his racist assumptions with some regularity. While decrying his boss's racism early on, for instance, Kingsblood notes, "[Mr. Prutt is] prejudiced against Scandinavians and the Irish and Hunkies and Polacks. He doesn't understand that we have a new America. Still and all, even hating prejudice, I do see where the Negroes are inferior and always will be." More straightforward still, "One thing is obvious: the whole biological and psychological make-up of the Negroes is different from that of white people, especially from us Anglo-Saxons (of course I have some French blood, too)."[63]

Kingsblood's romance and anxiety, dead certainty, complete ignorance, self-congratulatory liberalism, and ineradicable white-supremacism on race questions whirl in an ideological-emotional tempest when, on his genealogical research trip, the archivist first tells him (mistakenly, it turns out) that there is a possibility that one of his ancestors had been a Chippewa Indian. Kingsblood reels for a moment; then, "learnedly summing it all up,"

> Neil decided that (1), he probably had no Indian blood or Indian genes or whatever it was and (2), it wouldn't matter if he had, but (3), he wouldn't mention it to [his wife] and (4), recalling Gramma Julie's swarthy gracefulness, he was sure that [his daughter] and he were as Indian as Sitting Bull, and (5), he had now completely lost interest in the subject and (6), he was going to find out for certain, as soon as he could, whether he did have any Indian blood and/or genes.[64]

Lewis's comic tone here veils a profound insight into the texture of popular American racial thought: (1) an indefinite understanding of race ("genes or whatever it was"); (2) a proud but thin adherence to what Myrdal had called "the American creed" ("it wouldn't matter"); (3) a stubborn adherence to notions of hierarchy that Myrdal had called the "American dilemma" ("he wouldn't mention it"); (4) a belief in racial essentialism marked by physicality ("Gramma Julie's swarthy gracefulness . . . as Indian as Sitting Bull"); (5) and (6) an imperfectly repressed urgency as to race and its revealed truths ("he had now completely lost interest . . . he was going to find out for certain as soon as he could").

Kingsblood's response is more powerful still when his kinsman Xavier Pic's identity is established with certainty. When the archivist cheerfully tells him that he has made a mistake, and that the ancestor in question was not part Chippewa, but rather full-blooded Negro, Kingsblood remains poker-faced, thinking primarily of his "golden" daughter Biddy, who had been until that moment a Saxon. The narrative resumes after a chapter break, to find Kingsblood seated at a lunchcounter facing the new facts of his existence—"He was still in horror, beyond surprise now, like a man who has learned that last night, walking in his sleep, he murdered a man, that the police are looking for him." His sense of alienation was total: "He was apparently eating a sandwich."[65]

Having thus firmly established Neil Kingsblood's worldview and having set him squarely within a universe of racial "differences," Lewis critiques the race concept using the racial re-education of the ex-noncolored man as his vehicle. It is not just rac*ism* that Kingsblood revises as he remaps the world; it is race itself. The black people whom he avidly seeks out do not at all match his prior mental image of "Negroes"—even though, now, with a kind of proselyte's enthusiasm, he strangely wishes that they did. Upon his first visit to an African-American church, he vaguely hopes to find "tom-toms and jungle-dancing," but is disappointed and confused by the ordinariness (the whiteness, in his view) of the proceedings. It is "plain hell," he concludes, "to get myself nerved up to being a Negro and then find out there aren't any special Negro things *to* be." Even after his very first forays into the "black" world,

> Neil discovered that his sense of their being "colored," being alien, being fundamentally different from himself, had evaporated. Their similarity to one another in duskiness and fuzzy hair was so much less than their individual differences that they had already ceased being Negroes and become People, to wonder about, to love and hate.
>
> Evan Brewster was no longer ugly to him . . . and Neil saw dimly what a piece of impertinence it had been for the Caucasians to set up their own anemic dryness as the correct standard of beauty.[66]

This drastic revision of race as difference becomes more pointed later on, when Kingsblood (who through much of the novel has continued to pass among his white neighbors) announces the truth of his ancestry at a meeting of the august, whites-only Federal Club. In addition to the very fact of this white man's blackness itself, the language of Kingsblood's public disclosure takes apart the typical notions of racial fixity and repositions the biological fact of race in the realm of culture: he "resigns" from the white race; and when his wife, Vestal, chides him for this ill-conceived "public confession," he asserts that, knowing what he knows now about the two races and their moral character, he would "volunteer" to be a Negro, even if it turned out that there had been some kind of mistake in the genealogical archive.[67]

As with much of the antiracist writing in *Common Ground*, however, there is a sense in which this critical dismantling of the races actually *enforces* the notions of "white" and "black" while effacing the older paradigm of distinct white races. As white and black are the only categories held up for scrutiny and critique, they are reified beyond the no less hypothetical yet fully submerged categories like "Nordic," "Alpine," and "Mediterranean." Early on, Lewis refers to Kingsblood's neighbor, Nancy Pzort, as "a dollarless Slav"; Kingsblood grudgingly concedes (and so denies) that, "sure, lots of Jews are just like us—I guess"; or again, a local booster for beautiful, suburban Sylvan Park "privately advises" that the neighborhood is "just as free of Jews, Italians, Negroes, and the exasperatingly poor as it is of noise, mosquitoes, and rectangularity of streets."[68]

But as Kingsblood gets further and further into his personal investigations of the color line—and as the entire city becomes focused on his spectacular case and on the "Negro Problem" in general—concern about "Slavs," "Jews, Italians . . . and the exasperatingly poor" all but disappears. There are only white and black (even though Kingsblood's personal history demonstrates that there are not *even* white and black). Now unalterably a black man, the former white man arrives at this recognition himself in a daydream about a Southern-style confrontation: he could be kicked off a Tennessee bus by a "Mick conductor," a "hillbilly cop," and a "Wop detective," he muses. "This whole color code is nonsense," as one social philosopher tells him, "but it is so tied up with the old aristocratic class myth, like the D.A.R. or the English nobility . . . that you can't ignore it any more than you can syphilis, which it greatly resembles."[69]

In *Kingsblood Royal* no less than in the liberal social sciences, then, the project of exploding race as biological difference leads to a fixation on race as a web of social differences and distinctions; and this plane of analysis reifies "white" and "black" while effacing all distinctions among the former "white races." Unlike Schuyler, who self-consciously played with the slippages among the "Caucasian," "Nordic," and "Anglo-Saxon" races, Lewis rather *un*self-consciously falls back, by default, on "Caucasian" as a naturalized appellation. For Lewis, that is, race is not undone by the obvious constructedness of categories like Caucasian, Nordic, and Anglo-Saxon or by the evident ideological competition among them. Rather, it is undone by the fact that many "Caucasians" might in fact be "Negroes" without knowing it.

Lewis's frequent and unproblematic use of the term "Caucasian," then, is symptomatic of a baseline acceptance of a unified whiteness, insofar as there is in fact such a thing as whiteness at all: Neil possesses a "large, ruddy, Caucasian strength," a certain bank receives complaints about employing a "non-Caucasian," Ash Davis cannot find work as a chemist because employees might object to a "non-Caucasian," concerns are expressed regarding the prospect of a "non-Caucasian living here and lowering the social tone of the neighborhood," and, in the wake of Kingsblood's dramatic public disclosure, Vestal's family longs for her again to be "panoplied in Caucasian superiority."[70] Whiteness is seamless and whole, Lewis seems to argue, even if it may not in fact exist. As for Schuyler's Anglo-Saxons, Nordics, Hebrews, and Teutons, *Kingsblood Royal* seems to say, as some sage once said, a difference that makes no difference is no difference. Lewis's quarrel is not so much with the social conventions and acts of fabrication that go into the enforcement of the racial order, as with a more general failure to reckon with the facts of biology itself, whose messiness and hybridity render moot the notion of clean, nicely delineated races.

Contemporary reviews of *Kingsblood Royal* uniformly missed Lewis's intent. While the novel called for a searching reevaluation of the race concept—how many people, after all, were so certain of their own pedigree (not to mention their neighbor's) that they could speak with certainty of the existence of meaningful races and reliable racial boundaries?—reviewers decried *Kingsblood Royal* as "artificial, unconvincing, dull, and melodramatic." The key to Lewis's failure, as far as the New York *Times* was concerned, was his "virulent, grotesque portrayal of Neil's former friends." The small city of Grand Republic, Minnesota, apparently contained "more detestable skunks than any other city its size in America."[71] Whereas Lewis had intended to make the very notion of "white people" unstable and so untenable, contemporary ("white") readers were more inclined to object, simply, that *white people are not that bad*. (The objection itself is rather interesting, in an immediate context where the attempted integration of neighborhoods from Birmingham to Chicago to Redwood City had resulted in scores of residential bombings.) But contemporaries' insisting upon reified whiteness by their refusal to engage Lewis's dismantled whiteness was as much a product of mid-century racial liberalism as a product of the regressive regime of Jim Crow. By 1947—in the wake of the Double V, the March on Washington Movement, and the establishment of the Fair Employment Practices Committee (FEPC), and on the eve of *Shelly v. Kramer*—American liberalism was already deeply structured in black and white.

In *The Race Question and the Negro* (1944), amid a discussion of the "mythic" aspects of race as a category, John LaFarge set out to make some fine distinctions:

> There is no Breton *race*, but a Breton *people*. There is no French *race*, but a French *nation*. There is no Aryan *race*, but Aryan *languages*. There is no Latin *race*, but a Latin *civilization*.

In the Bobst (NYU) Library's copy of the book, directly below this passage, someone, sometime, scrawled in pencil: "But there is a white race, without any of the above." Who might have written this, and when? Was it someone writing soon after the book's publication, having recently imbibed Ruth Benedict's *Races of Mankind* and now certain that there were "three great divisions—the Caucasian, the Negroid, and the Mongoloid"? Was it a skeptical white student in the 1940s, objecting to LaFarge's discounting of patent racial reality? Was it a black student in the 1960s, protesting that there is no wishing away race in a setting where whiteness so clearly structures power regardless of the finer points of nationality, language, and civilization? Was it a white supremacist in the 1980s, insisting upon the existence of a unified, superior, and above all ineradicable racial whiteness? Was it a student of deconstruction in the 1990s, noting, in academic fashion, that LaFarge's conceptual scheme throughout the book tacitly reifies whiteness even as it argues that races are "hypothetical stocks, rather than living ones"?[72] The very indeterminacy of this unknown reader's response to LaFarge speaks volumes about the vicissitudes of whiteness in U.S. political culture in the twentieth century.

But whether the exchange gives voice to a mid-century protest against LaFarge's rendering of race as "myth," or a late-century objection to his tacit reifications of race in spite of himself, far clearer is the extent to which LaFarge's contention itself represents the road not taken in American race politics. American political life has been dominated not by the dismantling of race, but by reification and coalition. Racism itself, of course, has been organized precisely according to a conception of race-in-nature, and so progressives certainly did not invent the Caucasian—or any other—race. But in forging a new politics of racial justice along an axis of black and white, progressives did help to shift the most salient lines of racial identity, beginning at a moment when the consolidated whiteness of the new immigrants was not at all a foregone conclusion.

This is not to *blame* racial liberals for their efforts in race-based coalition politics. Nor should attention to the fluidity of racial whiteness suggest that the social realities now attending racial nonwhiteness can be altered without concerted political action, as if race itself can be conveniently wished away. George Schuyler was able to deconstruct race in the 1930s (like some of his counterparts in the 1990s) precisely because he was not engaged in the practicalities of political organizing after the fashion of the Communist Party. His insight that race is a congeries of public fictions still awaits praxis in the street-level realm of civic life.

But if race-based (and hence race-sustaining) politics are a practical necessity, it is still worth knowing what some of the ideological consequences of such politics have been. So deeply embedded is racialism in our national political culture that movements to alleviate racial tension on one front are likely to influence the racial chemistry on another, perhaps in unexpected ways. Negro rights activists' earliest accomplishments included their quiet revision of then-current conceptions of racial whiteness—a revision whose effects were protested nostalgically in an "ethnic revival" decades later, after the movement had actually made a few gains for African-Americans. In the meantime, non–Anglo-Saxon immigrants and their children were perhaps the first beneficiaries of the modern civil rights movement, in that the movement helped confer upon them a newly consolidated status as Caucasians in a political setting where that meant—and continues to mean—a great deal.

Are Jews/Italians/Greeks/Slavs/Portuguese/Letts "white"? *So far,* is the only answer whose certainty is not overstated one way or the other; and any realistic progressive politics on the part of these "white ethnics" must now rest squarely on an understanding of both the yes (they are white) and the no (their whiteness is merely contingent) which are historically embedded in that tentative reply. The affirmative, it turns out, owes something to the black civil rights struggle, and this is worth pondering, even if—*especially if*—coalition politics on the model of the black civil rights struggle is all that progressives are left with when it comes to putting ideas into action. No less than the white-supremacist logic of American expansionism, and no less than the racial contortions of the courts in upholding the racial logic of 1790, progressive civil rights agitation in the 1930s and after evaporated distinctions among the immigrant white races and thus helped to coin Caucasian whiteness on behalf of those non–Anglo-Saxons whose problematic status in the United States Robert Orsi, David Roediger, and James Barrett have aptly summed up in the phrase "inbetween peoples."[73]

I've noticed it in others—sometimes in Jews, just around the corner of attention. Everything is going well; they've forgotten the familiar feeling. Then
something you say prompts uneasiness in their eyes, the eyes of one hunted,
almost found, in danger . . .

You can generate that uneasiness in the eyes of almost any American, except a wealthy WASP: in Poles, Italians, Chicanos, Blacks, in Greeks, Armenians, the French . . . Unworthiness was stamped upon their souls. Red-hot
branding irons singe a calf's new skin. The trauma can be traced, reopened.

—Michael Novak, *The Rise of the Unmeltable Ethnics* (1971)

The fact of the matter is that Jews, however much we have accumulated the
trappings of American success, are not white. We are not white symbolically,
and we are not white literally . . . We are too much an oppressed people, still,
and too much a rejected people, even in this country, to accept the designation "white."

—Leonard Fein, "Israel's Crisis" (1968)

Epilogue: Ethnic Revival and the Denial of White Privilege

Whiteness has posed serious problems when it comes to narrating the
European immigrant saga. As Oscar Handlin noted in *Truth in History*
(1979), racism of the Anglo-Saxonist, pre-1930s variety influenced generations of American scholars: "In a world of biologically distinct species,
the natives of Sicily were as distinct from those of Norway as either were
from those of the Gold Coast. Impure blood, whether from Europe or
from Africa, threatened the Anglo-Saxon stock . . . Casual assumptions
about innate Anglo-Saxon superiority and about the racial differences
between the old and new immigrants uncritically penetrated the [schol-
arly] writing of the period."[1]

If Handlin seems to be assuming that the non–Anglo-Saxon races were
not "really" racially distinct (which indeed they had been, by consensus),

nonetheless he later recognizes the pitfalls in the other direction—the problem of anachronistically transporting the post–World War II white-black dualism backward in time. More recent historians began to rely far too heavily on the polarity of black and white, he cautions,

> after the civil rights struggle focused the concern of social scientists on the problem of color. The fact that most statistical data after 1940 fell into the categories of white and non-white, as well as the tactics of current controversy, eased acquiescence in the proposition that American population, past and present, fitted neatly into two distinct racial groups.
>
> . . . It may or may not have been correct to speak of "whites" or of the "white community" in New York or Chicago of the 1960s; it was grossly inaccurate to do so for those cities before 1930. In the repeated use of those terms, the historian forgot that they applied not to homogenous groupings, but to congeries of populations sharply divided among themselves.[2]

The challenge, then, is to devise a narrative line which can take account of racial changeability—to construct a drama whose first-act Celts, Slavs, and Ugro-Finns can reemerge as Caucasians before the final curtain, without diminishing *either* the power and the significance of that transformation for their ultimate social standing *or* the very real distinctions that had held sway and had structured their experience along the way. The challenge is not only to recognize the fluidity of race, but to find ways of narrating events, social movements, and the trajectory of individual lives in all their integrity along the convoluted path of an ever-shifting racial reality.

Doing justice to both the "whiteness" and the "racial distinctness" of the immigrant saga will prove difficult enough under any circumstances, so accustomed have we become to thinking of race as color. But the hunger for a usable past presents many temptations, and hence even more difficulties. Nowhere is this as plain as in the literature of the ethnic revival of the 1970s—an impulse whose energy derived from a distinctly "white" set of grievances and entitlements, but whose central tendency was to disavow "whiteness" in favor of group narratives that measured their distance from the WASP mainstream, or even, in some instances, that dwelt upon group oppression under the heel of Nordic America. If Handlin's representative historians were too quick to impose the black-white dualism upon an earlier period where it did not belong, others rightly pointed to the racial injuries and outrages endured by non-Nordics, but wrongly dragged the regime of Nordic-supremacism into the present, as though whiteness and the category "Caucasian" had had no purchase at all upon the nation's political life.

Michael Novak gave especially sharp voice to the otherwise diffuse ethnic revival. As he summarized the inchoate social movement among second-, third-, and fourth-generation Poles, Italians, Greeks, and Slavs in 1974, the "new ethnicity" entailed

> a growing sense of discomfort with the sense of identity one is sup-posed to have—universalist, "melted," "like everyone else"; then a growing appreciation for the political wisdom of one's own gut re-actions (especially on moral matters) and their historical roots; a growing self-confidence and social power; a sense of being discrim-inated against, condescended to, or carelessly misapprehended; a growing disaffection regarding those to whom one had always been taught to defer; and a sense of injustice regarding the response of liberal spokesmen to conflicts between various ethnic groups, espe-cially between "legitimate" minorities and "illegitimate" ones. There is . . . an inner conflict between one's felt personal power and one's ascribed public power: a sense of outraged truth, justice, and equity.[3]

The ethnic revival is thus a complex affair, combining ideological strands of anti-modernism, anti-elitism, cultural conservatism, and vaguely artic-ulated class-based grievances. As Micaela di Leonardo has argued, it also represents a distinctly post–civil rights brand of mobilization, in which, ironically, "key expressions of white resentment were couched in language consciously and unconsciously copied from blacks themselves."[4]

But among the fundamental elements of the ethnic revival is a certain dissonance in postwar whiteness: the emergent ethnics are white without actually *feeling* white; they are alienated from other whites, and are be-ginning to identify the reasons why; they feel themselves treated as non-whites, and are increasingly angry at white elites who deem their protests less "legitimate" than those of other nonwhites. (Once the unmeltable ethnics of the 1970s become the Reagan Democrats of the 1980s, the anger will increasingly turn on nonwhites themselves.) The "inner con-flict" which Novak describes represents, in part, a tension between non-whiteness ("one's felt personal power") and whiteness ("one's ascribed public power").

Novak's fullest treatment of the theme—indeed the most complete document of the ethnic revival extant—is *The Rise of the Unmeltable Ethnics* (1971). The book is both an anti-capitalist protest and an anti-modernist lament (Novak later recanted the former), in which "ethnicity" safely harbors a communitarian spirit so lacking in the nation's dominant culture. His is a protest from the margins against a cold, often ruthless "Anglo-Saxon" or "Nordic" hegemony. It is a protest, on behalf of Polish, Italian, Greek, and Slavic "ethnics," against those Nordic elites in the media, the academy, and elsewhere who would peg them as "backward," "stupid," and above all, "racist." White ethnics did not ask to be pitted against African-Americans in a competition for the scarce resources of the urban rustbelt, Novak argues. Many of the attitudes so blithely tarred as "racist" by Nordic elites from the comfort of their suburban homes and Ivy League institutions have nothing to do with race at all, but rather reflect a realistic concern for some very pressing dangers. Ethnics' enthusiasm for retaining the character of their "old" (that is, segregated) neighborhoods, for example, is traceable not so much to color prejudice as to a wise vigilance for their investment-in-property—a worry from which many Nordics have conveniently excused themselves by removing to their own (also segregated) suburbs on the urban periphery. There is a certain continuity in all this, for Novak: "those whom the grandfathers called 'hunkies' and 'dagoes' were now being called 'racists,' 'fascists,' and 'pigs,' with no noticeable gain in affection."[5]

Because black-"ethnic" relations lie so near the core of this entire complex of concerns, the whiteness of the white ethnic becomes once again unstable. Recounting the murder of Joseph Columbo by an African-American on Italian Unity Day, 1971, Novak wants to know, "Couldn't [blacks] distinguish a fellow sufferer under Nordic prejudice from a WASP?" Or again, ethnics are not unaware of the "peculiar forms of fear, envy, and suspicion across color lines. How much of this we learned in America by being made conscious of our olive skin, brawny backs, accents, names, and cultural quirks is not plain to us."[6]

Unmeltable Ethnics thus sits rather precariously astride the racial contradictions that, I have argued, constituted the early history of European immigration to the United States. On the one hand, the whiteness of white ethnicity is beyond question: "Standing in front of a crowded lecture hall, a speaker can scarcely single out ethnic differences. *Such differences as we have,* apart from race, *are mainly internal.*" "Ethnicity is not a matter of genetics; it is a matter of *cultural transmission,* from family to child."[7] That John F. Kennedy had attained the presidency a decade before and

Spiro Anagnostopoulos was the sitting vice president seemed to settle once and for all the question of the ethnics' "fitness for self-government." Their whiteness had been ratified by popular vote.

And yet, on the other hand, so pronounced is the social and psychological distance separating European immigrants and their children from the dominant Nordic mainstream that mere "ethnicity," for Novak, does not do justice to the full range of variegations in the American order. Poles, Italians, Greeks, and Slavs are "born into a history not white Anglo-Saxon and not Jewish; born outside what, in America, is considered the intellectual mainstream—and thus privy to neither power nor status nor intellectual voice."[8] If they are white, in other words, they are not *that* white. This is one of the structuring motifs of Novak's book and of the ethnic revival in general—a strange, voluntary throwback to the days of *Rollins v. Alabama,* when a court might rule upon the inconclusive whiteness of the Sicilian; a peculiar re-embrace of that logic by which Henry Cabot Lodge had viewed the immigrants as a bad biological investment for the nation to make; a surprising rejection of the racial certainty "Caucasian" as but a thin veneer that only imperfectly conceals the disunity of "white America" and that all too perfectly does conceal the real, *Nordic* supremacist basis of American social life.

Although Novak's excavation of the historic tyrannies endured by non-Nordics in America does recover some well-hidden skeletons, *Unmeltable Ethnics* is nonetheless enmeshed in a politics of disavowal that buries at least as much as it exposes. "One day on a platform," Novak writes,

> an American Indian was telling a group of Polish nuns and me what our ancestors did to *his* ancestors. I tried gently to remind him that *my* grandparents (and theirs) never *saw* an Indian. They came to this country after that. Nor were they responsible for enslaving the blacks (or anyone else). They themselves escaped serfdom barely four generations ago.[9]

The just-off-the-boat spirit of "the new ethnicity" necessarily acknowledges pan–white supremacism only in its most extreme forms (genocide and slavery), and fossilizes it safely in a past too distant to implicate any but the blood-soaked Nordic American. White ethnics may indeed be white, but their history is severed from the broader, structural history of whiteness in America. Novak's disavowal sometimes verges on a contempt for the claims of other non-Nordics: "The Molly Maguires lost twenty men to hangings by officials, and many others to gunshot, club, and jail in what they regarded as a legitimate 'war' against nativist America. In the Irish riot of 1863, between twelve hundred and two thousand New Yorkers (mostly Irish) died. Would that be called 'genocide' if it happened today?"[10]

Novak sounds the keynote in a chapter titled "The Nordic Jungle: Inferiority in America."[11] The piece draws liberally from Louis Adamic's *Laughing in the Jungle* (1932) in its rendering of "Nordic" supremacy, as if nothing much had happened in the intervening forty years—as if the conceptual category "Caucasian" had had no purchase whatsoever upon American politics and culture. This is an ideological sleight of hand. Here is "ethnic" history uncoupled from its most salient structural features. The move is at best mistaken, and at worst disingenuous. It is at once the brilliance and the damning limitation of *Unmeltable Ethnics* (like the ethnic revival in general) that the psychological dimension of identity politics and struggle—Novak's "inner conflict between one's felt personal power and one's ascribed public power"—takes precedence over structural features of the political landscape like legal codes, housing covenants, or Jim Crow practices. If one has not been allowed to *feel* "white," then one's whiteness does not amount to privilege.

In this formulation racial hierarchy has less to do with power than with self-esteem: remarking upon a distinct "uneasiness in the eyes" that he has observed among people of various backgrounds in certain social situations, Novak notes, "You can generate that uneasiness in the eyes of almost any American, except a wealthy WASP: in Poles, Italians, Chicanos, Blacks, in Greeks, Armenians, the French . . . Unworthiness was stamped upon their souls."[12] This line can work only where race is presumed to translate primarily into feelings of relative "worth" rather than into real power differentials. Only where whiteness has been rejected out of hand as an insignificant detail can grievances reduce to a matter of "unworthiness," and can "Chicanos, [and] Blacks," for instance, appear unproblematically in a list of aggrieved Poles, Italians, Greeks, Armenians, and French, as though these latter groups' becoming Caucasian meant nothing in the American milieu. As though, by virtue of their non-WASPness, these groups all occupied the same terrain in American political life.

Although Novak was only fleetingly concerned with the status of Jews as "white ethnics" (more often he numbered them among the privileged and contemptuous elites), the Jewish writer Leonard Fein was perhaps even more to the point on precisely Novak's theme: "We are too much an oppressed people, still, and too much a rejected people, even in this country, to accept the designation 'white.' "[13] More recently (1993), *Tikkun* editor Michael Lerner has similarly argued, "Jews can only be deemed 'white' if there is massive amnesia on the part of non-Jews about the monumental history of anti-Semitism."[14]

This disavowal of whiteness has become pronounced in recent years, particularly around the question of affirmative action. The notion that Jews, Letts, Finns, Greeks, Italians, Slovaks, Poles, or Russians are not *really* white has become suddenly appealing in a setting where whiteness has wrongly become associated with unfair *dis*advantage. It has not been my purpose in this book to help these arguments along—although, I confess, I am not altogether optimistic about the implications of deconstructing race at a moment when so many "free white persons" are anxious for various reasons to distance themselves from whiteness. (I join that race seminar leader cited at the outset in asking, "What happened to all the white people who were here just a minute ago?") Rather, it is my hope that in recognizing the historical fabrication, the changeability, and the contingencies of whiteness, we might begin to look in a new way upon race, the power relations it generates, and the social havoc it wreaks. Only then might we find our way to that political realm beyond racism that W. E. B. Du Bois significantly called *transcaucasia*.[15]

Notes
Acknowledgments
Index

Notes

Introduction: The Fabrication of Race

1. Mid-century examples include Ashley Montagu, *Race: Man's Most Dangerous Myth* (New York: Columbia University Press, 1942), and George Schuyler, "Who Is 'Negro'? Who Is 'White'?" *Common Ground*, Autumn 1940, p. 53. The more recent incarnation of the argument is exemplified by Barbara Fields, "Ideology and Race in American History," in J. Morgan Kousser and James McPherson, eds., *Region, Race, and Reconstruction* (New York: Oxford, 1982), pp. 143–178; James Davis, *Who Is Black? One Nation's Definition* (University Park: Pennsylvania State University Press, 1991); and Virginia Dominguez, *White by Definition: Social Classification in Creole Louisiana* (New Brunswick: Rutgers University Press, 1986).

2. Philip Roth, *The Counterlife* (New York: Penguin, 1988), p. 79.

3. Glenda Gilmore, *Gender and Jim Crow: Women and the Politics of White Supremacy in North Carolina, 1896–1920* (Chapel Hill: University of North Carolina Press, 1996), p. 71; Laura Doyle, *Bordering on the Body: The Racial Matrix of Modern Fiction and Culture* (New York: Oxford, 1994), pp. 27, 10–34; Joel Williamson, *A Rage for Order: Black-White Relations in the American South since Emancipation* (New York: Oxford, 1986).

4. *Rollins v. Alabama*, 92 So 35–36. On miscegenation see Peggy Pascoe, "Race, Gender, and the Privileges of Property: On the Significance of Miscegenation Law in the United States," in Susan Ware, ed., *New Viewpoints on Women's History: Working Papers for the Schlesinger Library 56th Anniversary Conference* (Cambridge: Schlesinger Library, 1994), pp. 99–122; Peggy Pascoe, "Miscegenation Law, Court Cases, and Ideologies of 'Race' in Twentieth-Century America," *Journal of American History*, June 1996, pp. 44–69; Eva Saks, "Representing Miscegenation Law," *Raritan*, Fall 1988, pp. 39–69.

5. John Brennan, *Erin Mor: The Story of Irish Republicanism* (San Francisco: P. M. Diers, 1892), pp. 35, 263.

6. David Katzman, *Before the Ghetto: Black Detroit in the Nineteenth Century* (Urbana: University of Illinois Press, 1973), p. 166.

7. Alfred Schultz, *Race or Mongrel?* (Boston: Little, Brown, 1908), p. 111.

8. Margaret F. Byington, *Homestead: The Households of a Mill Town* [1910] (Pittsburgh: University of Pittsburgh Press, 1974), p. 14 and passim.

9. David Levering Lewis, *When Harlem Was in Vogue* (New York: Oxford, 1979), p. 139; Ann Douglas, *Terrible Honesty: Mongrel Manhattan in the 1920s* (New York: Farrar, Straus, Giroux, 1995), p. 78; Jeffrey Melnick, *A Right to Sing the Blues* (Cambridge: Harvard University Press, forthcoming).

10. Alexander Saxton, *The Rise and Fall of the White Republic: Class Politics and Mass Culture in Nineteenth-Century America* (London: Verso, 1990), p. 14.

11. Michael Novak, *The Rise of the Unmeltable Ethnics* (New York: Macmillan, 1971); Michael Lerner, "Jews Are Not White," *Village Voice*, May 18, 1993, pp. 33–34; Paul Kivel, *Uprooting Racism: How White People Can Work for Racial Justice* (Philadelphia: New Society Publishers, 1996), p. 10.

12. Michael Omi and Howard Winant, *Racial Formation in the United States: From the 1960s to the 1980s* (New York: Routledge and Kegan Paul, 1987), p. 65.

13. The general absence of race from European immigration historiography to date has less to do with the history itself than with the birth of the subfield precisely at that moment in the mid-twentieth century when these varied racial groups were becoming Caucasian. Immigration historiography from Oscar Handlin on down has quietly participated in the deracination of Europeans. Oscar Handlin, *Race and Nationality in American Life* (Boston: Anchor, 1957), and *The Uprooted* (Boston: Little, Brown, 1951); John Higham, *Strangers in the Land: Patterns of American Nativism, 1865–1925* (New Brunswick: Rutgers University Press, 1955); Maldwyn Allen Jones, *American Immigration* (Chicago: University of Chicago Press, 1960). Even the most alert and sophisticated writers on the subject of race occasionally use the term "Caucasian" unproblematically, as though it reflected some bedrock racial reality. Among them are Eric Lott, Ann duCille, Sander Gilman, Susan Gubar, Michael Rogin, David Roediger, Virginia Dominguez, George Fredrickson, and Joel Williamson.

14. Matthew Frye Jacobson, *Special Sorrows: The Diasporic Imagination of Irish, Polish, and Jewish Immigrants in the United States* (Cambridge: Harvard University Press, 1995), Chapter 5; Matthew Guterl, "Bleeding the Irish White: The Irish Race Convention of 1916," unpublished seminar paper in the author's possession.

15. Ruth Benedict, "Obituary, Franz Boas," *Science* 97: 2507 (Jan. 15, 1943), p. 60.
16. Handlin, *Uprooted,* p. 3.

1. *"Free White Persons" in the Republic, 1790–1840*

1. Hugh Henry Brackenridge, *Modern Chivalry* [1792] (New York: American Book Co., 1937), pp. 6, 807–808.
2. Ibid., pp. 209, 38, 55–56.
3. Ibid., pp. 218–219.
4. Ibid., p. 596.
5. Ibid., p. 749; James Hall, "The Pioneers" (1835), quoted in Dana Nelson, *The Word in Black and White: Reading "Race" in American Literature, 1638–1867* (New York: Oxford, 1993), p. 57.
6. Theodore Allen, *The Invention of the White Race: Volume One: Racial Oppression and Social Control* (London: Verso, 1994); David Roediger, *The Wages of Whiteness: Race and the Making of the American Working Class* (London: Verso, 1991). See also David Roediger, *Towards the Abolition of Whiteness: Essays on Race, Politics, and Working-Class History* (London: Verso, 1994); James Barrett and David Roediger, "Inbetween Peoples: Race, Nationality and the New Immigrant Working Class," *Journal of American Ethnic History,* Spring 1997; Noel Ignatiev, *How the Irish Became White* (New York: Routledge, 1995).
7. Allen, *White Race,* pp. 23, 134–135, 185, 134.
8. Roediger, *Wages,* pp. 12, 13.
9. New York *Times,* July 17, 1863, p. 4; *Harper's Weekly,* Aug. 1, 1863, p. 482.
10. Sinclair Lewis, *The Man Who Knew Coolidge: Being the Soul of Lowell Schmaltz, Constructive and Nordic Citizen* (New York: Harcourt Brace, 1928), p. 124.
11. Tomas Almaguer, *Racial Fault Lines: The Historical Origins of White Supremacy in California* (Berkeley: University of California Press, 1994), pp. 52, 57, and passim; Eric Foner, *Free Labor, Free Soil, Free Men: The Ideology of the Republican Party before the Civil War* (New York: Oxford, 1970); Cheryl Harris, "Whiteness as Property," *Harvard Law Review* 106 (1993), p. 1707.
12. Quoted in Oscar Handlin, *Race and Nationality in American Life* (New York: Anchor, 1957), p. 105.
13. *Annals of Congress, Vol. 1, Abridgements of the Debates of Congress, 1789–1856* (New York: D. Appleton and Co., 1857), p. 184.
14. Ibid., pp. 184–190, 555–558.
15. Gunnar Myrdal, *An American Dilemma: The Negro Problem and Modern Democracy* (New York: Harper, 1944); Judith Shklar, *American Citizenship: The Quest for Inclusion* (Cambridge: Harvard University Pres, 1991), p. 14

and passim; Pierre van der Berghe, *Race and Racism: A Comparative Perspective* (New York: Wiley, 1967); Joel Williamson, *A Rage for Order: Black-White Relations in the American South since Emancipation* (New York: Oxford, 1986), p. 170.

16. Francis Newton Thorpe, *The Federal and State Constitutions, Colonial Charters, and Other Organic Laws of the States, Territories, and Colonies* (Washington: Government Printing Office, 1909), vol. VII, p. 3802; vol. V, p. 2753; vol. VI, p. 3211.

17. Ibid., vol III, pp. 1828–1829.

18. Ibid., vol. III, pp. 1682, 1630; vol. II, p. 765.

19. A. Leon Higginbotham, Jr., *In the Matter of Color: Race and the American Legal Process: The Colonial Period* (New York: Oxford, 1978), pp. 33, 109.

20. A. Leon Higginbotham, Jr., *Shades of Freedom: Racial Politics and the Presumptions of the American Legal Process* (New York: Oxford, 1996), p. 71.

21. *Annals of Congress,* vol. I, pp. 189.

22. *Annals of Congress,* vol. I, p. 566. On the importance of "savagery" to the constitution of citizenship, see esp. Robert Berkhofer, Jr., *The White Man's Indian* (New York: Vintage, 1978); Roy Harvey Pearce, *Savagism and Civilization: A Study of the Indian and the American Mind* [1953] (Berkeley: University of California Press, 1988); Richard Drinnon, *Facing West: The Metaphysics of Indian-Hating and Empire-Building* (New York: Schocken, 1980); Richard Slotkin, *Regeneration through Violence: The Mythology of the American Frontier, 1600–1860* (Middletown: Wesleyan, 1976).

23. Elaine Daney Carzo, ed., *National State Papers of the United States, 1789–1817* (Wilmington, Del.: Michael Glazier, 1985), vol. 13, p. 227.

24. Thorpe, *Constitutions,* vol. II, p. 779; vol. VI, pp. 3258–3259.

25. Ron Takaki, *Iron Cages: Race and Culture in Nineteenth Century America* (Seattle: University of Washington Press, 1979), esp. pp. 3–15; Benjamin Ringer, *"We the People" and Others: Duality and America's Treatment of Its Racial Minorities* (New York: Tavistock, 1983), traces the racial assumptions of republicanism into American law, defining a "dual terrain" consisting of "the people" and the republic's racialized "others."

26. M. N. S. Sellers, *American Republicanism: Roman Ideology in the United States Constitution* (New York: New York University Press, 1994), pp. 6, 96, 238, 244.

27. John R. Commons, *Races and Immigrants in America* (New York: Macmillan, 1907), p. 1.

28. Audrey Smedley, *Race in North America: Origin and Evolution of a Worldview* (Boulder: Westview, 1993), pp. 175–176; Edmund Morgan, *American Slavery, American Freedom: The Ordeal of Colonial Virginia* (New York: Norton, 1975), esp. Book 4; George Fredrickson, *White Supremacy: A Com-*

parative Study in American and South African History (New York: Oxford, 1981), pp. 124–129.

29. Gordon S. Wood, *The Creation of the American Republic, 1776–1787* (New York: Norton, 1969), pp. 30–31, 47, 49–50, 53–65, 68. For his full explication of republicanism, see pp. 46–90. On the intersection of race and working-class republicanism later in the nineteenth century, see Roediger, *Wages,* esp. pp. 56–60. On "Anglo-Saxondom" and political genius in republican thought, see also Reginald Horsman, *Race and Manifest Destiny* (Cambridge: Harvard University Press, 1981), pp. 9–77.

30. Gordon S. Wood, *The Radicalism of the American Revolution* (New York: Vintage Books, 1991), pp. 104–105.

31. Shane White, *Somewhat More Independent: The End of Slavery in New York City, 1770–1810* (Athens: University of Georgia Press, 1991), pp. 67–68, 71; Celeste Michelle Condit and John Louis Lucaites, *Crafting Equality: America's Anglo-African Word* (Chicago: University of Chicago Press, 1993), pp. 45, 40–68. For related treatments of independence, self-possession, and republicanism, see Christine Stansell, *City of Women: Sex and Class in New York, 1789–1860* (Urbana: University of Illinois Press, 1982); Sean Wilentz, *Chants Democratic: New York City and the Rise of the American Working Class, 1788–1850* (New York: Oxford, 1984); Linda Kerber, *Women of the Republic: Intellect and Ideology in Revolutionary America* (New York: Norton, 1986); and Thomas Dumm, *Democracy and Punishment: Disciplinary Origins of the United States* (Madison: University of Wisconsin Press, 1987).

32. Wood, *Radicalism,* p. 186. See also Leon F. Litwack, *North of Slavery: The Negro in the Free States, 1790–1860* (Chicago: University of Chicago Press, 1961), pp. 3–15; Bernard Bailyn, *The Ideological Origins of the American Revolution* (Cambridge: Harvard University Press, 1967), pp. 232–246.

33. Quoted in Gary B. Nash, *Race and Revolution* (Madison: Madison House, 1990), pp. 19, 142–143.

34. Theodore Parker, "The Aspect of Slavery in America" (1858), in *Saint Bernard and Other Papers* (Boston: American Unitarian Association, 1911), p. 276.

35. Smedley, *Race in North America,* pp. 222, 223; Williamson, *Rage,* pp. 6–7.

36. Higginbotham, *Shades of Freedom,* p. 36.

37. John P. Kaminski, *A Necessary Evil? Slavery and the Debate over the Constitution* (Madison: Madison House, 1995), p. 218; Winthrop Jordan, *White over Black: American Attitudes Toward the Negro, 1550–1812* (Chapel Hill: University of North Carolina Press, 1968), pp. 542–569.

38. Kaminski, *Necessary Evil,* pp. 247–248.

39. Ibid., pp. 214, 217–218, 220, 228.

40. Litwack, *North of Slavery,* pp. 15, 33, 65, 84; Leonard Richards, *"Gentlemen of Property and Standing": Anti-Abolition Mobs in Jacksonian America* (New York: Oxford, 1971).

41. Quoted in David M. Katzman, *Before the Ghetto: Black Detroit in the Nineteenth Century* (Urbana: University of Illinois Press, 1973), p. 34.

42. Ringer, *"We the People,"* pp. 103–107; Higginbotham, *Shades of Freedom,* pp. 7, 61–67.

43. J. H. Van Evrie, *Negroes and Negro Slavery: The First an Inferior Race: The Latter Its Normal Condition* (New York: Van Evrie, Horton and Co., 1863), p. 292.

44. Robert W. Johannsen, ed., *The Lincoln-Douglas Debates of 1858* (New York: Oxford, 1965), pp. 33, 128.

45. The best summary is David Fowler, *Northern Attitudes Towards Interracial Marriage: Legislation and Public Opinion in the Middle Atlantic and the States of the Old Northwest, 1780–1930* (New York: Garland, 1987), pp. 339–439.

46. Thorpe, *Constitutions,* vol. II, pp. 1003, 1009.

47. Ibid., vol. I, pp. 99, 271, 393, 414, 544; vol. II, pp. 1003, 1009; vol. IV, p. 1983; Gail Bederman, *Manliness and Civilization: A Cultural History of Gender and Race in the United States, 1880–1917* (Chicago: University of Chicago Press, 1995), p. 20.

48. Jordan, *White over Black,* pp. 3–43; William Cronon, *Changes in the Land* (New York: Hill and Wang, 1984); Alden Vaughn, *Roots of American Racism: Essays on the Colonial Experience* (New York: Oxford, 1995).

49. Bailyn, *Ideology,* p. 237; Vaughn, *Roots,* esp. pp. 3–102.

50. Smedley, *Race in North America,* p. 27; Thomas Gossett, *Race: The History of an Idea in America* (New York: Schocken, 1963).

51. Thomas Jefferson, "Instructions to Captain Lewis," collected in Merrill D. Peterson, ed., *The Portable Thomas Jefferson* (New York: Penguin, 1975), pp. 310–311; Gay Wilson Allen, ed., *The Portable Walt Whitman* (New York: Viking, 1973), p. 279.

52. Franz Boas, "The History of Anthropology" [1904], collected in George Stocking, Jr., ed., *A Franz Boas Reader: The Shaping of American Anthropology, 1883–1911* (Chicago: University of Chicago Press, 1974), pp. 25, 23–36.

53. David Spurr, *The Rhetoric of Empire: Colonial Discourse in Journalism, Travel Writing, and Imperial Administration* (Durham: Duke University Press, 1993), p. 112; Robyn Wiegman, *American Anatomies: Theorizing Race and Gender* (Durham: Duke University Press, 1995), pp. 21–42; Michel Foucault, *The Order of Things: An Archaeology of Human Sciences* (London: Tavistock, 1970); Smedley, *Race in North America,* p. 171.

54. In addition to Smedley, *Race in North America,* and Gossett, *Race,* see William Stanton, *The Leopard's Spots: Scientific Attitudes Toward Race in America, 1815–1859* (Chicago: University of Chicago Press, 1960); George Stocking, *Race, Culture, and Evolution: Essays in the History of Anthropology*

(Chicago: University of Chicago Press, 1968); George Stocking, ed., *Bones, Bodies, and Behavior: Essays on Biological Anthropology* (Madison: University of Wisconsin Press, 1988); Sandra Harding, ed., *The 'Racial' Economy of Science: Toward a Democratic Future* (Bloomington: Indiana University Press, 1993).

55. Josiah Nott, *Two Lectures on the Connection Between the Biblical and Physical History of Man* (New York: Bartlett and Welford, 1849), p. 5.

56. Ibid., p. 17.

57. Josiah Nott and George Glidden, *Types of Mankind* (Philadelphia: Lippincott, 1855), pp. 184–185.

58. Samuel Morton, *Crania Americana: A Comparative View of the Skulls of Various Aboriginal Natives of North and South America, to which Is Prefixed an Essay on the Variety of Human Species* (Philadelphia: J. Dobson, 1839), p. 5; Arthur Comte de Gobineau, *The Moral and Intellectual Diversity of Races: with Particular Reference to Their Respective Influence on the Civil and Political History of Mankind* (Philadelphia: Lippincott, 1856), p. 439; Arthur Comte de Gobineau, "Essay on the Inequality of Human Races," in Michael Bediss, ed., *Selected Political Writings* (New York: Harper and Row, 1970), p. 136.

59. James Cowles Prichard, *Natural History of Man* (London: Baillaire, 1855), pp. 5, 24, 713–714.

60. Charles Darwin, *The Descent of Man and Selection in Relation to Sex* [1871] (Princeton: Princeton University Press, 1981), pp. 238, 404.

61. Van Evrie, *Negro Slavery,* pp. 89, 108.

62. Ibid., pp. 178, 44.

63. Ibid., p. 66.

64. Morton, *Crania Americana,* p. 16.

65. New York *Times,* July 17, 1863, p. 4.

66. Reverend Hugh Peter quoted in Alden Vaughan, "Early English Paradigms for New World Natives," in *Roots,* p. 42; Fredrickson, *White Supremacy,* pp. 13–17; Allen, *White Race,* esp. chapters 1 and 2; Smedley, *Race in North America,* pp. 52, 85–90; Leonard Liggio, "The English Origins of Early American Racism," *Radical History Review* 3:1, 1–36.

2. *Anglo-Saxons and Others, 1840–1924*

1. Shih-Shan Henry Tsai, *The Chinese Experience in America* (Bloomington: Indiana University Press, 1986), chapters 3 and 4; Sucheng Chan, *Asian Americans: An Interpretive History* (Boston: Twayne, 1991), pp. 45–61; Lucy Salyer, *Laws Harsh as Tigers: Chinese Immigrants and the Shaping of Modern Immigration Law* (Chapel Hill: University of North Carolina Press, 1995), p. 13; Michi Weglyn, *Years of Infamy: The Untold Story of America's Con-*

centration Camps (New York: Morrow Quill, 1976); Roger Daniels, *Concentration Camps USA: Japanese Americans and World War II* (Hinsdale: Dryden, 1971); John Okada, *No-No Boy* [1957] (Seattle: University of Washington Press, 1995), p. 227.

2. Benjamin Franklin, "Observations Concerning the Increase of Mankind and the Peopling of Countries" [1751], in *The Autobiography and Other Writings by Benjamin Franklin* (New York: Bantam, 1982), p. 226.

3. Richard Henry Dana, Jr., *Two Years before the Mast* [1840, 1859] (New York: Signet, 1964), pp. 139, 161, 316, 344, 345.

4. On the draft riots, see below. Henry Cabot Lodge, "The Restriction of Immigration," *North American Review,* vol. 152 (1891), pp. 30–31, 32, 35; *Congressional Record,* vol. 65, part 6, p. 5923; Salyer, *Laws Harsh as Tigers,* p. 124.

5. John Higham, *Strangers in the Land: Patterns of American Nativism, 1865–1925* (New Brunswick: Rutgers University Press, 1955), chapter 6, "Toward Racism: The History of an Idea." In *Send These to Me: Immigrants in Urban America* [1975] (Baltimore: Johns Hopkins University Press, 1984), Higham also addresses the rise of Anglo-Saxonism and the late-century shift toward an "elaborate ideology" of racism along many axes, but here, too, "race" operates in his discussion as a mask for "an underlying concern about *cultural homogeneity.*" See esp. pp. 46–47, 149–150. See also Robert Singerman, "The Jew as Racial Alien: The Genetic Component of American Anti-Semitism," in David A. Gerber, ed., *Anti-Semitism in American History* (Urbana: University of Illinois Press, 1987), pp. 103–128.

6. U.S. Bureau of the Census, *Historical Statistics of the United States, Colonial Times to 1970, Bicentennial Edition* (Washington, D.C.: Government Printing Office, 1975), pp. 105–109, 117–118.

7. "Essay on the Inequality of Human Races," in Michael Bedliss, ed., Arthur Comte de Gobineau, *Selected Political Writings* (New York: Harper and Row, 1970), p. 161; J. H. Van Evrie, *The Negro and Negro Slavery* (New York: Van Evrie and Horton, 1863), pp. 52, 181.

8. Ruth Benedict, *Race: Science and Politics* [1940] (Westport: Greenwood, 1982), p. 126; Samuel Morton, *Crania Americana* (Philadelphia: J. Dobson, 1839), p. 16; Gobineau, "Inequality of the Human Races," p. 73, emphasis added; Theodore Parker, "The Aspect of Slavery in America" [1858], *Saint Bernard and Other Papers* (Boston: American Unitarian Association, 1911), pp. 271, 280, 276–277.

9. Josiah Nott, Appendix to Arthur Comte de Gobineau, *The Moral and Intellectual Diversity of Races: with Particular Reference to Their Respective Influence on the Civil and Political History of Mankind* (Philadelphia: Lippincott, 1856), pp. 468–469; Dale Knobel, *Paddy and the Republic: Ethnicity and Nationality in Antebellum America* (Middletown: Wesleyan University Press, 1986), p. 116.

10. Josiah Nott, *Two Lectures on the Connection Between the Biblical and Physical History of Man* [1849] (New York: Negro Universities Press, 1969), pp. 19, 43, 44.
11. Van Evrie, *Negro Slavery*, pp. 324–325.
12. Reginald Horsman, *Race and Manifest Destiny* (Cambridge: Harvard University Press, 1981), pp. 3–4, 11–17, 27–29; Thomas Gossett, *Race: The History of an Idea in America* (New York: Schocken, 1963), pp. 84–122; Glenda Gilmore, *Gender and Jim Crow: Women and the Politics of White Supremacy in North Carolina, 1896–1920* (Chapel Hill: University of North Carolina Press, 1996), pp. 67–68.
13. John Hawgood, *The Tragedy of German-America: The Germans in the United States of America during the Nineteenth Century and After* (New York: Putnam's Sons, 1940), p. 96; Albert Bernhardt Faust, *The German Element in the United States* (Boston: Houghton Mifflin, 1909), p. 434; Russell Kazal, "Irish 'Race' and German 'Nationality': Catholic Languages of Ethnic Difference in Turn-of-the-Century Philadelphia," paper delivered at the ASA, November 1996, p. 9 and passim.
14. Carl Wittke, *Refugees of Revolution: The German 'Forty-Eighters in America* (Philadelphia: University of Pennsylvania Press, 1952), pp. 181, 183; John Commons, *Races and Immigrants in America* (New York: Macmillan, 1907), p. 24; Kathleen Neils Conzen, "German-Americans and the Invention of Ethnicity," in Frank Trommler and Joseph McVeigh, eds., *America and the Germans: An Assessment of a Three Hundred Year History* (Philadelphia: University of Pennsylvania Press, 1985), vol. I, pp. 133–134, 136; Edward Lewis, *America: Nation or Confusion?* (New York: Harper and Bros., 1923), pp. 128–129; Faust, *German Element*, pp. 465–475; Russell Kazal, "*Volk, Nationalitat,* and *Rasse*: Philadelphia Germans and the Shifting Language of Race in the Era of World War I," paper delivered at the ASA, November 1995, p. 7; Peter Conolly-Smith, "The Translated Community: New York City's German-Language Press as an Agent of Cultural Resistance and Integration, 1910–1918" (Ph.D. diss., Yale University, 1996), p. 486.
15. Knobel, *Paddy*, pp. 80, 88, 90, 123, 68–103.
16. "The Fenian Idea," *Atlantic Monthly*, May 1866, pp. 574, 575; New York *Tribune*, June 26, 1877, p. 4.
17. F. Marion Crawford, *An American Politician* [1884] (New York: Macmillan, 1894), p. 18; Henry Childs Merwin, "The Irish in American Life," *Atlantic Monthly*, March, 1896, pp. 289, 294–295, 298.
18. Matthew Frye Jacobson, *Special Sorrows: The Diasporic Imagination of Irish, Polish, and Jewish Immigrants in the United States* (Cambridge: Harvard University Press, 1995), esp. chapter 5.
19. Hugh Quigley, *The Irish Race in California* (San Francisco: n.p., c.1865), p. 61; *Pilot*, Feb. 4, 1899, p. 4.
20. Elizabeth Gurley Flynn, *The Rebel Girl: An Autobiography: My First Life*

(1906–1926) (New York: International Publishers, 1955), p. 23; Jacobson, *Special Sorrows,* chapters 2 and 3.

21. Jeramiah O'Donovan Rossa, *Rossa's Recollections, 1838–1898* (New York: Rossa, 1898), p. 115; *Irish World,* May 7, 1898, p. 1; Matthew Guterl, "Bleeding the Irish White: The Irish Race Convention of 1916," unpublished seminar paper, Rutgers University, 1996.

22. Rossa, *Recollections,* p. 262.

23. Eleanor Leonard, "Three Days Reign of Terror, Or, The July Riots in 1863 in New York," *Harper's Magazine,* Jan. 1867, p. 3; Anonymous, *The Bloody Week: Riot, Murder, and Arson, By An Eye Witness* (New York: Coutant and Baker, 1863), pp. 4, 21; Edward Countryman, *Americans: A Collision of Histories* (New York: Hill and Wang, 1996), pp. 202–205.

24. New York *Times,* July 16, 1863, p. 1; *Harper's Weekly,* Aug. 1, 1863, pp. 484–485.

25. Iver Bernstein, *The New York City Draft Riots: Their Significance for American Society and Politics in the Age of the Civil War* (New York: Oxford, 1990), pp. 27, 25–42.

26. The line is from the preamble to the journal's "Platform of Principles," New York *Weekly Caucasian,* April 4, 1863, p. 2.

27. *Herald* quoted in Bernstein, *Draft Riots,* p. 36; *Harper's Weekly,* July 23, 1863, p. 466; New York *Tribune,* July 16, 1863, p. 1.

28. New York *Herald,* July 17, 1863, p. 1; July 14, 1863, pp. 1, 5; Bernstein, *Draft Riots,* p. 34.

29. David M. Barnes, *The Draft Riots in New York, July, 1863: The Metropolitan Police: Their Services During Riot Week, Their Honorable Record* (New York: Baker and Goodwin, 1863), p. 116; Vincent Colyer, *To the Memory of the Martyrs: Slain in the Riots of July, in the City of New York* (New York: Vincent Collier, 1863), p. 4.

30. New York *Times,* July 15, 1863, p. 4.

31. New York *Times,* July 17, 1863, p. 4; Rev. B. Peters, *Discourses on the Late Riots in New York City* (Brooklyn: Broach and Herring, 1863), pp. 5–6; New York *Tribune,* July 14, 1863, p. 1; July 15, 1863, p. 8; July 16, 1863, p. 8; July 17, 1863, pp. 1, 8; Anon., *The Bloody Week,* p. 1; Tomas Almaguer, *Racial Fault Lines: The Historical Origins of White Supremacy in California* (Berkeley: University of California Press, 1994), p. 108; Alden Vaughn, *The Roots of American Racism: Essays on the Colonial Experience* (New York: Oxford, 1995), pp. 3–54.

32. *Harper's Weekly,* July 23, 1863, p. 466; Aug. 1, 1863, p. 482; Aug. 8, 1863, p. 498.

33. *Atlantic Monthly,* Oct. 1864, p. 517; George Fredrickson, *The Inner Civil War: Northern Intellectuals and the Crisis of the Union* (New York: Harper, 1965), p. 115.

34. Anonymous, *The Volcano under the City: By a Volunteer Special* (New York: Fords, Howard, and Hulbert, 1887), pp. 9–10, 319–320. See also George A. Thayer, *The Draft Riots of 1863: A Historical Study* (n.l., n.p., c.1916), p. 4.

35. Quoted in Higham, *Strangers in the Land*, p. 66; "Italian Life in New York," *New York: A Collection from Harper's Magazine* (New York: Gallery Books, 1991), p. 240. On the "racial in-betweenness" of Italians in the United States, see also Robert Orsi, "The Religious Boundaries of an Inbetween People: Street *Feste* and the Problem of the Dark-Skinned Other in Italian Harlem, 1920–1990," *American Quarterly*, vol. 44, no. 3 (Sept. 1992), pp. 313–347; James Barrett and David Roediger, "Inbetween Peoples: Race, Nationality and the New Immigrant Working Class," *Journal of American Ethnic History*, Spring 1997.

36. New York *Times*, March 15, 1891, p. 1; March 16, 1891, p. 4.

37. See esp. Marco Rimanelli and Sheryl L. Postman, eds., *The 1891 New Orleans Lynching and U.S.-Italian Relations: A Look Back* (New York: Peter Lang, 1992); on the contours of the New Orleans affair, see also Humbert S. Nelli, *The Italians in Chicago, 1880–1930: A Study in Ethnic Mobility* (New York: Oxford University Press, 1970), pp. 130–132.

38. Rimanelli and Postman, *New Orleans Lynching*, pp. 1, 47, 58, 115, 116–117, 119, 142, and passim. On the White League, see Allen Trelease, *White Terror: The Ku Klux Klan Conspiracy and Southern Reconstruction* (Baton Rouge: Louisiana State University Press, 1971), pp. 131–136. In Louisiana's state constitutional convention in 1898, during deliberation over how to disfranchise blacks, the "blackness" of the state's Italians also became a point of discussion. Barret and Roediger, "Inbetween Peoples."

39. New York *Times*, March 18, 1891, p. 4.

40. New York *Times*, March 17, 1891, p. 2; Rimanelli and Postman, *New Orleans Lynching*, pp. 60, 91.

41. New York *Times*, March 17, 1891, p. 1; Rimanelli and Postman, *New Orleans Lynching*, p. 117.

42. New York *Times*, March 17, 1891, pp. 1, 2; March 21, 1891, p. 1. On the rhetorical might of "barbarism," "civilization," and "manhood" in American political discourse in this period, see Gail Bederman, *Manliness and Civilization: A Cultural History of Gender and Race in the United States, 1880–1917* (Chicago: University of Chicago Press, 1995), esp. chapter 2 on these terms as they were deployed around questions of lynching.

43. Henry Cabot Lodge, "Lynch Law and Unrestricted Immigration," *North American Review*, vol. 152 (1891), pp. 604–605.

44. Ibid., pp. 606, 607, 608.

45. *New York Detective Library*, April 25, 1891, vol. I, no.439, pp. 5, 9–10.

46. Ibid., pp. 11, 29.

47. Mark Twain, *Pudd'nhead Wilson and Those Extraordinary Twins* [1894]

(New York: Penguin, 1986), pp. 237–238, 145, 197–198, 64; Eric Sundquist, *To Wake the Nations: Race in the Making of American Literature* (Cambridge: Harvard University Press, 1993), pp. 261–263.

48. John H. Mariano, *The Italian Immigrant and Our Courts* (Boston: Christopher, 1925), pp. 36, 41; William Faulkner, *Light in August* [1936] (New York: Vintage, 1990), p. 225.

49. C. Vann Woodward, *Tom Watson, Agrarian Rebel* (New York: Rinehart and Co., 1938), p. 439; Seth Forman, "The Unbearable Whiteness of Being Jewish" (Ph.D. diss., SUNY at Stony Brook, 1996), esp. chapters 1 and 2; Eugene Levy, " 'Is the Jew a White Man?': Press Reaction to the Leo Frank Case, 1913–1915," *Phylon,* June 1974.

50. New York *Times,* Aug. 21, 1915, p. 4; Leonard Dinnerstein, *The Leo Frank Case* (New York: Columbia University Press, 1968); Jeffrey Melnick, "Ancestors and Relatives: The Uncanny Relationship of African-Americans and Jews" (Ph.D. diss., Harvard University, 1994); Woodward, *Tom Watson,* pp. 435–450; Joel Williamson, *A Rage for Order: Black-White Relations in the American South since Emancipation* (New York: Oxford, 1986), pp. 151, 240–244.

51. New York *Times,* Aug. 20, 1915, p. 4.

52. Dinnerstein, *Leo Frank,* pp. 42–44; Melnick, "Ancestors and Relatives," p. 177; Albert Lindeman, *The Jew Accused: Three Anti-Semitic Affairs (Dreyfus, Beilis, Frank) 1894–1915* (Cambridge: Cambridge University Press, 1991), p. 245. On Frank and his lawyers' reliance upon "whiteness," see Melnick, "Ancestors and Relatives," Part I.

53. Clergyman quoted in Levy, " 'Is the Jew a White Man?' " p. 214; Carey McWilliams, "How Deep Are the Roots?" (Part II), *Common Ground,* Autumn 1947, p. 7.

54. Melnick, "Ancestors and Relatives," pp. 69, 66; Dinnerstein, *Leo Frank,* p. 52.

55. Melnick, "Ancestors and Relatives," pp. 99–102, 119–121, 133; Woodward, *Tom Watson,* p. 438.

56. Melnick, "Ancestors and Relatives," p. 107.

57. Woodward, *Tom Watson,* p. 438; Lindeman, *Jew Accused,* p. 264.

58. Melnick, "Ancestors and Relatives," pp. 95, 109–110, 97, 115–116, 119–121.

59. Woodward, *Tom Watson,* p. 438.

60. Melnick, "Ancestors and Relatives," pp. 115–116, 119–121.

61. Woodward, *Tom Watson,* p. 435.

62. Melnick, "Ancestors and Relatives," p. 168.

63. Woodward, *Tom Watson,* p. 442.

64. Lindeman, *Jew Accused,* p. 264; Woodward, *Tom Watson,* p. 382; Dinnerstein, *Leo Frank,* pp. 64, 130–132.

65. Dinnerstein, *Leo Frank,* p. 144.
66. Lothrop Stoddard, *Racial Realities in Europe* (New York: Charles Scribner's Sons, 1924), p. 153; 61st Congress, 3rd Session, document no. 662, *Reports of the Immigration Commission, Dictionary of Races and Peoples* (Washington: Government Printing Office, 1911), pp. 104–106.
67. Michael C. LeMay, *From Open Door to Dutch Door: An Analysis of U.S. Immigration Policy since 1820* (New York: Praeger, 1897), pp. 38–72. On intelligence testing and the likes of H. H. Goddard see Stephen J. Gould, *The Mismeasure of Man* (New York: Norton, 1981), and Elazar Barkan, *The Retreat of Scientific Racism: Changing Concepts of Race in Britain and the United States between the World Wars* (Cambridge: Cambridge University Press, 1992).
68. Harry H. Laughlin, *Analysis of America's Modern Melting Pot: Hearings before the Committee on Immigration and Naturalization, House of Representatives, November 21, 1922* (Washington, D.C.: Government Printing Office, 1923), pp. 731, 757.
69. Quoted in Alan M. Kraut, *Silent Travelers: Germs, Genes, and the "Immigrant Menace"* (Baltimore: Johns Hopkins University Press, 1994), p. 34.
70. American Party, *Address of the American Republicans of the City of Philadelphia to the Native and Naturalized Citizens of the United States* [c.1844] (nl: np, nd), pp. 9, 11, Beinecke Library. The racial dimensions of early American nativism are still largely neglected in the scholarship. Most recently, compare Dale Knobel, *"America for the Americans": The Nativist Movement in the United States* (New York: Twayne, c.1996).
71. "Romanism and the Irish Race," *North American Review,* Dec. 1879, pp. 523, 527–528; Jan. 1880, p. 3.
72. Daniel Ullman, "The Constitution of the United States," The Daniel Ullman Papers, New York Historical Society, Reel no. 5, frames 174, 167, 230, 231.
73. Ibid., frames 169, 185, 193, 194, 198.
74. Ibid., frames 172, 173, 175, 176–177, 172, 180–181. On Daniel Ullman, see also Tyler Anbinder, *Nativism and Slavery: The Northern Know-Nothings and the Politics of the 1850s* (New York: Oxford, 1992), pp. 77–87, 106–107.
75. "Romanism and the Irish Race," p. 533.
76. James Russell Lowell, "Democracy" [1884], in *Essays, Poems, and Letters* (New York: Odyssey, 1948), p. 147; Francis Walker, "Restriction of Immigration," *Atlantic Monthly,* June 1896, p. 828.
77. *Congressional Globe,* Second Session, 41st Congress, part VI (June 22–July 15, 1870), pp. 5121, 5123.
78. Ibid., pp. 5123, 5155, 5125, 5150–5151, 5156.
79. Ibid., p. 5177.
80. Ibid., p. 5152.

81. John H. Wigmore, "American Naturalization and the Japanese," *American Law Review* 28 (1894), p. 821.

82. Ibid., pp. 822, 823, 827.

83. Henry Cabot Lodge, "The Restriction of Immigration," *North American Review,* vol. 152 (1891), pp. 30–31, 32, 35.

84. Barbara Miller Solomon, *Ancestors and Immigrants* (Chicago: University of Chicago Press, 1955); Higham, *Strangers in the Land;* Daniel Kevles, *In the Name of Eugenics: Genetics and the Uses of Human Heredity* (Berkeley: University of California Press, 1985), pp. 94–112; Kenneth Ludmerer, *Genetics and American Society: A Historical Appraisal* (Baltimore: Johns Hopkins University Press, 1972), p. 95; Layra Doyle, *Bordering on the Body: The Racial Matrix of Modern Fiction and Culture* (New York: Oxford, 1994), pp. 10–34.

85. Kevles, *In the Name of Eugenics,* pp. 45–56, 47; Ludmerer, *Genetics,* pp. 87–113.

86. Commissioner quoted in Lawrence H. Fuchs, *The American Kaleidoscope: Race, Ethnicity, and the Civic Culture* (Hanover: University Press of New England, 1990), p. 60; *Dictionary of Races or Peoples,* pp. 2–3.

87. *Dictionary of Races or Peoples,* pp. 54, 13, 23, 30, 69, 74, 104.

88. Ibid., pp. 22–23, 47, 69, 72, 82, 104, 109, 117, 127, 129.

89. Ibid., p. 84.

90. Reports of the Immigration Commission, *Statements and Recommendations Submitted by Societies and Organizations Interested in the Subject of Immigration* (Washington: Government Printing Office, 1910), pp. 107, 111.

91. Madison Grant, *The Passing of the Great Race; or, The Racial Basis of European History* (New York: Charles Scribner's Sons, 1916), pp. 80, 81, 15–16. Sales figures cited in Higham, *Strangers in the Land,* p. 271. Sinclair Lewis demonstrated both the hegemonic familiarity of Grant's pro-Nordic vision and its potential ruptures when, in 1928, he satirized his *Man Who Knew Coolidge* as a "Productive and Nordic Citizen."

92. Grant, *Passing of the Great Race,* pp. 80, 81.

93. Ibid., pp. 73, 30, 61.

94. Harry H. Laughlin, *Analysis of America's Modern Melting Pot: Hearings before the Committee on Immigration and Naturalization, House of Representatives, November 21, 1922* (Washington, D.C.: Government Printing Office, 1923), pp. 731, 757.

95. Harry H. Laughlin, *Immigration and Conquest* (New York: New York State Chamber of Commerce, 1939), p. 39.

96. *Eugenical News,* IX:2 (Feb. 1924), p. 21; New York *Times,* Jan. 7, 1924, p. 8. Celts often became honorary Nordics in this formulation, as for instance, when the Immigration Restriction League's John Langley averred, "Thirty or forty years ago most of the newcomers were Irish, Germans, and Scandina-

vians, which were in the main good material, and assimilable under republican ideals." *Statements and Recommendations Submitted by Societies and Organizations Interested in the Subject of Immigration,* p. 115.

97. New York *Times,* April 8, 1924, p. 18.

98. Laughlin, *Immigration and Conquest,* pp. 22, 55, 8.

99. Thurman Rice, *Racial Hygiene: A Practical Discussion of Eugenics and Race Culture* (New York: Macmillan, 1929), pp. 303, 308. See also Paul Poponoe and Roswell Hill Johnson, *Applied Eugenics* (New York: Macmillan, 1935), p. 291; Madison Grant, *The Conquest of a Continent; or, The Expansion of Races in America* (New York: Charles Scribner's Sons, 1933), pp. 1, 271; Edward M. East, *Heredity and Human Affairs* (New York: Charles Scribner's Sons, 1927), pp. 280, 290–291.

100. *Congressional Record,* 68th Congress, 1st Session, vol. 65, part 6, pp. 5914, 5915, 5647, 5648.

101. Ludmerer, *Genetics,* p. 106. On popular rallies and demonstrations against the Immigration Act, see the New York *Times,* Feb. 25, 1924, p. 1; Feb. 28, 1924, p. 4; March 3, 1924, p. 2; March 9, 1924, p. 9.

102. *Congressional Record,* vol. 65, part 6, pp. 5929–5930; New York *Times,* Jan. 14, 1924, p. 16.

103. *Congressional Record,* vol. 65, part 6, p. 5648.

104. Poponoe and Johnson, *Applied Eugenics,* p. 291; Thomas Gossett, *Race: The History of an Idea in America* (New York: Schocken, 1963), pp. 287–338; Thomas Dyer, *Theodore Roosevelt and the Idea of Race* (Baton Rouge: Louisiana State University Press, 1985); Bederman, *Manliness and Civilization;* Louise Newman, *White Women's Rights: The Racial Origins of American Feminism* (New York: Oxford, forthcoming).

105. Brander Matthews, *Americans of the Future and Other Essays* [1909] (New York: Books for Libraries Press, 1968), pp. 6–7, 20, 22.

106. Gossett, *Race,* pp. 198–227; Robert Bannister, *Social Darwinism: Science and Myth in Anglo-American Social Thought* (Philadelphia: Temple University Press, 1979), pp. 212–225; Richard Hofstadter, *Social Darwinism in American Thought* (Boston: Beacon, 1944), pp. 143–200; Walter LaFeber, *The New Empire: An Interpretation of American Expansionism* (Ithaca: Cornell University Press, 1964); Jack London, *The Sea-Wolf* [1904] (New York: New American Library, 1964), pp. 68–69, 24, 79; Frank Norris, *McTeague* [1899] (New York: Norton, 1977), pp. 25, 135.

107. Charles Chesnutt, *The Marrow of Tradition* [1901] (New York: Penguin, 1993), pp. 90, 289–290; James Weldon Johnson, *The Autobiography of an Ex-Colored Man* [1912] (New York: Penguin, 1990), pp. 111, 113, 116; Michael Denning, *The Cultural Front: The Laboring of American Culture in the Twentieth Century* (London: Verso, 1997), pp. 195–199.

108. Jacob Riis, *How the Other Half Lives* [1890] (New York: Hill and Wang,

1957); Stuart Anderson, *Race and Rapprochement: Anglo-Saxonism and Anglo-American Relations, 1895–1904* (Rutherford, N.J.: Fairleigh Dickinson University Press, 1981); Ann Douglass, *Terrible Honesty: Mongrel Manhattan in the 1920s* (New York: Farrar, Straus, Giroux, 1995); Miriam Hansen, *Babel and Babylon: Spectatorship in American Silent Film* (Cambridge: Harvard University Press, 1991), pp. 254–294; Melnick, "Ancestors and Relatives"; Jacobson, *Special Sorrows,* pp. 177–216.

109. *Good Housekeeping* article quoted in Ludmerer, *Genetics,* p. 104; Coolidge's proclamation in New York *Times,* July 1, 1924, p. 1.

3. Becoming Caucasian, 1924–1965

1. Quoted in Lucy Salyer, *Laws Harsh as Tigers: Chinese Immigrants and the Shaping of Modern Immigration Law* (Chapel Hill: University of North Carolina Press, 1995), p. 127.

2. *Education,* Jan. 1946, p. 259.

3. New York *Times,* April 8, 1924, p. 18.

4. Maldwyn Allen Jones, *American Immigration* (Chicago: University of Chicago Press, 1960), p. 307.

5. Council against Intolerance in America, *An American Answer to Intolerance, Teacher's Manual Number One, Junior and Senior High Schools, Experimental Form* (New York: CAIA, 1939), p. 81.

6. H. H. Laughlin, *Report of the Special Committee on Immigration and Alien Insane Submitting a Study on Immigration-Control* (New York: Chamber of Commerce, 1934), p. 43.

7. Los Angeles *Times,* July 12, 1930, p. 2; New Orleans *Times-Picayune,* July 14, 1935, magazine p. 5.

8. Dashiel Hammet, *The Maltese Falcon* (New York: Knopf, 1929).

9. *Common Ground,* Spring 1944, pp. 104–105; Spring 1945, p. 82.

10. John McGreevy, *Parish Boundaries: The Catholic Encounter with Race in the Twentieth-Century Urban North* (Chicago: University of Chicago Press, 1996), pp. 28–53; Michael Denning, *The Cultural Front: The Laboring of American Culture in the Twentieth Century* (London: Verso, 1997), pp. 192–199, 445–454.

11. Denning singles out the year 1942 as "a turning point in our dealings with all colored minorities," the beginning of a new racial formation. Denning, *Cultural Front,* pp. 36, 451; McGreevy, *Parish Boundaries,* pp. 78, 110.

12. *Chicago Sun,* Oct. 22, 1945. *Social Forces,* quoted in *Race Relations,* Jan. 1946, inside back cover.

13. Laura Z. Hobson, *Gentleman's Agreement* (New York: Simon and Schuster, 1947), p. 196.

14. Herbert Aptheker, ed., W. E. B. Du Bois, *Against Racism: Unpublished Es-*

says, Papers, Addresses, 1887–1961 (Amherst: University of Massachusetts Press, 1985), pp. 254–256; George Schuyler, *Black No More* [1931] (Boston: Northeastern University Pess, 1989).

15. New York *Times,* July 28, 1919, p. 4; David Levering Lewis, ed., *The Harlem Renaissance Reader* (New York: Penguin, 1991), pp. 110–117; Kelly Miller, *Radicals and Conservatives and Other Essays on the Negro in America* [1908] (New York: Schocken, 1968), p. 165.

16. Matthew Frye Jacobson, *Special Sorrows: The Diasporic Imagination of Irish, Polish, and Jewish Immigrants in the United States* (Cambridge: Harvard University Press, 1995).

17. Nikhil Pal Singh, "Race and Nation in the American Century: A Genealogy of Color and Democracy" (Ph.D. diss., Yale University, 1995); Paula Pfeffer, *A. Philip Randolph, Pioneer of the Civil Rights Movement* (Baton Rouge: Louisiana State University Press, 1990); Paul Kleppner, *Chicago Divided: The Making of a Black Mayor* (DeKalb: Northern Illinois University Press, 1991), pp. 15–63; Elazar Barkan, *The Retreat of Scientific Racism: Changing Concepts of Race in Britain and the United States between the World Wars* (Cambridge: Cambridge University Press, 1992), pp. 279–340.

18. Margaret Mitchell, *Gone with The Wind* [1936] (New York: Warner, 1993), p. 5.

19. *Report of the National Advisory Commission on Civil Disorders* (New York: Bantam, 1968), p. 1.

20. Lothrop Stoddard, *The Rising Tide of Color against White World-Supremacy* (New York: Charles Scribner's Sons, 1920), pp. 164–165.

21. Ibid., pp. 221, 235.

22. F. Scott Fitzgerald, *The Great Gatsby* [1925] (New York: Macmillan, 1991), pp. 17, 137; Walter Benn Michaels, *Our America: Nativism, Modernism, and Pluralism* (Durham: Duke University Press, 1995), pp. 23–29.

23. Lothrop Stoddard, *Reforging America* (New York: Charles Scribner's Sons, 1927), pp. 256–257.

24. Ibid., pp. 328, 284–325, 292.

25. Ruth Benedict, *Patterns of Culture* (Boston: Houghton Mifflin, 1934), p. 15; *Race: Science and Politics* [1940] (Westport: Greenwood Press, 1982), pp. 97–98.

26. Julian S. Huxley, *We Europeans: A Survey of "Racial" Problems* (London: Harper and Brothers, 1936), pp. vii, 215, 233; Barkan, *Retreat,* pp. 297–298.

27. CAIA, *Answer to Intolerance,* p. 84.

28. Ruth Benedict, *The Races of Mankind* [1943], in *Race: Science and Politics,* pp. 176–177. The work was also produced as a filmstrip, a traveling exhibit, and an animated cartoon.

29. Franz Boas, *Race and Democratic Society* [1945] (New York: Biblo and Tannen, 1969), pp. 6–14.

30. Ashley Montagu, *Race: Man's Most Dangerous Myth* (New York: Columbia University Press, 1942), pp. 4–5, 180–191.
31. Ashley Montagu, "What Every Child and Adult Should Know about 'Race,' " *Education,* Jan. 1946, pp. 262, 263, 264.
32. UNESCO, *The Race Concept: Results of an Inquiry* (Paris: UNESCO, 1952), pp. 11–15.
33. Ibid., pp. 30–31, 46.
34. Benedict, *Races of Mankind,* pp. 176–177.
35. Huxley, *We Europeans,* p. 86.
36. Robert E. Park, "The Nature of Race Relations" [1939], in *Race and Culture: Essays in the Sociology of Contemporary Man* (New York: Free Press, 1950), p. 81.
37. Yehudi O. Webster, *The Racialization of America* (New York: St. Martin's Press, 1992), p. 81.
38. Benedict, *Patterns of Culture,* p. 11.
39. My account of the exhibit is based on a panel-by-panel description in the *Monthly Summary of Events and Trends in Race Relations,* Oct. 1944, pp. 87–88. A slightly different version is summarized as an appendix to Ashley Montagu's *Race: Man's Most Dangerous Myth.* Benedict's *Races of Mankind* was also rendered as an eleven-minute cartoon, *The Brotherhood of Man,* by a group of Popular Front animators affiliated with the United Auto Workers. See Denning, *Cultural Front,* pp. 419–420.
40. Richard Slotkin, *Gunfighter Nation: The Myth of the Frontier in Twentieth-Century America* (New York: Harper, 1992), pp. 347–486; Ella Shohat and Robert Stam, *Unthinking Eurocentrism* (New York: Routledge, 1993); Alan Nadel, *Containment Culture: American Narratives, Postmodernism, and the Atomic Age* (Durham: Duke University Press, 1995), pp. 90–116.
41. Benedict, *Patterns of Culture,* pp. 5, 11, 13, 15; *Race: Science and Politics,* p. 113.
42. W. Lloyd Warner and Leo Srole, *The Social Systems of American Ethnic Groups* (New Haven: Yale University Press, 1945), pp. 286, 290–291.
43. Ibid., p. 294.
44. *In Re Halladjian,* 174 Fed 843.
45. W. E. B. Du Bois, *Dusk of Dawn: An Essay toward an Autobiography of a Race Concept* [1940] (New York: Schocken, 1960), p. 153.
46. *Race Relations,* Nov. 1944, p. 109.
47. Singh, "Race and Nation," p. 103; Stephen Steinberg, *Turning Back: The Retreat from Racial Justice in American Thought and Policy* (Boston: Beacon, 1995), pp. 21–49.
48. Quoted in Carey McWilliams, *Brothers under the Skin* [1942] (Boston: Little Brown, 1946), pp. 4, 301. See also Gary Gerstle, "The Working Class Goes to War," *Mid-America,* Oct. 1993, pp. 316–319.

49. "Why Negroes Should Oppose the War" [1939], in C. L. R. James et al., *Fighting Racism in World War II* (New York: Pathfinder, 1980), pp. 29, 31; Robert Mullen, *Blacks in America's Wars: The Shift in Attitude from the Revolutionary War to Vietnam* (New York: Pathfinder, 1973), pp. 51–60; George Roeder, Jr., *The Uncensored War: American Visual Experience during World War Two* (New Haven: Yale, 1993), pp. 43–79, 121–123.

50. McWilliams, *Brothers*, p. 35.

51. Louis Adamic, *From Many Lands* (New York: Harpers, 1939), p. 339; *Nation of Nations* (New York: Harper, 1944), p. 201.

52. *Survey Graphic*, "Color, Unfinished Business of Democracy," (Nov. 1942). Other issues devoted entirely to race include *Annals of the American Academy of Political and Social Science*, "Minority Peoples in a Nation at War" (Sept. 1942); *Journal of Negro Education*, "The American Negro in World War I and World War II" (Summer 1943); *Journal of Educational Sociology*, "The Negro in the North during Wartime" (Jan. 1944) and "Race Relations on the Pacific Coast" (Nov. 1945).

53. *Race Relations*, Oct. 1946, p. 66; June–Dec. 1948, pp.204–209.

54. Mary Dudziak, "Desegregation as a Cold War Imperative," in Richard Delgado, ed., *Critical Race Theory: The Cutting Edge* (Philadelphia: Temple University Press, 1995), p. 111; Joel Williamson, *A Rage for Order: Black-White Relations in the American South since Emancipation* (New York: Oxford, 1986), pp. 254–256.

55. Harvard Sitkoff, *A New Deal for Blacks: The Emergence of Civil Rights as a National Issue* (New York: Oxford, 1978) remains the best exemplar of a counternarrative. On the disposition of the courts "on the road to *Brown*," see A. Leon Higginbotham, Jr., *Shades of Freedom: Racial Politics and the Presumptions of the American Legal Process* (New York: Oxford, 1996), pp. 152–168.

56. By 1945 the number of active organizations stood at "over two hundred," concerning themselves with public education, surveys, pressure activities (like petition drives and protests), education, conferences, employment, recreation, delinquency, police administration, health, antitension campaigns, housing, and transportation. *Race Relations*, Jan. 1944, p. 2; March 1945, pp. 234–236; Nov. 1945, pp. 116–118.

57. *Race Relations*, Aug. 1943, p. 1; March 1946, p. 267; Nov. 1943, p. 6; Dec. 1943, pp. 7–8; May 1947, p. 320.

58. Ibid., July 1944, pp. 8–10; May 1947, pp. 301–302; Jan. 1947, p. 172; Dec. 1945, pp. 148–152; July 1947, p. 383; Feb. 1948, pp. 101, 102; April 1946, p. 289; July 1946, p. 363; Oct.–Nov. 1947, p. 33. Kleppner, *Chicago Divided*, pp. 4–44.

59. *Race Relations*, Dec. 1947–Jan. 1948, pp. 66–71; *Richmond News* quoted

p. 72; President's Commission on Civil Rights, *To Secure These Rights* (Washington: Government Printing Office, 1947).

60. *Congressional Record,* 82nd Congress, 2nd Session, vol. 98, part IV, pp. 4431–4432, 4441, 4409–4413, 4435, 4438.

61. David Reimers, *Still the Golden Door: The Third World Comes to America* (New York: Columbia University Press, 1985), pp. 63–90, 82.

62. Shohat and Stam, *Unthinking Eurocentrism;* Robert Rydell, *All the World's a Fair: Visions of Empire at American International Expositions, 1876–1916* (Chicago: University of Chicago Press, 1984), p. 65; Amy Kaplan and Donald Pease, eds., *Cultures of U.S. Imperialism* (Durham: Duke University Press, 1993).

63. Robert Lang, ed., *The Birth of a Nation* (New Brunswick: Rutgers University Press, 1994).

64. Kenneth Jackson, *The Ku Klux Klan in the City, 1915–1930* (New York: Oxford, 1967); Nancy MacLean, *Behind the Mask of Chivalry* (New York: Oxford, 1993); Kathleen Blee, *Women of the Klan: Racism and Gender in the 1920s* (Berkeley: University of California Press, 1992), p. 18; Michael Rogin, "His Sword Became a Flashing Vision: D. W. Griffith's *Birth of a Nation,*" in Lang, *Birth of a Nation,* pp. 250–293; Michaels, *Our America,* p. 67.

65. Robert L. Carringer, ed., *The Jazz Singer* [1925, 1927] (Madison: University of Wisconsin Press, 1979), pp. 94, 147. The reference to "Anglo-Saxon severity" is from the original short story upon which the movie is based, Sampson Raphaelson's "Day of Atonement."

66. *The Jazz Singer,* pp. 61, 63. On *The Jazz Singer* and whiteness, compare Michael Rogin, *Blackface, White Noise: Jewish Immigrants in the Hollywood Melting Pot* (Berkeley: University of California Press, 1996), pp. 45–70 and passim.

67. *The Jazz Singer,* pp. 80, 120.

68. Ibid., pp. 59, 85, 117, 127, 50, 115.

69. Ibid., p. 124.

70. Ibid., pp. 83, 133, 41.

71. Jeffrey Melnick, *A Right to Sing the Blues* (Cambridge: Harvard University Press, forthcoming); Rogin, *Black Face, White Noise;* David Roediger, *The Wages of Whiteness: Race in the Making of the American Working Class* (London: Verso, 1990), pp. 116–127; Eric Lott, *Love and Theft: Blackface Minstrelsy and the American Working Class* (New York: Oxford, 1993); Susan Gubar, *Racechanges: White Skin, Black Face in American Culture* (New York: Oxford, 1997), pp. 53–94; Alexander Saxton, *The Rise and Fall of the White Republic: Class Politics and Mass Culture in Nineteenth-Century America* (London: Verso, 1990), pp. 165–182; Jean Baker, *Affairs of Party:*

The Political Culture of Northern Democrats in the Mid-Nineteenth Century (Ithaca: Cornell University Press, 1983), pp. 225–243.

72. Schuyler, *Black No More,* pp. 30, 26, 28.

73. Ibid., pp. 46, 48, 31–32, 179.

74. Ibid., pp. 60, 44, 86, 122, 134.

75. Ibid., p. 65.

76. Ibid., pp. 152–153.

77. Ibid., p. 175.

78. Schuyler reiterated aspects of this critique in a piece for *Common Ground* in the fall of 1940. "No superstition is so prevalent in the U.S. as that pertaining to race," he began. "Who Is 'Negro'? Who Is 'White'?" *Common Ground,* Autumn 1940, p. 53.

79. Hobson, *Gentleman's Agreement,* pp. 64, 33, 34.

80. Ibid., pp. 101–102, 196.

81. Ibid., pp. 184, 154, 35.

82. Ibid., pp. 130–131, 122.

83. Ibid., pp. 65, 67.

84. Ibid., pp. 39, 96, 170–171, 179–180.

85. Ibid., pp. 138, 99.

86. Ibid., p. 212.

87. Jo Sinclair [Ruth Seid], *The Changelings* [1955] (Old Westbury: Feminist Press, 1985), p. 1.

88. *Blackboard Jungle,* MGM Studios, 1955.

89. Arthur Laurents, *West Side Story* [1957] (New York: Dell Publishing, 1965), pp. 137, 164–165, 178–179, 217, 167–168.

90. Herbert Simmons, *Corner Boy* (Boston: Houghton Mifflin, 1957), pp. 22, 259.

91. Benedict, *Race: Science and Politics,* p. 125.

92. Oscar Handlin, *Race and Nationality in American Life* (New York: Anchor, 1957), pp. 141, 145, 150, 175.

4. 1877: The Instability of Race

1. Henry James, *The American* [1877] (New York: Signet, 1980), p. 121.

2. Ibid., pp. 162–163.

3. Eric Foner, *Reconstruction: America's Unfinished Revolution, 1863–1877* (New York: Harper and Row, 1988); W. E. B. Du Bois, *Black Reconstruction in America, 1860–1880* [1935] (New York: Atheneum, 1992); Allen Trelease, *White Terror: The Ku Klux Klan Conspiracy and Southern Reconstruction* (Baton Rouge: Louisiana State University Press, 1971); Brian Dippee, *The Vanishing American: White Attitudes and U.S. Indian Policy* (Lawrence: Kan-

sas, 1982); Dee Brown, *Bury My Heart at Wounded Knee: An Indian History of the American West* (New York: Bantam, 1970); James Welch, *Killing Custer: The Battle of the Little Bighorn and the Fate of the Plains Indians* (New York: Penguin, 1994); Alexander Saxton, *The Indispensable Enemy: Labor and the Anti-Chinese Movement in California* (Berkeley: University of California Press, 1971); Gary Nash and Richard Weiss, eds., *The Great Fear: Race in the Mind of America* (New York: Holt, Rinehart and Winston, 1970); Ronald Takaki, *Iron Cages: Race and Culture in Nineteenth-Century America* (Seattle: University of Washington Press, 1979); Sucheng Chan, *The Asian Americans: An Interpretive History* (Boston: Twayne, 1988); Carey McWilliams, "How Deep the Roots," *Common Ground,* Autumn 1947, pp. 3–5; David Roediger, " 'The So-Called Mob': Race, Class, Skill, and Community in the St. Louis General Strike," in *Towards the Abolition of Whiteness* (London: Verso, 1994), pp. 85–116; Tomas Almaguer, *Racial Fault Lines: The Historical Origins of White Supremacy in California* (Berkeley: University of California Press, 1994); John Fiske, "The Races of the Danube," *Atlantic Monthly,* April 1877, p. 401.

4. Howard Winant, *Racial Conditions: Politics, Theory, Comparisons* (Minneapolis: University of Minnesota Press, 1994), p. 21.

5. Alexander Saxton, *The Rise and Fall of the White Republic: Class Politics and Mass Culture in Nineteenth-Century America* (London: Verso, 1990), p. 14.

6. Charles Dudley Warner, *In the Levant* [1877] (New York: Houghton Mifflin, 1901), p. 439.

7. Charles Dudley Warner, *Mummies and Moslems* (Hartford: American, 1876), pp. 31, 32, 40, 41.

8. Ibid., pp. 40, 41, 59, 106, 121–122, 234; *Levant,* pp. 16, 40, 107, 544.

9. *Levant,* pp. 63–64.

10. Ibid., p. 502; *Mummies,* p. 110.

11. *Mummies,* pp. 296, 234, 171.

12. Ibid., p. 213; *Levant,* p. 377.

13. *Levant,* pp. 165, 177–178; *Mummies,* pp. 276–277.

14. *Mummies,* p. 53.

15. *Levant,* pp. 62–63.

16. Ibid., pp. 63, 64, 127–128.

17. Ibid., p. 500; *Mummies,* p. 292.

18. *Levant,* p. 460.

19. *Mummies,* p. 390.

20. *Harper's New Monthly Magazine,* Sept. 1877, p. 637, emphasis added. (Hereafter *HNMM.*)

21. *Visitor's Guide to the Hall of Mammals in the American Museum of Natural*

History (New York: William C. Martin, 1883), p. 2. The Hall of Mammals opened in 1877; this is the earliest guide extant.

22. *HNMM,* April 1877, p. 776.

23. A. Von Steinwehr and D. G. Brinton, *An Intermediate Geography with Lessons in Map Drawing* (Cincinnati: Van Antwerp, Bragg, and Co., n.d. [c.1877]), p. 13.

24. New York *Herald,* March 27, 1877, p. 3.

25. *HNMM,* April 1877, p. 769.

26. *HNMM,* Feb. 1877, p. 387; April 1877, p. 676; May 1877, p. 873.

27. New York *Herald,* March 26, 1877, pp. 3–4.

28. Ibid., p. 3.

29. New York *Herald,* Nov. 14, 1877, pp. 5–6; Nov. 24, 1877, p. 3.

30. Ibid., Nov. 14, 1877, pp. 5–6.

31. Ibid., Nov. 24, 1877, p. 3.

32. New York *Times,* March 6, 1877, p. 1.

33. Ibid., p. 1. See, for example, Foner, *Reconstruction;* Du Bois, *Black Reconstruction;* Nina Silber, *The Romance of Reunion: Northerners and the South, 1865–1900* (Chapel Hill: University of North Carolina Press, 1993); Joel Williamson, *A Rage for Order: Black-White Relations in the American South since Emancipation* (New York: Oxford, 1986).

34. *Congressional Record,* 44th Congress, 2nd Session, vol. V, part 2, pp. 1404, 1405. On Louisiana in this period see also Foner, *Reconstruction,* pp. 262–264, 385–389, 550–555, 575–582; Du Bois, *Black Reconstruction,* pp. 451–484; A. Leon Higginbotham, Jr., *Shades of Freedom: Racial Politics and the Presumptions of the American Legal Process* (New York: Oxford, 1996), pp. 88–93.

35. Specific Louisiana "whites" who were presumably affected included Mayor Pastremski of Baton Rouge, Democratic supervisor O'Sullivan of La Fourche parish, and Max Aronson, a "white" who was allegedly "killed by a band of unknown negroes." *Congressional Record,* 44th Congress, 2nd Session, vol. V, part 2, pp. 1409, 1416, 1425, 1429. On the power of Louisiana's binary racial scheme in this period from the standpoint of Louisiana Creoles, see Virginia Dominguez, *White by Definition: Social Classification in Creole Louisiana* (New Brunswick: Rutgers University Press, 1986), pp. 133–148.

36. *Congressional Record,* 44th Congress, 2nd Session, vol. V, part 2, pp. 1409–1416.

37. Ibid., pp. 1432, 1429, 1407–1408.

38. Ibid., pp. 1444, 1445, 1463.

39. Ibid., pp. 1445, 1446, 1447, 1471.

40. Trelease, *White Terror,* pp. xl, 93–94.

41. Ibid., pp. 133, 136.

42. *HNMM,* Oct. 1877, p. 776; *The Rough and Ready Songster: Embellished with Twenty-five Splendid Engravings Illustrative of the American Victories in Mexico* (New York: Nafis and Cornish, c.1848), Beinecke Library.
43. *HNMM,* Nov. 1877, p. 813.
44. Richard Slotkin, *Regeneration through Violence: The Mythology of the American Frontier, 1600–1860* (Middletown: Wesleyan University Press, 1973), and *The Fatal Environment: The Myth of the Frontier in the Age of Industrialization, 1800–1890* (Middletown: Wesleyan University Press, 1985). See also Chapter 6 below.
45. *Congressional Record,* 44th Congress, 2nd Session, vol V. part 2, pp. 1347–1348, 1355, 1356.
46. Ibid., pp. 1055, 1057.
47. *Congressional Record,* 45th Congress, 1st Session, vol. VI, pp. 391–392, 393.
48. Stuart Creighton Miller, *The Unwelcome Immigrant: The American Image of the Chinese, 1785–1882* (Berkeley: University of California Press, 1969); Chan, *Asian Americans;* Takaki, *Iron Cages,* pp. 215–249; Almaguer, *Racial Fault Lines,* pp. 153–204; Patricia Nelson Limerick, *The Legacy of Conquest: The Unbroken Past of the American West* (New York: Norton, 1987), pp. 259–269; Saxton, *Indispensable Enemy;* Tsai, *Chinese Experience.*
49. *Congressional Record,* 44th Congress, 2nd Session, vol. V, part 3, pp. 2004–2005.
50. Quoted in *Memorial: The Other Side of the Chinese Question; Testimony of California's Leading Citizens* (Woodward and Co., 1886), pp. 8–9.
51. Esther E. Baldwin, *Must the Chinese Go? An Examination of the Chinese Question* (New York: H. B. Elkins, 1890), pp. 60–61.
52. John Swinton, *The New Issue: The Chinese-American Question* (New York: American News Co., 1870), p. 6.
53. New York *Times,* Aug. 6, 1870, p. 5.
54. Stephen Powers, "California Saved," *Atlantic Monthly,* Nov. 1871, p. 601.
55. Wilhelmina Harper and Aimee M. Peters, eds., *The Best of Bret Harte* (Cambridge: Houghton Mifflin, 1947), p. 180.
56. New York *Times,* April 3, 1877, p. 4; Almaguer, *Racial Fault Lines,* p. 170; Saxton, *Indispensable Enemy,* pp. 18, 196.
57. Roediger, *Abolition of Whiteness,* p. 88.
58. *HNMM,* Oct. 1877, p. 657.
59. Ibid., July 1877, p. 185; Feb. 1877, p. 362; Oct. 1877, pp. 729, 730.
60. *Harper's Weekly,* Jan. 1877, p. 318; March 1877, p. 513; *HNMM,* June 1877, pp. 38, 50.
61. *HNMM,* June 1877, p. 153.
62. Ibid., March 1877, pp. 487–488. On "French physiognomy," see also Dominguez, *White by Definition,* p. 133.

63. *HNMM,* Oct. 1877, pp. 784–785; Feb. 1877, pp. 467–468, 474; Jan. 1877, p. 312; July 1877, p. 321.

64. *Nation,* May 1877, p. 260; John Fiske, "Races of the Danube," *Atlantic Monthly,* April 1877, pp. 403, 404.

65. McWilliams, "How Deep the Roots"; John Higham, *Send These to Me: Immigrants in Urban America* [1975] (Baltimore: Johns Hopkins University Press, 1984), pp. 123–128, 117–152.

66. New York *Tribune,* June 20, 1877, p. 4.

67. New York *Commercial Advertiser,* June 19, 1877, p. 2.

68. *Nation,* June 28, 1877, p. 378.

69. New York *Daily Graphic,* June 21, 1877, p. 2.

70. New York *Evening Post,* June 20, 1877, p. 2.

71. New York *Tribune,* June 20, 1877, p. 4. (The headline "No Jews Need Apply" did capture a certain irony, as A. T. Stewart, whose estate now housed the Grand Union Hotel, was an Irish immigrant himself.)

72. New York *Tribune,* June 21, 1877, p. 8; June 27, 1877, p. 4.

73. *Harper's Weekly,* July 7, 1877, pp. 518–519.

74. New York *Tribune,* June 26, 1877, p. 4.

75. F. P. Dewees, *The Molly Maguires: The Origin, Growth, and Character of the Organization* (New York: Burt Franklin, 1877), pp. 9–13. The historian Walter Coleman endorsed this racial interpretation as late as 1936: in the coalmining regions of Pennsylvania "the growing numerical supremacy of the Irish . . . aroused the fears of the other groups and intensified the racial problems." *The Molly Maguire Riots: Industrial Conflict in the Pennsylvania Coal Region* (Richmond: Garrett and Massie, 1936), p. 20.

76. Slotkin, *Fatal Environment,* pp. 480, 482, 497.

77. Ibid., pp. 495, 492.

78. *Harper's Weekly,* Aug. 18, 1877, p. 368.

79. Quoted in Slotkin, *Fatal Environment,* p. 485.

80. Quoted in Ibid., p. 483.

81. James, *American,* p. 32.

82. Ibid., pp. 5, 6, 83, 120, 105, 212.

5. Looking Jewish, Seeing Jews

1. Johann Fredrich Blumenbach, *On the Natural Varieties of Mankind* [1775, 1795] (New York: Bergman, 1969), p. 234.

2. In Morris U. Schapps, ed., *A Documentary History of Jews in the United States, 1654–1875* (New York: Schocken, 1950, 1971), pp. 1–2.

3. Henry James, "Glasses," *Atlantic Monthly,* Feb. 1896, p. 145; William Boelhower, *Through a Glass Darkly: Ethnic Semiosis in American Literature*

(New York: Oxford, 1987), pp. 17–40, 21; Henry James, *The American Scene* [1906] (n.l.: Library of America, 1993), pp. 425–427. See also Karen Brodkin Sacks, "How Did Jews Become White Folks?" in Steven Gregory and Roger Sanjek, eds., *Race* (New Brunswick: Rutgers University Press, 1994), pp. 79–85.

4. Melanie Kaye/Kantrowicz, *My Jewish Face and Other Stories* (San Francisco: Spinster-Aunt Lute, 1990); Philip Roth, *The Counterlife* (New York: Penguin, 1988), p. 79.

5. Charles Dudley Warner, *In the Levant* [1877] (New York: Houghton Mifflin, 1901), pp. 177–178. Emphasis added.

6. *North American Review*, 152 (1891), p. 128. On "white Jews" see Louis Binstock, "Fire-Words," *Common Ground*, Winter 1947, pp. 83–84, and Laura Z. Hobson, *Gentleman's Agreement* (New York: Simon and Schuster, 1947), pp. 154–155.

7. F. Marion Crawford, *The Witch of Prague* [1891] (London: Sphere Books, 1974), p. 186.

8. Matthew Frye Jacobson, *Special Sorrows: The Diasporic Imagination of Irish, Polish, and Jewish Immigrants in the United States* (Cambridge: Harvard University Press, 1995), pp. 102–105, and " 'The Quintessence of the Jew': Polemics of Nationalism and Peoplehood in Turn-of-the-Century Yiddish Fiction," in Werner Sollors and Marc Schell, eds., *Multilingual America* (New York: New York University Press, forthcoming); John Efron, *Defenders of the Race: Jewish Doctors and Race Science in Fin-de-Siecle Europe* (New Haven: Yale University Press, 1994).

9. Hasia Diner, *In the Almost Promised Land: American Jews and Blacks, 1915–1935* [1977] (Baltimore: Johns Hopkins University Press, 1995), pp. 8–9.

10. Madison Grant, *The Passing of the Great Race: or, The Racial Basis of European History* (New York: Scribners, 1916), pp. 15–16; James William Gibson, *Warrior Dreams: Violence and Manhood in Post-Vietnam America* (New York: Hill and Wang, 1994), p. 72.

11. Ludwig Lewisohn, *The American Jew: Character and Destiny* (New York: Farrar, Straus and Co., 1950), p. 23.

12. Sander Gilman, *The Jew's Body* (New York: Routledge, 1991), chapter 7; Sacks, "How Did Jews Become White Folks?"

13. James Shapiro, *Shakespeare and the Jews* (New York: Columbia University Press, 1996), pp. 36, 168, 169, 170; see pp. 167–193 on early modern English conceptions of nationality and the Jewish alien.

14. Frederic Cople Jaher, *A Scapegoat in the New Wilderness: The Origins and Rise of Anti-Semitism in America* (Cambridge: Harvard University Press, 1994), pp. 17, 82, 87–88, 106, 112. For Jaher's view of the Christian roots of the Jew as "Historical Outsider," see pp. 17–81 passim.

15. Jaher, *Scapegoat*, p. 133.

16. Ibid., pp. 222, 232; on the worsening image, see pp. 170–241; on the proto-racialism of older stereotypes, see pp. 192–194. John Higham, *Send These to Me: Immigrants in Urban America* [1975] (Baltimore: Johns Hopkins University Press, 1984), p. 123. Jeffrey Melnick notes an interesting swing in American discourse between the Jew as "mongrel" and the Jew as racially "pure"—both are bad. *A Right to Sing the Blues* (Cambridge: Harvard University Press, forthcoming).

17. New York *Sun,* April 24, 1893, p. 6.

18. Higham, *Send These to Me,* pp. 117–152. On Jews and the racial sciences see Robert Singerman, "The Jew as Racial Alien: The Genetic Component of American Anti-Semitism," in David Gerber, ed., *Anti-Semitism in American History* (Urbana: University of Illinois Press, 1987), pp. 103–128, and below.

19. John Higham, "Ideological Anti-Semitism in the Gilded Age," and "The Rise of Social Discrimination," in *Send These to Me,* pp. 95–116, 117–152. On "status panic" and American anti-Semitism, see p. 141.

20. Efron, *Defenders,* p. 63.

21. Michael Bediss, ed., Arthur Comte de Gobineau, *Selected Political Writings* (New York: Harper and Row, 1970), p. 102; William Stanton, *The Leopard's Spots: Scientific Attitudes toward Race in America, 1815–59* (Chicago: University of Chicago Press, 1960), pp. 147–148; George Stocking, ed., *Bones, Bodies, Behavior: Essays on Biological Anthropology* (Madison: University of Wisconsin Press, 1988); Thomas Gossett, *Race: The History of an Idea in America* (New York: Schocken, 1963).

22. Quoted in Efron, *Defenders,* p. 51.

23. Josiah Nott, *Types of Mankind* (Philadelphia: Lippincott, 1855), pp. 117, 118; John P. Jeffries, *Natural History of the Human Races* (New York: Edward O. Jenkins, 1869), p. 123.

24. Joseph Jacobs, *Studies in Jewish Statistics, Social, Vital, and Anthropometric* (London: D. Nutt, 1891), p. xxx.

25. Ibid., p. xxviii; Efron, *Defenders,* pp. 58–90, 59.

26. Jacobs, *Jewish Statistics,* pp. v, xiv; Efron, *Defenders,* pp. 79–80; Maurice Fishberg, *The Jews: A Study of Race and Environment* (n.l.: Walter Scott, 1911); Sander Gilman, *The Case of Sigmund Freud: Medicine and Identity at the Fin de Siecle* (Baltimore: Johns Hopkins University Press, 1993), pp. 11–68; Sander Gilman, *Freud, Race, and Gender* (Princeton: Princeton University Press, 1993), pp. 12–48.

27. Quoted in Louise Mayo, *The Ambivalent Image: Nineteenth-Century America's Perception of the Jew* (Rutherford: Fairleigh Dickinson University Press, 1988), p. 77.

28. James Russell Lowell, "Democracy" [1884], in *Essays, Poems, and Letters* (New York: Odyssey Press, 1948), p. 153.

29. Oliver Wendell Holmes, "At the Pantomime" [1874], in *The Poetical Works*

of Oliver Wendell Holmes (Boston: Houghton, Mifflin and Co., 1949), vol. 2, pp. 210–213.

30. Mayo, *Ambivalent Image,* pp. 44, 53, 54.

31. New York *Times,* April 25, 1913, p. 3.

32. Mayo, *Ambivalent Image,* pp. 75–76, 154; Howells quoted in Bernard Richards, "Abraham Cahan Cast in a New Role," in Cahan, *Yekl, the Imported Bridegroom, and Other Stories* (New York: Dover, 1970), p. vii.

33. Mayo, *Ambivalent Image,* pp. 58, 156, 172; Stoddard quoted in Michael Rogin, *Blackface, White Noise: Jewish Immigrants in the Hollywood Melting Pot* (Berkeley: University of California Press, 1996), p. 89. The Dillingham Commission was uncharacteristically sanguine regarding Jews' prospects for assimilation in 1911, asserting that "the Jews of to-day are more truly European than Asiatic or Semitic." Nonetheless, the report did note that "Israelites" were "preserving their own individuality to a marked degree." *Reports of the Immigration Commission: Dictionary of Races and Peoples* (Washington, D.C.: Government Printing Office, 1911), pp. 73, 74.

34. Efron, *Defenders,* pp. 123–174.

35. Quoted in Gilman, *The Jew's Body,* p. 179.

36. Emma Lazarus, *An Epistle to the Hebrews* [1887] (New York: Jewish Historical Society, 1987), pp. 9, 20, 21, 78, 80.

37. Jacobson, *Special Sorrows,* pp. 97–111; Melnick, *A Right to Sing the Blues.*

38. Ludwig Lewisohn, *The Island Within* (New York: Modern Library, 1928), p. 43.

39. Ibid., pp. 103–104, 146, 154–155, 168.

40. Ibid., pp. 148, 346.

41. Laura Browder, "*I Am a Woman—And a Jew:* Ethnic Imposter Autobiography and the Creation of Immigrant Identity," paper delivered at the ASA annual conference, Kansas City, November 1, 1996.

42. Leah Morton [Elizabeth Stern], *I Am a Woman—and a Jew* [1926] (New York: Markus Wiener, 1986), pp. 347, 62, 193, 360. The text also contains racialized references to Irish and Polish immigrants and to Nordic natives, pp. 175, 245, 299.

43. Frantz Fanon, *Black Skin, White Masks* [1952] (New York: Grove Wiedenfeld, 1967), p. 115.

44. Albert Nock, "The Jewish Problem in America" *Atlantic Monthly,* July 1941, p. 69 (emphasis added). In rebuttal, see Marie Syrkin, "How Not to Solve the 'Jewish Problem,' " *Common Ground,* Autumn 1941, p. 77.

45. Deborah Lipstadt, *Beyond Belief: The American Press and the Coming of the Holocaust, 1933–1945* (New York: Free Press, 1986), pp. 59–60, 88, 93, 157. See also Elazar Barkan, *The Retreat of Scientific Racism: Changing Concepts of Race in Britain and the United States between the World Wars* (Cambridge:

Cambridge University Press, 1992), chapter 6; Stefan Kuhl, *The Nazi Connection: Eugenics, American Racism, and German National Socialism* (New York: Oxford, 1994).

46. Deborah Dash Moore, *To the Golden Cities: Pursuing the American Jewish Dream in Miami and L.A.* (New York: Free Press, 1994), p. 55; Sacks, "How Did Jews Become White Folks?" pp. 86–98; Rogin, *Blackface, White Noise,* p. 265; Nikhil Pal Singh, " 'Race' and Nation in the American Century: A Genealogy of Color and Democracy" (Ph.D. diss., Yale University, 1995); Douglass Massey and Nancy Denton, *American Apartheid: Segregation and the Making of the Underclass* (Cambridge: Harvard University Press, 1993), pp. 51–54.

47. Moore, *Golden Cities,* pp. 227–261; Alan Nadel, *Containment Culture: American Narratives, Postmodernism, and the Atomic Age* (Durham: Duke University Press, 1995), pp. 90–116. On the racial dynamics of American involvement in the Middle East, see also Soheir A. Morsy, "Beyond the Honorary 'White' Classification of Egyptians: Societal Identity in Historical Context," in Gregory and Senjak, *Race,* pp. 175–198.

48. Arthur Miller, *Focus* (New York: Reynal and Hitchcock, 1945), pp. 175, 26.

49. Ibid., p. 182.

50. Ibid., pp. 142–150, 147.

51. Ibid., pp. 149, 150.

52. Ibid., pp. 142–150, 149, 150. The issue was pressing in Finkelstein's America just as it was in Itzik's Poland: according to the historian Hasia Diner, more than a hundred anti-Semitic organizations formed in the United States in the 1930s. Diner, *Almost Promised Land,* p. 241.

53. Miller, *Focus,* pp. 33, 28–35.

54. Ibid., pp. 34–35.

55. Ibid., pp. 34, 174, 117.

56. Ibid., p. 24.

57. Ibid., p. 25.

58. Ibid., pp. 67, 66.

59. Theodore Herzl, *The Jewish State* [1896] (New York: Dover, 1988), p. 92.

60. Miller, *Focus,* pp. 82–83, 134.

61. Ibid., pp. 215, 216.

62. Rogin, *Blackface, White Noise,* pp. 265–266; Sacks, "How Did Jews Become White Folks?" pp. 92–98.

63. Miller, *Focus,* pp. 138, 177.

64. Raphael Patai and Jennifer Wing, *The Myth of the Jewish Race* (New York: Scribner's, 1975); Michael Lerner, "Jews Are Not White," *Village Voice,* May 18, 1993, pp. 33–34.

65. Miller, *Focus,* p. 217.

6. The Crucible of Empire

1. Edgar Allan Poe, *The Narrative of Arthur Gordon Pym of Nantucket* [1838] (New York: Penguin Books, 1975), pp. 84–85, 93, 189, 212; Dana Nelson, *The Word in Black and White: Reading "Race" in American Literature, 1638–1867* (New York: Oxford, 1993), pp. 100–101.

2. Howard Winant, *Racial Conditions: Politics, Theory, Comparisons* (Minneapolis: University of Minnesota Press, 1994), p. 21.

3. John Finerty, *Warpath and Bivouac or the Conquest of the Sioux* [1890] (Norman: University of Oklahoma Press, 1994), p. xix.

4. Ibid., pp. xix–xx.

5. Quoted in Kathleen Neils Conzen, "German-Americans and the Invention of Ethnicity," in Frank Trommler and Joseph McVeigh, eds., *America and the Germans: An Assessment of a Three Hundred Year History* (Philadelphia: University of Pennsylvania Press, 1985), vol. I, p. 136. On nonwhite responses to American empire, see Willard Gatewood, *Black Americans and the White Man's Burden, 1898–1903* (Urbana: University of Illinois Press, 1975); Amy Kaplan, "Black and Blue on San Juan Hill," in Amy Kaplan and Donald Pease, eds., *The Cultures of US Imperialism* (Durham: Duke University Press, 1993), pp. 219–236.

6. Albert Beveridge, "March of the Flag," in Daniel J. Boorstin, ed., *An American Primer* (New York: Mentor, 1966), p. 647; Richard Welch, Jr., *Response to Imperialism: The United States and the Philippine-American War* (Chapel Hill: University of North Carolina Press, 1979), p. 101.

7. Matthew Frye Jacobson, *Special Sorrows: The Diasporic Imagination of Irish, Polish, and Jewish Immigrants in the United States* (Cambridge: Harvard University Press, 1995), pp. 191–192, 182–200.

8. Reginald Horsman, *Race and Manifest Destiny: The Origins of American Racial Anglo-Saxonism* (Cambridge: Harvard University Press, 1981), pp. 9–24, 77, 166–186, 174. See also Walter LaFeber, *The New Empire: An Interpretation of American Expansion, 1860–1898* (Ithaca: Cornell University Press, 1963), pp. 62–101; Ernest Lee Tuveson, *Redeemer Nation: The Idea of America's Millennial Role* (Chicago: University of Chicago Press, 1968), pp. 137–186; Patricia Nelson Limerick, *The Legacy of Conquest: The Unbroken Past of the American West* (New York: Norton, 1987), pp. 259–292; Richard Drinnon, *Facing West: The Metaphysics of Indian-Hating and Empire-Building* (New York: Schocken, 1980), esp. part IV; Thomas Dyer, *Theodore Roosevelt and the Idea of Race* (Baton Rouge: Louisiana State University Press, 1980), pp. 45–68; Thomas Gossett, *Race: The History of an Idea in America* (New York: Schocken, 1963), pp. 310–338.

9. Horsman, *Race and Manifest Destiny*, pp. 174, 219; Frederick Merk, *Mani-*

fest Destiny and Mission in American History (New York: Vintage, 1966), p. 46.

10. Richard Hofstadter, *Social Darwinism in American Thought* [1944] (Boston: Beacon, 1955), p. 154; LaFeber, *New Empire,* pp. 72–80; Tuveson, *Redeemer Nation,* pp. 166–167, 137–175 *passim.*

11. *Irish World,* May 21, 1898, p. 1.

12. *Abend Blatt,* Feb. 6, 1900, p. 4.

13. *Abend Blatt,* May 7, 1898, p. 2; July 21, 1898, p. 2.

14. *Catholic Citizen,* Oct. 1, 1898, p. 4; Feb. 18, 1899, p. 4; *Irish American,* Feb. 4, 1899, p. 4.

15. *Pilot,* March 25, 1899, p. 1.

16. *Pilot,* Oct. 1, 1898, p. 4; *Irish World,* June 11, 1898, p. 2.

17. *Pilot,* Feb. 4, 1899, p. 1.

18. *Irish World,* May 7, 1898, p. 1.

19. *Irish World,* March 5, 1898, p. 4; *Irish American,* April 8, 1899, p. 4.

20. *Irish World,* June 11, 1898, p. 2; *Transcript* quoted in *Pilot,* April 22, 1899, p. 4.

21. *Irish American,* March 4, 1899, p. 4.

22. *Yiddishes Tageblatt,* May 10, 1898, p. 1; Jan. 18, 1899, p. 7; Jan. 20, 1899, p. 7; Jan. 24, 1899, p. 7.

23. *Kuryer Polski,* April 22, 1899, p. 4; May 2, 1899, p. 4.

24. Horsman, *Race and Manifest Destiny,* pp. 244, 276.

25. Christopher Lasch, "The Anti-Imperialist as Racist," in Thomas Paterson, ed., *American Imperialism and Anti-Imperialism* (New York: Crowell, 1973), pp. 110–117; Richard Welch, Jr., "Twelve Anti-Imperialists and Imperialists Compared: Racism and Economic Expansion," in Ibid., pp. 118–125; Robert Beisner, *Twelve against Empire: The Anti-Imperialists, 1898–1900* (Chicago: University of Chicago Press, 1968); Daniel Schirmer, *Republic or Empire: American Resistance to the Philippine War* (Boston: Schenckman, 1972); Stuart Creighton Miller, *"Benvolent Assimilation": The American Conquest of the Philippines, 1899–1903* (New Haven: Yale University Press, 1982).

26. *Abend Blatt,* Nov. 15, 1898, p. 4.

27. *Dziennik Chicagoski,* Jan. 23, 1899, p. 2.

28. *Catholic Citizen,* Nov. 12, 1898, p. 4.

29. *Catholic Citizen,* Sept. 10, 1898, p. 4. This sentiment was shared by Stephen Wise's *American Israelite;* see Jeanne Abrams, "Remembering the *Maine:* The Jewish Attitude toward the Spanish-American War as Reflected in *The American Israelite," American Jewish History,* LXXXVI:4 (June 1987), p. 454. See also David Noel Doyle, *Irish Americans, Native Rights, and National Empires* (New York: Arno, 1976).

30. *Catholic Citizen,* Aug. 27, 1898, p. 4.

31. *Catholic Citizen,* Dec. 10, 1898, p. 4.

32. James Jeffrey Roche, "The White Wolf's Cry," in *The V-A-S-E and Other Bric-a-Brac* (Boston: Richard Badger, 1900), pp. 59–60.

33. *Pilot,* July 1, 1899, p. 4.

34. *Pilot,* Feb. 25, 1899, p. 4.

35. *Pilot,* Dec. 24, 1898, p. 4.

36. *Irish American,* April 22, 1899, p. 4. See also *Zgoda,* May 5, 1898, p. 4; Aug. 25, 1898, p. 4.

37. *Yiddishes Tageblatt,* Jan. 16, 1899, p. 4.

38. U.S. Dept. of Labor, *Federal Textbook on Citizenship Training; Vol III: Our Nation* (Washington, D.C.: Government Printing Office, 1924, 1935), p. 1.

39. Quoted in Susanne Klingenstein, *Jews in the American Academy, 1900–1940: The Dynamics of Intellectual Assimilation* (New Haven: Yale University Press, 1991), p. 40.

40. Henry Adams, *The Education of Henry Adams* [1905] (Boston: Houghton Mifflin, 1961), pp. 411–412.

41. Theodore Roosevelt, *The Winning of the West* [1889–1896] (Lincoln: University of Nebraska Press, 1995), vol. I, pp. 1–14.

42. Elsewhere he negotiated precisely the racial problems raised by urbanization and immigration, touching upon the "dull brains of the great masses of these unfortunates from southern and eastern Europe," or delineating the "Mediterranean," "Slavic," "Jewish," "Alpine," and "Teutonic" races among the growing population. Frederick Jackson Turner, "The Significance of the Frontier in American History" [1893], in *The Frontier in American History* (Tucson: University of Arizona Press, 1986), pp. 1–4, 11; Turner, "Pioneer Ideals" [1910], *Frontier,* p. 278; "Social Forces in American History" [1910], *Frontier,* p. 316.

43. Francis Parkman, The Conspiracy of *Pontiac and the Indian War after the Conquest of Canada* [1851] (Lincoln: University of Nebraska Press, 1994), Vol. I, pp. 41–44. For powefully racialized interpretations of U.S. history, see also John Fiske, *American Political Ideas* (New York: Harper and Bros., 1885), *The Beginnings of New England: The Puritan Theocracy and its Relations to Civil and Religious Liberty* (London: Macmillan, 1889), *The Discovery of America* (Boston: Houghton Mifflin, 1892), and *A History of the United States for Schools* (Boston: Houghton Mifflin, 1907).

44. Thomas Wentworth Higginson, *A Larger History of the United States of America* (New York: Harper and Bros., 1886), p. 1.

45. Thomas Wentworth Higginson, *Young Folks' History of the United States* (Boston: Lee and Shepard, 1876), p. 37.

46. Parkman, *Pontiac,* vol. I, p. 1.

47. Turner, "Significance of the Frontier," *Frontier,* p. 1.

48. Roosevelt, *Winning of the West,* vol. I, p. 1.

49. Abraham Cahan, *Historie fun die fereynigte shtaaten* (New York: Forverts, 1912), vol. I, p. 3.
50. Parkman, *Pontiac,* vol. II, p. 313.
51. Thomas Wentworth Higginson, *A Book of American Explorers* (Boston: Lee and Shepard, 1877), p. v.
52. Higginson, *Young Folks' History,* pp. 1, 13, 14–15, 23–24.
53. Ibid., pp. 328–329; Higginson, *Larger History,* p. 192 (emphasis added), 406–430, 408, 415–416.
54. Roosevelt, *Winning of the West,* vol. III, pp. 43–45.
55. Ibid., vol. I, pp. xxxi–xxxvii.
56. Finerty, *Warpath and Bivouac,* pp. 16–17.
57. Ibid., pp. 75, 165, 180. Elsewhere Finerty differentiates between the "mercurial temperament" and "Celtic dash" of the Irish soldier and the congenital "docile, cool" demeanor of the German; he likewise refers to "our cosmopolitan army," including "all the races of Europe" (pp. 306–307).
58. Finerty, *Warpath and Bivouac,* pp. 68, 69 (emphasis added), 238, 109.
59. Ibid., p. 235.
60. Ibid., pp. xix–xx.
61. Higginson, *Larger History,* pp. 415–416.
62. Turner, "The Problem of the West" [1896], *Frontier,* p. 219.
63. Turner, "Pioneer Ideals" [1910], *Frontier,* p. 280; "Social Forces in American History" [1910], *Frontier,* p. 316.
64. *Eugenical News,* IX:2 (Feb. 1924), p. 21.
65. *Catholic Citizen,* July 30, 1898, p. 4.

7. Naturalization and the Courts

1. *In re Dow* 213 F. 355, 364 (E.D.S.C. 1914).
2. Ibid. at 365.
3. *Terrace v. Thompson* 274 F. 841, 849 (1921).
4. Cheryl Harris, "Whiteness as Property," *Harvard Law Review* 106 (1993), pp. 1709–1791; A. Leon Higginbotham, Jr., *Shades of Freedom: Racial Politics and the Presumptions of the American Legal Process* (New York: Oxford, 1996), pp. 108, 115; Pricilla Wald, "Terms of Assimilation: Legislating Subjectivity in the Emerging Nation," in Amy Kaplan and Donald Pease, *Cultures of United States Imperialism* (Durham: Duke University Press, 1993), pp. 59–84; Derrick Bell, "Property Rights in Whiteness—Their Legal Legacy, Their Economic Costs," in Richard Delgado, ed., *Critical Race Theory: The Cutting Edge* (Philadelphia: Temple University Press, 1995), pp. 75–83; Ian Haney Lopez, *White by Law: The Legal Construction of Race* (New York: New York University Press, 1996), pp. 197–202; Wilcomb Washburn, *Red Man's Land/*

White Man's Law: The Past and Present Status of the American Indian [1971] (Norman: University of Oklahoma Press, 1994); Benjamin Ringer, *"We the People" and Others: Duality and America's Treatment of Its Racial Minorities* (New York: Tavistock, 1983); Mary Frances Berry, *Black Resistance / White Law: A History of Constitutional Racism* [1971] (New York: Penguin, 1994); Charles Lofgren, *The Plessy Case: A Legal-Historical Interpretation* (New York: Oxford, 1987); A. Leon Higginbotham, Jr., *In the Matter of Color: Race and the American Legal Process: The Colonial Period* (New York: Oxford, 1978).

5. Michael O'Malley, "Specie and Species: Race and the Money Question in Nineteenth-Century America," *American Historical Review* 99:2 (April 1994), pp. 369–395; Nell Irvin Painter, "Thinking about the Languages of Money and Race: A Response to Michael O'Malley, 'Specie and Species,' " Ibid., pp. 396–408.

6. *In re Thind* 268 F. 683, 684 (D.Or. 1920).

7. *Dow* at 355, 364.

8. *In re Feroz Din* 27 F. 2nd 568 (N.D.Cal. 1928).

9. On law and the legal epistemology of race see also Lopez, *White by Law;* Virginia Dominguez, *White by Definition: Social Classification in Creole Louisiana* (New Brunswick: Rutgers University Press, 1986), pp. 23–55.

10. *In re Ah Yup* 1 F. Cas. 223 (C.C.D.Cal. 1878).

11. Ibid. at 223, 224.

12. Ibid. at 224; Los Angeles *Times,* July 24, 1910, p. 3.

13. *Ah Yup* at 224.

14. *In re Camille* 6 F. 256.

15. *In re Kanaka Nian* 6 Utah 259, 260 (Ut. 1889).

16. *In re Po* 28 N.Y. Supp. 383, 384 (City Ct. 1894).

17. *In re Rodriguez* 81 F. 337, 354–355 (W.D.Tex. 1897).

18. Ibid. at 337–338, 340.

19. Ibid. at 345, 347.

20. Ibid. at 350.

21. On the vagaries of Mexican "racial" identity in the United States, see Ian Haney Lopez, "The Social Construction of Race," in Delgado, *Critical Race Theory,* pp. 191–203; Tomas Almaguer, *Racial Fault Lines: The Historical Origins of White Supremacy in California* (Berkeley: University of California Press, 1994), pp. 45–104; Neil Foley, *White Scourge: Mexicans, Blacks, and Poor Whites in Texas Cotton Culture* (Berkeley: University of California Press, 1997); Suzanne Obler, *Ethnic Labels, Latino Lives: Identity and the Politics of (Re)Presentation in the United States* (Minneapolis: University of Minnesota Press, 1995); Martha Menchaca, *Mexican Outsiders: A Community History of Marginalization and Discrimination in California* (Austin: University of Texas Press, 1995); Douglas Monroy, *Thrown among Strangers:*

The Making of Mexican Culture in Frontier California (Berkeley: University of California Press, 1990); Camille Guerin-Gonzales, *Mexican Workers and American Dreams: Immigration, Repatriation, and California Farm Labor, 1900–1939* (New Brunswick: Rutgers University Press, 1994), pp. 51–75. The Ninth Circuit Court of Appeals ruled in 1947 that Mexican children could not be segregated in California schools because they were "of the Caucasian race" and therefore did not come under the existing segregation law. *Summary of Events and Trends in Race Relations*, May 1947, pp. 325–326.

22. *In re Halladjian* 174 F. 834, 844–845 (C.C.D.Mass. 1909).
23. Ibid. at 845, 834.
24. Contrast the Dillingham Commission, which—though classifying Armenians as an "Aryan" race—noted striking similarities between the Armenian and the "Malay." *Reports of the Immigration Commission: Dictionary of Races and Peoples* (Washington: Government Printing Office, 1911), p. 16. In 1919 M. Vartan Malcom would argue that modern historiography, philology, and anthropology all proved "beyond a question of doubt that the Armenians are Aryan and belong to the same racial stock as all European peoples." *The Armenians in America* (Boston: Pilgrim, 1919), pp. 7–8.
25. *Halladjian* at 835, 837.
26. Ibid. at 837, 840, 838.
27. Ibid. at 842.
28. Ibid. at 843.
29. *In re Mudarri* 176 F. 465, 466 (C.C.D.Mass. 1910); *Halladjian* at 837–838.
30. *Mudarri* at 466–467.
31. *Ozawa v. United States* 260 U.S. 178, 180–185 (1922); Lopez, *White by Law*, pp. 80–86; James Lesser, "Always 'Outsiders': Asians, Naturalization, and the Supreme Court," *Amerasia* 12 (1985–86), p. 83.
32. *Ozawa* at 187, 188.
33. Ibid. at 195.
34. Ibid. at 197, 198, 178.
35. *Thind* at 683, 684.
36. *United States v. Thind* 261 U.S. 204, 209, 211.
37. *Ex parte Shahid* 205 F. 812, 813, 815 (emphasis added), 816 (E.D.S.C. 1913).
38. *Dow* at 355, 365.
39. *In re Ellis* 179 F. 1002, 1004 (D.Or. 1910).
40. *Dow* at 355; 211 F. 486.
41. *Dow v. United States* 226 F. 145, 147, 148 (4th Cir. 1915).
42. *United States v. Cartozian* 6 F. 2nd 919, 920, 921, 922 (D.Or. 1925).
43. *United States v. Ali* 7 F. 2nd 728, 732 (E.D.Mich. 1925).
44. *In re Yamashita* 30 Wash 234, 238–239 (1902).
45. *Halladjian* at 839. See also John H. Wigmore, "American Naturalization and the Japanese," *American Law Review* 28 (1894), pp. 818–827, 822.

46. *United States v. Balsara* 180 F. 694, 695 (2nd Cir. 1910).
47. Ibid. at 695–696.
48. *In re Young* 198 F. 715, 716 (W.D.Wash. 1912).
49. *In re Sadar Bhagwab Singh* 246 F. 496, 499, 500, 497–498 (E.D.Pa. 1917).
50. *United States v. Ali* 7 F. 2nd 728, 731 (E.D.Mich. 1925). See also *In re Mohan Singh* 257 F. 209 (S.D.Cal. 1919), which held that "the Hindus of India, as members of the Aryan branch of the Caucasian race, are 'white persons.' "
51. *Morrison v. California* 291 U.S. 82, 85 (1934).
52. Lopez, *White by Law,* appendix A, pp. 207–208.
53. *Delavigne v. Delavigne* 402 F. Supp. 363 at 367 note 4 (1975).

8. The Dawning Civil Rights Era

1. Quoted in Harvard Sitkoff, *A New Deal for Blacks: The Emergence of Civil Rights as a National Issue—the Depression Decade* (New York: Oxford, 1978), p. 62.
2. Ibid., p. 50; Douglass Massey and Nancy Denton, *American Apartheid: Segregation and the Making of the Underclass* (Cambridge: Harvard University Press, 1993), pp. 51–54.
3. James Ford, *Hunger and Terror in Harlem* (New York: Harlem Section CP, 1935), p. 13; New York University Tamiment Library, microfilm reel 1768, item 2336. (Hereafter, TL reel no.:item no.)
4. John LaFarge, S.J., *The Race Question and the Negro: A Study of the Catholic Doctrine of Interracial Justice* (New York: Longmans, 1944), p. 74; Louis Adamic, *From Many Lands* (New York: Harper, 1939), p. 301.
5. Sitkoff, *New Deal,* pp. 158–159.
6. Mark Naison, *Communists in Harlem during the Depression* (New York: Grove, 1983), pp. 5–10.
7. James W. Ford, *The Negro Industrial Proletariat of America* (Moscow: Red International of Labor Unions, n.d. [1928]), TL 1768:2338.
8. Naison, *Communists in Harlem,* pp. 17–19, 45–47; Robin D. G. Kelley, *Race Rebels: Culture, Politics, and the Black Working Class* (New York: Free Press, 1994) p. 109; Sitkoff, *New Deal,* pp. 142–143, 139–168; James Smethurst, *The New Red Negro* (New York: Oxford, forthcoming), chapter 1.
9. James S. Allen, *Negro Liberation* (New York: International Publishers, 1932, 1938), pp. 4–5, TL 1744:87; Harry Haywood, *Black Bolshevik: Autobiography of an Afro-American Communist* (Chicago: Liberator Press, 1978), pp. 346–347.
10. Allen, *Negro Liberation,* pp. 13, 21, 29–30. As Earl Browder announced years later, blacks ultimately favored "their complete integration into the American nation as a whole." *Communists in the Struggle for Negro Rights* (New York: New Century, 1945), pp. 19–20. The Black Belt Thesis, it should

be noted, had somewhat double-edged implications: if it trumpeted the importance of Negro liberation for the workers' struggle, it also limited legitimate black nationalism to a particular region of the South.

11. Earl Browder et al., *The Communist Position on the Negro Question* (n.l.: n.p., n.d.), p. 39, TL 1752:798; *Daily Worker,* Feb. 24, 1931, p. 4.

12. Allen, *Negro Liberation,* pp. 26, 27.

13. Ibid., p. 45.

14. Browder, *Communist Position,* pp. 45, 56–64; Communist Party, *Foster and Ford for Food and Freedom* (n.l.: n.p., n.d. [1932]), p. 12, TL 1768:2335; Earl Browder, *The Communist Party and the Emancipation of the Negro People* (New York: Harlem Section CPUSA, 1934), p. 2, TL 1752:795.

15. James S. Allen, *Smash the Scottsboro Lynch Verdict!* (New York: Workers' Library, 1933), pp. 11–12; Haywood, *Black Bolshevik,* pp. 358–363; James Goodman, *Stories of Scottsboro* (New York: Vintage, 1994), pp. 27–29, 47–52, and passim; Dan T. Carter, *Scottsboro: A Tragedy of the American South* (Baton Rouge: Louisiana State University Press, 1969), pp. 137–173.

16. Goodman, *Stories of Scottsboro,* p. 48. Although never as electrifying a cause for white Communists, the Italian invasion of Ethiopia in 1935 became yet another occasion for "practical work" in interracial alliance and protest. James Ford noted with satisfaction that such antifascist demonstrations of "Negro and white people" and other interracial meetings had even included some Italian immigrants. James Ford, *Communists and the Struggle for Negro Liberty* (New York: Harlem Section, n.d.), p. 44, TL 1768:2332.

17. Haywood, *Black Bolshevik,* pp. 351, 352, 342–363.

18. Ibid., p. 353; Interview with Maud White Katz, Oral History of the American Left, series I, no. 130, TL.

19. Allen, *Negro Liberation,* pp. 33, 42–43, 44; Browder, *Communist Position,* pp. 5, 11; George Blake, "The Ideological Struggle against White Chauvinism" (New York: New York State Communist Party, 1950), TL 1750:579; Harold F. Gosnell, *Negro Politicians: The Rise of Negro Politics in Chicago* (Chicago: University of Chicago Press, 1935), pp. 340–342.

20. CPUSA, *Race Hatred on Trial* [1931], p. 4, collected in Bernard Johnpoll, ed., *A Documentary History of the Communist Party of the United States* (Westport: Greenwood, 1994), vol. II, pp. 393–440; Haywood, *Black Bolshevik,* pp. 349–358; Naison, *Communists in Harlem,* pp. 47–49.

21. *Race Hatred on Trial,* pp. 7, 8, 9–10.

22. *Daily Worker,* Feb. 25, 1931, p. 2.

23. New York *Times,* March 2, 1931, pp. 1–2; *Race Hatred on Trial,* p. 3.

24. *Race Hatred on Trial,* pp. 13, 16–22.

25. Ibid., p. 32; Naison, *Communists in Harlem,* p. 48.

26. *Race Hatred on Trial,* p. 38.

27. New York *Times,* March 3, 1931, p. 12; March 4, 1931, p. 28; March 5,

1931, p. 3; *Daily Worker,* March 3, 1931, p. 2; March 5, 1931, p. 1; March 13, 1931, p. 1.

28. Gosnell, *Negro Politicians,* p. 341; Sitkoff, *New Deal,* p. 156.

29. New York *Times,* March 2, 1931, p. 1.

30. *Race Hatred on Trial,* pp. 38, 4.

31. *Daily Worker,* Feb. 26, 1931, p. 4.

32. Allen, *Negro Liberation,* pp. 4–5.

33. *Daily Worker,* Feb. 26, 1931, p. 4; James W. Ford, *Anti-Semitism, the Struggle for Democracy, and the Negro People* (New York: Workers' Library, 1939), p. 17; Communist Party, *Communists and the Struggle for Negro Rights* (New York: New Century, 1945), p. 18; Naison, *Communists in Harlem,* p. 49. Harold Cruse has argued that "Negro Liberation" was the fulcrum by which Jewish Communists ascended within the Party and by which they tacitly defended a brand of distinctly "Jewish" Communism—largely at the expense of blacks themselves. See *The Crisis of the Negro Intellectual: A Historical Analysis of the Failure of Black Leadership* [1967] (New York: Quill, 1984), pp. 162–165, 147–170 passim.

34. Hasia Diner, *In the Almost Promised Land: American Jews and Blacks, 1915–1935* (Baltimore: Johns Hopkins University Press, 1977), p. 139.

35. Browder, *The Communist Party,* pp. 9–10; Sitkoff, *New Deal,* p. 165.

36. Haywood, *Black Bolshevik,* pp. 357, 358.

37. New York *Times,* Feb. 28, 1931, p. 22.

38. John Caswell Smith, Jr., "Each Man Is an Island," *Common Ground,* Summer 1947, pp. 61–73, 63.

39. Thomas J. Harte, "Catholic Organizations Promoting Negro-White Relations in the United States" (Ph.D. diss., Catholic University, 1947), pp. 11, 12, 46–50, 94–95; John LaFarge, *Interracial Justice: A Study of Catholic Doctrine of Race Relations* (New York: America Press, 1937), and *The Race Question and the Negro: A Study of the Catholic Doctrine on Interracial Justice* (New York: Longmans, 1944); Sitkoff, *New Deal,* p. 266; John McGreevy, *Parish Boundaries: The Catholic Encounter with Race in the Twentieth-Century Urban North* (Chicago: University of Chicago Press, 1996).

40. Sitkoff, *New Deal,* pp. 60–65, 161–165. On Popular Front politics as race politics, see Michael Denning, *The Cultural Front: The Laboring of American Culture* (London: Verso, 1997), pp. 445–454, 466–467.

41. New York *Times,* July 21, 1935, p. 23; Sitkoff, *New Deal,* pp. 91, 109, 102–138, 169–189.

42. *Summary of Events and Trends in Race Relations,* Nov. 1945, pp. 116–120.

43. Charles Silberman, *Crisis in Black and White* (New York: Random House, 1964); Lerone Bennet, *Confrontation: Black and White* (Chicago: Johnson, 1965); William Brink and Louis Harris, *Black and White: A Study of U.S. Racial Attitudes Today* (New York: Simon and Shuster, 1967); Andrew Bill-

ingsly, *Black Families in White America* (Englewood Cliffs: Prentice-Hall, 1968); Paul Mitchell, *Race Riots in Black and White* (Englewood Cliffs: Prentice-Hall, 1970); Thomas Cottle, *Black Children, White Dreams* (Boston: Houghton Mifflin, 1974); James Comer, *Beyond Black and White* (New York: Quadrangle, 1972); Donald Check, *Assertive Black, Puzzled White* (San Luis Obispo: Impact, 1976); Morris Rosenberg, *Black and White Self Esteem: The Urban School Child* (Washington: American Sociological Association, 1971); Sara Blackburn, ed., *White Justice, Black Experience Today in America's Courtrooms* (New York: Harper and Row, 1971).

44. Carey McWilliams, *Brothers under the Skin* [1942] (Boston: Little, Brown, 1946).

45. Ibid., pp. 7, 8, 9, 299 (emphasis added), 11, 14, 17, 19, 28–49, 305.

46. Louis Adamic, *My America* (New York: Harpers, 1938), p. 249.

47. Louis Adamic, *Nation of Nations* (New York: Harpers, 1944), p. 6; Louis Adamic, *From Many Lands* (New York: Harpers, 1939), pp. 298, 347–349.

48. Adamic, *My America*, pp. 187–259; *From Many Lands*, pp. 291–301.

49. *Common Ground*, Autumn 1940, p. 66.

50. Adamic, *My America*, p. 219.

51. Adamic, *From Many Lands*, p. 302.

52. Adamic, *Nation of Nations*, pp. 217, 219.

53. Adamic, *From Many Lands*, p. 293.

54. Smith, "Each Man Is an Island," p. 67.

55. *Common Ground*, Winter 1945, pp. 33–34.

56. *Common Ground*, Autumn 1943, pp. 7–12, 13–26, 37–52.

57. Marie Syrkin, "Jim Crow in the Classroom," *Common Ground*, Summer 1944; Langston Hughes, "I Thank You for This," and Louella MacFarlane, "The Faint Dawn Quickens," *Common Ground*, Autumn 1944. For Adamic on anti-alienism, see *Common Ground*, Autumn 1940, p. 63. Denning notes a similar shift in *Common Ground*, though he attributes it to the rising influence of Carey McWilliams and the waning influence of Louis Adamic. *Cultural Front*, p. 449.

58. *Common Ground*, Winter 1949, p. 36.

59. Adamic, *Nation of Nations*, p. 197; Brewton Barry, "A Southerner Learns about Race," *Common Ground*, Spring 1942, p. 89; George Schuyler, "Who Is 'Negro'? Who Is 'White'?", *Common Ground*, Autumn 1940, p. 53.

60. Random House also announced this as "the book that will jolt the nation!" New York *Times*, May 23, 1947, p. 21.

61. Sinclair Lewis, *Kingsblood Royal* (New York: Random House, 1947), pp. 104, 99, 179.

62. Ibid., p. 180.

63. Ibid., pp. 59, 12, 13.

64. Ibid., p. 62.

65. Ibid., p. 65.
66. Ibid., pp. 99, 97.
67. Ibid., pp. 230–231.
68. Ibid., pp. 18, 29, 10.
69. Ibid., pp. 100, 110.
70. Ibid., pp. 22, 260, 270, 304, 319; also 23, 196, 224.
71. New York *Times,* May 23, 1947, p. 21.
72. LaFarge, *Race Question,* pp. 19, 12.
73. James Barrett and David Roediger, "Inbetween Peoples: Race, Nationality, and the New Immigrant Working Class," *Journal of American Ethnic History* (Spring 1997); Robert Orsi, "The Religious Boundaries of an Inbetween People: Street Feste and the Problem of the Dark-Skinned 'Other' in Italian Harlem, 1920–1990," *American Quarterly* 44 (Sept. 1992).

Epilogue: Ethnic Revival and the Denial of White Privilege

1. Oscar Handlin, *Truth in History* (Cambridge: Belknap Press of Harvard University Press, 1979), p. 387.
2. Ibid., p. 393.
3. Michael Novak, "The New Ethnicity" [1974], in *Unmeltable Ethnics: Politics and Culture in American Life* (New Brunswick: Transaction, 1995), p. 347.
4. Micaela di Leonardo, "White Ethnicities, Identity Politics, and Baby Bear's Chair," *Social Text* 41 (Winter 1994), p. 175; Jonathan Rieder, *Canarsie: The Jews and Italians of Brooklyn against Liberalism* (Cambridge: Harvard University Press, 1985); Nathan Glazer and Daniel Moynihan, *Beyond the Melting-Pot: The Negroes, Puerto Ricans, Jews, Italians, and Irish of New York City* (Cambridge: MIT Press, 1963); Joseph Ryan, ed., *White Ethnics: Life in Working-Class America* (Englewood Cliffs: Prentice-Hall, 1973); Andrew Greely, *The Irish Americans: The Rise to Money and Power* (New York: Warner, 1981).
5. Novak, "New Ethnicity," p. 349.
6. Novak, *The Rise of the Unmeltable Ethnics* (New York: Macmillan, 1971), pp. 5, 72.
7. Ibid., pp. xv, xviii, emphasis in original.
8. Ibid., p. 63.
9. Ibid., p. xx.
10. Ibid., p. 298.
11. Ibid., pp. 85–136.
12. Ibid., p. 85.
13. Quoted in Seth Forman, "The Unbearable Whiteness of Being Jewish: Black

Americans in the Jewish Mind, 1945–1972" (Ph.D. diss., SUNY at Stony Brook, 1996), chapter 4, p. 120.

14. Michael Lerner, "Jews Are Not White," *Village Voice,* May 18, 1993, p. 33.
15. Herbert Aptheker, ed., W. E. B. Du Bois, *Against Racism: Unpublished Essays, Papers, Addresses, 1887–1961* (Amherst: University of Massachusetts, 1985), pp. 254–256.

Acknowledgments

Man, I've had a lot of help!

The origin of this project dates, quite precisely, to a conversation in Bob Lee's office when I was a graduate student at Brown in 1987. I have lost touch with Bob through most of the actual research and writing; but with any luck at all his imprint on the project will be as evident to the reader as it is to this writer. I am still very grateful.

I had the good fortune to cross paths for a year with Nikhil Singh in the history department at SUNY Stony Brook. He has been among my most energetic readers, discussants, and advisors ever since. From the few times we carpooled back and forth from Long Island to Manhattan, to the many hours floating ideas over coffee or beer, he has illuminated something about race, history, and culture for me virtually every time we have spoken. His friendship and intellectual engagement have meant a great deal to me; his mark on my work is immense.

Several people have read the manuscript or portions of it, and have offered invaluable advice, dissent, encouragement, leads, and caveats: Donna Gabaccia, Gary Gerstle, Robert Johnston, Jeff Melnick, Louise Newman, Rachel Rubin, Bernard Schwartz, Jim Smethurst, Judy Smith, Katy Stewart, and David Waldstreicher. William Weir showed me the way around a law library and commented extensively on Chapter 7; he also helped me overcome many a "general protection fault," as my computer and I did battle under a set of rules I never fully understood. Ken Jacobson gave the manuscript a tremendously close, line-by-line critique. The book is much better for having passed through his hands. I am grateful for his help; but even more, I am grateful for the way our conversations over the years have given meaning to the word *kinship*. My editor, Aida Donald, my copy-editor, Christine Thorsteinsson, and the anonymous reviewers for Harvard also made many improvements to the manuscript. David Roediger generously shared unpublished material with me, and he offered some important, kind words at a critical juncture. Gail Bederman, Peter Connolly-Smith, Joseph Entin, Seth Forman, Kevin Gaines, Eric Goldstein, Matthew Guterl, Russ Kazal, Kio Stark, Michael Topp, Alys Weinbaum, and Mark Weiner all shared ideas and material with me in ways that made a big difference.

I worked in two different departments while this book was in progress; I have strong attachments to both, and, certainly, my work has profited by my connection to both. I want to thank my colleagues at Stony Brook and Yale, whose interest in my work has improved it in many tangible and intangible ways. Special thanks to Jean-Christophe Agnew, Michael Barnhart, Nancy Cott, Ruth Schwartz Cowan, Michael Denning, Paula Hyman, Gene Lebovics, Patricia Pessar, Bill Taylor, Nancy Tomes, Alan Trachtenberg, Barbara Weinstein, Laura Wexler, and Bryan Wolf. I also want to thank Iona Man-Cheong, Ira Livingston, Kathleen Wilson, Nick Mirzoeff, Paul Gootenberg, Franny Nudelman, Robert Johnston, and David Waldstreicher, not only for their intellectual engagement, but also for good humor and emotional sustenance. Carlo Corea spent many hours chasing down microfilmed material for this project, always with good cheer and a keen eye; Katy Stewart helped to gather illustrations; and Marina Moskowitz helped to compile the index. I also want to thank the students in "Assimilation and Pluralism," "American Roots," "Expansionism and American Culture," and " 'Race' and 'Races' in American Studies." Funny that *we* should be known as *their* teachers.

I have presented pieces of this research at Stony Brook, Yale, Columbia, New York University, Princeton, Wesleyan, and at the ASA and OAH. I am indebted to the many anonymous members of these audiences who pushed me to sharpen my formulations or to redirect my inquiries. Some of these commentors did not remain anonymous to me. I'll take the opportunity to thank Joshua Brown, Deborah Dash Moore, Michael Salmon, Ellen Schrecker, Christine Stansell, and Mary Helen Washington. I spent the fall of 1994 in residence at Wesleyan University's Center for the Humanities, and I am especially indebted to Betsy Traube for making my stay there so productive. While there I also benefited by my proximity to Henry Abelov, Ann duCille, Sean McCann, Claire Potter, Jessica Shubow, Becky Thompson, Khachig Tololyan, and the other visiting Fellows that term, Bill Cohen, Dan Cohen, Judith Goldstein, Jane Margold, and Jim Scott.

I began the intellectual work that would become this book in 1987; I began the actual writing in 1994. In the course of those years many books on various aspects of whiteness appeared—David Roediger's *Wages of Whiteness,* Vron Ware's *Beyond the Pale,* Ted Allen's *Invention of the White Race,* Alexander Saxton's *Rise and Fall of the White Republic,* Ruth Frankenberg's *White Women, Race Matters,* Noel Ignatiev's *How the Irish Became White,* Ian Haney-Lopez's *White by Law,* Michael Rogin's *Black Face, White Noise,* and at least eight or ten volumes, it seems, by Sander Gilman. Frankly, this steady stream of related publications was at times an irritation. But though they may have robbed it of its initial novelty, this book is far better for having been developed in dialogue with these writers. They represent my most devoutly wished—if toughest—audience.

This research was funded in part by an NEH Fellowship for University Teachers (grant number FA-32398-94); and the final preparation of the manuscript was aided by a Morse Fellowship from Yale University.

As ever, my parents, Sarah Frye Jacobson and Jerry Jacobson, were encouraging and supportive far beyond the call. They each read the manuscript with a refreshingly uncritical eye. Every author should have at least two such readers.

And finally, this book is dedicated to my new family, Fran, Nick, and Tess. Francesca Schwartz has been a sharp critic and a profoundly provocative sparring partner, as we've debated the ways in which "psyche" and "culture" intersect. She might not win me over as far as she'd like to her views, but still I have learned more from her than she will probably ever suspect. Our conversations have always helped me to bring order to the chaos of my own incipient thoughts; and if there is a shred of persuasiveness to anything I have written here, it is because I have consciously addressed myself to Fran's astute and unflagging skepticism. Not least, she has also been an enlivening spirit in the day-to-day combat that is life in New York. Nick and Tess, for their part, have consistently thrown a good deal of chaos back into whatever semblance of order I ever manage to attain. But a splendid chaos it is. They may threaten to gobble up my entire writing day one dinosaur puzzle at a time, but ultimately it is they who redeem the days, too—every single one. I wonder if they'll ever know how profound has been their lesson to me, that a book is just a book.

Index